Interviewing Art and Skill

Jeanne Tessier Barone
Indiana University Purdue University Fort Wayne

Jo Young Switzer
Manchester College

Allyn and Bacon
Boston • London • Toronto • Sydney • Tokyo • Singapore

My work in the creation of this book and my joy at its completion is dedicated to the memory of Eileen Steen McCullough Tessier, who taught me to ask questions and seek answers to them.

—*Jeanne Tessier Barone*

To my parents,
John F. Young and the memory of Miriam Kindy Young, who taught me to respect differences, explore inquisitively, and work persistently.

—*Jo Young Switzer*

Series Editor: Carla Daves
Editorial Assistant: Mary Visco
Cover Administrator: Suzanne Harbison
Composition Buyer: Linda Cox
Manufacturing Buyer: Louise Richardson
Marketing Manager: Lisa Kimball

 Copyright © 1995 by Allyn & Bacon
A Simon & Schuster Company
Needham Heights, Massachusetts 02194

Library of Congress Cataloging-in-Publication Data

Barone, Jeanne Tessier, 1947–
    Interviewing art and skill / Jeanne Tessier Barone, Jo Young
  Switzer.
        p.   cm.
    Includes bibliographical references and index.
    ISBN 0–205–14088–2 (alk. paper)
    1. Interviewing. 2. Intercultural communication. I. Switzer, Jo
  Young.
  BF637.I5B27   1995
  158' .39—dc20   94–23849
                                                              CIP

Printed in the United States of America

10   9   8   7   6   5   4   3   2   1   99   98   97   96   95   94

Photo Credits: p. 7: N. R. Rowan/ Stock Boston; p. 16: L. Delvingne/ Stock Boston; p. 20: Ted Soqui/ Impact Visuals; p. 36: John Coletti; p. 42: Bob Daemmrich/ Tony Stone Images; p. 62: Will Faller; p. 87: Peter Southwick/ Stock Boston; p. 118: Clark Jones/ Impact Visuals; p. 124: John Coletti; p. 147: Tom Benton/ Impact Visuals; p. 159: Rick Bowmer/ AP Wide World Photos; p. 175: Owen Franken/ Stock Boston; p. 187: John Coletti; p. 206: Charles Gumpton/ Tony Stone Images; p. 209: Loren Santow/ Impact Visuals; p. 243: John Coletti; p. 266: Seth Joel/FPG; p. 277: John Coletti; p. 306: Jeffery M. Meyers/ Stock Boston; p. 324: Seth Joel/ FPG; p. 355: Hazel Hankin/ Stock Boston; p. 363: Elizabeth Simpson/ FPG; p. 383: Loren Santow/ Impact Visuals; p. 393: Jonathan A. Meyers/FPG.

Contents

Preface

Whose life is not affected, often and intimately, by interviews? In the workplace, in the marketplace, in physicians' offices and our children's classrooms, in the privacy of counseling sessions and in the public forum of the media, we see and take part in interviews on many of the days of our lives. *Interviewing Art and Skill* represents a new exploration of these ubiquitous interactions. It is an exploration that increases our understanding of the interview in all of its contexts and from the points of view of *all* of the parties who enter into these important dialogues.

We began with the goal of creating an interviewing text that was succinct and "user friendly" and that placed the art of interviewing within the broader context of basic communication theory. We also sought to present an approach to interviewing that synthesized interviewing concepts and principles, while at the same time specifying the unique needs of particular settings and situations. In addition, we wanted to create a text that speaks to the increasing cultural diversity and globalism of the present age and the new emphasis in business on team concepts in the workplace. Finally, we sought to develop a text that readers can employ in a variety of organizational settings as a standard reference work for ongoing guidance through the theoretical and practical realities of interviewing. We believe we have accomplished these goals in *Interviewing Art and Skill*.

Our text is organized into five parts. **Part I** covers the foundations of the interview, with a chapter on basic communication principles and a chapter on the listening skills, which are so vital to the success of any interview. **Part II** covers basic interviewing principles with chapters on interview process and structure, the power of questions, and the issues of diversity and cultural understanding in interviewing. **Part III** explores, in turn, three kinds of information-gathering interviews—journalistic interviews, research interviews, and job search information-gathering interviews. **Part IV** examines persuasive interviews, with chapters on the selection interview, disciplinary and appraisal interviews, and a chapter on the ethics of persuasion in interviews that focuses in particular on the sales interview. **Part V,** finally, treats a variety of assistance interviews, from employee intervention interviews to diagnostic and counseling interviews, respectively.

In every section and in every chapter, we have focused on the needs and goals of both interviewers and interviewees. In addition, throughout the text, we have emphasized the importance of diversity—cultural, ethnic, gender—as a logical and necessary extension of the more basic need to be open to the other, which is a skill vital to effective participation in interviews. At every level of text-writing—in our language, our examples, our illustrations, and our sample interviews—we have tried to create a text that models acceptance and avoids ethnocentrism and stereotyping.

In our development of this text, we were guided by several important beliefs, the first of which is that understanding enhances good decision making. Participants who understand the complexity of the interview are more likely to make effective choices in whatever interview settings they find themselves and in whatever roles they occupy in those interviews.

Second, we believe that *who* is in school should affect the way that textbooks are written. At many universities across the nation, the *who* in school is changing: the average age of college students is rising. We wrote this text with the understanding that it will serve new kinds of learners, including growing populations of older and international students on campuses and growing numbers of persons in need of retraining and new skills in the workplace. In our desire to meet the needs of the changing university population, we asked a broad range of students at several universities to help us identify essential aspects of content and form in the creation of this text. In addition, we sought the input and assessment of the text needs of individuals in various organizational settings who are confronted with the need to engage in interviews.

The outstanding features of *Interviewing Art and Skill* are these:

- Interviewing grounded within the broader context of basic communication principles and listening skills.
- An emphasis on the realities of globalism and cultural diversity.
- An emphasis on synthesis, which identifies continuities across interview settings and situations.
- The incorporation of examples, interviews, and photographs that relate to both traditional and "new majority" learners, including older, disabled, and international students.
- Interviews considered from the point of view of both interviewer and interviewee, so that a practical and applicable understanding of each interviewing context is offered to all readers, regardless of whether they will ever act as interviewers in these contexts.
- Up-to-date legal information regarding the impact on interviews of The Americans with Disabilities Act of 1990 and the Civil Rights Act of 1991.
- Exploration of interviewing as a team process as well as the traditional dyadic process.

Additional features of interest and practical value include:

- Thought-provoking introductory interviews at the start of each chapter which draw readers in, hint at the complex realities of the interviewing process, and serve as a useful referent for later discussions.
- Chapters begin with chapter goals and end with chapter summaries, which are features requested by students in research conducted in the process of preparing the text.
- Discussion questions and suggested activities provide provocative probing of the complexities of interviewing contexts.
- Up-to-date recommendations of related readings at the end of each chapter.
- Examples and photographs which vary the position power of people of various gender and ethnic backgrounds.
- Typography which accentuates key concepts and wide external margins for notetaking and a clean, uncrowded look.
- A summary chapter at the end of the text which synthesizes the principles and quidelines of each of the individual chapters.
- Content which has been classroom-tested by multiple instructors employing various approaches to learning.

We are pleased with the results of our labors, and we hope you, our readers, will be, too. We have made one discovery in the process of creating this text; that is, perfection is elusive. This text, like all labors of love, is an evolving entity which we expect will continue to be strengthened by dialogue. It is our hope that our readers—students, teachers, and professionals alike—will share their reactions and suggestions about this edition with us so that we can make any subsequent editions better and more responsive to the needs of our various audiences.

Interviewing Art and Skill was written with the advice and assistance of many people, beginning with our editor, Stephen P. Hull; Brenda Conaway, editorial assistant, and the reviewers provided by them whose comments encouraged and strengthened our work. Dean David Cox of the School of Arts and Sciences at IPFW provided encouragement and funding assistance for the preparation of the manuscript. Gabrielle Ginder, David Switzer, and Jane Banks, our colleagues and friends, read various portions and versions of our manuscript and offered valuable feedback, editing, and support. Our associate and friend Tammy Davich provided invaluable assistance in the preparation and handling of the manuscript. Jean Short assisted in the development of supplemental materials, and Kathy Magaña and Lisa Sandstrom offered the benefit of their experience in two of our opening chapter interviews. In addition, Jo Young Switzer's interviewing students at Manchester College and IPFW and Jeanne Tessier Barone's students in interviewing and business and professional speaking classes at IPFW deserve our acknowledgement and thanks. They have informed, challenged, and strengthened our understandings of interviewing, communication, and teaching in ways that have contributed to all that is best about this book. As for what is not, the authors alone take full responsibility.

Individually, the authors would like to offer these additional acknowledgements:

From Jo Young Switzer: Thanks to my friends whose support kept this task in perspective: Barb Young-Miller, Paula Moscinski, Noreen Carrocci, Carol Albright, Marcia Benjamin, Denny Varwig, and Rowan Keim Daggett. Special thanks to my family whose lives were affected by the time and focus that this book required: to John for his schedule flexibility, help with dinner, and comments like, "it really looks good"; to Sarah for her affirming nonchalance that, of course, mothers write books; and to Matt for his expanding horizons. Special gratitude to Dave for his loving listening, brains, and steady encouragement.

From Jeanne Tessier Barone: To my friends Gabrielle, Jude and Denis, Susie and Skip, and Jamie, for seeing me through; to my friend Judy Rieser, who has always had faith in me; to Robin, Marilyn and Al, for friendship and support spanning twenty years; to Mom and Dad, Kathy and Joe, Bob and Kathy, Mary and Steve, Erin, Jan and Mary Jeanne, for being at my side; and to my sons, Stephen and Benjamin, and my daughter Shelley, for encouraging, tolerating, challenging, loving, and giving me great joy.

J. T. B.   J. Y. S.

Part I

Foundations

Chapter 1
Introduction to Interviewing

Chapter 2
Listening and Perception in Interviews

Chapter 1

Introduction to Interviewing

"If there's a trick to interviewing, its engaging in conversation, having a cup of coffee."
—Studs Terkel, in "The Real Studs,"
Chicago Tribune, April 5,
1992, Arts Section, 19

Edward Campbell Hawley is appearing before Judge Katherine Levine in regard to the death of his younger sister, Julia. District Attorney Charles Ma has called Edward forward for questioning. In this preliminary hearing, conducted in the judge's chambers, the district attorney is trying to get more information than the police investigation has provided. The following interview occurs as District Attorney Ma talks to the young suspect, Edward Hawley.

Ma: Have a seat here, please, Edward.
(Edward sits in the chair near the Judge and crosses his arms, his eyes downcast.)

Ma: Edward, please tell us your full name.
(Edward glares at the District Attorney through heavy brown hair that almost obscures his eyes.)

Edward: You just said it. Why should I?

Judge: Mr. Hawley, answer Mr. Ma.

Edward: (Glaring at the judge) Ed Hawley.

Ma: Is your full name Edward Campbell Hawley?

Edward: Yeah.

Ma: Edward, do you know why you're here today?

Edward: I ain't stupid.

Judge: Mr. Hawley, please just answer Mr. Ma's questions directly.

Ma: Why are you here today, Edward?

Edward: Because I whacked my sister.

Ma: What do you mean, you "whacked" your sister, Edward?

Edward: I threw her out the window, dummy. I killed her! You guys already know all this.

Ma: Is it your sister, Julia, you're talking about, Edward?

Edward: I ain't got no other! (Laughs harshly)

Ma: How old was Julia, Edward?

Edward: Six.

Ma: And did you throw her out the window on purpose?
(Edward shrugs his shoulders.)

Judge: Answer the question, Mr. Hawley.

Edward: Yeah, I threw her out on purpose.

Ma: Why?

Edward: Because she was bugging me, and I was sick of it.

Ma: Did you think about where you were at the time, Edward? Did you realize you were on the sixth floor of your apartment building?

Edward: I've been living there ten years, stupid—you think I don't know how many floors it is?

Judge: Mr. Hawley!

Ma: It's all right, Judge. I don't mind. I'd just as soon go on.
(Judge Levine nods in agreement.)

Ma: What did you think would happen when you threw Julia out the window, Edward?

Edward: (Laughs again) I thought she'd fly, dummy. How stupid are you?

Ma: (Smiles) What did you really think would happen, Edward? I want to know what you were thinking at the time you threw her out.

Edward: Look. She was bugging me, and I told her to quit. She didn't shut up, so I threw her out the window. So what?

Ma: What did you think would happen to Julia when you did that, Edward?

Edward: (Laughs) I thought she'd hit the ground with a splat and never bug me again. And I was right!

Ma: Are you sorry you made that choice, Edward?
(Edward shakes his head and looks away.)

Ma: Please answer me out loud, Edward. Are you sorry you pushed Julia out the window?

Edward: Nah. Not really. Except for her scream.

Ma: What scream is that, Edward? What scream do you mean?

Edward: I didn't like the way she screamed my name.

Chapter Goals

- Define the interview.
- Present communication principles that operate in interviews.
- Introduce key communication terms that characterize interviews.
- Identify obstacles to effective communication in interviews.
- Identify differences between interviews and other kinds of communication.

Introduction

When we hear the word *interview,* most of us think only of job interviews; but in fact, interviews are commonplace. Lawyers such as Charles Ma interview people in courts of law every day. Journalists interview governmental officials in times of crisis. Physicians interview patients in order to make diagnoses and parents interview teachers about their children's progress in school. Furthermore, social workers interview clients to determine eligibility and needs, and students interview professors about assignments. Therefore, we rarely go through a week without being involved in at least one interview. Interviews are both highly varied and highly specialized forms of human communication. They require certain skills and understandings, such as the formulation and use of questions, that are different from those required for ordinary interpersonal communication.

In this chapter, we will define an interview and then focus on several basic principles about communication that apply to interviews, as well as to other forms of communication. Students who have studied communication before will recognize some of these fundamental principles. Others who are new to the field of communication will learn these principles for the first time. By considering how interviewing is based on certain fundamental communication principles, we can appreciate the ways in which interviewing operates as one specialized form of communication. For example, one general principle about communication is that it is an imperfect process. Understanding this allows us to know why it was important for Charles Ma to ask Edward what he meant when he said that he had "whacked" his sister. When the attorney tried to clarify the definition of "whacked," he was trying to make the communication less imperfect. Hence, the imperfection of communication affects interviews. This chapter will take several such communication principles and apply them specifically to interviewing.

We will also look at what differentiates interviews from other types of communication. While interviews share many qualities with other forms of communication, they are also different from them in very specific ways. We need to understand, for example, that during interviews people are often more concerned about the impressions that they are making than in everyday communication. In the case of Edward Hawley, his hostility toward Mr. Ma was an attempt to present himself as being tough and unafraid. Therefore, the similarities and dissimilarities between interviewing and other forms of communication are important, and they will be the foundation for this book.

Reasons for Studying Interviews

Although the study of human communication is thousands of years old, the specific study of communication in interpersonal and business settings is a relatively new phenomenon.[1] The study of interviews, as a unique form of communication, is even more recent, with the earliest communication-based textbooks on interviewing appearing in the 1960s. What has led to this attention on interviews?

Interviews play a powerful role in contemporary communication. The employment interview, for example, is a component in over 90 percent of all selection decisions in the United States.[2] Skopec estimates that U.S. companies conduct more than 250 million selection interviews annually.[3] Add to those numbers all of the parent-teacher conferences, visits to physicians, and interactions with researchers, social workers, journalists, and sales persons, and it is clear that interviews are ubiquitous.

When we participate in any specific communication this often, we benefit by understanding it more accurately. Understanding the complexities of interviewing allows us to make more informed choices when we participate in interviews. Since our ability to interview effectively affects not only job success but also health care, social services, education, business interactions, and the quality of social knowledge, it makes sense that we need to learn all we can about interviewing.

Understanding the interviewing process increases our options. If our understanding of an interview is superficial, then our choices about appropriate behavior are limited. For example, if we consider the job interview solely as a situation where the applicant is "on trial" before an employer, who will judge whether to

Interviews are highly varied forms of communication. This athlete is being interviewed as part of a mandatory drug test.

choose the person for the job, then when we are applicants for jobs, our attention will be focused only on how to make the best impression on this potential employer. As a result, we may direct our energies towards dressing well, having an attractive resume, giving the "preferred" answers to questions, and creating a positive impression. An employer may also have a similar limited view of the interview, with the belief that only the applicant is "on trial" for the job.

However, if we understand that the selection interview is a two-way interaction with *both* the applicant and the employer "on trial," we approach it differently. The applicant will be less likely to focus solely on making a good impression and will focus on whether it is a good organization for which to work. To accomplish this, the applicant will go to the interview after doing research about the company. The applicant should have some questions ready to ask. Thus, in addition to evaluating the applicant, the employer will also work to present the organization in a favorable light to the applicant, realizing that both of them are "on trial." In other words, both the applicant and the employer will exercise wider options in the interview. Understanding the complex process of communication in the interview opens doors and increases our choices.

The Interview Defined

An **interview** is a communication interaction between two (or more) parties, at least one of whom has a goal, that uses questions and answers to exchange information and influence one another. Let us talk about the various elements of this definition one at a time.

First, to be considered an interview, at least *two parties* need to participate. In most situations, interviews involve exactly two parties. These two parties typically assume the roles of interviewer (i.e., the party that conducts the interview) and interviewee (i.e., the party being interviewed). However, contrary to popular belief, two parties sometimes means more than two people. While it is common for an interview to involve just two people, it is also possible to have more. In this chapter's opening interview, for example, both Attorney Ma and Judge Levine are part of the interviewer party. Another example from a different setting might be a company that uses quality control circles in its manufacturing division. In this situation, an entire quality circle with six or seven employees may interview a job applicant. But overall, even in this situation there are still just two parties—the interviewers (the quality circle members) and the interviewee (the job applicant)—although there are more than two individuals.

In some circumstances, there may be more than two parties, particularly when different people bring contrasting goals to the interview. Consider a situation where three individual department heads, each with their own professional needs, jointly interview a candidate for a position. Even though the department heads' goals might differ, they all serve as interviewers. However, in another sense, they are *not* one "party," since their goals are different and conflict. In this interview, there are more than two parties. Generally, however, interviews have two parties—the interviewer and the interviewee.

Second, this definition of an interview suggests that at least one of the interview parties must bring a **goal** to the interview. A goal represents the purpose that the party wants to accomplish during the interview. In the interview between the District Attorney Ma and Edward Hawley, it is clear that Ma has a goal—to discover if, and in what frame of mind, Edward killed his sister. It is less apparent whether Edward had a goal.

An interview goal depends on the nature of the interview. A social worker's goal might be to get accurate information about income and child care, while a television reporter's goal might be to get a good five-second sound bite for the five o'clock news. Many times both parties have a goal or purpose, such as in a job interview. In this case, the employer has the goal of choosing the best applicant, and the applicant wants to get the job offer.

Third, an interview—unlike other forms of communication—is **dominated by questions and answers.** Questions and answers form the heart of the interview process, with either or both parties asking questions and the other party answering them. No other kind of communication relies so heavily on questions and answers to achieve its end.

Questions involve the use of words and symbols to convey and solicit meanings. With such **verbal communication,** we code our thoughts into words and other symbols to convey meaning. Andersen explains that "... Symbolic communication is a socially learned system of arbitrary signs and ... is voluntary, socially shared, capable of logic analysis."[4] Using words and other symbols to formulate and ask interview questions is a social activity that uses "a system of arbitrary signs" (symbols understood by others) to analyze information and share meanings. Words (symbols) both represent ideas and thoughts (their representational function) and present opportunities to create new ideas and thoughts (their presentational function).[5] In other words, words represent what we intend to communicate (e.g., "please sign this form"), *and* words help us to understand ourselves and our ideas in new ways (e.g., "when I told you that Sheila was hardworking, I suddenly realized that we need another reporter who is really hardworking!"). Words also function representationally and presentationally in these ways, in interviews. The ways thoughts are coded into symbols has an impact both on how others understand them and how people understand themselves and use them to generate new ideas.

Nonverbal messages are all the messages that people express in ways other than words. Nonverbal behaviors have the potential for forming communicative messages, but they only become communication when another person interprets the behavior and assigns it meaning.[6] Unlike verbal messages, many nonverbal behaviors do not have precise meanings. Nonetheless, nonverbal behaviors such as touch, proximity, promptness, smell, facial expressions, eye gaze, and gestures allow meaningful communication between interview participants. In the opening interview, Edward Hawley's shrugs, glares, and hard laughter were all nonverbal messages. These nonverbal behaviors conveyed messages about his attitudes and emotions. His nonverbal messages "spoke" at least as loudly as his words. Extensive research about nonverbal behavior supports the notion that nonverbal communication is a powerful way to send messages.[7] Therefore, both verbal and nonverbal communication affect questions in interviews.

Finally, interviews involve **mutual influence.** The process of interviewing includes two parties, each of whom influence (persuade) the other. Charles Ma attempted to persuade Edward Hawley to explain his sister's violent death. Edward Hawley attempted to persuade Charles Ma that he was not intimidated or remorseful. Mutual influence utilizes both verbal and nonverbal messages. Using a combination of verbal and nonverbal messages, both parties in an interview try to inform and influence the other. This is apparent in a parent-teacher conference, where both parties are using verbal and nonverbal messages to communicate. The teacher may describe the student's behaviors (verbal) and simultaneously show examples of the student's work (nonverbal). Moreover, the teacher may use the tone of her voice to stress to the parents the seriousness of certain student behaviors (nonverbal).

Mutual influence is present, sometimes in much more subtle ways, in all kinds of interviews. Sometimes this influence is overt, and other times it is limited to the subtle influence that results from exchanging information. In a health care interview, for example, a dietitian works to influence the patient to adopt a healthier diet. At the same time, the patient influences the dietitian's explanation by showing understanding or misunderstanding. If the dietitian says, "avoid sodium," and the patient looks puzzled, the patient's facial expression influences the dietitian to give a more specific explanation about avoiding sodium. Therefore, mutual influence pervades every interview.

To summarize, interviews have elements in common: two or more parties, a goal held by at least one of the parties, questions and answers, and mutual influence by the parties involved. Let us turn our attention now to some general communication principles that apply to interviewing.

General Communication Principles

Interviewing as a Transactional Process

Some terminology in the field of communication still sounds familiar to people who have never studied it. In academics, however, everyday terms can carry precise meanings. For instance, two words, *transactional* and *process,* have specific meanings in communication. **Transactional** means both parties in the interview act as senders and receivers of messages simultaneously.[8] Each person influences and is influenced by the other. For example, as an interviewing class professor lectures to a class, students' responses influence the lecture. If students appear attentive, the professor may be energized and pleased at the focused attention. If the students act tired or bored, the professor may try to add more enthusiasm to the presentation. The professor's lecture influences the class, and the class influences the professor's lecture.

Older views of communication once described communication as a linear activity in which one person sent a message to another person, with the second person passively waiting to receive it. This sender-receiver concept was termed *linear* because the sending and receiving of messages was seen as a sequential, one-way process. First, one person sent the message, a second person received the message, and the receiver formed a response. The word *linear* comes from the same root, *linea,* as the word *line.* Linear views of communication depicted messages as going one way on a time line, with the receiver acting only as the recipient of the message.

Flaws in this linear model can be seen in an example of patient-physician interaction in which the patient tells his physician about his sore throat. The patient (sender) conveys the message, "My throat hurts when I swallow," (message) through the channel of spoken word (channel) to the physician (receiver). Using this model, the two parties then switch roles, and the physician becomes the sender and the patient the receiver.

What is wrong with this concept of the interview? Clearly, several critical components of interviewing are missing, most notably immediate feedback. While only one person may be talking at any given moment in an interview, both parties are sending messages continuously. These messages are not all oral (spoken) and verbal, but they are still messages. For example, when the patient describes his sore throat, the physician is watching him, listening to him, perhaps taking notes, and conveying messages of attentiveness. Also, the physician may be looking for visual evidence of fever or swollen glands. Their communication is transactional because they are simultaneously senders and receivers of the messages. They are exchanging messages. The patient is talking, and the physician is communicating even as the patient speaks. Likewise, when the physician speaks, the patient continues to communicate—nodding, frowning, wincing—even as he listens to the physician. When we describe an interview as a transaction, it is important to remember that the communication involves a simultaneous two-way exchange of messages.

An interview is also a **process,** a common word with a surprisingly precise meaning. The process view of communication suggests that communication involves ongoing transmission of meaning.[9] Communication never stops completely, as long as the participants remain in the communication setting. While linear models of communication perceive communication as an event that starts and stops, process implies dynamism. The cliche "communication breakdown" describes an impossible situation (wherever two or more parties are present), because it implies that the communication can stop. On the contrary, communication can become less effective; but when people are in each other's presence, communication *cannot* stop.

For example, consider the experience of a couple on a date at a restaurant thirty minutes from home. As they eat the meal, a serious disagreement arises. They argue, but do not resolve the disagreement. They leave the restaurant furious with each other and then have to get into the car for the long drive home. Neither of them speaks. The silence is filled with tension. Some people would say that they had a breakdown in communication because no one is speaking. Actually, intense communication is occurring. Perhaps it is not effective communication, but it is communication nonetheless. In interviews, as elsewhere, communication is continuous. As long as the participants are aware of each other, it never stops completely.[10]

Dance's early writings describe communication as a process with no beginning and no ending.[11] In other words, the communication that occurs in any interview is just one segment of an ongoing communication in which both participants have been involved during that day. The early linear view suggested that interviews occurred in a kind of vacuum; that is, an interview occurred quite apart from the rest of the communication in which the participants were involved. Interview communication, however, is simply one portion of the larger daily communication lives of the participants. So while a selection interview may officially begin when the employer greets the applicant, the communication in that interview occurs within the context of those two persons' days. The job applicant, for example, may have just had an argument with the parking attendant, resulting in her late arrival at the office. Or the employer may have just received a resignation from an employee and may know that this position is suddenly available. Their official one-hour interview will be just one hour amid the ongoing communication processes in their lives.

Interviews are transactional processes because they are two-way interactions with continuous feedback between the parties. While only one person may be speaking, both parties will be continually sending verbal and nonverbal messages and providing feedback to one another. While verbal messages start and stop, nonverbal feedback is continuous. This simultaneous exchange moves the interview from the flat linear view and places it into the much livelier, more dynamic context of ongoing process and message exchange.

Messages as Purposive and Nonpurposive

Whenever we communicate face-to-face, some of our messages are intended, and some are not. In interviews, as in other communication settings, a **purposive message** is one that reflects a person's goals. A person's goals can be objectives the person is aware of and consciously wants to achieve, or unconscious objectives the person moves toward somewhat automatically without thinking about them or setting them as explicit goals.[12] Unconscious goals are consistent with what the person intends, but the person has not identified them actively and said, "this is what I want to achieve." A physician's purposive message might be to use a firm handshake before an interview to demonstrate energy and competence. Another example of purposive messages is a newspaper journalist asking carefully prepared questions of a local politician. In the opening interview, District Attorney Ma's questions were purposive. All these behaviors help the interviewers achieve their goals.

Some messages, however, are **nonpurposive;** that is, they communicate meanings to receivers, even though the sender does not mean to send them. For example, appearances often convey a message, even though the person sending the message may not mean it. A job applicant might have a cold, sweaty palm when she shakes the interviewer's hand. Her cold, wet hand sends the message, "I'm nervous," even though she does not intend to send that message. The journalist who asks well-prepared questions (purposive messages) might mispronounce the politician's name accidentally (nonpurposive message). Edward Hawley may have intended to call Attorney Ma "stupid" (purposive message), but he may not have intended to communicate fear by folding his arms across his chest (nonpurposive message). Whether messages are purposive or nonpurposive, people who receive the messages get information from them. As Andersen notes, "Both unintentional and intentional messages are meaningful to receivers."[13]

Messages also convey different levels of meaning. Every message in an interview contains two levels: content messages and relational messages.[14] A **content message** focuses on the actual topic at hand. The topic of the interview is its content message. For example, a parent-teacher conference is an interview in which the content messages center on a student's performance. The content may be about classroom assignments, grades, or behavior. **Relational messages** are used by the two interviewing parties to let the other know how they define their relationship. Relational messages can be about status (who has the more important role in this interview) and about affect (feelings toward the other). In a parent-teacher conference, if the teacher sits behind the desk in a comfortable adult-sized chair and has the parents sit in child-sized chairs, the teacher sends a message, perhaps unintentionally, about their relationship. The relational message may be: "I'm the teacher and I'm the expert here. You should listen to me."

Affect messages tell how one feels about the person, and they can include obvious signs, such as smiling or frowning. Edward Hawley's multiple references to Charles Ma as "dummy" and "stupid" sent a message about how he felt about the man and his authority. If the teacher at a school conference smiles at the parents in their little chairs, the relational messages are that the teacher considers himself to be of higher status (the bigger chair) and that he has positive affect or emotion toward the parents (he smiles genuinely).

Whether our messages are purposive or nonpurposive, content or relational, they are sometimes contradictory. Sometimes the verbal communication message may contradict the nonverbal message. In a medical interview, if a patient winces but says, "That doesn't hurt" when touched, the patient is sending contradictory messages. The wincing conveys the message "This is painful," while the verbal message "That doesn't hurt" says something different. The nonpurposive nonverbal message, the wince, contradicts the purposive verbal message, the oral statement. Interview participants can also send contradictory relational and content messages. A supervisor wearing an expensive suit, elegant shoes, and a $500 watch who tells an employee during the appraisal interview, "Hey, we've all got money problems," is sending a contradictory message. The clothing and watch suggest that the supervisor has plenty of money. The statement suggests that the supervisor wants the worker to believe they are both on very lean budgets. Therefore, components of messages can be contradictory.

In interviews, both purposive and nonpurposive messages are conveyed. Moreover, purposive and nonpurposive messages send information about content and relationship, including both status and affect messages.

Interviews as Rule-governed

In all communication contexts and situations, people follow rules. These rules can be formal rules such as social workers insisting that clients "take a number" so that they can be called in turn, or they can be informal rules such as patients knowing not to sit in the physician's chair in the examining room. When rules are explicit (i.e., stated outright) they are relatively easy to follow because they are direct and clear. It is easy for a guest on a television talk show to follow rules such as "wear bright-colored clothes," "be at the makeup room an hour before the show," and "remember to mention your new book." Even spontaneous television news interviewers give instructions like these to their interviewees, such as "look at me, not at the camera."

It is harder to understand and comply with implicit rules, or norms. Most rules operating in interviews are implicit: they are norms. **Norms,** unstated and powerful guidelines about what behaviors are typical and appropriate, affect many of our communicative choices. A norm in a television interview might be that the interviewee should not sit down until the host points to the chair. Interviewees who violate this norm often feel uncomfortable when they get questioning looks from the regular participants on the show (i.e., the people who know the norms). Norms affect many aspects of interviews—whether to use formal or informal names for the other party, how close to sit to the other, and how much eye gaze to establish. Let us look at several studies about norms that affect interaction in interviews so their impact is apparent.

Sussman and Rosenfeld found dramatic cultural differences in norms about how close an individual should sit near a partner in interactions between two people.[15] When the people in their study were paired with someone from their own country, Japanese interview partners sat considerably farther apart from each other than did the partners from Venezuela. Pairs of Americans sat at an intermediate distance. In other words, the norms about how far to sit from an interview partner differed from culture to culture.

Other norms are present across a variety of interview settings. For example, norms about conversational turn-taking affect interviews. Turn-taking, the process of knowing when it is time to speak and when it is time to listen, is learned during childhood.[16] The norms about turn-taking are complicated. In an interview setting where the two parties are strangers, knowing when it is time to speak and when it is time to listen may be difficult. Moreover, norms people expect to be operating may not work as people expect. In the U.S. culture, conventional norms suggest that people expect the higher status party to control turn-taking. Higher status individuals can control turn-taking by interrupting. Much of the research about interruptions has been about gender differences, which are often related to status differences. Do men and women interrupt their partners at an equal rate, both in same-sex or opposite-sex pairs? In her studies of task-oriented conversations, Hawkins found that people expected men to interrupt more than women.[17] Actual studies of such interactions have yielded mixed results. In same-sex pairs, researchers have found no significant differences in the levels of interruptions.[18] Moreover, in mixed-sex pairs, Dindia found that women interrupted men and men interrupted women at comparable rates.[19] These research findings hint at the complexity of turn-taking norms. What people expect the norms to be may not be reflected in people's behaviors.

As strangers enter interviews, they need to know the turn-taking norms. Does the higher status person have the unwritten right to interrupt the other? In a disciplinary interview in a job setting, successfully figuring out these norms can help the employee. If the supervisor, the higher status party, assumes that lower status parties should not interrupt those higher than themselves, then employees will be wise to wait for the supervisor to finish speaking.

Another norm operating in some interviews is known as the **norm of reciprocity.** This norm suggests that when one party provides a particular kind of information, the other party should reciprocate, or give back, similar information. For instance, an informal interview between two young attorneys exploring a partnership might begin this way:

Janet: Hi. Conrad? I'm Janet Frisch. Glad to meet you (Shakes hands).
I thought you might have a tough time getting here today because the traffic's so bad. When the Cubs are in town, it's hard to get within a mile of here.

Conrad: I took the bus, so it wasn't a problem. Sure is crowded though.

Janet: I'll bet. It's great to work near Wrigley though—at least I think so.

Conrad: Me, too. I slip away to Saturday games whenever I can.

Janet: So do I! It's kind of therapeutic to go to the ballpark and yell for the Cubbies when the pressure gets high here at the office. Well, speaking of the office, let's talk about setting up our own shop.

Conrad: Sounds good to me. I'm ready to talk.

Both parties in this interview reciprocate in the exchange by focusing on the same topics and providing information at about the same level of intimacy. When Janet talked about traffic, a very superficial rapport-building topic, Conrad responded in kind. When she talked about recreation, he did, too. When she moved the conversation to the business topic, he immediately made the switch to the same level. The norm of reciprocity guided their interaction. In interviews where the roles are fairly equal, the norm of reciprocity operates from superficial levels (e.g., greetings and light conversation) to the deepest levels of intimacy.

In other settings, the norm of reciprocity does not operate. Reciprocity is not present in interviews where the roles dictate that one person shares information while the other does not, such as a physician-patient diagnostic interview. Physicians expect patients to share private, personal information, but patients do not expect physicians to respond by telling about their own personal health problems. The norm of reciprocity that operates in many interviews does not operate in these types of interviews.

Norms are culturally specific. Each culture and subculture has its own norms, such as the distance norms mentioned earlier that govern interactions. In North American cultures sustained eye contact is a norm, whereas in some African cultures the norm is for people to avert their gazes.[20] When an interview involves parties from different cultures, different norms may be in place for each party, and this increases the possibility for misunderstanding and confusion. A medical interview between a nurse from a culture that discourages open expressions of pain and a patient from a highly expressive culture may pose problems. The nurse may assume that the patient's moans indicate excruciating pain because of an assumption that the patient would bear the pain quietly if it were possible. The patient, on the other hand, may not even be aware of moaning because moaning is an automatic response to any discomfort. Because norms are culturally determined and varied, inferences made by interview participants from different cultures may be inaccurate.

As with all communication, interviews involve norms. Unlike formal written rules, norms are informal and implicit. Nonetheless, they are powerful influences during interviews. Because they vary from one culture to another, norms are often misinterpreted and misunderstood. If interview participants are from different cultural backgrounds, they need to be aware of the increased possibilities for misunderstanding.

Interviews as Imperfect Processes of Communication

Although communication has been defined in many ways, one commonly accepted definition of effective communication is *shared meaning*. This definition suggests that when both parties have communicated effectively, then they both are likely to understand the message in the same way. They *share* the meaning. Obviously, perfectly shared meaning seldom occurs.

In interviews, shared meaning is unlikely for several reasons. We will refer to some of these reasons as communication obstacles. **Communication obstacles** are commonly called *noise*, but the broader term *obstacles* better describes the things that can interfere with the accurate reception of a message. For example, obstacles can be environmental. **Environmental obstacles** are physical noises and distrac-

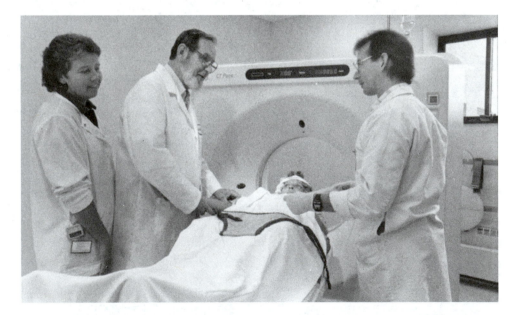

A patient's nervousness can be a psychological obstacle to a clear understanding of the doctor's information.

tions in the interview setting that interfere with effective communication. They can include sounds such as telephones ringing or voices outside the door. Environmental obstacles also affect interviews in other ways. Consider interviews that sometimes occur in the hallways of shopping malls. Many retail store managers do not have the space to conduct appraisal interviews with their employees inside the stores. Therefore, in order to provide their workers with privacy from other employees, the managers conduct performance reviews while sitting on benches in public mall corridors. The distractions of chattering people, the smell of caramel corn, nearby research interviewers asking questions about buying habits, and crying babies make these appraisal interviews more difficult. They can simply make it difficult for the interview participants to hear each other. They can also make concentration difficult. Environmental obstacles include any type of physical barrier to clear communication.

Psychological obstacles, sometimes called *internal noise,* are factors inside the communicators that interfere with their clear understandings of messages. A person's own nervousness can be an obstacle. If a patient is nervous in a diagnostic interview with a surgeon, it could make it more difficult for the patient to concentrate on the physician's explanation of the scheduled surgery. Moreover, general misperceptions about the self and the other person can also affect the degree to which an interview is effective. If the interviewer's self image is different from the interviewee's perception, the communication may be impaired. For example, if a student complains to a professor about sexual harassment by a lab assistant, the student may assume that the professor knows how to handle such complaints. But, in fact, a professor may not be clear about what to do or say. The professor may not know the pertinent laws or how to discern the facts of the situation. The professor's self-image in this situation might be one of uncertainty and confusion. So while the student may perceive the professor as an expert, the professor's self-image could be one of a confused listener. This difference could lead to different expectations on the basis of their perceptions—the student seeking answers from a perceived expert who cannot supply them and a professor feeling unsure and insecure.

A third factor affecting the abilities of interview participants to reach shared meaning is **cultural obstacles;** that is, misunderstandings of intended meanings as a result of different cultural backgrounds and experiences. **Stereotyping,** the act of forming ideas about a group of people and then applying these impressions to an individual member of the group without checking whether they really fit, is one kind of cultural obstacle. Often, interviewers will respond to their interviewees (and vice versa) as stereotyped members of a group in their evaluative responses to those interviewees.[21] De la Zerda and Hopper found that employees who interviewed Mexican Americans for supervisory and technical positions reached more positive-hiring evaluations for those persons who had "standard-sounding" speech (i.e., less accented speech) than those who spoke with heavier accents.[22] Similarly, Gill and Badzinski found that American listeners evaluated American nonaccented speakers more positively than persons with accents.[23] If interviewers interact more with their stereotypes about the interviewees based on their accents, rather than with the interviewees themselves, the resulting impressions will be compromised. Stereotyping from accented speech leads interviewers into less effective communication.

Stereotypes about any groups—African Americans, older people, women, Asians, welfare recipients, the clergy, college students, persons with disabilities—can hurt communication in any interview. By dealing with the other party as a stereotype rather than as a unique individual, the interviewer sacrifices important information about the other person, information that would be helpful in increasing communication accuracy. For example, if an employment interviewer assumes that an older person is inactive just because of age, the interviewer might omit questions about mobility and activity levels. The impression based on this stereotype, however, might be wrong. Not asking means that accurate information necessary for making a good decision may be lost.

Stereotypes and labels affect interviews negatively when the answers to questions are assumed without checking the accuracy of our assumptions. We may assume, for instance, that a humanities graduate might not know the technical vocabulary of computer science and consequently might not check out the person's academic and professional background with regard to technical computer skills. Without checking the accuracy of our assumption, these assumptions might be acted on by not extending an invitation for a job interview to a highly qualified person. Any stereotyped label can be confusing when used to shut out information that contradicts an assumption. If an employer wants to hire a computer liaison and assumes that all humanities graduates are "long-haired guitar players," then the label "humanities graduate" alone might close the employer's mind to the suitability of that applicant. In fact, that person might be a very qualified and attractive candidate.

Different vocabularies are another form of cultural obstacle that come from differences in educational backgrounds and experiences. Consider this medical interview:

Physician: I'm going to order a GTT for you, John.

Patient: A GTT? Is that for my heart?

Physician: No (Laughing). Your heart is fine. This is a GTT, not an EKG.

Patient: Oh, I see.

The patient's lack of knowledge about what GTT means (glucose tolerance test to check for diabetes) interferes with his ability to share meaning with the physician. The physician's culture, the medical world, contains a vocabulary not shared by the patient who does not know medical test names by their acronyms.

Also, interviews can be affected by obstacles such as different cultural meanings for symbols. People attribute different meanings to words and to nonverbal emblems; that is, nonverbal behaviors that replace or stand for words. A nonverbal emblem like the *OK* sign made by touching the forefinger to the thumb does not mean *OK* in all cultures. In fact, in some cultures, it is an obscene gesture.[24] Likewise, even fairly obvious and simple words do not mean the same to everyone. If a job interviewer asks an applicant, "How was your attendance record at your previous job?" and the applicant responds, "Good," one might assume that the parties had communicated clearly. The applicant, however, might have said "good" because he did not exceed the maximum sick days allowed, whereas using the maximum number of sick days might not have been at all what the prospective employer would characterize as "good." In fact, if the interviewer checked with the previous employer and learned that the applicant consistently used the maximum number of sick days, the employer might decide that the applicant had lied in answering the question. Even the simplest words and phrases can be equivocal in their meanings.

Environmental, psychological, and cultural obstacles interact in interviews to affect communication in three distinctive ways. First, in most interviews the two parties are relative strangers. As a result, arriving at accurate understandings of messages with strangers is especially difficult because perceptions are just being formed. At the earliest stages of relationships, the two parties have little common ground to help them form accurate interpretations of the other's messages. In the process of meeting and seeking to understand others, people form **perceptions** of them. Perceptions are the results of noticing, organizing, and interpreting stimuli. **Person perception,** the process of noticing, organizing, and interpreting people, includes three basic stages: (1) selection (what we notice about the other), (2) organization (how we arrange the information we have about the other), and (3) interpretation (the sense we make of the information we have). First, in interviews, perceptions of the other party are affected by various factors, including each individual's implicit personality theories. **Implicit personality theory** is the tendency for humans to view other people in terms of groups of personality characteristics.[25] People group certain personality characteristics with other characteristics. If a person has one particular characteristic, the assumption is that they have other characteristics that go along with that one. For example, if a television news reporter is aggressive, the assumption is that she is also impatient and smart. If a nurse has children, the assumption is he is also kind, understanding, and flexible. Implicit personality theories vary from individual to individual, but our perceptions of others are affected by our own implicit personality theories.

Impressions of others are also affected by assumptions about human behavior, stereotypes, mood, level of knowledge, expectations, and past experiences. In interviews, the process of person perception influences the entire interaction. Often these interpretations about the other party are not accurate, but they still affect the interactions.

Second, despite traditional norms about what should happen during an interview, each person's individual responses are unknown to the other party. The uncertainty caused by the pressure to understand the situation and its norms

Pressure to understand a situation results in increased anxiety and uncertainty.

heightens anxiety and decreases the likelihood of shared meaning. Sometimes, communication results from the human need to reduce the anxiety resulting from this uncertainty. Indeed, **uncertainty reduction theory** is a theory based on the belief that people communicate in order to reduce their uncertainty about situations. Some degree of certainty about people and situations enables better predictions about what will happen and how to act. In order to interview effectively, for example, "one must be able to both predict how one's interaction partner is likely to behave, and, based on these predictions, to select from one's own repertoire those responses that will optimize outcomes in the encounter."[26]

The more opportunities people have to interact, the more information they gain about the other and the more they can reduce their uncertainty about the person. In interviews, contacts with relative strangers increase uncertainty because so little information has been shared. Of course, the context of the interview provides the parties with some information.[27] Teachers interviewing parents during parent-teacher conferences have some initial information about the parents because of the context. They know the parents are interested enough to attend the interview, and they know the parents want to share their impressions with the teacher. The context itself provides some information, but communication between the teacher and parents will provide additional information that will help reduce uncertainty.

Many interviews are interactions that have high levels of **anxiety.** Interview participants such as job applicants, ill patients, and persons seeking counseling are often worried about their impressions with the interviewers. As a consequence, their defensiveness makes them more confused about the messages they receive.[28] A common experience in medical diagnostic interviews is for the nervous patient who is introduced to the nurse or physician to forget the person's name immediately. This is not a problem of not hearing the name when it is spoken. When sound waves interfere with reception of messages, most people ask the other person to repeat the name. The problem with remembering names in these situations stems more from tension and nervousness.

Environmental, psychological, and cultural obstacles, and other misperceptions can decrease the effectiveness of any interview. Environmental obstacles can interfere with an ability to hear in the interview, and psychological obstacles can distract people from giving their complete attention to the interview. Likewise, cultural obstacles and other misperceptions may lead to false assumptions about the other party. Three distinctive characteristics of interviews—forming perceptions of strangers, reducing uncertainty about the other person and the situation, and feeling anxious about making a positive impression—work together to make it difficult for the parties in many interviews to reach shared meaning.

Where Interviews Fit into Communication Contexts

Interviewing is a specific type of communication that shares characteristics with other kinds of communication, yet it has qualities unlike those in other contexts. Communication is often categorized into the contexts shown in Figure 1.1.

What ways are these communication contexts different? One way of understanding these differences is to examine each kind of interaction with regard to specific communication characteristics. These contexts can be defined, for example, on the basis of the characteristics described in Figure 1.2.

Using these characteristics, consider two university students who meet for lunch at the campus union. Their time together is purely social.

Mass Communication	television, radio, print media
Public Communication	political addresses, lectures
Organizational Communication	communication in large organizations such as hospitals, corporations
Small Group Communication	quality control circles, volunteer work groups, juries
Interpersonal Communication	family and friends
Intrapersonal Communication	message sent by the self to the self

FIGURE 1.1

Number of persons involved	Are there few or many?
Proximity of persons	Are they close together or far away?
Nature of the feedback	Is it immediate or delayed?
Communication roles	Are roles informal or formal?
Adaptation of the message to this particular receiver	Are messages tailored to the other specifically or generally?
Goals and purposes	Are goals unstructured or structured?

FIGURE 1.2 Characteristics of Communication Contexts

Adapted with permission from Trenholm, Sarah, *Human Communication Theory*, 2nd ed. (Englewood Cliffs, NJ: Prentice Hall, 1991), 20. Used by permission of Prentice-Hall Publishers.

How many people are involved?	Few (two friends)
How near are the interactants?	Close (side by side)
Is the feedback immediate or delayed?	Immediate (verbal and nonverbal)
Are the communication roles formal or informal?	Informal (casual friends)
Are the messages adapted to the receivers?	Specifically (respond to friend individually)
Are the goals unstructured or structured?	Unstructured (no goals)

This set of characteristics places lunch between friends as a form of interpersonal communication because it is between two friends, seated close together, who are able to give direct and immediate feedback to one another and to listen to each other without specific goals in mind.

Now let's describe interviewing by using these same characteristics (see Figure 1.3). Most interviews have few participants—most commonly two. Participants in interviews communicate in close proximity, usually face to face, although sometimes interviews occur over the telephone. This, of course, influences the nature of the feedback that they can give to each other. With the exception of telephone interviews, participants are in constant face-to-face message exchange. Even telephone interviewers and interviewees have immediate oral feedback to their messages. As a result, they can give immediate feedback, verbal and nonverbal, to one another. A patient in a medical diagnostic interview may not understand the reason for a particular medication. In this situation, the patient can ask immediately about the reason for the medication. Moreover, even if the patient does not ask overtly, the physician may notice the patient's perplexed facial expression and offer a more complete explanation. The feedback is immediate.

Number of persons involved	Two parties
Proximity of participants	Near (except telephone interviews)
Nature of the feedback	Immediate (verbal and nonverbal)
Communication roles	Formal (interviewer and interviewee)
Adaptations of messages to other	Specific (except in survey interviews)
Goals and purposes	Structured (at least 1 has goal)

FIGURE 1.3 Dimensions of Communication in Interviews

Adapted with permission from Trenholm, Sarah, *Human Communication Theory*, 2nd ed. (Englewood Cliffs, NJ: Prentice Hall, 1991), 20.

Moreover, communication roles in interviews are relatively formal. One party communicates in the role of interviewer, and the other acts as interviewee. In some interviews, these roles are associated with formal occupations such as a counselor interviewing a client, a student interviewing a professor, or a newspaper reporter interviewing a sports figure. At other times, the parties occupy less specific occupational roles. In fact, the roles of interviewer and interviewee can be interchanged during an interview. This often happens during selection interviews when the interviewer, near the end of the interview, says, "Now let's hear your questions for me," and the interviewee responds, "Yes, I'd like to ask you how you train new employees." For the next several minutes, the applicant becomes the interviewer, and the employer becomes the interviewee. In interviews, the two roles—interviewer and interviewee—are always present, but they are sometimes interchanged.

Interviews allow the participants to adapt messages specifically to the other party. Unlike televised political speeches where the speaker can do little during the speech to adapt to the nature of the particular audience, interview participants can adapt as much as they choose to the other party, even as the interview progresses. A nurse can adapt to a hearing impaired patient by speaking louder. A supervisor can discipline a worker who is frequently late with the degree of toughness necessary to motivate that worker. Therefore, interviews provide for specific and immediate adaptation to the other.

Finally, the goals and purposes of interviews are often structured. At least one of the interview participants always has a purpose for conducting the interview. This degree of purpose and structure contrasts with an informal interpersonal interaction, where two friends having coffee together communicate spontaneously about whatever issues arise. In an interview, at least one party (and often both) has a purposeful reason for participation. Interviewing, therefore, has many of the same characteristics of interpersonal communication where two parties speak face to face to discuss issues. Interviewing differs from interpersonal because the parties have more specific goals and because they use so many questions and answers in their discussion.

Type of Interview	Primary Purpose	Secondary Purpose	Interviewer Qualities	Interviewee Qualities	Outcome/ Success
Journalistic	gather info	entertain, report the news	able to do research, listen, record accurately, probe	expertise, good listener, articulate on issues	good story that draws readers & viewers
Research	gather info to learn about a population	apply info to specific needs	consistent, accurate, good listener	willing to participate, honest	valid & reliable data
Persuasive	sell idea or product	maintain interviewer credibility, assess customer needs	able to assess needs of other, persuasive, energetic	perceived need, willing to listen	successful sale to satisfied customer
Selection (employment)	gather information, evaluate	promote self, employer	knowledge of job and law, able to listen and assess	preparation, self-confidence, self-awareness	find good match
Appraisal (employment)	evaluate work, give feedback, motivate	set goals, decide merit	able to plan, research, listen, be objective	able to assess self, set goals, receive feedback	accurate evaluation and goal-setting
Disciplinary (employment)	give feedback about problem, motivate to change	seek info to decide course of action	able to confront, document, be honest	able to get feedback, listen, admit error, change	appropriate plan of action is decided
Diagnostic	seek info to help in identifying problem	get facts relevant to problem	knowledge-able, able to probe, non-judgmental	willing to participate, honest, forthcoming about symptoms	accurate diagnosis of interviewee's problem
Counseling	offer opportunity for self-knowledge and change	feedback, suggest options	positive regard, good listener, non-judgmental	willing to participate, felt need to change, honest	growth and change in interviewee

FIGURE 1.4   Types of Interviews

Types of Interviews

This text will focus on many types of interviews. In order to get a sense of the range of this book's interview contexts, Figure 1.4 gives an overview. This chart summarizes the types of interviews, their primary and secondary goals, qualities that are essential for interviewers and interviewees in each type, and the measure of success for the specific interview context. While reading the text, each type of interview will be encountered and the ways to work effectively within each interview context will be explained.

Interviewing as an Art

Many people believe that interviewing is a skill that is learned in much the same way that one learns how to use a computer keyboard. Once certain mechanical skills are accomplished, some people believe there is nothing more to learn. Skills are techniques or tools, and interviewing skills involve knowing the techniques of interview structure, question wording, and functions of questions. Learning about interviewing as a skill means learning these techniques. But as any music lover knows, learning how to use a piano keyboard involves not only mechanical skills, but many artistic subtleties as well. Art involves performance that goes beyond mechanical techniques. This book will focus on interviewing both as skill and art. Knowing interviewing techniques alone does not make a good interviewer. Rather, a good interviewer knows the basic skills *and* brings an appreciation for the individual dynamics of each unique interviewing situation, thereby understanding that interviewing is also an art. An artful interviewer adapts to each interview differently and appropriately. Compare some interviews done by a local television news team with interviews done by a national television network. Observe that local news personnel may use the right techniques, but their interviews sometimes appear clumsy and amateurish. They may use good interview structure, but they may not adapt well when the interviewee does not cooperate. They may ask good questions, but of the wrong people. In contrast, national television personnel, especially those with extensive experience, often conduct interviews that appear effortless. As experienced interviewers demonstrate, once the basic skills are learned, the best interviewers move beyond the skill level to adapt artfully to the important individual characteristics of each interview and each interviewee.

Summary

Interviewing, a communication interaction in which two or more parties, at least one of whom has a goal, use questions and answers to share information and to influence one another, is both a skill and an art. Like other contexts of communication, interviews are imperfect transactional processes governed by rules, including both purposive and nonpurposive messages. Three types of obstacles —environmental, psychological, and cultural—hinder the abilities of interview participants to communicate effectively. Interviews represent one particular type of communication context, and there are many types of interviews within that context.

Discussion Questions

1. Consider interviews that you have witnessed or experienced. Describe several of them and decide which participants brought goals to the interviews. What were their goals?

2. What were the goals of District Attorney Ma, Edward Hawley, and Judge Levine in the opening interview? Were these goals the same or different? Would it have been possible for all three of them to achieve their goals?

3. Discuss some of the norms that operate in selection interviews. Contrast them to norms that are present in medical interviews.

4. From your experience, what are some environmental, psychological, and cultural obstacles that you have experienced in interviews?

5. Describe a common stereotype of some group on your campus. What characteristics are typically attributed to this group? Compare those characteristics to an individual you know who is in the group.

Activities

1. Using the definition of interview presented in the chapter, develop a list of all the interviews in which you have participated during the last month. In groups of three to four, compare your lists and discuss whether the results support the statement "we rarely go through a week without being involved in at least one interview."

2. Interview a member of your class for five minutes learning as much as you can. Then switch roles. After you are finished, discuss whether your interviews contained all the major components of an interview: at least two parties, mutual influence, and a predominance of questions and answers.

3. Locate an interview in a film, book, or on tape. In a four to five page paper, analyze the interview, identifying its component parts. In particular, describe the number of parties,

their goals, purposive and nonpurposive messages, content and relational messages, norms, and obstacles.

4. In groups of five to six, discuss your stereotypes of university professors. Develop a list of the primary characteristics of this "type." After you are finished, compare your list with those of other groups in the class. Discuss similarities and differences between them. On what basis were the characteristics developed in each group?

5. Using the classification scheme about different types of communication, identify what type of communication is occurring in your interviewing class during a typical class period. To do so, identify the separate components of the class (number and proximity of interactants, immediacy of feedback, etc.) and place your class into the classification scheme.

Related Readings

Ailes, Roger. *You are the Message.* New York: Doubleday, 1988.

Gouran, Dennis, Miller, Larry, and Wiethoff, William. *Mastering Communication*, 2nd ed. Boston: Allyn and Bacon, 1994.

Gudykunst, William B. *Bridging Differences: Effective Intergroup Communicaton.* Newbury Park, CA: Sage, 1991.

Littlejohn, Stephen W. *Theories of Human Communication*, 4th ed. Belmont, CA: Wadsworth, 1992.

Miller, A. (ed.). *In the Eye of the Beholder: Contemporary Issues in Stereotyping.* New York: Praeger, 1982.

Trenholm, Sarah. *Human Communication Theory*, 2nd ed. Englewood Cliffs, NJ: Prentice Hall, 1992.

Endnotes

1. W. Charles Redding, "Stumbling Toward Identity: the Emergence of Organizational Communication as a Field of Study," Kevin L. Hutchinson (ed.). *Readings in Organizational Communication* (Dubuque, IA: William C. Brown Publishers, 1992), 2–44.

2. G. Johns, *Organizational Behavior: Understanding Life at Work*, 2nd ed. (Glenview, IL: Scott Foresman, 1988).

3. Eric W. Skopec, *Situational Interviewing* (New York: Harper and Row, 1986), p. 48.

4. Peter Anderson, "Consciousness, Cognition, and Communication," *The Western Journal of Speech Communication 50* (1986), 92.

5. See, for example, John Stewart, "A Postmodern Look at Traditional Communication Postulates," *The Western Journal of Speech Communication 55* (1991), 354–79; and Gadamer, Hans-Georg, *Truth and Method*, 2nd rev. ed., Joel Weinsheimer and Donald G. Marshall, trans., (New York: Crossroad, 1989), 549.

6. Virginia P. Richmond, McCroskey, Hames C., and Payne, Steve K., *Nonverbal Behavior in Interpersonal Relations*, 2nd ed. (Englewood Cliffs, NJ: Prentice Hall, 1991), 7.

7. For extensive discussion of this issue see Richmond, *et. al* (1991); Burgoon, J.K., Buller, D.B., and Woodall, W.G., *Nonverbal Communication: The Unspoken Dialogue* (New York: Harper and Row Publishers, 1989).

8. William W. Wilmot, *Dyadic Communication*, 3rd ed. (New York: Random House, 1987), 11–14, 95–96.

9. For an introduction to discussion of process, see Frank E.X. Dance, "The 'concept' of communication," *Journal of Communication 20* (1970), 201–210.

10. Peter A. Andersen, "When One Cannot not Communicate: A Challenge to Motley's Traditional Communication Postulates," *Communication Studies 42* (1991), 310.

11. Dance (1970).

12. Motley (1990), 4.

13. Andersen (1991), 321.

14. Paul Watzlawick, Beavin, Janet, and Jackson, Don, *Pragmatics of Human Communication: A Study of Interactional Patterns, Pathologies, and Paradoxes* (New York: Norton, 1967).

15. Nan M. Sussman, and Howard M. Rosenfeld, "Influence of Culture, Language, and Sex on Conversational Distance," *Journal of Personality and Social Psychology, 42* (1982), 66–74.

16. H. Sacks, Schegloff, E., and Jefferson, G., "The Simplest Systematics for the Organization of Turn-taking for Conversation," *Language 50* (1974), 696–735.

17. Katherine Hawkins, "Interruptions in Task-oriented Conversations: Effects of Violations of Expectations by Males and Females," *Women's Studies in Communication* (1988), 1–20.

18. See, for example, E.B. Rogers and A. Schumacher, "Effects of Individual Differences on Dyadic Conversational Strategies," *Journal of Personality and Social Psychology 45* (1983), 700–05; C. Trimboli, and M.B. Walker, "Switching Pauses in Cooperative and Competitive Conversations," *Journal of Experimental Social Psychology 20* (1984), 297–311.

19. Karen Dindia, "The Effects of Sex or Subject and Sex of Partner on Interruptions," *Human Communication Research 13* (1987) 345–71.

20. P. Byers, and H. Byers, (1972). "Nonverbal Communication and the Education of Children." In C.B. Cazden, V.P. John, and D. Hymes (eds.) *Functions of Language in the Classroom.* (New York: Teachers College Press), 20–21.

21. Frederick Williams, *et. al. Explorations in the Linguistic Attitudes of Teachers* (Rowley, MA: Newbury House, 1976).

22. Nancy de la Zerda and Robert Hopper, "Employment Interviewers' Reactions to Mexican American Speech," *Communication Monographs 46* (1979), 131.

23. Mary M. Gill and Diane M. Badzinski, "The Impact of Accent and Status on Information Recall and Perception Formation," *Communication Reports 5* (1992), 99–106.

24. Richmond, *et. al.,* (1991), 296–97.

25. For discussion of implicit personality theory, See Daniel M. Wegner, and Robin R. Vallecher, *Implicit Psychology: An Introduction to Social Cognition* (New York: Oxford University Press, 1977).

26. Charles R. Berger, "Communicating Under Uncertainty," Michael E. Roloff, and Gerald R. Miller, eds. *Interpersonal processes: New Directions in Communication Research* (Newbury Park: Sage Publications, 1987), 41.

27. See Charles R. Berger and R. J. Calabrese, "Some Explorations in Initial Interaction and Beyond: Toward a Developmental Theory of Interpersonal Communication," *Human Communication Research 1* (1975), 99–112; B.R. Rubin, "The Role of Context in Information Seeking and Impression Formation," *Communication Monographs 44* (1977), 81–90.

28. Jack R. Gibb, "Defensive Communication," *Journal of Communication 11* (1961), 141–48.

Chapter 2

Listening and Perception in Interviews

*"Anyone who listens is fundamentally open. Without this kind of
openness to one another there is no genuine human relationship."*
—H.G. Gadamer, Truth and Method, translated by W.
Glen-Doepel, J. Cumming, and G. Barden (London:
Sheed and Ward, 1979), 324. As quoted and cited
in Gemma Corradi Fiumara, The Other Side
of Language: A Philosophy of Listening
(London: Routledge, 1990), 28.

Brett Wiznecki's father and mother divorced when he was seven years old. His father soon remarried, moved to another state, and had two sons with his second wife. Brett seldom saw him.

When Brett was twelve, he joined the wrestling team at school and quickly became devoted to the team coach, Winston Jones. He began arriving early for practice and finding excuses to stay after the other boys had gone home. One afternoon, Brett and the coach had this conversation:

Coach: Here early again, Brett? Don't you ever stop at your locker or talk with the girls after school?

Brett: No.

Coach: Are you really all that crazy about crawling on the mat?

Brett: (shrugged) I don't know. Maybe.

Coach: Well, here, you can help me put the mats out.

Brett: Sure. Great.
As they worked, the two continued talking.

Coach: So, are you excited about our first meet?

Brett: Yep.

Coach: Your folks gonna come see you wrestle?

Brett: No. I mean, well, maybe my Mom will.

Coach: How about your Dad? Won't he want to see you?

Brett: (angrily) Not a chance.

Coach: Why's that? Don't you two get along?

Brett: How could we? I never see him.

Coach: Your folks divorced?

Brett: (nodded)

Coach: Your Dad live here in town?

Brett: (Shook his head no)

Coach: Hmm. That must make it kind of rough for you.
When did you see him last?

Brett: Two years ago. He's got new kids now.

Coach: He's remarried then?

Brett: (nodded again)

Coach: I bet you miss him.

Brett: (shrugged and looked away)

Coach: It's gotta be hard sometimes, not having your Dad around.

Brett: (shrugged again)

Coach: Well, you know, I'll be rooting for you at our matches—all my wrestlers feel like sons to me.

Brett: (looked up at the coach but didn't speak)

Coach: Hey, you know, it's kind of nice having help putting these mats out and picking them up again when we're done. If you don't mind doing it, I'd be glad to have your help before and after practice every day. That sound okay to you?

Brett: (smiling) Yeah. Sure.

Coach: Great. It's settled then. You're my "before and after" assistant. Maybe once in awhile, if we get stuff put away quickly, we can even shoot a few baskets together before you go home. How's that sound?

Brett: (smiled broadly) Great, Coach. That would be great.

Chapter Goals

- To explore the relationship between listening and perception.
- To appreciate the need for effective listening and accurate perception in interviews.
- To understand basic listening and perceptual processes.
- To recognize obstacles to listening and perception.
- To develop effective listening and perception checking skills for use in the interview.

Introduction

From the moment we're born, we learn by listening and seeing. We listen and see long before we speak. In fact, for most of us, it was through listening that we learned to speak and through seeing that we learned to communicate nonverbally. Those who cannot hear learn to speak with difficulty. Those who cannot see do not employ the same nonverbal skills. Listening and seeing are so much a part of how we grasp our world—its language and meanings, our relationships, and even learning itself—that they are tools we tend to take for granted, both as individuals and as a culture. For most of us through most of our lives, how we listen and how we perceive (see) go untaught and unexamined.

In the previous informal interview, Coach Winston Jones' goal was to learn why Brett Wisznecki was so eager to arrive and hesitant to leave wrestling practice. Through careful observation and gentle probing, Coach Jones was able to determine that Brett was bothered by his Dad's absence. Coach Jones employed both listening and perceiving in his encounter with Brett.

Listening and perceptual skills are the essential tools of the interviewer; they are vital to the success of the interviewing process. Only through accurate perception and effective listening can we hope to attain our goals in interviews. In this chapter we will explore the importance of listening and perception to the art of interviewing. We will begin by examining the relationship between listening and perception. Next, we will discuss the elements of listening and perception, by exploring the processes and levels of these related skills. Then, we will examine the obstacles to effective listening and perception and the principles and skills we can use to become effective listeners in interviews and elsewhere.

Listening and Perception Defined

Though often discussed and studied separately, listening and perception are essentially the same processes. **Perception** is the process of gathering and interpreting information through the senses. The word *perception* is derived from the Greek word *percipere,* which means to thoroughly seize or apprehend. As stated in chapter 1, perception is a multistaged process involving the selection, organization, and interpretation of stimuli or information. Usually, the process of perception is most closely linked with the reception, organization, and interpretation of visual stimuli (i.e., the things we see with our eyes), but in its broadest sense **perception** refers to all of the ways we take in, process and evaluate sensory information.

One important finding of perception research is that the previously established attitudes of the perceiver affect both what is noticed and how he or she interprets what has been observed.[1] This phenomenon is known as **selective perception.** Weaver extended this notion of selective perception to the understanding of listening with the term *selective exposure,* suggesting that attitudes such as the desire to seek information affect what and how we hear.[2] In the areas of perception and listening, the prior attitudes and judgments of the receiver affect both what is received and the interpretations that result. Bostrom writes, "Individuals vary widely in their ability to receive information, and the causes of this variation are poorly understood. Clearly messages, contexts and media all affect the reception of messages. But individual differences in receiving ability still account for large differences in communication effectiveness."[3]

While the words hearing and listening are often used interchangeably, they are not the same. **Hearing** is the auditory reception of sound waves, while listening involves far more than receiving sounds. **Listening** is the creative, intentional, and dynamic process of selectively receiving and attending to both aural and visual stimuli for the purpose of interpreting and responding appropriately to the messages and meanings of the other.[4] This definition, which includes both aural and visual reception of stimuli, demonstrates just how closely listening and perception are intertwined.

We listen and perceive most effectively when we use our eyes and ears and an open mind together. Like perception, listening involves more than actively attending (paying attention) to the messages of the other. It also involves the organization and interpretation of meanings inferred from those messages. As we shall see, listening also involves such actions as responding appropriately and clarifying our understanding through feedback. Without these ongoing responses on the part of a listener, communication would end before understanding began. Let us examine our definition of listening more closely and draw parallels to the process of perception.

Listening Is Creative

Listening involves bringing our imaginations, past experiences, and knowledge to bear on the stimuli we receive for the purpose of understanding. In a sense we can say that in the interview at the start of the chapter, Coach Jones' act of listening really began when he wondered about and imagined the reasons why Brett might be coming around so early and staying so late. The first step in the coach's listening was imaginative, it was the act of creatively wondering about Brett's actions. Perception, too, involves curiosity; that is, the thoughtful turning of one's focus toward an object, person, or situation, and bringing to bear our own past experiences and observations in the ongoing process of exploring our world.

Listening Is Intentional

It is impossible to listen well unless we intend to do it. The word *intend* comes from the Latin word *intendere,* which means to stretch toward or aim for. We can hear without intending to do so, but the act of listening requires the purposeful reaching for meaning. In the same way, we can receive visual and other stimuli without focusing on them, but it is the act of focusing that brings our organizational and interpretive powers into play. It is obvious that Coach Jones, for example, sought to understand the reason for Brett's presence through purposeful, careful questioning. Both listening and perception require deliberate focus.

Listening Is Dynamic

The listening process involves energy and life. Listening is not a passive process. The Greek root word for *dynamic* means powerful. Listening is a powerful act. It took committed energy on Coach Jones' part to learn the reason for Brett's presence. Likewise, if Brett had not listened well to the coach's questioning but had only shrugged or looked away, it is not likely the interview would have arrived at a successful conclusion.

Listening Is a Process

Each of these three qualities of listening—creativity, intentionality, and dynamism—gives meaning to our sense of listening as a *process* because listening is never an instantaneous act. It is ongoing and occurs over time. It involves refinement and exchange. We have already seen that perception, too, is an ongoing process of selecting (or focusing), organizing (or arranging) what has been perceived, and actively interpreting (or making sense of) what has been observed.

Listening Is Selective

We hear or see (receive) and pay attention to (attend to) aural and visual stimuli selectively. The process of listening, like the process of perception, is always selective; we never listen to everything that is going on around us simultaneously. There are always more sounds, movements, and thoughts surrounding us than we can assimilate. As listeners and perceivers, we continually edit out those sights and sounds that are not of interest or which we do not need to hear. Sometimes we consciously decide to pay attention to certain stimuli and ignore others, and sometimes we filter out unwanted information without even knowing we are doing it.

In our opening interview, for example, we can imagine that other sights and sounds surrounded and broke in on the exchange between Coach Jones and Brett (e.g., students going in and out, class bells ringing, people talking in nearby offices, and, of course, the sight and sounds of the wrestling mats being dragged and slapped into place on the floor). Both participants had to remain focused on the sight and sounds of the other in order to communicate effectively. As we listen and perceive, we filter out what is extraneous to the message to which we are attending. Listening well and perceiving effectively involve selecting and paying attention to the most relevant stimuli for our purposes or goals. Within the interview process, it is essential that we select and attend to the information that best serves our purposes.

Listening Is Visual as well as Aural

Like perception, listening is both a visual and aural process that involves our eyes and minds as well as our ears. As mentioned in chapter 1, much of the information we send one another is not carried on sound waves but in nonverbal messages such as facial expressions, gestures, and movements. We can see this in the opening interview; there are several occasions when Brett answers the coach's questions or statements without uttering a sound. To listen effectively, Coach Jones had to monitor Brett's nonverbal responses as well as the boy's vocalizations. The coach listened both to Brett's silence and to his spoken words. Interviews involve listening to silent as well as spoken messages; this involves paying attention to what we can see as well as what we can hear. Here, too, we can see the overlap between what is traditionally thought of as perception and the process of listening.

Listening Involves Interpretation

Both perception and listening involve interpretation. Not only do we pay attention to necessary aural and visual stimuli as we listen, but we also strive to make sense of what has been communicated. For example, imagine yourself standing near a man at a bus stop who seems to be talking to himself, waving his hands randomly, and lurching to left and right as though struggling for balance. Observing him, you compare his behavior to previous experiences and associations. Depending on your associations and on other factors, such as how the man is dressed and how he smells, you may interpret his actions to mean that he is drunk. On the other hand, you could look at that same set of communicative behaviors and interpret them to mean that this man at the bus stop is mentally ill, eccentric, or that he has severe cerebral palsy and is simply trying to talk to you. Therefore, it is through our *interpretation* of stimuli that we give meaning to the sights and sounds we receive from the world around us. All communication involves interpretation, although successful communication involves accurate interpretation of the messages received.

We cannot be sure of the validity of our interpretations unless we test them. **Perception checking** involves rephrasing and clarifying what we think we heard, saw, or understood in order to be sure our perceptions are accurate. For example, a child tells her teacher, "I feel bad," and the teacher responds by asking, "Are you feeling sick to your stomach?" The teacher is checking her understanding that the child's message "I feel bad" means that the child feels physically ill. This is an example of perception checking. Perception checking is an essential tool for an interviewer.

Listening Involves Response

"Listening to another, taking in, receiving, or accepting from another are often seen as passive. However, they all generate a response, for one never merely passively receives, one also reacts. The reaction can take many forms."[5] Listening involves responding appropriately to the communication of another. While it may not be a part of our everyday understanding of the listening process to include a listener's responses, we can easily see how vital the element of response is to the listening process. For example, imagine trying to tell a friend about an embarassing personal problem, one you want to talk about but also find difficult to express. If your friend gives you his full attention, nodding and vocally assuring you that he's listening and that he understands your embarassment and concern, you are likely to keep talking and to say all that you want or need to say about the problem. If, on the other hand, your friend sits staring out the window as you talk and doesn't respond either verbally or nonverbally, it is unlikely that you will continue speaking.

A listener's ongoing responses assure that there will be something to which to listen. Fiumara writes, "It is the capacity of paying heed to a story that allows the unfolding of its meaning. . . ."[6] The author goes on to suggest that "the child begins to speak *because* the adult listens."[7] Listening involves a set of responses in relation to the other which invite speech and welcome the expression of meanings. Appropriate listening responses include verbal and nonverbal messages as well as silence. The measure of an effective listener includes the ability to respond appropriately to what has been said. A person who attends to another's messages but gives no response cannot be an effective listener because without appropriate responses the speaker cannot be sure the message has been received.

Coach Jones used question after question in the process of determining why Brett stayed so long at wrestling practice. These questions were as much a part of the coach's ongoing listening skills as the way he paid attention to what Brett said. In fact, without those questions that continued to probe for understanding, there would have been little to which to listen, and the conversation between the coach and the boy would have ended before understanding was obtained.

An effective listener has the ability to respond appropriately to what has been said.

Therefore, questions are an essential listening tool for the interviewer. They are the vehicle used by the interviewer to move forward, to explore ideas in depth, and to obtain all necessary information. The role of questions in the interviewing process will be discussed in detail in chapter 4.

It is clear from our exploration of the definitions of listening and perception that there is more involved in these processes than simply being in the vicinity of others and seeing them or hearing whatever passes from their lips to our ears. Now let's examine more closely the specific aural, visual, and mental elements of listening and perception.

The Elements of Listening and Perception

The Aural Process

Hearing is a vital and complex element in listening and perception. We hear through a complicated system of movement of sound waves into our ears that are "translated" into electrical impulses interpreted by our brains. A variety of impairments to the hearing process can affect listening and perception in the interview. In addition, it is important to note that ". . . hearers are not passive transformers. Hearers may also have intentions."[8]

No two individuals hear the same. How and what we hear is affected by unique physiological limitations. Millions of individuals in the United States suffer significant hearing loss, including several million people who are considered deaf. There are many more whose hearing is affected by physiological factors such as tinnitus (ringing in the ears) or progressive hearing loss caused by the aging process or exposure to loud noises in the environment.[9] In fact, there is increasing concern in the U.S. culture about hearing loss among the young as a result of noise pollution. The Deafness Research Foundation, for example, estimates that 61 percent of first-year college students have a measurable hearing loss, as opposed to an estimated 4 percent of sixth graders.[10] "In the United States, nearly 8 million of the 39 million school children may have varying degrees of hearing loss in one or both ears. The degree of hearing loss need only be minimal to cause educational deficit. By the time many hard of hearing children finish elementary school, they are two or more years behind academically."[11] Obviously, it would be unwise to assume that everyone we encounter hears what we hear, even when we are thinking solely in terms of the reception of sound waves.

Moreover, many people are either unaware or embarassed by their own hearing impairments. As a result, persons with hearing impairments may not acknowledge their impairment in social situations, including in interviews. In the interviewing process, it is important for both parties to be alert to potential hearing difficulties which may not be fully known or acknowledged.

We do not hear in a vacuum. Ours is a noisy world, and the process of listening is often conducted in environments in which multiple sources of sound compete for our attention. Phones ring, footsteps and voices resound in hallways outside office doors, planes resonate overhead, radios blare, and computers hum—and all while we are trying to communicate with one another. Berg writes, "Excessive noise and reverberation in classrooms . . . are major contributors to listening and learning difficulties experienced by school children. Poor classroom acoustics cause even normal students to have listening difficulty."[12] Silverstone lists "high ceilings, hard walls, hard floors, parallel walls, hard ceilings, and reflective windows" as common causes of excessive noise levels in buildings.[13] One or more of these features are common in many settings in which interviews routinely take place.

We are continually engaged in filtering the sounds that vibrate in our ears, focusing on some and ignoring others, through selective attention. Some of us are better at this task than others. Two people may be involved in an interview in a room in which "piped-in" instrumental music is playing; one may not "hear" the music, while the other may find it difficult to think clearly because the music seems so intrusive. We hear, respond, and filter types of sounds differently. The aural process is selective.

The Visual Process

Both listening and perception employ our eyes as well as our ears. We already know that much of the information we receive when we communicate comes from nonverbal messages. We make important judgments about the communication of others on the basis of how they dress and move, how they look at us or look away, whether they gesture freely, or tightly clasp their hands. Though we're seldom aware of doing it, we continually combine the stimuli we receive from aural and visual sources in an effort to determine what other people are really saying and whether or not they are credible. The visual aspect of the listening process focuses our awareness and attention on the nonverbal communication of the other person.

Bostrom and Searle write that it is "natural" for aural and visual messages to be transmitted simultaneously and that most often these messages are consistent. When messages are inconsistent, however, these authors suggest that most listeners choose one channel to pay attention to and many exhibit a possible preference for the visual channel. The authors conclude, "Whether or not it is sensible to treat listening as aural processing alone is a vital question."[14] Listening involves more than aural processing.

In interviews our goals sometimes include assessing the credibility, competence, or even health of the other person. Nonverbal cues are of particular importance in these efforts. When attempting to assess the honesty of another, European Americans tend to observe whether, how often, and for what intervals of time the other person "looks us in the eye." In job interviews, when seeking to know how another would handle a certain situation, we describe it and observe the comfort or nervousness with which the other responds. When assessing the health of another in a medical setting, we may look at and touch the other's body, seeking signs or symptoms of disease. The art of interviewing would be made much more difficult if we could not see each other face to face.

Eye contact is a vital aspect of listening and perception, especially within interviews. Hickson and Stacks report many interesting findings about what residents of European U.S. culture "hear" and perceive when they listen with their eyes. First, these authors report a relationship between the amount of eye contact a person exhibits and their self-esteem. Those with high self-esteem maintain increased eye contact with the sender in the presence of *positive* messages, while those with low self-esteem maintain increased eye contact with the sender in the presence of *negative* messages. Second, the authors cite evidence that averted gaze on the part of a listener is most often perceived as an indication of boredom. Third, the authors report findings that persons with high gaze (i.e., persistent eye contact) are perceived by their observers as attentive, capable and strong, mentally healthy, and with good social skills.[15]

Friedman summarizes various research findings on what can be learned through visual channels. The findings reported include: (1) that clothing choices indicate both self-perceptions and the impressions wearers hope to convey; (2) that facial cues reveal feelings and body cues reveal feeling intensity; and (3) that body movements turned toward or away from another reveal like or dislike for the other, respectively.[16]

De Paulo writes, ". . . there are no perfect one-to-one correspondences between particular nonverbal behaviors and specific states or meanings. For instance, although people who like each other often gaze into each other's eyes, they do not always do so; and though gazing is often interpreted as a sign of liking, it is not always construed in this way."[17] There is wide variation, especially across cultures, in the ways listeners perceive the visual cues provided by eye contact patterns, but there is also considerable evidence that eye contact provides useful and varied information about the other.

Likewise, facial expressions are an ongoing and vital source of perceived information in interviews. We observe emotions in the faces of others and make judgments about their warmth and approachability on the basis of facial expressions. Often we perceive a sense of the tension or comfort of the other person through the tension or relaxation that is evident in facial muscles. There is evidence that facial expressions of basic emotions are the same across cultures; there are also cross-cultural consistencies in how facial expressions are perceived.[18]

Smiling is a particularly potent form of facial expression. De Paulo reports numerous research findings concerning the smiles of politicians engendering positive attitudes and responses in voters; the ability of smiles to soften legal judgments against law breakers; and the use of smiles to "apologize, neutralize, and appease." DePaulo also provides evidence that women smile much more than men.[19]

In addition to finding meanings in such visual cues as facial expressions and eye gaze, listeners observe and interpret these and other visual cues in an ongoing effort to clarify understanding of the meanings in the aural messages received. If a colleague says, "Really, I'm not a bit angry" while scowling and speaking through clenched teeth, we may decide that he or she is angry indeed. We continually seek to decipher the actual or intended meanings of others not only through their facial expressions, gestures, gaze and tone of voice, but also through observing and interpreting their clothing, movements, posture, and even where they place themselves physically in relation to others.

We cannot possibly do justice to the wealth of information available about and gained through nonverbal communication, but we can at least be aware that there is much information to be gained through our eyes when we listen to the communication of others. Our ability to understand and interpret correctly the communication of others is enhanced when we collect as much information as possible from various sources. To listen without looking would be to rob ourselves of a rich source of information. As interviewers, we must structure interviews so that we have the fullest possible visual access to those people we interview, making sure that we can see as well as hear our interviewees clearly.

The Mental Process

We are not just passive recipients of stimuli, whether aural or visual. Rather, we select, focus, arrange, label, and ultimately interpret what we see and hear. As interviewers, we make decisions—even before the interview begins—about what to ask, what to listen for, and how to assess and categorize the information we receive. After the interview, this process continues as we seek a diagnosis or arrive at a decision about an interviewee. The mental aspects of listening and perception are as influential as the stimuli that prompt the mind to work. They include such important elements as selective attention, attitudes and goals, and even the apprehension or nervousness of the perceiver/listener.

All of us make different decisions about which stimuli to give meaning and the meanings we give. The process of individual selection of information is not fully understood, but we know it is affected by both our capacity to absorb information and by the decisions we make about what merits our attention. One interviewer may insist that she can accurately assess a man's financial status by looking at his shoes, while another may not notice shoes at all. One interviewer may listen for facts, dates, and details while another may listen for a general coherence of thought and clarity of focus. Some of us "tune in" when we hear a story being told and "tune out" when we hear numerical equations, and others do the opposite.

Borden suggests that human beings have different "cognitive styles" that vary greatly in relation to the willingness of the individual to see and accept information or ideas that do not fit with her/his expectations.[20] Every listener and perceiver appears to be predisposed to attend to certain kinds of messages and to ignore others. Some researchers speculate that part of the difference in selectivity between human beings may be due to differences in which hemisphere of the brain of an individual is dominant.[21]

Even the level of anxiety we experience at a given moment affects what and if we hear.[22] Our ability to attend to and comprehend another's communication is affected negatively by our own level of uncertainty or apprehension in various situations. Because interviews—especially job-search, appraisal, medical and counseling interviews—are often anxious events, this aspect of aural receptiveness is important. It suggests that as listeners we need to work harder at listening when we are anxious and that as interviewers we should take special care to make sure our statements and questions are understood when we know or suspect that our interviewee is experiencing anxiety.

In addition to all of the mental factors that affect what we listen to, there are various ways in which we interpret stimuli differently. The sense we make of the stimuli that we encounter is affected by our own past experiences, which form the framework against which we test and measure new information we receive. Each time we encounter new information, we try to see how this information fits with what we already know or believe. Each of us brings different connotative meanings to every word we utter.

Each of us also carries within us those clusters of ideas about people and human traits known as *implicit personality theories*, which were discussed in chapter 1. Our personal responses to what we see and hear are as intricate and varied as we are. We will talk more about these differences in chapter 5, "Achieving Diversity," when we discuss the concepts of culture and frame of reference. The interpretive aspect of the listening process is intensely individual and varied.

The Importance of Feedback to the Listening Process

When we consider that individual listeners attend to, hear, and interpret information differently, it is easy to understand why feedback is an essential part of the listening process. Unless we build a framework for checking our perceptions and interpretations against what the other person intended, we have no way of assessing the validity of what we heard or saw. **Feedback,** the ongoing verbal and nonverbal responses of a listener to a speaker, provides that framework. In addition, feedback is the tool used to communicate to one another that we are listening, interested, and want to hear more. Without feedback, a vital framework for listener response, interaction would cease quickly.

When one person talks and another nods with understanding, it is feedback. When one says, "I'm feeling down," and another replies, "Is something depressing you?" it is feedback. When a job applicant answers a question about his job history by saying, "It's pretty spotty," and the interviewer replies, "Tell me what you mean when you say it's spotty," it is feedback, too. In fact, as we shall see in chapter 4, interviewers frequently employ a particularly useful form of feedback known as the *probing question*, which essentially allows the interviewer to say, "Please tell me more."

Feedback allows us to encourage others to speak. More importantly, it allows listeners to make sure that they have understood the other correctly. Feedback is as essential to the listening process as our ears, eyes, and minds in attempting to receive and make sense of what the other seeks to share.

Listening for Various Purposes

When we listen to our favorite musicians on our radios or stereos, we can do so with ease by floating in and out of the music as we please, without any pressure or obligation to hear every note or interpret correctly the messages the musicians are seeking to convey. When we listen to a lecture on which we will be tested, however, we may be under considerable pressure to hear, record, and understand the lecture correctly if we hope to do well on the test. When we interview a medical client to whom we must convey the news that he has a terminal illness, we may need to take particular care to ensure that he has heard and understood our message and to respond sensitively to how he seems to receive the news. We listen differently and for different purposes, depending on our needs and the needs of the situation.

Within the particular setting of the interview, we must always listen carefully, but what we attend to and listen for will vary according to the goals we have set for that situation. The goal of a journalistic interview, for example, is generally to gather information. The goals of selection and appraisal interviews within the workplace are usually to gather information and to evaluate the other on the basis of that information. The goal of a medical interview is to offer diagnosis and support to the other. Every interview involves goals, and interviewers must listen differently depending on those goals.

For example, if a journalist conducts an interview of a famous writer in order to write an essay on how writers write, she may ask some questions of a biographical nature but she will be listening in particular for statements by the author about how he engages in and completes the act of writing. If a mother is seeking a doctor for her children, she wants to listen for both evidence of pediatric expertise and compassion for children in the doctors she interviews. In order to be effective listeners within interviewing settings, we need to know in advance what we are listening for. Then we must listen with an eye and ear toward meeting the goals with which we entered into the dialogue.

Obstacles to Effective Listening In Interviews

We can characterize the various types of obstacles to effective listening as environmental, psychological, and cultural. These obstacles to effective listening are particular forms of the environmental, psychological, and cultural obstacles to communication we discussed in chapter 1. In addition, lack of preparation is an additional obstacle that can seriously impede the effectiveness of an interviewer. Let's look briefly at each of these types of obstacles and how they affect the interview.

In any listening situation, obstacles exist. Preparation for an interview will alleviate some obstacles.

Environmental obstacles to effective listening exist in the setting where the interview is taking place. Environmental obstacles include such elements as poor lighting, uncomfortable or inadequate seating, spatial arrangement problems (e.g., participants seated too close or too far away), room temperatures (e.g., too warm or too cold) that are distracting, and sound distractions (background music, voices in the hall, a jackhammer pounding on the pavement outside, etc.). In essence, any aural, visual, or tactile aspect of the environment that impedes the ability of either participant to remain focused on the other can be considered an **environmental obstacle.** Figure 2.1 summarizes some common environmental obstacles.

Psychological obstacles, on the other hand, exist within the minds of the participants. Included in the category of psychological obstacles to listening are such factors as an upset or imbalanced mental state that makes it hard to focus on the other person, an unwillingness to participate that results in a refusal to listen, and even symptoms such as headaches or stomachaches that distract a participant from listening well. Any or all conditions that cause inner disturbances in the thought processes of the participants and therefore exist as obstacles to good listening are **psychological obstacles.** Figure 2.2 summarizes some common psychological obstacles.

Cultural obstacles are barriers or hindrances to effective listening that exist by virtue of cultural differences between the participants in the interview. Cultural differences include not only language and meaning differences in verbal and nonverbal communication, but also differences in values, expectations, and beliefs that might impede effective communication of meanings. For exam-

Problems with Lighting	Too dark, too bright, too glaring, too harsh
Problems with Seating	Uncomfortable chairs, disproportionate chairs, furniture which squeaks or tips, desks or other furniture which create physical barriers between interview parties
Problems with Spatial Arrangements	Chairs too close together or too far apart, crowded or cluttered space and surfaces
Problems with Room Temperature	Too cool, too warm, too drafty, too stuffy
Problems with Sound	Intrusive background music, beepers, telephones ringing, street noises
Problems with Visual Distractions	Cluttered desks or tables, distracting objects, moving objects, movement or persons around the interview setting

FIGURE 2.1   Some Environmental Obstacles to Effective Listening

Obstacles	Examples
Mental Disturbances	Mental illness, agitation, preoccupation, depression, poor self-concept
Disturbing Physical Symptoms	Headache, stomach ache, shortness of breath
Unwillingness or Reticence	Shyness, fear, forced participation
Self-involvement	Inability to remain focused on others, narcissism

FIGURE 2.2   Some Psychological Obstacles to Effective Listening

Note: This list is not exhaustive; it is an illustrative sampling.

ple, a study of the use of eye contact in the United States indicates that increased eye contact by a speaker enhances listener perceptions of speaker credibility.[23] Within other cultures, however, sustained eye contact is perceived as an invasion of privacy or a challenge to authority. The Hopi Indians perceive direct eye contact as offensive.[24] Milroy reports various research findings of cultural differences in the interpretation of messages, even within different ethnic groups in US culture.[25] Any time there are cultural differences between participants in an interview, these differences pose obstacles to effective listening unless they are understood by both parties. Figure 2.3 expresses common cultural obstacles to effective listening. We will talk more about these kinds of obstacles in chapter 5.

Obstacles	Examples
Language Obstacles	Different native tongues, different word meanings, different accents or patterns of speech
Nonverbal Obstacles	Different norms about space, time, touch, status, gestures, eye contact, dress, bearing
Belief and Value Differences	Different cultural values about work, family, responsibility; different beliefs about reality, society, roles of men and women

FIGURE 2.3   Some Cultural Obstacles to Effective Listening

Note: This list is not exhaustive; it is an illustrative sampling.

Finally, our ability to listen well in an interview is affected by the degree to which we are prepared. As interviewers, we need to set clear goals in order to assess and plan. As interviewees, we have a responsibility to consider in advance what we want to learn and to share in the interview. The teacher at a parent-teacher conference may want to discover why Emily seems so tired every day. Emily's parents, on the other hand, may be hoping to learn why Emily is having recurring nightmares about getting in trouble at school. In both cases, the participants will know better what to ask and listen for if they have planned their goals in advance and considered how to attain them. To the extent that they come into the interview unprepared, both interviewer and interviewee are more likely to be distracted by irrelevant information and other obstacles.

Principles of Effective Listening

Let's turn now to a brief summary of the basic principles of effective listening that are vital to successful interviews. These principles include setting goals, listening with multiple senses, eliminating or adapting to obstacles in the interview, and keeping records. Each of these principles describes essential listening tools for interview participants.

Setting Goals for Listening

How do we set goals for listening in an interview? Listening goals are related to, but are not the same as, interview goals. In an employee search, for example, the over-riding goal of the interviewer might be to find the best candidate for the job from among the available pool of applicants. This is an interview goal, but it is not a listening goal. For these interviews, the employer's listening goals might include: (1) listening for evidence of those qualities sought in an employee: friendliness, good social skills, word processing skill, a commitment to career, and a history of successful academic and work performance; (2) listening for evidence of qualities or histories that would be detrimental to a candidate's fulfillment of the job such as problems with past employers, difficulty in interpersonal interaction, or poor academic performance in job-related areas; and (3) listening for evidence of preparation for the interview, prior research into the company, and questions about the job that indicate interest and intelligence.

A psychotherapist conducting a diagnostic interview with a new patient, on the other hand, might set listening goals seeking: (1) evidence of depression and/or delusional thinking, (2) history of prior hospitalization for mental illness, (3) evidence of drug or alcohol abuse, and (4) hostile or suicidal thought patterns. In any interviewing situation, the more clearly the interview participants assess their needs in advance, the more likely they are to learn them.

Listening with All the Senses

We have already described in detail the degree to which listening effectively engages the whole person—eyes, ears, mind, and voice—in the process of focusing on the other person's messages. One of the basic goals we must set for ourselves in interviews, therefore, is to listen with our whole selves engaged. This takes planning and commitment. Interviewers must focus intently to keep their eyes, ears, and minds attending to the other person. Likewise, interviewers must (1) develop and sustain question and response patterns that assure the other they are listening, (2) probe for needed information, and (3) use feedback to check understanding. To remain focused on another for a sustained period of time takes great energy. As interviewers, we will know we have listened well if, when the interview is over, we have obtained the information we needed, have confidence in the accuracy of our information, and are exhausted from the effort.

Adapting to Listening Obstacles

Part of the planning process for interviews must include finding out in advance what listening obstacles exist and attempting either to eliminate or compensate for them during the interview. This requires a step-by-step assessment of the interview setting and conditions.

It is the responsibility of the interviewer to locate and arrange the interview environment. Settings must be chosen that are free from as many environmental obstacles as possible. A private office with a closed door, for example, is preferable to an open setting where other conversations may intrude on the interview. The interviewer can minimize interruptions by posting a sign on the door or asking another employee to prevent intrusions. Phone calls should be held or re-routed. Televisions, radios, stereos, and even office equipment should be turned off to minimize background environmental noise.

As much as possible should be done to create a comfortable interview setting. Chairs should be arranged at a comfortable distance, allowing clear face-to-face interaction. Lighting should allow both parties to see one another with ease without harshness or glare. Visual distractions such as clutter and other unnecessary stimuli should be removed. Understanding the impact of anxiety on the outcome of an interview, the interviewer should create an environment that allows the interviewee to be as comfortable and relaxed as possible.

If there are environmental obstacles that cannot be eliminated, interviewers should do whatever they can to compensate and alleviate the distraction (e.g., closing the window to shut out jackhammer noise, or employing quiet background music to block out harsher noises from the street). If lighting is poor, chairs should be arranged by the window. If the activity of others is visible through a window or doorway, chairs should be arranged so that neither person is looking directly at the area of activity. If the phone rings, it should be answered quickly and the interviewer should say no more than is necessary to end the call. We can never control our environment completely, but we can overcome its most glaring weaknesses and create a space within it for successful listening.

Likewise, interviewers should take time to eliminate or compensate for whatever psychological obstacles they are experiencing. If they feel burdened by many tasks needing attention, they may need to take a few minutes before the interviewee arrives to make a list of those tasks so that they can set them aside to focus on the interview. If they don't feel well enough to concentrate, they should reschedule the interview. If pressured for time, they may want to affirm mentally before beginning that the information sought in the interview is worth the time. It should be a part of the interviewers' routine preparation for an interview to assess beforehand their psychological state and take whatever steps are necessary to enter the interview clear-headed and focused.

And finally, an interviewer should be aware of the potential for cultural obstacles in the interview and seek to compensate for them. An interviewer cannot eliminate cultural differences, but with sensitivity they can clarify what differences exist and recognize their potential power. We will say more about the interviewer's responsibility for effectively handling cultural differences in chapter 5.

Record-keeping: An Interviewer's Essential Listening Tool

When we attend a lecture, the content of which we will be tested on at a later date, we are likely to bring with us a pen and paper to record the important details of the lecture. Unless we happen to possess a perfect memory, we would not want to entrust the lecture information to our memories alone, but we would supplement our sometimes unreliable mental capacities with a written record. In fact, even writing information can be an effective tool for aiding our memories because by doing so we have perceived the information in both aural and visual forms.

The interviewer seeks information necessary to accomplish a specific goal, and it's of too great importance to entrust it to memory alone. Abundant anecdotal evidence exists about the imperfect nature of human memory—statements misquoted by reporters, differing views of family history by different family members, differing eyewitness accounts of single events, etc. We have all had experiences of remembering words or conversations differently from someone else present at the time. Human beings not only forget pieces of information, but we also often remember events or interactions inaccurately. In other words, we not only sometimes lose information stored in our memories, but we also have a tendency to reconstruct the information we store.

As a result, the quality of interview decisions can be eroded if we rely only on our memories to retain the information we need. As interviewers, therefore, we have a responsibility to document carefully the information that we receive in ways that allow us to retrieve it completely and accurately.

The task of record keeping within the context of an interview, however, is not an easy one. The most common effective forms of record keeping in interviews are (1) note taking, (2) electronic recording, and (3) limited reliance on memory.

Bostrom cites research that supports the value of note taking and the reviewing of notes to enhance memory, retention, and recall.[26] Note taking provides a written record of the interview, and it also affects the flow of the interview process. If we take notes, the act of note taking slows the exchange of information in the interview because the interviewer must take time to write information down. Also, when writing, an interviewer cannot pay attention to the visual messages of the interviewee or even listen fully to aural messages. For this reason, many interviewers develop a checklist or interview recording form that allows them to make short (but coherent) notations. Two examples of these forms are included near the end of the chapter. Other interviewers may develop a personal shorthand to help them record important information as quickly as possible. Still others may do away with handwritten notes during the actual interview and instead make careful notes as soon as the interview is over.

Interviewers who use note taking as their record keeping tool should prepare for the note-taking process in several ways. First, it is important to have the necessary materials ready before the interview begins. Second, interviewers should consider using a checklist or evaluation form; it makes brief notations possible and clear. Third, interviewers should work to develop a simple and personal shorthand that allows them to record information quickly. An example of such a shorthand is a physician's use of the initials "URI" to refer to an upper-respiratory infection. Note taking can only be an effective record-keeping tool for the interviewer if it is implemented so that interruptions of the interview process are minimal and do not distract from the interviewer's primary focus on the interviewee.

Another available method of record keeping to the interviewer is to record the interview on audio or videotape. This method provides a complete record of the spoken portions of the interview and allows for retrieval of complete and accurate information as needed. Electronic recording is particularly useful in interview situations where completeness and accuracy are necessary because of legal issues.

There are disadvantages, however, to this method of record keeping. Chief among these disadvantages is the potential for adding to the anxiety level of interviewees by introducing the presence of recording equipment. Of course, it is unethical to record interviews without the knowledge and consent of all parties. Relying on recording equipment also adds the burden of making sure that the equipment is operating correctly before each interview. If the equipment fails, interruption of the interview or lost information may result. Another distinct problem with this method is the large amount of time necessary to retrieve the information. An interviewer who has recorded an interview by note taking can quickly retrieve a key piece of information. On the other hand, if this same interviewer has recorded the interview electronically, retrieving a piece of information may necessitate listening to or viewing the entire interview in order to locate that same information.

Interviewers who want to use electronic-recording methods should take several steps to insure the effectiveness of their efforts. First, they should make sure the equipment is ready and operating correctly before the interview begins. Second, they should obtain the consent of the interviewee in as unthreatening a manner as possible before the interview, referring to the recording matter-of-factly and explaining that their desire to record the interview has to do with wanting to remember the information accurately that the interviewee will provide. Third, they should place the recording equipment so that it is visible but not intrusive. Microphones should be placed to one side of the interview parties rather than directly between them, where they may be a constant focus of attention. At the same time, the operating equipment—the tape recording unit or the video-taping equipment—should be sufficiently visible to the interviewer so that he or she can observe and correct any problems that might develop. Fourth, if possible, the interviewer should make notes on his or her interview guide concerning where in the interview certain information was provided. This will be helpful later in retrieving specific information from the recordings. Taping equipment with a visible counter can be particularly useful for this purpose.

As we have already noted, memorization is a faulty recording tool. Few of us can remember accurately the order and details of a conversation, even an important one, minutes after the conversation has ended. It is because of the flawed nature of our memories and the unreliability of our perceptions that so many errors and conflicts in communication occur. Only those interviewers who have remarkably trustworthy memories should rely on memory alone—or even primarily—as a record-keeping tool.

With this in mind, however, it is possible for an interviewer to rely on memory in several useful ways. Because memory has the advantage of causing no intimidation to the interviewee or distraction to the interviewer, an interviewer can rely on short-term memory to store as much information as possible until the interview is over to write it all down. This use of memory is most effective when coupled with some form of note taking.

Journalists, for example, frequently rely upon their memories when conducting information-seeking interviews, but at the same time, they record at once certain vital details—dates, times, particularly pithy remarks—to preserve accuracy. As another example, a psychiatrist in a diagnostic interview with a distraught emergency patient might not have access or wish to employ record-keeping tools in the course of the interview. However, she may decide to remember certain phrases the patient has used that seem to articulate the essential cause of the patient's crisis. At best, brief and specific pieces of information can be easily stored in and accurately retrieved from memory. With effective note taking, however, it becomes easier to reconstruct segments of interviews accurately on the basis of brief segments of information that are recorded. Memorization as a record-keeping tool works best in conjunction with one of the other tools.

Overall, the best means an interviewer has available for listening well and remembering accurately is to prepare written materials in advance that allow quick, simple notations during the interview. Then, as soon as the interview is over, these skeletal notes can be fleshed out with more detailed observations, impressions, questions, and concerns resulting from the encounter. The use of this method becomes easier with experience, as the interviewer develops a personal system for making notes. Some sample forms for use in specific interviewing situations are found in Figures 2.4 and 2.5.

Greeting	Direct/indirect
	Nervousness
	Handshake
	Eye Contact
Questions	Symptoms
	Duration
	Depression?
	Suicide?
	Delusions?
	Anxiety?
	Fear?
	Hospitalizations
	Dates/duration
	Medications
	Alcohol
	Drug history
	Over-Counter
	Expressed Concerns
Close	Reassurances sought
	Reassurances provided
	Next visit or follow-up plan

FIGURE 2.4   Sample Interview Recording Form: Initial Counseling Session

Candidate: **Date:**

Nonverbals:

    Handshake

    Posture

    Dress

    Eye gaze

    Nervous Habits

Questions:

    Tells about self

    Knows about co.

    Appeals about job

    Best job, why?

    Worst job, why?

    Career goals

    Academic achievements

    Response to conflict scenario

    Response to leadership scenario

    Personal qualities response

Qualities observed

Aggressive	Assertive	Confident
Competent	Direct	Honest

FIGURE 2.5   Sample Interview Recording Form: Job Candidate Selection

Summary

Listening well and perceiving accurately are vital to the success of an interview. Listening is an ongoing process of receiving and attending to aural and visual stimuli and responding appropriately and interpreting accurately. Listening is a creative, dynamic, and active process requiring energy, attention and commitment on the part of the listener. Numerous environmental, psychological, and cultural obstacles impede effective listening in any situation, as does a lack of preparation on the part of the parties involved. It is the responsibility of the interviewer to anticipate, eliminate, or compensate for obstacles encountered in interviews.

Listening well requires careful goal setting and prior planning. For the interviewer, the listening process is not complete without a system of record keeping (note taking, electronic recording, memorization, or some combination of these methods) that ensures accurate interpretation of the information collected. The dual qualities of effective listening and accurate perception are essential to the interviewer's art and skill.

Discussion Questions

1. Has there been a time recently when you misunderstood someone else's meaning or they misunderstood yours? Describe one of those occasions and decide how a perception check might have corrected the problem.

2. Which visual listening cues do you pay the most attention to when you listen? Do you watch eyes, hands, mouths? Do you check body movements or look at jewelry or clothes? Compare what you notice to what others notice when they listen.

3. What forms of feedback do you use most often when you listen? Do you nod your head, smile, or verbally respond? What forms of feedback do you look for in those who are listening to you? How do the two compare?

4. What listening goals would you set for yourself if you were asked to be involved in a search for a new dean of students? What would you be listening for in interviews with candidates?

5. If you were being interviewed for a job, how would you feel about your interview being tape recorded? What would you want to know about when and where the tape would be replayed? What would you as an interviewer say to someone you wanted to record electronically to make them feel comfortable with the idea?

Suggested Activities

1. Sometime today, take time to sit alone in a public setting of your choice — inside or outside, on campus, in a restaurant, library or car, at an intersection, in a busy hallway or in a parking lot. Once there and settled in, with pen and paper, spend five minutes listening to everything you can hear. Try to identify every sound and jot it down. If you hear sounds you cannot identify, jot those down, too, describing them as best you can: "clanging noise," "dull thud," etc. Try to record all the visual stimuli you encounter, too, as well

as your interpretations of what you have heard and seen. To the best of your ability, avoid becoming distracted by your thoughts and feelings; focus entirely on listening. When your time is up, make note of how you feel after listening intently for this period of time.

2. In one class today, spend the entire period watching for, attending to, and making note of psychological obstacles that get in the way of your listening. As soon as you detect internal distractions, make note of them in the margin of your class notes and then set them aside. Count how many obstacles you detected in the class period—25 obstacles in 50 minutes, for example—and determine from this the number of psychological obstacles per minute you experienced. Compare your ratio of obstacles per minute to those of your classmates. Are you more or less distracted by psychological obstacles than your peers?

3. With a group of your classmates, take a survey of the environmental obstacles to effective listening which exist in your classroom—poor lighting, noise, uncomfortable seating, crowding, etc. Then, as a group, design a classroom setting which would eliminate as many obstacles as possible and would encourage effective listening. Compare your design with those of other classmates.

Related Readings

Bostrom, Robert N. *Listening Behavior: Measurement and Application.* New York: The Guilford Press, 1990.

Donaghy, William C. *The Interview: Skills and Applications.* Salem, WI: Sheffield Publishing Company, 1984.

McGregor, Graham, and White, R.S., eds. *The Art of Listening.* London: Croom Helm, 1986.

Roach, Carol A. and Wyatt, Nancy J. *Successful Listening.* New York: Harper & Row, 1988.

Steil, Lyman K., Summerfield, Joanne, and de Mare, George, *Listening: It Can Change Your Life.* New York: John Wiley & Sons, 1983.

Wolvin, Andrew and Coakley, Carolyn Gwynn. *Listening.* 4th ed. Dubuque IA: William C. Brown, 1992.

Endnotes

1. Bostrom, Robert N. *Listening Behavior: Measurement and Application* (New York: The Guilford Press, 1990), 5.
2. Bostrom (1990), 5
3. Bostrom (1990), 1.
4. Andrew Wolvin and Carolyn Gwynn Coakley, *Listening,* 4th ed. (Dubuque IA: William C. Brown 1992), 69–109.
5. Jean Baker Miller, *Toward a New Psychology of Women,* (Harmondsworth: Penguin), 1978, 58.
6. Gemma Corradi Fiumara, *The Other Side of Language*: *A Philosophy of Listening,* translated by Charles Lambert (London: Routledge, 1990), 72–3.
7. Fiumara (1990), 118.
8. John Pellowe, "Hearer's Intentions," in McGregor, Graham and White, R.S., eds. *The Art of Listening* (London: Croom Helm, 1986), 12.
9. Wolvin and Coakley (1992), 78–88.
10. Wolvin and Coakley (1992), 87.
11. Frederick S. Berg, *Facilitating Classroom Listening* (Boston: College Hill Press, 1987), 1.
12. Berg (1987), p. v.
13. D.M. Silverstone, "Considerations for listening and noise distraction." In P.J. Sleeman and D. Rockwell (eds.), *Designing Learning Environments* (New York: Longman, 1982), 79.

14. R. N. Bostrom and B. Searle, "Encoding, Media, Affect, and Gender," in Bostrom (1990), 25–41.

15. Mark L. Hickson III and Don W. Stacks, *Nonverbal Communication*, 2nd ed. (Dubuque IA: William C. Brown, 1989), 140–44.

16. Paul G. Friedman, *Listening Processes: Attention, Understanding, Evaluation* (Washington DC: National Education Association, 1986), 20-21.

17. Bella M. De Paulo, "Nonverbal Behavior and Self-Presentation," *Psychological Bulletin 111*, No. 2 (1992), 225.

18. De Paulo (1992), 205–6.

19. De Paulo (1992), 225–27.

20. George A. Borden, *Cultural Orientation: An Approach to Understanding Intercultural Communication* (Englewood Cliffs NJ: Prentice Hall, 1991), 65–76.

21. Wolvin and Coakley (1992), 145–150.

22. Hauser, Barker, and Hughes, "Receiver Apprehension and Listening Comprehension: A Linear or Curvilinear Relationship," *The Southern Communication Journal*, Fall 1990, 62–70.

23. Hickson and Stacks (1989), 141.

24. Larry Samovar and Richard Porter, *Communication Between Cultures* (Belmont CA: Wadsworth Publishing Company, 1991), 199.

25. Lesley Milroy, "Comprehension and Context: Successful Communication and Communication Breakdown," McGregor and White (1986), 36.

26. Bostrom (1990), 29.

Part **II**

The Nature of
the Interview

Chapter 3

Interview Process and Structure

"What it's really all about is bringing my logical analytic skills to bear in the service of human understanding"
—Nancy Singer, as quoted in Sally Helgesen, The Female Advantage: Women's Ways of Leadership (New York: Doubleday, 1990), 246.

Terry Redman, a student in an introductory political science class, has just arrived at the office of her professor, Dr. Oberstadt. She has not met him personally because the class is a very large lecture. She knocks on his door.

Terry: Do you have a minute?

Professor: In a second. Let me get done with this paragraph.
(Several minutes pass while Terry stands outside the door.)

Professor: Oops! Still here? Come on in. What can I do for you?

Terry: I'm Terry Redman ... from your afternoon class? You may not know me because there are so many people. I sit near the door.

Professor: Uh huh?

Terry: Well, I'm not sure how to start.

Professor: Start what? What do you need?

Terry: (Taking a deep breath) I need to tell you about Mike Vollmer, your graduate assistant? He's my discussion leader, and he keeps asking me to come to his apartment. He says I need his help to review for the test and that I should study with him on the weekends. He asks me to go out for drinks after almost every class. I try to leave right away, but he asks me to wait and says he needs to see me.

Professor: This really surprises me.

Terry: I got an A on the first test, but Mike said that without his help there's no way I can pass the second one. He said he grades all your tests and that I can't pass without his help. He told our discussion group we should take all our questions to him and never bother you, so I wasn't sure about coming to see you.

Professor: (Sits up quickly) He said that?

Terry: Yes. (Sighs) I'm worried about what's going to happen. I don't want to go out with him, but if I don't, I'm afraid he'll flunk me.

Professor: Okay. I see. Let me think here. I think it might be best if you'd go to see the university's affirmative action director. I think maybe she's the one who can help you. Let me find her number here. (He looks around for the telephone book.) Here it is 866–2728. Her name is Sue Northmueller. I'll write it down for you.

Terry: Will this get me in trouble? I mean, what will she do? Will Mike find out?

Professor: I won't tell him, and I know she won't. So unless you will tell him, he won't know.

Terry: I'm really worried about what he'll do if he finds out.

Professor: Listen, you talk to Sue. I'll keep an eye on your grades to make sure he doesn't lower them. Now tell me your name again.

Terry: Terry Redman. R-E-D-M-A-N.

Professor: Well, let me know what Sue suggests. I'm not sure what to do about this myself, so I'll wait to hear from you.

Terry: Thanks. I hope Mike doesn't find out about me coming here. I'm really worried about my grade.

Professor: I'll take care of that. You just let me know what you hear from Sue.

Terry: OK. Thanks.

Professor: Take care.

Chapter Goals

- To understand the interaction between the knowledge of interviewing and the art of using that knowledge in an interview.
- To be able to plan and use appropriately the three basic components of the interview: the opening, body, and conclusion.

- To know how to make effective choices about the degree of control in an interview.
- To be able to recognize, strategically select, and use the four most common methods for question sequencing.

Introduction

As a context for communication, interviews are rampant with uncertainties about many things; namely, who the other party is and how that person will act, possible outcomes, unfamiliar norms, and other unpredictable events that might occur during the actual interview. In the interview at the beginning of this chapter, Terry Redman faced uncertainty about how her professor would respond to her concern. Would he believe her? Would he seem to care? Would he laugh at her or belittle her? In other interviews, there are even practical uncertainties like "Will my tape recorder work this time?" and "Will I be able to find the right room?" As previously discussed, interviewing involves both skill and art. As artists, we can never be sure in advance whether we can create the interview we imagine. Like artists, though, we greatly enhance our chances of creating what we envision when we bring certain skills to the interview; namely, planning, organizing, and preparation skills.

This chapter will introduce the practical skills necessary to structure interviews. These skills include what you need to know to plan and conduct interviews. The chapter will include types of interview structures, the degree of control that the interviewer chooses to use, and question sequences. Understanding these skills is a good beginning, but it is only a beginning. Basic skills are necessary— but not sufficient—for becoming an effective interviewer. They are the foundation; the artistic structure must be carefully managed by the skilled interviewer within the interview itself.

A common mistake made by some people who write about interviewing is that they provide specific facts and practical guidelines, but they go no further and create, in effect, "how-to" manuals for interviewers. These authors create the impression that all you need to know about interviewing are the most basic skills, such as how to dress for a job interview, how to give answers that create a positive impression, or how to make the sale. The "skills" approach to interviewing is an important part, but only part of the complete interviewing process.

Moreover, not all interviewers receive even this minimal skills approach to training. Posner, for example, found that less than 60 percent of interviewers who conducted recruiting interviews on university campuses had formal training in interviewing techniques.[1] Consider interviews in which you've participated, perhaps for part-time employment. Many interviewers for major fast food chains, for example, receive only a basic introduction to the skills of interviewing. They may know enough to ask a series of standard questions; but despite this basic understanding, most do not know the art of interviewing. They haven't learned how to take the basic technical understanding and apply it flexibly, in a wide variety of settings with a wide variety of people in order to get the specific information they need from each applicant.

Interviews with people who have the skills but do not understand the art of interviewing are often unsatisfying. An example of the contrast between an interviewer with skills only and someone who understands both the art and skill of interviewing comes from a woman who recently underwent surgery. During the presurgery consultations, she met with her surgeon who spent considerable time explaining the surgery, its risks, and predicted recovery pattern. He answered her questions carefully and kept eye contact as they talked. Even in the brief visit he had with her ten minutes before surgery, he stood where she could see him, asked her if she had questions, answered them, and assured her that "things look good."

Because surgery was on a Friday and this physician had the weekend off, the woman's weekend encounters were with his partner who rushed through their interviews, checked her incisions as they talked, and asked minimal questions such as "Are you able to swallow?" He got the information he needed about her physical condition, but the patient found the interactions much less reassuring. Both physicians knew the "skill" of interviewing; they knew how to structure a diagnostic interview. Only one, however, knew the *art* of interviewing, and the patient experienced the difference.

An effective interviewer will use skills to adapt creatively and appropriately to the specific needs of individual interviews. For most of us, trying to learn the art of interviewing is challenging; we find the skills approach more comfortable because it is more concrete. For those of us whose introduction to interviewing has been limited to skills, this book will undergird that foundation of learning and will also provide assistance to become more gifted at the art of interviewing.

Interview Goal

In an interview, at least one (and often both) parties have a goal or goals. They have ideas of what they want to accomplish with the interview. These goals guide their actions during the interview. Ideally, everything they do in the interview will move them toward achieving their goals. Without clear goals, the participant in the interview may meander through various topics without a sense of direction. Moreover, if the interviewer does not have clear goals, the questions may not obtain the information needed. Examples of several specific interview goals follow:

Journalistic interview	To get the mayor's reaction to the announcement of the automotive plant closing for use in the evening television news
Medical interview	To tell the veterinarian all of Tiger's symptoms so that the vet can prescribe the appropriate cure
Selection interview (employer)	To find the best individual to fill this job by learning whether the person has experience using spreadsheets and conducting statistical analyses

Selection interview (applicant)	To learn about the company and get a job offer by asking about the job description, company's economic stability, and by creating a good impression on the interviewer

All beginning interviewers should articulate their goals for interviews. **Interview goals** are the objectives that interview participants plan to achieve during the interview. Goals are generally written as infinitive phrases, like those in the previous examples, which begin with the word *to*. Goals usually include one main purpose. Notice that three of the sample goals are unified; that is, they all have one key purpose. The last goal, the selection interview from the applicant's perspective, contains two parts; namely, the applicant wants (1) to learn about the company and (2) to get an offer. At times, interview goals will have multiple focii; but generally, an interview participant who has a unified (one key idea) goal statement will be more likely to conduct an effective interview than someone who does not have a goal. Specific goals allow the interview participants to focus on what they hope to accomplish in interviews.

Types of Control in an Interview

Who needs to learn about interview structure? Many people assume that only the interviewer is concerned with interview structure and organization. Actually, both parties in the interview exchange roles, and often both parties have goals they are seeking to achieve within the interview. So both need to be concerned about organization.

Interviewers have a particular interest in interview structure because their roles usually have the most directional control. Planning for the direction of the interview generally falls to the interviewer. **Directional control** refers to the power of the interview participant to influence the substance of an interview, including what information is introduced, what topics are covered, and what topics are omitted. Directional control is analogous to deciding the route of a journey. Like a journey, preparation about the direction of the interview takes place before the actual interview. Obviously, a professional interviewer, such as a social worker whose job is to process new client application interviews all day, pays attention to directional control because of the need to direct the interview to obtain certain information. Consideration must be given to the time available, what questions to ask, and which to omit. These decisions affect the success of the interview and influence whether the interview goals are met. It is obvious that interviewer planning affects the interview.

Interviewees exert directional control less frequently. For example, job interviews often include a time for an applicant to ask questions. How well an applicant has prepared for this moment by formulating good questions influences whether the job is offered. In this situation, the interviewee exerts directional control by deciding what topics to raise during the time available for applicant questions. In the chapter opening interview, if we consider the professor the interviewee, we could say that the professor had some directional control through the information he sought, the questions he asked, and the information he provided about a course of action; but the student had more.

Despite the fact that the interviewee usually exerts less directional control than the interviewer, the interviewee has another kind of control; that is, informational control. **Informational control** is exactly what it says. It is control over how much, and what kind of data are shared. Regardless of what questions are asked, an interviewee can answer them either completely or evasively. A classic example of assertive informational control by an interviewee was apparent in the answers given by then Vice President George Bush in his live television interview with Dan Rather in January 1988. As CBS news anchor, Rather had pressed repeatedly for details about Bush's involvement in the Iran Contra affair, but Bush used large portions of the limited interview time (which was live via satellite) insisting instead that Rather ask him about education and "this great country of ours." Rather exerted directional control by persistently questioning Bush about Iran Contra, but Bush exerted even stronger informational control by giving only the information that he wanted to share.

Interviewees in other settings also demonstrate informational control. Several years ago, for example, national television attention was focused on Chicago where over 10,000 people applied for 1,000 positions in a new Sheraton Hotel that was opening. ABC's morning news report interviewed the hotel manager and an appli-

Often, both parties in an interview have goals they are trying to achieve.

cant who had stood in line in sub-zero weather from 2 a.m. until morning in order to apply for a housekeeping job. The reporter asked the applicant why he had arrived so early. Standing directly beside the hotel manager, who could obviously influence the hiring decision, the applicant answered that he had hotel experience and had always dreamed of working for such a prestigious hotel as Sheraton. His use of informational control in that interview probably increased his chances of being hired.

Both parties in an interview have power. The interviewer traditionally has more directional control, and the interviewee usually has more informational control, but these roles and areas of control can be exchanged during the interview. It is clear, therefore, that both parties in an interview have an ongoing responsibility for its organization and its outcome.

Two Active Parties in Each Interview

Both the interviewer and interviewee actively prepare, participate in, and evaluate interviews. Some people mistakenly believe that only interviewees prepare for interviews, as in job interviews, by getting a good resume ready, dressing well, and anticipating questions that might be asked. Other people tend to think that only interviewers need to prepare, as in the case of parent-teacher conferences where only the teacher needs to prepare. Actually, both parties prepare carefully for their roles in interviews.

Preparation

The interviewer prepares first by setting goals for the interview. These goals help the interviewer to decide how structured the interview will be, how much control will be exerted, and how the interview will be conducted. Most skilled interviewers prepare in advance. Sometimes watching effective professional media interviewers like Oprah Winfrey or Larry King can lead to the false impression that good interviewing is easy. On the contrary, it is only because these persons are both so well prepared and experienced that their interviews look so simple. It is like watching the ease with which the best Olympic divers enter the water almost without a splash; their preparation and practice makes the dive look easy. Good interviewers, like good athletes, must bring preparation and practice to the interview process to create an equally smooth performance. For the interviewer, the process of preparation includes not only goal setting, but also careful planning of the structure of the interview. (We will look more closely at the interview structure in a moment.)

Interviewees also prepare, but they prepare differently. The best interviewees prepare by (1) anticipating questions to be asked and considering ways to answer them, (2) knowing what they want to include in the interview, (3) practicing possible answers to difficult questions, (4) making appropriate choices (if necessary) about dress and punctuality, and (5) generating appropriate energy and focus for the actual interview. An example of interviewee preparation is provided in Figure 3.1.

Sample situation: Preparing for an interview with an Internal Revenue Service Tax Auditor

1. **Anticipate questions.**	What will the Internal Revenue Service auditor want to know? What documents should I have with me? What will I say if they ask about the educational expenses?
2. **Include all important information.**	What additional possible deductions could I have included? What else do I want to ask the auditor?
3. **Practice answers**	If they ask about the tuition remission, I tell them how my company only reimburses classes in computer science, not in engineering, and I'll show the booklet with that information.
4. **Make appropriate choices about dress, formality, and punctuality.**	When I meet with the IRS auditor, I plan to wear clean, conservative, and not extravagant clothes. I'll get there ten minutes early and will shake hands firmly.
5. **Generate energy and focus.**	I'm really worried about this interview, so my nervousness is making me energetic. I want to make sure that I get a good night's sleep beforehand so I can be sharp and clear with the auditor.

FIGURE 3.1   How Interviewees Prepare

Both interviewers and interviewees can learn that as their verbal interaction increases, the high levels of uncertainty that characterize the initial phase of the interview subside.[2] Moreover, as their uncertainty decreases and they both become aware of the potentially positive outcomes that can result from the interview, the more verbal communication they will have.

Participation

In effective interviews, both parties participate actively; but again, they have different ways of doing it. The interviewer acts as a kind of host, taking responsibility for beginning the interaction, initiating introductions, moving the interview from one part to another, and providing closure. The interviewer chooses what questions to ask and considers possible probes (i.e., follow-up questions) as a part of directional control. While experienced interviewers may not always prepare specific questions ahead of time, the rest of us must do so. Inexperienced interviewers who "wing it" undermine their own interview goals. Asking the necessary questions and wording them in ways that elicit the most informative responses are not easy tasks even with careful preparation. They are almost impossible to accomplish spontaneously. With proper preparation, however, even an inexperienced interviewer can participate in an interview with clear focus and effectiveness.

The interviewee participates differently. The primary focus of the interviewee is often on making an accurate and positive impression. **Impression management** refers to the ways that persons present themselves in order to create a particular impression in the minds of others. Interviewees work hard to manage their impressions. Some examples of interviewee impression management include speaking with good grammar in a job interview and describing medical symptoms completely in a medical diagnostic interview. The interviewee creates an impression by a variety of verbal and nonverbal behaviors. The interviewee also spends much of the actual interview adapting to the norms of the interviewer and the situation. In the opening interview, for example, the student, Terry Redman, adapted to the professor's lack of questions by volunteering more information about the difficulties she was experiencing with the graduate assistant. As mentioned in chapter 1, many norms are present in interviews. The interviewee's participation in the interview includes discerning and responding appropriately to the norms in that interaction.

Evaluation

Finally, both the interviewer and interviewee evaluate interviews when they are over. Did the interview accomplish its specific and different goals? If so, why? If not, why not? The more specific and focused the goals, the easier it is to assess whether they were achieved. A reporter whose goal was to get a good quote from the secretary of agriculture can judge with ease whether that goal was met. Either she got a good quote, or she didn't. Other questions help determine interview success. Did the interview obtain the desired information? Did the interview result in the information needed to make an effective decision? Diagnosis? Sale? Conclusion? Published story? Does this interview meet the participant's needs for the present? For the future? Who believes the interview was effective—the interviewer, the interviewee, both, or neither? These and hundreds of other questions help both parties judge the effectiveness of the interview on the basis of how well or how poorly they accomplished their goals. Evaluations include both the short-term and long-term success of the interview. In summary, both the interviewer and interviewee prepare for interviews, participate actively in them, and evaluate them when the interview is over. Let us look now at how interview structure affects all these activities.

Interview Structure

Even when they seem conversational and informal, interviews have structure and organization. Generally, interviews have three basic sections: the opening, body, and conclusion. The three segments differ in the amount of time they require, but each serves important functions for the interview. Let us look at the three sections individually to identify their purposes and suggest ways to use them effectively.

Interview Opening

An interview opening is critically important to the overall success of the interview because it sets the tone for the entire interview. This tone, or atmosphere, can be casual, formal, friendly, or hostile. What happens in the first several minutes of an interview shapes the impressions that the two parties have of one another and of the interview itself. In the opening interview for this chapter, for example, we can see that the professor did very little to help the student feel welcome and comfortable. In fact, he forgot about her while she waited in the hall. It is likely that this awkward opening affected the student's uncertainty about the rest of the interview. Schlenker's overview of research about how people manage their impressions shows that individuals often choose to exhibit certain behaviors in order to impress others.[3]

Social science research has identified a phenomenon called primacy effect that helps explain the importance of the opening of an interview. The **primacy effect** suggests that information received early in a relationship has a more powerful impact on the impressions formed by the participants than information received later. Jones and Goethals have noted that primacy effects have a consistently strong influence on impression formation.[4] Because primacy effects appear quite prevalent in person perception,[5] interview participants should be aware of their power. Early in any encounter, persons engage in many behaviors that shape impressions. For example, they nod, smile, shake hands, fiddle with shirt buttons, speak clearly, speak breathlessly, slouch, and stand erect. Impressions formed on the basis of early behaviors are powerful, both positively and negatively, in determining the eventual outcome of the interview. In a recent parent-teacher conference, a teacher began the conference by showing the parents of a third grader samples of the child's worksheets and artwork. After looking at some of the sheets, the parents realized they were not their daughter's work, but had another third grader's name on them. The teacher, understandably embarrassed, leafed through other piles of papers on her desk, was unable to find this child's work, and finally said, "Well, let me just tell you about her work." This kind of disorganization early in the interview had a significant impact on the rest of the interview. Although the parents continued to interact with the teacher, she seemed very disorganized to them. They may have spent the remainder of the interview wondering if the information they were receiving was really about their daughter. Because the confusion occurred early in the interview and was sustained later, this impression is an example of primacy effect. An interview opening shapes the outcome of the interview because it has a powerful impact on the ways that the two parties view one another thereafter.

An interview opening serves four important functions: (1) to exchange mutual introductions, (2) to motivate the interviewee to participate, (3) to establish a good working relationship between the two parties, and (4) to provide a preview of what will occur during the interview. These four functions—introductions, motivation, establishing relationship, and providing preview—should guide both parties in their decisions about what they should do during the opening. Let's look at these four functions separately.

Exchange of introductions is a simple and fundamental way to begin any interview. While it takes almost no time, it is an essential beginning. In most interviews, the parties simply introduce themselves to one another. If they are strangers, sometimes they will identify themselves by the organizations they represent. The parties often begin the interview by identifying themselves directly: "I'm Christina Nowaski. I've been with the station for four years" or "I'm Frank White from the Internal Affairs Department." It is important that interview participants know the name and role of the other participant. If the two already know one another, then their names and roles do not have to be stated explicitly.

These introductions do more than just establish the participants; they may also set the level of formality that governs the remainder of the interview. If a teacher introduces himself to parents as "Mr. Gabet," he is setting a different level of formality for the interview than if he says, "I'm Mr. Gabet, but please call me Parke." Interviewers often make deliberate choices about the level of formality in their introductions as a means to achieve their goals. For example, sales interviewers who sell so-called "big ticket" items like automobiles often try to set a casual tone in their interviews to create an impression of friendship that will subtly pressure the interviewee to purchase a car. Often, they will learn the customer's first name and call the customer by that name repeatedly. Some situations call for increased formality rather than informality. For example, in a disciplinary interview on a job, an interviewer may create a very formal tone for the interview. If a worker has committed a safety violation such as parking a vehicle in a dangerous position near an airplane, a supervisor who is a personal friend with the worker might conduct the mandatory disciplinary interview in a very formal, scripted way so that it is short, effective, clearly job specific, and does not interfere negatively with their relationship.

Second, introductions are the time to *motivate* interviewees to participate in the interviews. Many times interviewers are reluctant to talk. For example, survey research interviewers who conduct interviews in shopping malls often find it difficult to find people who will answer their questions. As a result, they often use the beginning sentence or two of their introduction to tell the prospective interviewee about a reward for participation. This reward may be tangible, such as coupons, free parking, or even cash. In other interviews, the rewards may be intangible, "You are so experienced in this area that we really need your help" or "You'll really make our work easier if you answer these five questions." The introduction is the portion of the interview where, if necessary, the interviewer motivates the interviewee to cooperate and participate.

Establishing a working relationship is also important to the success of any interview. Each party needs the cooperation of the other in order to achieve the goals. Interviews based on friendly interaction obviously offer greater opportunity for harmonious working relationships, but even interviews that are not friendly require mutual cooperation for interview goals to be met. An interrogation interview between police and a robbery suspect requires some measure of cooperation in order for police to achieve their goal of gaining accurate information. A professional interview between an adoption agency and an attorney needs cooperation from both sides in order to reach their mutual goal of a suitable and legal adoption. Establishing a good working relationship, therefore, does not mean that the two parties are necessarily friends; it means that the parties make communication choices that allow them to work together to achieve their individual goals.

There are many ways to establish a good working relationship. One almost universal activity that helps to establish a working relationship is rapport building. **Rapport** (the *t* is silent) is a French word meaning relationship. It is the word on which the slang term, *rap,* meaning to talk, is based. Interview participants build rapport in the first several minutes by participating in basic greeting rituals such as, "Hello, how are you?" "I'm fine, thanks. And you?" These ritualized messages help to begin a flow of interaction that continues into the interview. While they do not provide significant information, they are a part of a culturally specific greeting ritual that opens the channels for continued interaction. The opening of an interview involves the use of greeting rituals, introductions, and an established level of formality to build rapport and create an interview tone that will carry through the interview.

Finally, the opening of the interview also *previews* what is to follow in the interview. This preview functions as an orientation to the structure of the interview. It tells both parties what to expect during their time together. One of the parties, usually the interviewer, offers a preview of what will occur. This preview generally includes the following information:

1. Expectations for what the interview will accomplish. "Today I hope we can look at your performance records for the last quarter and figure out ways to help you develop more efficient use of travel time."
2. Probable length of the interview (if pertinent). "Reviewing these numbers should only take us 30 minutes or so. I know you need to get back out on the road tonight, so let's plan to be done by 2 o'clock."
3. How the information will be used. "When we figure out ways to save some dollars, we'll have you try it for a month before we make any formal agreement about the new plans. I'm not going to write this in your personnel file until we see how it works for a month."
4. Where this interview fits into the bigger picture. "The way I see it, this is a planning interview, not a performance review. I want to work with you to prevent lost time on the road. I hope this will eventually improve your performance evelutions."
5. When and if the interviewee can talk and ask questions. "I want to hear your ideas today. I'm not trying to force something on you that won't work for you. Let's start through the records together. Stop me if I misunderstand your fig-

ures and give me your input on this as we go along. I want to work with you to prevent lost time on the road. I hope this will eventually improve your performance evaluations."

Interviewers can use a variety of methods to achieve their purposes. Both verbal and nonverbal messages affect rapport building and the degree of formality in interviews. Notice how the interviewer in the following excerpt from an initial medical examination conducts introductions, establishes a working relationship and previews the interview.

Nurse: Hi, Mr. Heath. I'm Chris Richards and I'll be doing your preliminary workup today before you see Dr. Keltner. (Looks out between the blind on the window.) It still looks cold outside.

Heath: Man, it's freezing. I heard the chill factor's minus twelve.

Nurse: That's cold all right! The sign at the bank said "zero" when I came in at eight, and the radio guy said the chill factor then was minus twenty, so look at the bright side, maybe it's warming up!

Heath: Maybe, but it's still too cold for me.

Nurse: No kidding. Anyway, let me tell you what's going to happen. First, we'll get you changed into an examining robe and then I'll come back and get some background information from you. I'll also check your blood pressure, heart rate—you know, the basics. Then Dr. Keltner will come in. He usually takes about half an hour to examine you. The whole thing will last about an hour. Either Dr. Keltner or I will be glad to answer your questions at any time as we go along, okay? Well, here's the examining gown—you'll need to put it on. I'll leave while you change. You can put your clothes on that table there. I'll be back in about five minutes. I'll knock before I come in. Okay?

Notice that this interview opening achieves its basic purposes. The parties are introduced, the nurse creates a good working relationship with the patient by making small talk about the weather and establishing a tone of friendly formality, and then previews the diagnostic interview by telling what to expect. An opening does not have to be long to accomplish these three purposes. Once the opening is complete, the interviewer moves to the actual questioning phase of the interview, which is known as the *body* of the interview.

Body of the Interview

The body of the interview, like the body of a speech, is the core of the interview. It is in the body of the interview that both parties work to achieve their basic goals. As a result, this is usually the part of the interview that takes the most time. In essence, the body is where the essential work of the interview is done.

For the interviewer, preparing for the interview focuses primarily on what will occur during the body. One effective way to prepare for the body of the interview is to develop an **interview guide,** a page which includes the interviewer's goal and a list of the major questions to ask during the interview. The specificity and completeness of the interview guide will be determined in part by the interviewer's goal. This goal, in turn, determines the degree of directional control that the interviewer chooses to exert. Interviewers can decide to exert almost no control at all on an interview or they can exert tight control, depending on their goals. The degree of control in interviews and interview guides is best described as a kind of continuum (see Figure 3.2).

Let us examine these degrees of control, looking first at the left extreme on the continuum, the **highly scheduled standardized** interview guide. A highly scheduled standardized interview, most commonly seen in survey research (e.g., market research) where responses are entered into a computerized data base, has a set list of questions for the interviewee to answer. Most standardized interviews, because they are used for research and are designed to generate quantifiable responses, have questions that restrict the answers that can be given. Most require very brief answers, usually just one word. The interviewers who conduct these interviews must state the questions exactly as they are worded on the interview guide. All interviewees are asked exactly the same questions in the same way. Hence, this type of guide is called *standardized.* The questions and the answer options are highly consistent.

A less controlled kind of interview guide is the **highly scheduled** guide. This kind of guide also contains the questions that the interviewer plans to ask in the actual interview, including follow-up questions. Because highly scheduled interview guides are used in situations in which several interviewees are interviewed about the same topic, they still follow a strict format. For example, if an organization is screening six candidates for a job opening, an initial screening interview might be highly scheduled. Using this highly scheduled guide, the personnel director might interview all six, compare their answers to the same set of questions, and decide on the basis of this comparison which candidates to invite for the final round of interviews. The primary difference between the highly scheduled interview guide and the standardized guide is the degree of flexibility possible in the answers that can be given. An interview using a highly scheduled

| Highly scheduled standardized | Highly scheduled | Moderately scheduled | Topic List | Nonscheduled |

FIGURE 3.2   Degree of Control in the Interview

guide does not necessarily quantify the responses, but the standardized guide does. The standardized guide does not vary at all, and the highly scheduled guide is more flexible.

Even less restrictive is the **moderately scheduled** interview guide, the most common type of guide used by beginning interviewers. A moderately scheduled interview guide includes a list of all major questions to be covered and some possible follow-up questions. This type of guide forces the interviewer into careful preparation but allows the interviewer to make adaptations as needed in the actual interview. For the novice interviewer, a moderately scheduled interview guide provides the best of both worlds—good preparation and flexibility. A moderately scheduled interview allows the interviewer to exert appropriate control, to follow a flexible, logical sequence of well worded questions, and to probe for longer answers when necessary. An example of a moderately scheduled interview guide prepared by an interviewing student is provided as follows.

Moderately Scheduled Interview Guide

Goal: To Learn How Local Umpires are Selected for Little League Games

Possible Questions

1. How long have you been a Little League umpire?
2. What kind of requirements are there for Little League umpires in this state?
   (If he says something about license),
   How do you get that license?
   Do you have to renew the license each year?
3. What kind of training did you get to become an umpire?
   (If he says there's training locally),
   Do you keep going to the clinics?
   Do you ever teach in the clinics?
4. Why do you think we're having trouble finding enough umpires to cover all the Little League games?
   (If he says poor pay),
   What amount do you think umpires should get? Why?
   (If he says fans),
   What could be done to make the fans less abusive?
5. What other ideas do you have about the umpire shortage in town?

An interview guide that falls between those that are scheduled and those that are unscheduled is the **topic list** guide. An interviewer with a topic list guide enters the interview with a list of possible issues to raise during the interview but without any actual questions written out. For example, a pregnant woman visiting her obstetrician for a routine prenatal visit might prepare a topic list guide with concerns she has. It might include: (1) waking up to urinate, (2) a "catch" in her side, (3) childbirth classes. The list reminds the patient to ask questions about these topics during the interview.

The least restrictive kind of interview structure is the **nonscheduled** interview guide. This kind of guide has no questions prepared in advance. An interviewer using a nonscheduled guide still has an interview goal but does not prepare specific questions in advance. This kind of approach is used effectively by certain types of mental health counselors who want their clients' problems to shape the interview. These kinds of nondirective therapies are closely associated with the work of Carl Rogers.[6] For such nondirective counselors, their questions emerge entirely from issues raised by the interviewees, the clients. In such a setting, a nonscheduled guide is appropriate. Counselors who use nonscheduled guides have usually received years of training in how to conduct such counseling.

Nonscheduled interview guides are not appropriate, however, when interviewers simply have not planned ahead for the interview. Interviewers who try to conduct interviews without advance planning about goals, structure, questions, and related issues will often find that the unplanned nonscheduled approach introduces several serious problems: (1) the interview may wander away from the topics that need to be covered so the interviewer never achieves the interview goal, (2) the interviewee may withhold important information because the interviewer does not think to ask about it, (3) the interview cannot be replicated for comparison purposes because its form will be unique for each interviewer. Only highly skilled and experienced interviewers use the nonscheduled approach effectively. Beginning interviewers are well advised to adopt at least a moderate schedule for their interview guides.

An interviewer's decision about which type of schedule to use depends on the goal of the interview. If the goal is to gather information that can be compared across large numbers of interviewees (e.g., consumer research survey), then the highly scheduled standardized guide will best meet that need. If the goal is to gather information that can be compared across smaller numbers of interviewees (e.g., initial screening interviews), then a highly scheduled guide will work well. If the goals of the interview are to gather information in a way that provides flexibility but also allows the interviewer to maintain directional control (e.g., journalistic, diagnostic, selection, appraisal, and sales interviews), then the moderately scheduled interview is best. When the interview is informal, a topic list guide may be adequate for reminding participants of issues that they want to discuss. Finally, if the purpose is to provide nondirective counseling in which the interviewer responds almost entirely to the interviewee's agenda, then the nonscheduled guide will be most effective.

Question Sequences

In all interviews, even nonscheduled ones, interviewers can be more effective when they use carefully sequenced questions. In the next chapter, we will discuss specific characteristics and wordings of questions; but for now, let us examine the impact that the arrangement of the questions has on the interview. Artful interviewers design question sequences that help them to achieve their interview goals.

The most common kinds of question sequences used by skilled interviewers are the funnel, inverted funnel, parallel path, and quintamensional sequences.

Funnel Sequence

The funnel sequence gets its name from the shape of a funnel, which is large at the top and becomes increasingly narrow at the bottom. A **funnel sequence** of questions begins with broad questions and moves to increasingly narrow, or focused, questions; hence, its name. The advantage of using a funnel sequence is that the initial questions are usually fairly easy to answer because they are more general, thus helping to loosen up the interviewee. Another advantage of this sequence is that it allows the interviewer to uncover issues and subject areas that might be missed if the interview began with specific questions. When opening questions are broad and open, the interviewee is free to give general responses which, in turn, allows the interviewer to ask more specific questions about the interviewee's issues. As this sequence unfolds through the interview, the interviewee's answers are increasingly thorough and precise. An example of a funnel sequence is provided in Figure 3.3.

The funnel sequence is best used when the interviewee is willing to speak freely and is knowledgeable enough about the topic to respond well to broad questions at the outset. Some interviewers build their interviews around a series of funnels, with one funnel sequence for each major topic in the interview. Using a funnel is less helpful when the interviewee is unfamiliar with the topic or wants to withhold information. In those situations, a different approach is more likely to be effective.

Tell me about your current job responsibilities.

Why did you choose to work in that kind of position?

What has been the most challenging problem you've encountered in your work?

How did you handle it?

What would you do differently if you were faced with that problem again?

FIGURE 3.3   Funnel Sequence

Inverted Funnel Sequence

An inverted funnel sequence is the exact opposite of the funnel sequence. In the **inverted funnel sequence,** the interviewer begins with specific questions and moves toward more general ones. The inverted funnel sequence is effective in situations in which the interviewer wants to answer the question "why?" For example, in a police interview, an investigator might begin by asking about a specific situation ("Did you steal the car?") and then move to the more general issue of why the interviewee acted as he or she did ("Where were you going? What did you think would happen then?") The interviewer asks, in essence, about a specific response that the interviewee gave in the past and then probes to determine the causes for the action (see Figure 3.4).

The inverted funnel sequence allows an interviewer to learn about the reasons for an interviewee's responses. This sequence also makes it possible to find out what a person does or believes. The inverted funnel sequence is also helpful when interviewees are reticent or reluctant to participate in the interview. Since the inverted funnel begins with questions that can be easily answered with few words, quiet or uncooperative interviewees who might not answer more general questions may be willing to answer questions that are narrower.

Parallel Path Sequence

The **parallel path sequence** employs a series of questions that are comparable in structure and scope. In this sequence, the actual order of questions is less important than the fact that they are all equally broad or narrow. For example, a survey research interview involving a series of questions about the beverages consumers drink might use this parallel path sequence:

- Do you drink milk daily?
- Do you drink orange juice daily?

> When did you first start to feel this sense of panic?
>
> Where were you when it happened?
>
> Try to describe the feeling to me as exactly as you experienced it.
>
> How has this problem changed the way you schedule your day?
>
> What are the types of things that you worry about most?
>
> How do these feelings of panic fit into the rest of your life?

FIGURE 3.4   Inverted Funnel Sequence

- Do you drink carbonated beverages daily?
- Do you drink iced tea daily?

A somewhat different kind of parallel path sequence is employed in traditional journalistic interviews which ask *Who? What? When? Where?* These questions do not necessarily build on one another, but follow similar paths, like the prongs on a fork, to arrive at the "handle," or the complete picture of the situation that the journalist is covering.

In its purest form, the parallel path sequence does not use probes. Instead, it focuses on the answers to a series of similar and equally important questions (see Figure 3.5).

Quintamensional Design Sequence

The **quintamensional design sequence,** named because it is built around five (quinta) dimensions (mensional), was designed by George Gallup in 1947 as a means to gather information about the intensity of attitudes held by large numbers of people.[7] It has been used extensively since then by the Gallup Organization for its survey research. This series of five questions, always presented in a particular order, begins with a question, the *awareness step*, designed to determine how well the interviewee is informed about a particular issue. The second step, the *uninfluenced attitudes step*, asks interviewees to talk about the issue in their own words without prompting from the interviewer. The third step involves a "yes/no" question that seeks to discover the interviewee's specific response to the issue. The fourth step asks for the interviewees' reasons for their response. Finally, a fifth step is a question that attempts to measure the intensity of the interviewees' attitude about the issue. (see Figure 3.6.) The quintamensional design sequence is effective in obtaining information about attitudes from large numbers of people in an efficient manner. This brief five question design can provide insight into what people believe, why they believe it, and the intensity of those beliefs. The quintamen-

---

Whom did you just bring in for questioning?

What crime are these boys being questioned about?

When did the robbery occur?

Where did the robbery take place?

Why are these boys considered suspects in the robbery?

FIGURE 3.5 Parallel Path Sequence

Awareness Step	Tell me what you know about university assistance for learning disabled students.
Uninfluenced Attitude Step	What would you see as this university's responsibility, if any, to learning disabled students?
Specific Attitude Step	Do you approve or disapprove of the university's current assistance programs for learning disabled students?
Reasoning Step	Why do you feel this way?
Intensity of Attitude Step	On a scale of one to ten, how strongly do you feel about this issue?

FIGURE 3.6   Quintamensional Design

sional design is used primarily for research interviews. It is rarely used in other contexts.

Most of the choices about question sequencing are made when the interviewer prepares the interview guide, but as the actual interview is being conducted, it is likely in some cases that the sequencing will need to be adapted on the spot. This happens, for example, when an interviewee answers a question before the interviewer has asked it. The interviewer then adapts by reordering the remaining questions on the interview guide. Sometimes, because of interviewee responses, only the first question on the actual interview guide is actually asked during the actual interview. The art of interviewing requires both careful planning *and* flexibility to make appropriate adaptations to the specific needs of the particular interview.

To summarize, the body is the content core of the interview where both parties employ questions and answers to achieve their goals. The body is characterized by a series of questions and answers organized in a sequence designed to achieve those goals. Prior to the interview, the interviewer also plans the degree of control that will be exerted over the interview. This plan results in an interview that uses highly scheduled standardized, highly scheduled, moderately scheduled, topic list, or nonscheduled guides. Question sequences help achieve the interview goal. These include the funnel, inverted funnel, parallel path, and quintamensional. When the work of the interview body is complete, the interviewer moves into the conclusion.

Conclusion of the Interview

The conclusion of the interview serves three important functions: (1) to summarize the interview, (2) to finalize the business of the interview, and (3) to end the interview with a sense of completion, or closure. Even though these functions are all important to the successful completion of an interview, the conclusion itself does not take much time. Like that opening, the conclusion is important and brief. Let us look at the three functons of the conclusion individually and consider methods that can be used to achieve them.

First, an interviewer uses the conclusion to **summarize** what has happened during the interview. This summary, which may be as brief as one or two sentences, highlights the main issues that have been discussed. The summary reviews the interview content. Here are two examples of brief interview summaries:

Supervisor: (to employee during quarterly appraisal interview) "Before we finish up, let me touch on what we've covered today . . . let's see, we looked at your sales record for the last quarter . . . um . . . we talked about you driving up to Boulder to check out the new garages there. And we set a goal of a 2% increase for the next quarter. Did I miss anything?"

Professor: (to student academic advisee) "I appreciate your coming in to talk with me about your grade problems. Let me summarize what we've talked about and you tell me if this is how you remember it. You think your grades have suffered because you've been working so many hours at your job that you've missed a lot of classes. You're going to talk to your boss and try to get better hours. Then you'll talk to your professors about it, and you'll start going to every class. Anything else?"

A summary gives both parties the opportunity to check their perceptions to see that they remember the interview content accurately. It also reinforces the key ideas and decisions from the interview. As these examples show, the interviewer who conducts the summary can invite the interviewee to make additions or corrections.

The second function of the conclusion is to **finalize the business** of the interview. If some issues have not been resolved during the body, the conclusion gives both parties an opportunity to complete that work. For example, are there any questions that are still unanswered for either party? Are both parties clear on what will happen next? What outcomes are projected? Let us look at another sample conclusion to see how this process of finalization might occur in an actual interview.

Employer: (speaking to an applicant who is a finalist for a job) "This interview has given me a good chance to talk with you about your work experience and training and for you to ask me questions. Now let me tell you what will happen next. I have one more applicant to interview this week. We'll make our decision on Friday, and I'll be in touch with you about whether you get the offer or not early next week. If you don't hear from us, just call the secretary. Now do you have any questions about this timetable before we finish up? No? Well, then (standing and shaking hands), it's been good to talk with you. We'll be in touch early next week."

Notice that in this sample, the employer gives a brief and general summary of what they have done during the interview, tells what the applicant can expect to happen next, and gives the interviewee a chance to ask more questions. All these actions help finalize the business of the interview.

The third function of the conclusion, to **bring the interview to a close,** is also evident in the previous example when the interviewer stood, shook hands, and made a general closing statement. The interviewer takes the lead—both verbally and nonverbally—to end the interview, continuing to serve as a kind of host to the interview. The conclusion allows the host to complete the interaction and, metaphorically or literally, to show the "guests" to the door. Professional interviewers use a variety of methods to convey clearly to interviewees that the interview is over. Let us look at some additional examples:

Employer: It's been good talking with you today (Standing up). Once we complete the rest of the interviews next week, we'll contact you. Thanks for your time today (Shaking hands).

Physician: Well, take these antibiotics until they are done and I think you'll feel much better (hand on door knob as if to leave the examining room). Give me a call if you're not better in a week (Exits room).

Reporter: (Looking directly at a victorious basketball coach in the locker room) Coach, congratulations again on this great win (Turns away and looks into television camera). This is Randy Ventrella from Channel 24 Sports saying "good-bye for now."

All of these interviewers clinch their interviews in different ways. The employer gives the interview a sense of finality by summarizing, standing up, and saying "thanks for your time...." The physician gives some final advice, "give me a call if you are not better in a week," and uses two nonverbal behaviors, standing with hand on doorknob and exiting through the door, to indicate that the interview is finished. The reporter says "congratulations again" and then turns to the camera to conclude the interview. All combine verbal statements and nonverbal behaviors that say in a variety of ways "this interview is finished."

Giving the interview a sense of completion is a responsibility that falls to the interviewer. Beginning interviewers should plan a conclusion that summarizes, finalizes, and clinches the interaction.

After the Interview

Many people believe the interview "is over when it's over," that is, when the parties leave the interaction. In some types of interviews, however, either or both of the parties need to follow up on what happened in the interview, and in that sense, the interview is not complete until the follow-up work is done.

Following the face-to-face interaction, an interview participant may need to do additional work to bring closure to the interview. After a medical diagnostic interview, for example, the physician may end the face-to-face interaction

Medical interviews	<ul><li>Patient takes medicines as prescribed.</li><li>Patient comes back for the follow up visit in two weeks.</li><li>Office calls patient with lab results.</li></ul>
Journalistic	<ul><li>Reporter sends copy of article to interviewee.</li></ul>
Selection interview	<ul><li>Applicant sends thank you note.</li><li>Interviewer lets applicants know outcome of the selection process.</li></ul>
Parent-teacher conference	<ul><li>Teacher follows through on recommendations like switching child from one reading group to another.</li><li>Parents set aside time to read nightly to child.</li></ul>
Counseling	<ul><li>Client agrees to keep a journal recording her dreams.</li></ul>

FIGURE 3.7   Types of Interview Follow Up

saying, "Just wait here while my nurse writes the prescription. She'll bring it in to you as soon as it's ready." The physician then needs to make sure that the nurse gets the prescription to the patient promptly. The interview is incomplete until this "after interview" behavior is completed. The nature of the specific interview determines whether and what follow up is needed. Listed in Figure 3.7 are some of the types of follow up that might be appropriate for various kinds of interviews.

When we participate in interviews as interviewers or the interviewees, it is important for us to ask whether and what follow up is needed after the interview. If it is appropriate, interview follow up may increase the long-term effectiveness of the interview.

Summary

Effective interviewers combine their knowledge of basic information about interviews (skills) with an ability to adapt appropriately to the unique needs of individual interviews (art). One of the first decisions that an interviewer makes when planning an interview is the degree of control to exert to accomplish the interview goal. The range of control varies from highly scheduled standardized (i.e., pre-worded questions asked identically of all interviewees) to highly scheduled (i.e., questions prepared in advance and asked of several different interviewees); moderately scheduled (i.e., general questions and potential probes prepared in advance but adaptable to what occurs in the interview); topic list (i.e., a list of issues about which to ask); and finally, to nonscheduled interview guide (i.e., interviewer brings no prepared questions to the interview).

The interview itself has three distinct sections: opening, body, and conclusion. The opening of the interview, important because it can shape the outcome of the remainder of the interview, has four primary functions: introductions, motivation for the interviewee to participate, establishment of a good working relationship, and preview of the interview. The body of the interview, the question-and-answer portion of the interview in which both parties work to attain their goals, is organized around a sequence of questions determined by the interviewer's goal. The most common sequences are funnel, inverted funnel, parallel path, or quintamensional. After the work of the body is complete, the interviewer moves the interview to conclusion. The primary functions of the conclusion are to summarize the interview, complete any unfinished business, and end the interview with a sense of closure.

Discussion Questions

1. When you welcome a guest into your home, what do you say and do to make that person feel comfortable? What parallel actions could you use to build rapport in the opening phase of a journalistic interview? A job interview? A medical diagnostic interview?

2. Suppose you had the opportunity to interview anyone you would like to meet. Who would it be? What would your goal for the interview be? Compare your goal to those of others in your class who might interview the same person.

3. Which question sequence seems most like the normal pattern of questioning used in everyday conversations? Why?

4. Imagine that you are a reporter for the campus paper. You have been assigned the task of interviewing a professor accused of sexually harassing students. What form of interview guide would you use? Why?

5. Give an example of an interview that you have witnessed in which directional control overpowered informational control. Then, give an example from an actual interview in which informational control overpowered directional control.

Activities

1. Individually or in groups of two to four, decide which of the following persons you would most like to interview: Gloria Steinem, Michael Jordan, Bill Clinton, or Jodie Foster. Decide on your interview goal. Develop two interview guides which employ different question sequences. Decide which of the two guides would be more likely to result in an effective interview and why. Be able to defend your decision.

2. Listen to a television or radio interview of your choice. Analyze the interview in a way that answers these questions: Who was the interviewer? Who was the interviewee? What were the goals of the parties? What type of interview guide was used? Tell how you know. What question sequences were employed? Who had directional control? Who had informational control?

3. Prepare three different interview guides (a funnel, an inverted funnel, and a parallel path) for an interview between a reporter and the president of your college or university.

4. Individually or in groups of two to four, prepare a moderately scheduled interview guide for an interview with a local health food store owner about vegetarianism. Prepare the interview goal, five to six primary questions, and five to six possible probes.

Related Readings

Ayres, Joe. "The Impact of Communication Apprehension and Interaction Structure on Initial Interaction." *Communication Monographs 56* (1989), 75–88.

Knapp, Mark L., Hart, Roderick P., Friedrich, Gustav W., and Shulman, Gary M. "The Rhetoric of Good-bye: Verbal and Nonverbal Correlates of Human Leave-taking." *Speech Monographs 40* (1973), 182–98.

Krivonos, Paul D., and Knapp, Mark L. "Initiating Communication: What Do You Do When You Say Hello?" *Central States Speech Journal 26* (1975), 115–25.

Endnotes

1. Barry Z. Posner, "Comparing Recruiter, Student and Faculty Perceptions of Important Applicant and Job Characteristics," *Personnel Psychology 34* (1981), 329–39.

2. Michael Sunnafrank, "Predicted Outcome Value During Initial Interactions: A Reformulation of Uncertainty Reduction Theory," *Human Communication Research 13* (1986), 3–33.

3. Barry R. Schlenker, *Impression Management: The Self-Concept, Social Identity, and Interpersonal Relations* (Monterey, CA: Brooks/Cole Publishing Company, 1980).

4. E. E. Jones, and G. R. Goethals, "Order Effects in Impression Formation: Attribution Context and the Nature of the Entity," Jones, E. E., Kanouse, D.E., Kelley, H.H., Nesbitt, R.E., Valins, S., and Weiner, B. *Attribution: Perceiving the Causes of Behavior* (Morristown, PA: General Learning Press, 1972), 27–46.

5. Petronio, Sandra, Jess K. Alberts, Michael L. Hecht, and Jerry Buley, *Contemporary Perspectives on Interpersonal Communication* (Madison, WI: WCB Brown & Benchmark, 1993), 46.

6. See Carl R. Rogers, *A Way of Being* (Boston: Houghton Mifflin, 1980); Carl R. Rogers, "The necessary and sufficient conditions of therapeutic personality change," *Journal of Consulting Psychology 21* (1957), 95–103.

7. George Gallup, *A Guide to Public Opinion Polls* (Princeton, NJ: Princeton University Press, 1948), 40–49.

Chapter 4

The Power
of Questions

The thoughtful interviewer will word questions so as to:

- *Probe, not cross-examine.*
- *Inquire, not challenge.*
- *Suggest, not demand.*
- *Uncover, not trap.*
- *Draw out, not pump.*
- *Guide, not dominate.*

The test of your questions is not merely, "How much information did I get?" but, equally important, "How subtly did I guide the exchange?"
—Balinsky & Burger, The Executive Interview: A Bridge to People (New York: Harper, 1959), 59.

The student knocks on the door of her academic adviser.

Adviser: (Looks up.) Oh, hi, Lisa! I haven't seen you since last semester! You look like things are agreeing with you.

Lisa: Yeah, it's going great. I'm here to sign up for next semester. Are you ready for me?

Adviser: Sure. Come on in and make yourself comfortable. Have a seat (opens drawer of file cabinet). Let me just pull your file, and we'll get started (finds Lisa's file). Okay, let me just look over this . . . um . . . are you still taking the fifteen hours you signed up for this semester?

Lisa: Yup.

Adviser: Then, (working quickly on her calculator) it looks like you'll be a senior next semester. Seems like only yesterday you were in my fundamentals class.

Lisa: Boy, that was a long time ago. I was really a mess then.

Adviser: It's amazing what a little maturity will do. Looks from your transcript that you're really doing well. What courses do you have in mind for fall?

Lisa: Well, I have to take the two more required courses to finish my major because I want to do the internship next spring.

Adviser: (Jotting things down as Lisa speaks.) Okay. So you need the theory course. Let's see, what's the number? Oh, I've got it, number 388. And the advanced production class is 348. Got it. What else?

Lisa: For my writing minor, I have to take the advanced administrative writing class. It's number W-411. It's a five-credit class. I've heard it's a real bear.

Adviser: Getting that writing minor is a great idea. I'll bet it helps you writing papers even now.

Lisa: No kidding. You wouldn't believe the difference between how I write papers now and how I did when I was a freshman.

Adviser: It'll help you get a job, too. Companies are always complaining that their employees can't write. You can put your resume together so the minor really stands out. I think it was worth all the extra work.

Lisa: Yeah. Sometimes I wondered, especially when a couple of my friends chose real blow-off minors. They had almost no work at all. Here I was trying to do eighteen hours of pure writing classes. But I'm glad I did—if I can survive W-411!

Adviser: That means you need one more class. What do you have in mind?

Lisa: Well, I'm not sure.

Adviser: Have you looked over the course schedule book? You can choose anything at all since your requirements will be done.

Lisa: That's amazing. Anything at all—man, I've never been in this situation! Usually, I have almost no choice! Let me see. Gee, I don't have a clue. What do you think I should take?

Adviser: It's your choice, Lisa. You can decide.

Lisa: I've taken all the courses in the major that I really like. I'm *not* going to take another writing class, since I've already taken almost everything they offer and W-411 will be more than enough of that! Gee, let me see (leafs through schedule book). Wow! (Looks up at adviser.) I just don't know.

Adviser: Here's one way to work at it. Next year may be the last time in your life when you can take courses in things that you want to learn just for the heck of it.

Once you're graduated, you can take continuing education courses or courses at the public library, but most people don't. So this is your chance. What would be interesting to study just because you enjoy it?

Lisa: (Continues to look through scheduling book.) Gee, here's a course in philosophy that looks good. Nope, it's at the same time as the theory class. (Keeps looking.) Here's a course in contemporary American art that sounds interesting. I don't know much about art. Nope, it has a course prerequisite. Gee. Any suggestions?

Adviser: Another idea is to try to think about a course you've taken that was really a good course. Then we could see if there is a course in that same field that you might want.

Lisa: Well, you'll think I'm nuts, but I love the course I'm taking this semester, Geography 110. I put off taking a science class because I thought I couldn't handle it. I took Geography because it sounded easier than physics or astronomy. But I really like it. We're studying weather right now, and it even makes watching the local news more interesting. Is there a course in Geography? (Turns schedule book pages) . . . nope. Darn it.

Adviser: (Looking at the schedule book, too.) Here's a course in Meteorology. Whoops, it has a prerequisite.

Lisa: (Looking closely at schedule book.) Yeah, but the prereq is Geography 110—that's what I'm taking now.

Adviser: Well, what do you think?

Lisa: Let's see about the time. It's at 7:30 in the evening, Tuesdays and Thursdays. That'll work. My other courses all end by 4:30. Hey, this will be great! It's the same professor, too; and he's really good about explaining things so even people who aren't science nuts can understand.

Adviser: So, do you want to go with it?

Lisa: Yup. That'll be good—two courses in my major, the writing class, and meteorology. Looks good.

Adviser: I think it does too. Nice combination of classes. Go ahead and fill out your registration form.

Lisa: (Hands form to Adviser.) Okay, here you go. That was easy.

Adviser: Yes, it was. (Signs form.) Here you go (hands it to her). Now if there are any scheduling problems or classes that are closed, get back to me. I'll be here till five every day this week.

Lisa: Thanks a lot. I'll see you around.

Adviser: See you later, Lisa.

Chapter Goals

- To learn about the effect of questions on the nature of the answers received in an interview.
- To identify types of questions.
- To understand the functions and appropriate uses of open and closed questions.
- To identify interview situations that require secondary probes.
- To differentiate among different types of probes.
- To learn to minimize practices that create invalid interview answers.

Introduction

Questions and answers dominate interviews. In fact, the definition of interviewing refers to the prominent role that questions and answers play in interviews. There is no doubt that questions are absolutely central to the success or failure of interviews. Poor questions elicit poor answers. Unclear questions elicit unclear answers. Focused questions elicit focused answers. The quality of the question plays a powerful role in determining the quality of the answer. In the opening interview, Lisa's academic adviser used questions skillfully to guide Lisa to an independent decision.

In order to decide what to ask about and how to ask it, the questioner, usually the interviewer, needs to consider several important issues:

- What is my goal in this interview?
- Is the other party able to help me reach that goal?
- If able, is the other party motivated to help me reach my goal?
- How can I best adapt my questions to the other party so that I can achieve my goal in this interview?

The last consideration, adapting questions so that the goal can be attained, is the primary focus of this chapter.

Although both parties ask questions in interviews, the bulk of the responsibility for questioning usually belongs to the interviewer. It is the interviewer who most uses questions to achieve the interview goal. Writers about interviewing believe that an interviewer should generally do only 20–30 percent of the talking during an interview.[1] Beginning interviewers often talk much more than this. Why? Often, because inexperienced interviewers are not clear about their purposes and may not have prepared their questions in advance they spend too much time stating, restating, and explaining their questions. Consider this excerpt from a campus television sports reporter interviewing a university volleyball player immediately after a big upset win over the reigning NCAA champions:

Reporter: I have with me here the game's MVP (name appears across bottom of screen). What an upset! What an upset! I mean, the fans are going wild, and you guys must be absolutely wild that you pulled this off. Now, let me ask you . . . in the third match, you were down five and they were really beating you down the middle . . . and man, oh, man, you stayed with it. Now let me ask you, it seemed like you really closed down their star player. I mean, he wasn't able to do anything like he did in the tournament last year. I don't think he had more than five assists. You really shut him down. Now how did you do that on a night like this? What a night! What a night! Now, let me ask you, it really must be a thrill to be chosen MVP in a game like this.

Player: It really is, and the fans really helped us! They were like an extra player on the team.

Reporter: Well, great win! Back up to the booth.

This novice interviewer forgot that the purpose of the interview was to hear from the volleyball champion. In his excitement and lack of preparation, he literally forgot to wait for the answers to his questions. In an interview, the interviewer's purpose is likely to be met when the interviewee provides thorough answers to a comprehensive set of questions. In order for that to happen, the interviewer needs to *prepare* the questions well, *state* them clearly, and *wait* for the responses.

Questions can function as a means of exerting directional control in an interview.

The Purposes of Questions

Most people associate questions with getting information and think that questions serve only that one purpose. We use questions in problem-solving situations in which we need information. If we can't find our friends' apartment from the directions they have provided, we go to the service station and ask the cashier, "Where is Second Street from here?" We use questions to get information. If we didn't hear the weather report on television, we ask our roommates, "How cold did she say it was going to be today?" Again, we use questions to get information.

In interviews, questions serve many different functions, only one of which is to *get* information. Questions also affect the *level of rapport* in the interview. When questions are asked in a way that appears natural and conversational, the rapport between the two parties is enhanced. When the questions appear artificial and stilted, the rapport becomes more stilted also. Recent research on uncertainty reduction has found that increases in levels of disclosure like that which can occur within the first several minutes of an interview reduce the participants' anxiety about the situation.[2] Moreover, if the interview parties find that they like one another, the uncertainty drops even more, and rapport is more easily developed.[3] Experienced interviewers use questions in a way that appears conversational so the interviewees can relax and respond naturally; sometimes interviewees almost forget that they are participating in an interview. Third, questions also affect the *degree of formality* in interviews. Again, if questions sound conversational and seem to flow naturally from the responses of the interviewees, then the interview will seem less formal. If the questions are asked in a rapid sequence and if the interviewer seems to move to each question in succession without paying close attention to the response, then the interview will seem much more formal. Police interrogation and survey research interviews, for example, have formal tones in part because of the rapid-fire succession of questions (see Figure 4.1).

Fourth, questions function as the means by which the interviewer exerts *directional control*. Well-prepared interviewers know what topics they want to cover in the questions, how the questions will be worded, and in what order they will be asked. This allows them to control the direction of the interviews. They are in charge of which topics will be included and omitted from the interview. Fifth, another area related to directional control is that the questions allow the interviewer to *suggest an acceptable answer*. That is, when interviewers ask very broad questions, responses will likely be quite broad also. If the interviewer's questions are specific, the answers will likely be specific, too. The interviewer can make sure to ask questions in a way that moves the interview toward the goal. Finally, questions *encourage responses*. If questions are asked in a way that is interesting and clear, the interviewee is motivated to answer. Questions serve as motivators for the interviewee.

Then, questions serve many purposes. They gather information and affect rapport, level of formality, directional control, range of acceptable answers, and the interviewee's motivation to participate. Questions are stated both as interrogative sentences (e.g., "Does your elbow hurt when you bend it?"), and as declara-

1. Get information
   "Describe the pain in your stomach to me."

2. Affect the level of rapport
   "Overnight travel is tough for everybody, I think. Tell me, Nate, how much travel you've had to do in your present job."

3. Establish level of formality
   "Hello, Mr. Payton. Please sit over here. I would like to speak with you today about your loan application."

4. Support the interviewer's directional control
   "Are you going to support the school superintendent's new publication policy?"
   "What do you say to the other members of the board who accuse you of censorship?"
   "Will the school board vote on this policy tonight?"

5. Suggest an acceptable type of answer
   "Did you resign or were you released?"

6. Encourage responses
   "Tell me what it was like talking to your biological mother the first time after you had located her."

FIGURE 4.1   The Purposes of Questions

tive sentences (e.g., "Tell me about the problem you just had with the customer"). Good questions allow interviewers to achieve their goals while poor questions undermine those goals.

Questions: Breadth of Response

Questions are divided into various types depending on the breadth of the answer that is allowed by the question. If a question allows a very broad response (e.g., "How are you doing this semester?"), it is considered an **open question.** If a question demands a narrow answer (e.g., "Which did you enjoy more, your history class or your computer science class?"), it is considered a **closed question.** Open questions allow the interviewee to choose the response categories more freely, and closed questions allow the interviewer to choose the response categories. Labeling questions as open or closed, however, can be confusing. Many questions are not strictly open or strictly closed. Many questions, in fact, fall somewhere between those two extremes. In actuality, there is a continuum of questions ranging from extremely open to extremely closed. Figure 4.2 contains a look at the continuum about questions. See how different questions along the continuum are worded and how they work. Look first at the left side of the continuum.

FIGURE 4.2   Breadth of Questions Continuum

Highly Open

Highly open questions introduce general topics and give very few restrictions about how the interviewee can answer them. In other words, the interviewee has enormous range of what is acceptable for an answer. A common highly open question that selection interviewers use in employment interviews is "Tell me about yourself." That question is highly open because the interviewee is free to answer it in almost any fashion—in a few words or many, naming qualities or experiences, including past, present, and/or future. The range of acceptable responses is very wide.

At times, open questions are about more specific issues, but they still allow interviewees complete freedom in how to answer. A highly open question, therefore, can be very general (e.g., "Tell me about yourself.") or more focused (e.g., "Tell me your views on the tax structure."). Both questions allow the interviewee complete flexibility in how to respond, but one is on a very general topic and one on a much more specific topic. They are both highly open.

Moderately Open

Moderately open questions ask about a narrower topic and can often be answered with a briefer response than is needed to answer a highly open question. Sometimes, an interviewer will use a moderately scheduled question in order to get a more focused response to a question that had been asked earlier. For example, after asking a job applicant to "Tell me about yourself," an interviewer might ask, "Tell me more about the setbacks in your academic career that you mentioned." The interviewee still has a fairly broad range of options, but the question is more focused and may be answered more succinctly.

Both highly and moderately open questions are useful in situations in which the interviewee will benefit from the interviewer's focused and individualized attention. A hospital patient, for example, needs interactions that provide information, comfort, and reassurance. Anthony and Carkhuff identify four human relation skills which increase interviewer competence in the health care context.[4] They are also applicable to many other contexts. These authors believe that a good health care interviewer must demonstrate *attending* skills (i.e., showing the patient attention because he or she is a unique person), *responding* skills (i.e., behaviors that convey the interviewer's understanding of the patient's situation), *personalizing* skills (i.e., statements that allow the patient to better understand their role in the recovery process), and *initiating* skills (i.e., interview statements that incorporate problem solving to motivate the patient to take an active role in recuperation). Open questions allow these four skills to work in those interviews requiring personalized focus on the interviewee.

Let us look at several open questions that demonstrate Anthony and Carkhuff's categories:

Attending: "Good morning, Mrs. Garcia. I see from the chart that you had a pretty rough night last night. That must have been frightening. Tell me how you felt."

Responding: "Let's get the incision cleaned. It looks pretty sore. I admire your courage through this surgery. How are you feeling today?"

Personalizing: "When you need medication for the incision pain, you can just push this button over here. It will give you some pain medication, but it won't ever let you have too much or enough to get addicted. Think you know how to work it?"

Initiating: "This is the information from the physical therapist. Like she told you, this is a great rehabilitation program that requires lots of hard work from you. How do you feel about getting started on it?"

Moderately Closed

Generally, a **moderately closed question** seeks particular information and responses. In fact, moderately closed questions can often be answered in a few words. For example, "How long did you attend Long Beach State before you transferred to Utah?" and "What kinds of science courses did you take besides your major?" are moderately closed questions. They require brief answers. Notice that there is a fairly large gap between the breadth of answer allowed in a moderately open question compared to a moderately closed one. A moderately closed question seeks a response of only several words while a moderately open question will tolerate a lengthier answer. It is because of this gap between moderately open and moderately closed questions that we have left a visual gap on the model in Figure 4.2.

Highly Closed

A **highly closed question** seeks a one-word answer. This kind of question is used when the interviewer wants precise, specific information. For example, "How many management courses have you taken?" is a highly closed question. "How many years did it take you to complete your degree?" is another example of a highly closed question. Both can be answered with just one word, in these cases, a particular number.

Bipolar

Bipolar questions allow the interviewee to choose between two opposite answers. The word *bipolar* means just that—two (*bi*) opposite poles (*polar*). The most common bipolar question is the "yes/no" question (e.g., "Did you vote in the last election?" "Did you eat seafood yesterday before your stomach got upset?"). Other kinds of bipolar questions are also possible: "Did your G.P.A. go up or down after you got your night job?" "Are you taller or shorter than this mark on the wall?"

Types of questions, open and closed, fall on a continuum between those that are extremely open and extremely closed. An effective interviewer chooses the question type or combination that best accomplishes the interview goal. Ideally, these choices take into account the topic, the relationship between the parties, the interviewee, and the goal. Each basic type of question, whether open or closed, presents both advantages and problems.

Open Questions

Open questions, whether they are moderately or highly open, offer interviewers several unique opportunities to achieve certain interview goals. Among the advantages of open questions are these:

1. Open questions generate a wide variety of information. Generally, interviewees who respond to open questions provide much information, some of which the interviewer expects and some of which is unexpected yet useful. An example of a question that is likely to elicit a rich response is "Tell me what led you to this career in law enforcement."

2. Open questions allow the interviewee to volunteer information. As mentioned earlier, in a response to an open question, an interviewee may volunteer potentially valuable information that may not have been at all what the interviewer had in mind. If the person who was asked about what led him to his career in law enforcement volunteers that he was in serious trouble with the law when he was a teenager, the interviewer may gain unanticipated insights (see Figure 4.3).

3. Open questions allow the interviewee to answer a question in depth. An interviewee's response to an open question may answer the "why's" about a situation. The responses may give insights into the interviewee's motivation. Interviewees can answer open questions as long as they wish, and that length often allows for in-depth responses.

4. Open questions allow the interviewer to obtain a spectrum of information about the interviewee's attitudes, knowledge level, and values. For example, through mispronounced words an interviewee might demonstrate a low level of knowledge, the awareness of which might be valuable to the interviewer. A job applicant who claims to know various word processing programs may be

1. Generate a wide variety of information

2. Allow interviewee to volunteer information

3. Encourage in-depth responses

4. Provide the interviewer with much information about the interviewee's attitudes, knowledge, and values

5. Encourage interviewee participation and involvement

6. Allow the interviewee to relax and talk

FIGURE 4.3   Advantages of Open Questions

asked "What word processing do you know?" If she only answers "word processing," rather than a specific word processing program, then her lack of knowledge is apparent to a screening interviewer.

5. Open questions encourage the interviewee to participate. By their very nature, open questions elicit longer answers from the interviewee. Implicitly, an open question communicates "I want to hear your ideas on this" and allows for a greater degree of interviewee creativity, input, and control.

   Rapport is an important component of the success of open questions. Friendly greetings and identification of common interests helps build interview rapport. Likewise, research about development of **interpersonal coordination,** the ways people "mesh their flow of behaviors with each other,"[5] finds that nonverbal movement coordination correlates directly with the rapport that people experience.[6] That is, as interview partners develop more coordination between their nonverbal behaviors, the more rapport they report.

6. Because they encourage participation and a wide range of acceptable answers, open questions allow the interviewee to relax. For this reason, open questions are often a good way to start an interview.

Open questions are particularly appropriate in certain situations such as when the interviewee is relaxed and talkative, the interviewer wants indepth responses, and there is no need for direct comparison between different interviewees. For example, a journalist interviewing a cooperative interviewee to get in-depth responses for a story will find open questions best in this situation. Likewise, an employer interviewing a job candidate, one of two finalists for a job, will also find open questions useful.

With so many advantages, it would appear that open questions are the best kinds of questions to use in all interviews. These advantages, however, come at a price. While open questions encourage participation and elicit in-depth responses, they also present potential problems.

1. Open questions may provide too much information. When an interviewee is highly talkative, the interviewer may get much more information about a topic than is needed or desired. Television reporters, for example, face this problem with interviewees who take the entire air time to comment just on the opening question. They may tell the reporter far more than necessary about the topic introduced in one question and make it impossible for the journalist to ask about other important issues.

2. Open questions take time. Because an open question sets few limits, interviewees can talk as long as they want. As a result, open questions may be more time consuming than the interview goal warrants or the interviewer can allow.

3. Answers to open questions are difficult to quantify. Answers to open questions cannot be coded and changed into numerical data; thus, quantitative analysis cannot be done. If the interviewer's purpose includes the need for quantifiable data, open questions are not useful.

4. Answers to open questions are hard to compare. Because interviewees' answers may cover vastly different topics, open questions are also difficult to compare for evaluation purposes when interviewers need to rank one response over another such as comparing the responses of several job finalists. Questions cannot be easily repeated so that the results are comparable.

5. Open questions make the interview harder for the interviewer to control. This lessening of control occurs simply because the interviewer gives so much range to the interviewee in terms of what is an acceptable answer. As a result, the interviewee's informational control increases. At times, the interviewee's answers can also demonstrate directional control.

6. Open questions can result in lost or hidden information. If an interviewee answers an open question in an unexpected way, the interviewer may end up not obtaining the information he or she thought would be provided. Also, because an interviewee has more control when answering open questions, the interviewee who has something to hide can do so more easily when free to choose and edit the response. An example of this that poses problems for employers who are interviewing job candidates is that job candidates with something to hide (e.g., they have been fired from a previous job, have a poor attendance record, or have a poor G.P.A.) may not bring up those topics unless specific questions about them are asked. As a result, open questions make it easy for interviewees to "lose" this information and not provide it to the interviewer.

7. It is hard to use multiple interviewers reliably with an interview guide that has mostly open questions. When questions are open, controlling for differences among interviewers is difficult because probes are so important in developing complete responses to open questions. In an interview project with multiple interviewers, it is unlikely that they will use probes in comparable ways as one another. As a result, the answers to the questions may vary so much that comparison is very difficult.

8. Open questions are especially difficult when interviewers are not prepared. Wording open questions does not come naturally to most people. Novice

1. Generate too much information

2. Take too much time

3. Elicit nonquantifiable answers

4. Generate responses that are difficult to compare

5. Sacrifice some interviewer control

6. Can result in lost or hidden information

7. Are difficult for multiple interviewers to use effectively

8. Are difficult to word clearly on the spot

FIGURE 4.4   Problems with Open Questions

interviewers who have not prepared in advance are likely, when developing questions on the spot, to word them as closed rather than open questions. Listen to your own questions to other people during normal interaction. It is very likely that most of the questions, even when you want to receive broad and open responses, will be worded in a way that restricts the answers to them. For example, you might typically say, "Did you hear what the weather is supposed to be tomorrow?" when you really want the answer to the question, "What weather is predicted for tomorrow?" (see Figure 4.4).

Open questions present both advantages and problems for interviewers. Generally, the more open the questions, the more powerful the advantages for interviewers who want in-depth responses. Likewise, the more the questions are open, the more potential exists for problems when interviewees talk too much or hide information. In interview situations where an interviewee is reluctant to speak or where the interviewer needs a large quantity of focused information that can be compared among interviewees, then closed questions may be more appropriate.

Closed Questions

Questions on the end of the continuum where the answers are more restricted (i.e., closed questions) present a contrasting set of advantages and problems. In direct contrast to open questions, closed questions offer different characteristics that are distinctly advantageous in some interviewing situations (see Figure 4.5).

1. Closed questions gather a lot of information in a short period of time. Because the answers elicited are short, closed questions are an efficient way to get

1. Produce much information in a short time

2. Maintain interviewer directional control

3. Easy to quantify

4. Can be used effectively by inexperienced interviewers

5. Generate much data about behaviors and attitudes quickly

6. Useful with reluctant interviewees

FIGURE 4.5   Advantages of Closed Questions

necessary information quickly. A political campaign may need to assess the level of support their candidate has in a particular community. A telephone survey of 250 citizens may provide this information, but surveying so many people is only financially feasible if the questions are closed and the interviews are brief.

2. Closed questions give more control to the interviewer. Closed questions do not allow the interviewee to stray from the focus of the question. Since most closed questions can be answered in a few words, it is easy to see how the interviewer maintains better control of the questions, scope of the answers, and timing of the interview.

3. The answers to closed questions are easy to quantify. Answers to closed questions can be coded and compared, since the answers are so restricted. For example, if fifty people participate in interviews in which they can only respond "yes" or "no," keeping record of their answers and comparing their responses is not difficult. Consequently, closed questions are easy to replicate. Replicating, or repeating, a series of closed questions is possible. In fact, if the question is highly closed, many different interviewers can pose the same question and receive answers that can be compared reliably with one another. This is why closed questions are used frequently in research interviews with multiple interviewers.

4. Closed questions are easy for beginning interviewers. Many closed questions are used in specific applications like market research and political polling. In these situations, closed questions, particularly those that are highly closed, are prepared in advance of the interview by a project director rather than the actual interviewer. The actual interviewer's responsibility is simply to ask the questions, often to hundreds of different interviewees over a period of time. In these circumstances, the questions are prepared in advance by experienced question writers. Inexperienced interviewers are often hired to do the actual time-consuming interviewing. Beginners can often do this task very well because their role is simply to ask these prepared closed questions to each interviewee.

5. Closed questions are useful when the interviewer is more interested in the interviewee's views or actions than in-depth motivations. For example, an interviewer may want to know for whom the voter would vote if the election took place next week. A one word name would satisfy that interviewer's need for information.

6. Closed questions are effective when the interviewee is reluctant to speak freely because the questions are generally nonthreatening and easy to answer: "Have you bought detergent in the last week?" "If so, tell me if you bought any of these brands? All? Tide? Yes? Wisk? Other?" Interviewees may be reluctant to speak for a variety of reasons: shyness, obstinance, or speech impairment. Regardless of the reason, closed questions provide a way for an interviewee to answer briefly and easily. Thus, closed questions are particularly effective with reluctant interviewees.

These advantages—getting lots of information, ease of quantification, and greater interviewer control—are offset by potential problems associated with closed questions (see Figure 4.6). Let us look at those problems and then consider what kinds of situations are best suited to closed questions.

1. Closed questions may elicit too little information. At times, knowing the answer to a specific factual question, "For whom would you vote if the election were tomorrow" may not be as important as the *why?* Moreover, because they limit what the interviewee can say, the answers to open questions may be incomplete. That is, the interviewee may be allowed to report actual voting behavior but not the intensity of the belief.

2. They may provide invalid data. Question validity refers to the ability of the question to get an accurate answer. In fact, some authors say that "the best synonym for *validity* is *accuracy*."[7] For interviewers, the most important kind of validity is called **measurement validity;** these are answers from the interviewees that actually reflect what the interviewer is attempting to learn. For example, when an interviewer conducts a door-to-door survey about voting

---

1. May generate insufficient information

2. May produce invalid responses

3. Are not adapted to individual interviewees

4. Accept answers to questions that interviewees have not understood

5. Provide no information about intensity of beliefs

6. Do not build rapport

FIGURE 4.6   Problems with Closed Questions

preferences, it is important to be sure that the interviewees understand the wording of the questions. If they do not understand the wording, they may still answer. Their answers are then invalid because the interviewer doesn't know whether the answers reflect actual voting behavior or limited vocabulary comprehension. The wording of closed questions often makes them invalid. Moreover, a question may be worded in such a way that only two answers are given as options, but the interviewee's authentic response may be a third answer. If the closed question does not allow for this third answer, the question will not receive a valid answer. Closed questions, by their very structure, do not allow much flexibility in response. This is why the wording of closed questions is so important and so difficult. This difficulty is also the reason why many closed questions, despite the fact that they appear objective, lack validity.

3. Closed questions, by their nature, are not adapted to individual interviewees. For example, as mentioned previously, survey interviews often include many closed questions that are designed to be understood by hundreds of possible respondents. Unless a question is worded well, an interviewee may not be able to provide valuable information that the interviewer can use. For example, if an employer asks, "Which is more important to you in a job—earnings or advancement," a highly qualified candidate who also has a large family of young children would not be free to respond that "flexibility of hours and on-site day care are most important to me." Closed questions that include words that are not understood by the interviewees are also examples of poor adaptation to respondents.

4. Likewise, closed questions allow interviewees to answer even if they don't understand the questions. In response to a closed question, an interviewee's ignorance about a topic may not be apparent. For example, if an interviewer asks "Do you agree with the president's economic policy," the interviewee may say "Yes" without knowing the policy. This situation is analogous to student performance on true/false examinations. There may be a question about which the student knows absolutely nothing, but with the true/false option, there is still a 50 percent chance of being correct. Closed questions allow an interviewee to answer questions even when ignorant of their meaning. Such answers have no validity.

5. Closed questions do not allow an interviewee to express intensity of the feeling or belief about the topic. While closed questions may help an interviewer determine whether the interviewee supports a municipal bond issue, they may not be able to assess whether the interviewee believes the bond issue is an important matter.

6. Closed questions do not develop rapport. Because closed questions are controlled by the interviewer and require only short answers, the give-and-take of the interaction is lopsided. A tone of formal interrogation can easily develop. The interviewer asks a long question, and the interviewee says one or two words in reply. The pattern repeats. Such a pattern may well cause the interviewee to become defensive.

Closed questions can be helpful in achieving the interview goal in situations in which a lot of specific information is needed; multiple interviewers will be asking the questions; answers will be coded, quantified, and analyzed; and the interviewer needs control. In these kinds of situations, the advantages associated with closed questions will aid the interviewer. In situations that do not have these characteristics and/or with those interviewers who lack the ability to prepare clear and bias-free closed questions, the problems associated with closed questions will amplify the interview's problems and will generate invalid results.

To summarize, questions vary in the degree to which they allow full expression from the interviewee. When they allow a full range of possible answers from the interviewee, they are open questions. When they restrict those answers, they are closed questions. Determining whether to use open or closed questions depends on interview goals and the methods by which the questions are going to be asked. Interviewers who need in-depth responses from interviewees may use only open questions. Interviewers who need a large quantity of comparable information from many different interviewees may use only closed questions. In general, the interviewers utilize a combination of open and closed questions to obtain a balance of both specific and general information, to sustain rapport, and to allow the interviewees some meaningful choice and control.

Types of Questions

Rarely does an interviewer ask just one question in an interview. An interviewer asks a series of questions, and these questions appear in a particular sequence, or order. The overall sequencing of questions in the interview was discussed in chapter 3. There are, however, in addition to the structural sequence patterns (i.e., funnel, inverted funnel, parallel path, and quintamensional), two types of questions that are used in all interviews. These types are known as primary questions and probes, or secondary follow-up questions.

Primary Questions

Primary questions introduce topics and make sense when they stand alone. An interview often includes more than one topic, and primary questions are the first questions asked about any topic in the interview. A primary question also stands alone. That is, a primary question makes sense if you hear it by itself outside the context of the interview. Examples of primary questions could be: "Tell me about your experience with hyperbaric nursing." "Before we enroll you in an exercise class, I need to ask you whether you've had a doctor's examination in the past six months." Although we are reading these questions outside the context of an interview, they clearly introduce a topic and are understandable by themselves.

Primary questions are the questions most easily controlled by an interviewer because they can be prepared in advance. An interviewer knows what topics to cover and can word these questions to get the fullest and clearest possible responses from the interviewee. An interviewer adapts to what is known about an interviewee's knowledge, interests, attitudes, and actions on issues while preparing the questions. If the interviewer knows that the interviewee has an extensive background in a particular technical area, the interviewer does not have to define all terms and explain basic information because assumptions can be made that the interviewee already understands it. For example, a nurse talking with a new patient about her symptoms may need to ask more extensive questions than when talking to a patient who has been in the office with the same health problem for several years. After interacting with the familiar patient over time, the nurse knows the patient's knowledge about the illness, attitudes about it, and level of cooperation with the treatment. The nurse does not know these same things about the new patient. Thus, the questions will be modified to get information about those things. Adapting the primary questions to the interviewee's knowledge, attitudes, and interests is a sign of a well-prepared interviewer.

Primary questions must be clearly understandable to the interviewee. It is easy to ask questions that are overly complex. For example, listen to the following question, which was not carefully worded and prepared: "I see here you worked at the Chrysler dealership when they first opened up. How would you say it was—working for a new dealership with the older dealerships all around you. I mean, was it hard working for Chrysler when they were getting all that bad press and your dealership was the new kid on the block?" Interviewers who have not given adequate attention to the wording of primary questions sometimes begin asking the question and then find themselves caught in a tangle of complicated explanations which the interviewees cannot follow. Primary questions should contain only one idea and be easily understood. The clearer the questions, the better the answers. Now listen to a clearer primary question: "I see you worked at the Chrysler dealership when they first opened up. Tell me how it was working for a new dealership in an established market."

Primary questions must be unambiguous. When words or phrases are not readily understandable, interviewees will have a difficult time responding to them with the types of answers the interviewers are seeking. If a word or phrase is unclear, the interviewee is still likely to answer the question, but the answer may not correspond to the question that the interviewer intended to ask. For example, listen to the ambiguity in the following question asked by a reporter talking to a coach: "There were some really great plays in that game. Tell me how you felt when the big one happened." Now let us look at a clearer rephrasing of the same question: "There were some really great plays in that game. Tell me how you felt when Ochoa took it down the center for the win."

Primary questions also need to avoid **jargon;** that is, highly technical language. In any given field, jargon is a kind of sub-language that people in that field use frequently. It saves time for them because they can use short, technical words without having to give long explanations, since their coworkers know what they mean. A common problem for interviewers is that they often are so familiar with the jargon of their fields, they forget that not everyone knows what it means. Because people do not like to reveal their ignorance on a topic, they may pretend to understand what the unfamiliar jargon means and answer the question without really understanding it. Occupational jargon can pose problems in many fields, including medicine, computers, education, sports, and politics. Let us look at an example from a sales representative in a computer store: "This is a good printer for your needs. It has forty different fonts, incremental font size, and all the trimmings. Does your word processing software have the driver that works with this printer?" Contrast that question with one that clarifies jargon for the customer: "This looks like a good printer for you. It can print many different fonts—those are styles of type—in lots of sizes. One thing we need to check is whether your word processing software can adapt to this particular printer. Would you check in the manual you have there to see if your software has what's called a *driver* so that it can interact with this printer?"

Effective interviewers prepare for their interviews with primary questions that contain one clearly stated idea that avoids or explains unfamiliar language or technical jargon.

Probes

Probes, or secondary questions, do not have the same function as primary questions. **Probes** are questions that follow up on answers already given to elicit more complete information. Obviously, probes cannot always be planned in advance, since they require adaptation to specific interviewee responses. In order to develop effective probes, careful listening on the part of the interviewer is essential. Chapter 2 provided extensive information about listening skills. Those skills are essential for interviewers who want to use probes effectively. Beginning interviewers often reveal their inexperience by the absence of probes in their interviews.

Probes are necessary when the interviewer needs more information. The need for more information may stem from a variety of sources. First, an interviewee *may not have answered the question*. He or she may have misinterpreted the question, given an answer that was not sensible, or deliberately evaded answering a question. For example, in a conference with parents, a school principal might have asked: "Does Michelle eat well at home?" The parents might respond: "She seems like all she wants to do is watch TV all the time." They may be evading the question because they do not have enough food to give Michelle. Whether the answer is incomplete because the interviewee did not understand the primary question or did not want to answer it, a probe is in order.

A probe is also in order when an answer is *incomplete*. Sometimes interviewees respond to questions but do not provide any amplification or detail in their answers. The interviewer may need more information, and a probe will be required. For example, if, in response to the inquiry about whether Michelle ate well at home, her parents had said, "She has a good appetite," a probe would be in order to determine how much Michelle really ate at home.

A third circumstance when probes are needed occurs when an answer is *superficial*, and the interviewer wants to learn more about the reasons behind the answer. A commonly experienced probe in this situation is when a patient sees a physician, and the physician opens the interaction with "Well, how are you today?" Since that question is a standard greeting ritual, a patient may answer "just fine" despite being very ill. The physician who hears this polite, superficial response will follow with a probe, "The nurse says you have been vomiting. What else has been going on?" This probe allows the physician to learn more than the original superficial answer told.

A fourth reason to probe is that an answer *may not be clear.* In situations where the interviewer does not understand a response, a probe will help clarify. For example, a local politician talking to a reporter might answer a primary question with: "If we can get approval for the extension of the local option tax, then we can work on the infrastructure problems that are pressing." If the reporter does not understand how the local tax and the infrastructure problems are related, a probe to clarify is in order: "Tell me how the tax extension would help with specific infrastructure problems."

Finally, if an answer is *wrong,* an interviewer may ask another question to give the interviewee the opportunity to correct an obvious error. For example, if an interviewer has looked at a job applicant's resume and knows that the applicant has worked for the state government for ten years, the interviewer may probe if the applicant reports to have worked for the state government for two years: "You mean you've only worked for the state government for two years?" "Oh, no, what I meant to say was I have been in my current position there for two years. I've worked for the state for ten years." Notice how the probe straightens out the inaccurate answer.

In all of these circumstances, probes can help clarify answers to primary questions. Probes allow interviewers to dig deeper into answers given by their interviewees (see Figure 4.7).

Probes take many different forms and can be categorized according to the different functions they serve for the interviewer. Probes provide amplification, accuracy checks, summaries, and opportunities to ask unasked or unanswered questions. Let us look at these different functions separately.

Amplification Probes

One of the most common functions of probes is to amplify something that the interviewee has said in an earlier response. **Amplification probes** ask the interviewee to expand on an answer. Amplification probes are those that ask for more explanations, examples, or elaboration. The following example shows how an amplification probe can elicit more information:

Employer: Tell me about how well you've done on improving your problem with being late.

Employee: Okay, I guess. I mean, I tried to do better.

Employer: (Amplification probe) Specifically, what did you do last week to get here on time?

When question is not answered:

"Let me ask that again so I can understand what you mean. Tell me what happened after the professor handed out the examinations."

When an answer is incomplete:

"Okay, I understand that you said you worked on the line at Gemco for two years. Tell me specifically what your duties on the line were."

When an answer is superficial:

(Physician) "Tell me more exactly what you mean when you say `It hurts kind of every where.'"

When an answer is unclear:

"I don't understand what you mean when you say that you're partly for and partly against the annexation. Tell me more about your views."

When an answer is wrong:

"You said that you had been with the Army for four years, but your resume says three. Is four what you meant to say?"

FIGURE 4.7   Sample Probes in Circumstances When They are Necessary

Employee: Well, the main thing is I had Bruce pick me up on his way to work.

The amplification probe in this appraisal interview was asked to get more complete information than the interviewee provided in the initial response. By asking for more specific, focused information, the employer was able to secure the information needed to proceed effectively with the interview.

Amplification probes can be employed in several ways. First, they can be *straightforward questions* as in the previous example. The interviewer needed more specific information and asked for it explicitly. Amplification probes can also be used in the form of nudges. **Nudging probes** are those that ask for more information by giving several words that encourage the interviewee to say more. The following example contains a nudge that prods the student teacher to elaborate on an earlier statement:

Supervisor: Your student teaching seems to be going fine. How are you feeling about it?

Student teacher: All right, I guess. I've been pretty well prepared for my classes. Kids can get a little hyper, but they're only third graders. But my supervising teacher—she's a little hard to work with.

Supervisor: (nudge) She is?

Student teacher: Yeah, she tells me exactly what I have to teach every day and doesn't let me do anything creative like we learned in methods class. I feel like I'm just a substitute rather than a student teacher.

The nudge from the supervisor was an amplification probe. The mild push in the words "she is?" motivated the student teacher to explain in more detail his problems with the supervising teacher. This amplification allowed the interviewer to collect additional useful information.

A last technique used for amplification probes is *silence.* Many times interviewers encourage interviewees to amplify their responses by sitting silently and waiting for a longer answer. Although many people find silence disconcerting, it is an effective tool in an interview. An interviewee may feel uncomfortable with silence and may voluntarily go on to explain an answer more fully if the interviewer has the patience and courage to await a more complete response silently.

Amplification probes, whether in the form of outright questions, nudges, or silence allow an interviewer to get additional information from an interviewee.

Accuracy Checking Probes

Probes are also used to check the accuracy of answers, including both the accuracy of what the person said and the accuracy of interviewer's understanding. One of the techniques most helpful in communication in general is the **perception check,** the process by which we check whether our understanding of a message is accurate by asking the person who sent it. For example, in a classroom setting, a teacher might say to a student, "You look confused. Are you?" The student can then say, "Yes, I didn't understand that last example." This check on the teacher's perceptions, which the teacher seeks out, allows the teacher to affirm the accuracy of her perception that the student was confused. Moreover, it allows the teacher to go back and explain the concept again.

Accuracy checking probes serve the same purposes. By reflecting the answer to the interviewee, the interviewer checks to see (1) what the interviewee meant, and (2) whether the interviewer understood it accurately. It allows an interviewee to confirm, deny, adjust, and clarify what was said. Because accuracy checking probes reflect previous answers back to the interviewees, they are sometimes called *mirror probes.* Accuracy checking probes can also add to rapport in an interview because they demonstrate that the interviewer has been listening carefully and is authentically interested in getting accurate understanding from the interviewee. Let us look at an example:

Physician: I'm going to send you to the lab for these tests.

Patient: (accuracy-check) To the lab? The one here?

Physician: Right, the lab here on the first floor of our clinic.

Patient: (accuracy-check) Does the clinic run the lab? I mean does it do its own testing?

Physician: Yes, and I think they do the best work in town.

Summary Probes

Summary probes are secondary questions within the interview that provide an up-to-date account of what the interviewer thinks has happened in the interview. Summary probes can occur throughout the interview, but they are most likely to occur after a series of questions on one topic. They allow an interviewer to summarize what has been said, and, equally important, they allow the interviewee to check the accuracy of the interviewer's summary. Effective summary probes allow the interviewer to state her/his understanding of what has occurred, demonstrate careful attention, and encourage further interaction on the topic if it seems warranted. Below is an example of a summary probe:

School Counselor: (To parents) Let me see if I've got this all down. We're going to transfer Alisha to the advanced math class and switch her from 4th period Spanish to 1st period Spanish with the same teacher. I'll take care of the transfer this afternoon. Is that everything we decided?

Summary probes perform several valuable functions in an interview. They allow checks about agreement on decisions, and they convey to the interviewee that the interviewer is listening carefully and ascribing importance to what the interviewee has said.

Clearinghouse Probes

The last type of probe to be considered is the clearinghouse probe, which is a probe designed to "clear the house," or the interview, of any unasked questions. **Clearinghouse probes** allow both parties, but particularly the interviewee, to raise questions, topics, or issues that haven't been addressed yet in the interview. They allow the interviewee to ask questions that haven't been covered, give more complete explanations of earlier answers, or fill in any perceived gaps in the information provided. Here are some brief examples of clearinghouse probes.

Teacher: (To parents) So far, I've been doing most of the talking here. What questions do you have about Moshe's progress this year?

Loan officer: (To loan applicants) Okay, I think that wraps up all the questions I need to ask you about your loan application. Now what questions do you have about the terms of the loan or the application process?

Reporter: That gives me all the information I think I need for the story. Is there anything else you want to add that you think I should know?

Amplification Probes

- Straightforward questions
- Nudges
- Silence

Accuracy Checking Probes

- Perception check
- Mirror probes

Summary Probes

Clearinghouse Probes

FIGURE 4.8   Types of Probes

Clearinghouse probes give the interviewee one last chance to add anything that may have been omitted from the body of the interview.

As we have seen, probes serve many important functions in interviews, particularly the functions of amplification, accuracy checking, summary, and the clearinghouse role (see Figure 4.8). The effectiveness of probes depends on the interviewer's ability and motivation to listen closely to the interviewee's answers. Perhaps it is because beginning interviewers are focused so much on themselves and their questions that they find it difficult to concentrate on the answers and they often underuse probes. Experienced interviewers, on the other hand, use probes extensively to increase the quality and accuracy of the information they receive and to convey to their interviewees their interest in what the interviewees have to say.

Question Validity

The elements of questions that we have discussed so far in this chapter—degree of openness (open/closed) and type of questions (primary/secondary)—are based on the fundamental premise that the interviewer wants the most valid information possible. In general terms, the issue of **validity** is concerned with the degree to which we are actually measuring what we want to be measuring. In interviews, validity refers to whether the answers we receive are clear and accurate responses to our questions. In order to understand the importance of validity, take a minute to examine the following questions. See if you can determine the validity problem in each of them.

Professor: (To student currently enrolled in class) How do you like my lectures?

Car sales representative: You know about fuel-injection, don't you?

Collection agency representative to delinquent customer: Have you paid your bill or must we take legal action on this?

The specific problems with these questions vary, but they share one common weakness; namely, the answers they elicit are not likely to be valid. Why? A student enrolled in a professor's class has many reasons not to give an honest answer to the professor's direct question, "How do you like my lectures?" If the student says the lectures are poor, for example, the professor's feelings might be hurt and the student's grade lowered as a result. With the car sales representative's question, "You know about fuel injection, don't you," the customer risks appearing ignorant if he answers "no." With the collection agency representative's question, it is quite likely that a customer would say, "The check's in the mail" rather than give an honest response which could result in legal action. Each of these questions pose problems with the validity of the answers they would elicit.

Three different interview problems can impair the validity of the interview—social desirability effect, leading questions, and problem questions. Let us consider these individually.

Social Desirability Effect

Social desirability effect refers to the pressure that people commonly experience to give answers that seem socially acceptable. Socially desirable answers are those that seem to mesh with existing social norms. For example, in U.S. culture, people often under report the amount of alcoholic beverages they consume because the culture in general frowns on excessive consumption of alcohol. Socially desirable answers provide invalid information because they don't tell what the interviewee really believes or does. Rather, they tell what the interviewee thinks he or she *should* do or believe. Imagine that a nutritionist came to your interviewing class to conduct sample interviews. The nutritionist calls you up in front of the class and begins with the question, "What did you have for breakfast?" This seemingly harmless question can, in many circumstances, elicit a socially desirable response. If you had an oat bran muffin, orange juice, and decaffeinated tea, you might answer honestly because you assume your breakfast matched what a nutritionist would consider to be socially desirable. If, on the other hand, you ate a piece of leftover blueberry pie and washed it down with a Coke™, or if you ate nothing at all, the pressure for social desirability might lead you to give an invalid answer. You might say, "I don't remember," or "I think I just had some cereal" rather than "I had pie and Coke™." The pressures to provide socially desirable answers influences interviews about sexual preference and controversial topics like abortion. But this same pressure for social desirability can exert more unexpected influence on seemingly noncontroversial topics, such as personal hygiene, than people realize.

Let us look at a few examples of questions that exert pressure for socially desirable answers. The question, "Did you vote in the last election?" includes pressure for a socially desirable answer because citizens of the United States are "supposed" to vote. A question about voting behavior that exerts less pressure for a socially desirable answer would be, "Please tell me which of these you did in the last mayoral election: did not vote, voted for Bronowski, or voted for Melton." In this question, "did not vote" is presented as a valid option. The question, "Do you eat a lot of butter, fried foods, and other high cholesterol foods?" includes pressure for a socially desirable answer because current norms for healthy eating say these foods should be avoided. A question that exerts less pressure might be, "Tell me what you eat on a typical day."

If an interviewer is asking questions on a topic about which there are existing social norms, the questions need to be worded to minimize the pressure to conform to what is socially desirable. This adaptation of questions can vary markedly from one interviewee to the next. In some social groups, for example, it is highly desirable to attend religious services regularly. In other groups, it is socially undesirable to admit to regular attendance at religious services. Having background information about the interviewee in advance allows the interviewer to word questions in such a way to minimize the effect of socially desirable answers.

Leading Questions

Leading questions actually suggest a desired response from the interviewee. As worded, leading questions provide hints to the interviewee about what answer the interviewer wants to hear or considers correct. In most cases, when asked a leading question, an interviewee will respond to this interviewer bias by answering in the direction suggested by the interviewer, whether or not that answer is authentic. Leading questions pressure interviewees to answer in a way that conforms with what the interviewer has suggested.

Leading questions can be worded in ways that are blatantly leading or quite subtle. Blatantly leading questions are often prefaced with information that shows the interviewer's bias. For example, a principal speaking to an applicant for a teaching job at Central High might say: "Here at Central High, we think all teachers should support the school and attend at least two sports or cultural events each week. What do you think about attending school activities in the evening?" Another example from a sales representative to a potential corporate customer would be: "Your boss, Senior Vice President Simpson, said that you would be happy to meet with me anytime. Do you have some time now?" Notice that the prefatory phrases in each of these questions suggest a correct response. In suggesting this, the interviewer reduces the likelihood that the interviewees will disagree.

Leading questions often incorporate emotionally charged language to convey the correct answer. An interviewer for a campus paper, for example, asked a resigning student senator to ". . . comment on the student body president's complete domination of student government activities." Implicit in the words "complete domination" was an invitation to the senator to criticize the president.

Surveys by members of consumer groups to voters sometimes incorporate emotionally charged wording: "Who would you say is responsible for the recession? Average middle-class citizens or rich, greedy business owners?

Questions that incorporate leading language are fairly obvious; that is, the interviewer's bias is apparent. As a result, the interviewee is pressured to answer as the interviewer suggests is appropriate. Examples of leading questions include: "Isn't that about the worst article you've ever read?" "How do you feel about this ridiculous annexation that will double our property taxes?" "Are you in favor of killing babies?" The answers that people give to questions like these are not valid because the interviewer has imposed so much bias onto the questions that the interviewee is not free to respond authentically. Even if the interviewee agrees completely with the bias of the questioner, it is impossible to sort out the authentic agreement from unauthentic answers.

Questions can also be leading by omitting some response options. Leading questions can sway respondents to particular answers by giving an incomplete set of possible responses. A telephone survey from a member of the House of Representatives demonstrated this bias. His interviewer asked voters in the district: "How much of an increase should we implement in military allocations in the next budget? 10 percent increase? 20 percent increase? 25 percent increase? 50 percent increase?" Because no options were provided for "no increase" or "decrease," interviewees were led to answer in a way consistent with the political preferences of the representative. For questions to allow valid, bias-free answers, all possible answer options must be included. This is why, as we will discuss later in the book, many researchers avoid bipolar questions and provide, instead, a set of options to their interviewees. Let us look at some examples of leading questions and then examine neutral rewording of the same ideas:

Leading:

"You would plan to stay here with our firm for at least five years, wouldn't you?"

Neutral Rewording:

"What are your career plans for the next five years?"

Leading:

"Wasn't the Odiorne report terrible? I couldn't believe it—there were even spelling errors."

Neutral Rewording:

"What did you think of the Odiorne report?"

Leading:

"Does your leg hurt a lot down here by the ankle too?"

Neutral Rewording:

"Does your leg hurt anywhere else?"

There are certain limited situations in which leading questions can actually help interviewers get accurate and valid information. One such situation is when interviewees are being asked to share information that is embarrassing or incriminating. Research about sexual practices, for example, may intentionally incorporate leading questions because these questions can offer assurances to the interviewee that the interviewer believes that millions of normal, healthy people engage in a variety of sexual practices.[8] Thus, an interviewer in this case might say: "Sexually active adults engage in a variety of interesting sexual practices. How would you describe some of yours?" In situations where interviewees might believe they are violating social norms when they report their behaviors honestly, interviewers can design questions so that broader social norms are obvious. The interviewee may then feel free to speak about what might otherwise have been embarrassing topics (see Figure 4.9).

Problem Questions

Other specific types of questions can threaten the validity of answers. Interviewers who can identify and avoid these kinds of questions are more likely to attain valid, meaningful, and understandable responses. Questions that include more than one question, are too long or too short, contain jargon, or contain both an open and a closed question are all problematic for interviewers. Let us look at these one at a time to identify clearly the types of problems they create. This will aid our understanding of ways to reword such questions to avoid the problems they create.

Double-barreled Questions.   These questions, like a double-barreled gun, shoot out two questions at once. As a result, the interviewee has a problem deciding which question to answer. The interviewee may answer just one of the questions and forget the other. The interviewee also may become so confused that neither question is answered well. A guideline for interviewers in all situations is that each question should contain one and only one inquiry. If

---

1. Questions that encourage social desirability effect

2. Leading questions

3. Problem questions

   - Double-barrelled
   - Too long
   - Too short
   - Jargon
   - Combination of open and closed

FIGURE 4.9   Questions that Impair Validity

multiple questions need to be asked, they should be asked separately. Below is an example of a double-barreled question:

Reporter: How long have you been the disciplinary director here at the school and what is your experience with these kinds of student fights?

Here is how the question could be reworded to avoid the problem:

Reporter: How long have you been the disciplinary director here? (Later) What is your experience with these kinds of student fights?

Double-barreled questions confuse interviewees. Responsibility falls to the questioner, usually the interviewer, to separate the parts of the question so that each question contains one, and only one, inquiry.

Questions That Are Too Long.   Questions that are very long are also difficult for an interviewee to answer. Part of the difficulty with long questions stems from the fact that they are harder for interviewees to comprehend because there is too much information to absorb at one time. Interviewees generally work quite hard to follow and respond to content of questions, and a long, confusing question makes their work unnecessarily challenging. Let us look at a question that is too long:

Marriage counselor: You two seem to have a firm and loving commitment to one another, and because of that I need to ask you whether you've felt this strain, this tension, this divisiveness between you coming a long time ago, and did it evolve slowly over time, or did it happen suddenly? I mean, was the tension something that came up very quickly, happened gradually over a long period of time, or has it been there all along?

Here is a more concise rewording of the same basic question:

Marriage counselor: Tell me whether the tension you're feeling now came on gradually over the twelve years or whether it seemed to develop fairly suddenly.

Questions That Are Too Short.   Questions can also be so short that the interviewee cannot understand them easily. Any question needs to include enough detail so that the interviewee understands clearly what the interviewer wants to hear. Correcting an overly short question is fairly easy. If the interviewer adopts the perspective of the interviewee and asks "Will the interviewee know what I'm talking about here?" then the question length can be adapted so it is appropriate. For example, instead of asking, "What about income?" a social worker might say, "I need to know what your income was last year."

Questions that are too long or too short can be confusing to interviewees. Interviewers who want to get full and authentic answers need to tailor the length of their questions so that interviewees understand what is being sought and can provide information accurately.

Jargon.   A problem mentioned earlier was jargon; that is, the use of technical language. Even college and university students have jargon: prereqs, credit hours, TA's, GPA, etc. Once you're a member of a group, jargon doesn't sound like jargon any more. To the outsider, however, it is like another language. An interviewer who wants to share meaning with an interviewee will either avoid the use of jargon that the interviewee doesn't understand or explain its meaning. An example of a question that contains jargon follows:

Nurse: Have you been to pre-op to be prepped yet?

A suitable "translation" of the jargon might be:

Nurse: Have you been to the pre-operation area yet where they will shave you and get you ready for surgery?

Overuse of jargon leads to misunderstanding and fear. When an interviewee does not understand what is going on, anxiety will rise because people want to present themselves as intelligent and knowledgeable. When they cannot understand jargon, they worry about appearing stupid. That feeling can generate nervousness which will, in turn, hurt the interview. Interviewers must consider the perspective of the interviewee and either avoid or explain jargon.

Combination Questions.   Inexperienced interviewers sometimes phrase questions that combine open questions with closed questions. Most typically, they begin with an open question, perhaps one that they have prepared in advance and then change the question, midway through asking it, to a closed one. Here is an example: "Tell me about your work in security for Paul Simon's tour in Africa, I mean, did you run into trouble?" This interviewer has combined an open question, "Tell me about your work in security for Paul Simon's tour of Africa" with a closed question "Did you run into trouble?" The interviewee may decide to answer only the second question, the closed question, which really is not the better question. Or the interviewee might just say "yes." Combining questions nearly always dilutes the effectiveness of the interaction and results in lost information. An interviewer who begins with an open question should stay with that wording. An interviewer who begins with a closed question should, likewise, stay with that wording. And, as always, an interviewer should ask one question at a time.

Summary

Questions are the primary tools by which interviewers accomplish their goals. Interviewers can vary the range of acceptable answers by asking questions that range from highly open to highly closed, and even bipolar forms. Moreover, interviewers can sharpen their effectiveness by combining primary questions with probes (amplification, accuracy-checking, summaries, and clearinghouse) to get the most authentic and thorough responses. To encourage valid responses, interviewers should avoid leading questions, questions that elicit socially desirable answers, and certain kinds of problem questions (double-barreled, too long, too short, jargon, and combination).

Discussion Questions

1. What are the primary functions of questions? Which of these functions are present in the interview at the start of chapter 4?

2. What question have you recently been asked which troubled you? What about the question bothered you? Is there a way the question could have been worded differently that would have made it more acceptable? If so, how?

3. Give an example of each of these types of questions: highly open, moderately open, moderately closed, highly closed, and bipolar.

4. Suppose you had the opportunity to interview someone you consider to be the most influential person in the world today, but you would only be able to ask three questions. What questions would you ask? Identify what types of questions they are.

5. Which type of questions allow the interviewer the most control? Under what circumstances would such questions be useful? Conversely, which type of question allows the interviewee the most control? In what circumstances would those questions be especially useful?

Activities

1. Select a published interview and make a copy for yourself. On the margins of your copy, indicate probes that you would insert to get fuller answers than the actual interviewer did. Identify these probes by function.

2. Have all members of your class think of closed questions they want to ask someone in the class. Go around the room, asking and answering the closed questions. Then do the same for open questions. Discuss which of the two types was most satisfying for learning more about your colleagues.

3. In groups of two to four, prepare a list of five invalid questions as described in the chapter. Rewrite each of the questions to remove the validity problem.

4. Individually, or in groups of two to four people, prepare three primary questions and a possible probe for each that you would ask if you had the chance to interview the President of the United States for fifteen minutes.

5. Prepare questions that you believe would produce valid answers on these topics: the interviewee's exercise habits, the interviewee's views on abortion, and the interviewee's personal experience with cheating.

6. Prepare a one-page guide to preparing questions that summarizes as concisely as possible the problems and potential of various question types.

Related Readings

Dohrenwend, Barbara S. "Some Effects of Open and Closed Questions on Respondents' Answers." *Human Organization* 24 (1965) 174–84.

Killenberg, George M., and Anderson, Rob. *Before the Story: Interviewing and Communication Skills for Journalists.* New York: St. Martin's Press, 1986.

Payne, Stanley L. *The Art of Asking Questions.* Princeton, NJ: Princeton University Press, 1951.

Stewart, Charles J., and Cash, William B., Jr. *Interviewing Principles and Practices,* 6th ed. Dubuque, IA: William C. Brown, 1991.

Endnotes

1. Charles J. Stewart and William B. Cash, Jr., *Interviewing: Principles and Practices,* 7th ed. (Dubuque, Iowa: Brown and Benchmark, 1994), 5.
2. William Douglas, "Uncertainty, Information-seeking, and Liking During Initial Interaction," *Western Journal of Speech Communication* 54 (1990), 75–76.
3. William Douglas, (1990), 76.
4. William A. Anthony and Robert R. Carkhuff, *The Art of Health Care: A Handbook of Psychological First Aid Skills,* (Amherst, MA: Human Resource Development Press, 1976).
5. Frank J. Bernieri, "Coordinated Movement and Rapport in Teacher-student Interactions," *Journal of Nonverbal Behavior* 12 (1988), 120.
6. Frank J. Bernieri, (1988), 132.
7. Lawrence R. Frey, Carl H. Botan, Paul G. Friedman, and Gary L. Kreps, *Investigating Communication: An Introduction to Research Methods,* (Englewood Cliffs, NJ: Prentice Hall, 1991), 118.
8. A. C. Kinsey, *et al. Sexual Behavior in the Human Male,* (Philadelphia: W. B. Saunders, 1948), 53–55.

Chapter *5*

Achieving Diversity

"In real life, the most practical advice for leaders is not to treat pawns like pawns, nor princes like princes, but all persons like persons."
—James MacGregor Burns, as quoted in William Safire and Leonard Safir, Leadership (New York: Simon and Schuster, 1990), 202.

Janet Carrera, a social worker for the Department of Human Services of Gary, Indiana, has been asked to interview Catandra Washington, a sixteen-year-old mother of two who is seeking financial assistance for herself and her children. This is their first actual meeting, although they spoke briefly on the phone when Catandra called to make the appointment.

Janet: Miss Washington? I'm Mrs. Carrera. Please come in.

Catandra: Mrs.

Janet: Yes, that's right. Mrs. Carrera. Come in.

Catandra: No, I mean I am Mrs.—Mrs. Washington.

Janet: Oh, I see. I'm sorry. I thought you were here to see about aid for unwed mothers.

Catandra: No, I'm here for aid for myself and my children, but I'm married—well, I was.

Janet: You were married. I see. Is your husband gone then?

Catandra: Yes. He's gone, ...

Janet: And left you with the kids? (Smiling sympathetically) So many men seem to do that here in this community. . . .

Catandra: No. He died.

Janet: Oh, I'm sorry. I didn't realize . . . Recently?

Catandra: (Nodding) Four months ago.

Janet: I'm sorry. May I ask how it happened? Drugs? Gangs?

Catandra: (Shaking her head angrily) No! He fell off a ladder. He was painting a house. What's the problem here?

Janet: (Defensively) Excuse me? I thought you were the one with the problem. I thought that's what brought you here. But I must say I'm confused by what you've told me so far.

Catandra: Look. My name is Catandra Washington. I have two kids, twins, two years old. My husband and I got married three years ago. He was a good man. He died in a fall four months ago, and now I have to support my kids on my own. I'm here to find out what kind of help I can get until I finish school. I have a job, but it isn't enough to support us. I'm not some welfare queen. I'm just a hard-working woman who needs some help until I can get on my feet again."

Janet: (After a pause) Mrs. Washington, please forgive me. I guess I made some wrong assumptions about your situation. Can we begin again?

Catandra: Sure. Okay. Fine. I need to know what kinds of help are available for someone like me.

Chapter Goals

- To appreciate the impact of culture on our perceptions of reality and others in interviews as elsewhere.
- To recognize the importance of cultural, subcultural, racial and gender diversity in interviews.
- To develop guidelines for moving beyond stereotypes and communicating successfully across cultures
- To understand ways to implement existing legislation to foster and maintain diversity in the workplace.

Introduction

Each of us grows up with a way of looking at the world that developed as a result of the particular place, time, and circumstances into which we were born. A significant aspect of how we perceive the world is determined by our culture of ori-gin—the language, values, beliefs and attitudes, politics, laws, and social organi-zation—which defines the society in which we live. Part of our world view, too, is affected by our race or ethnicity,[1] our gender, and the particular human subcul-tures of which we are a part. Even within cultures and subcultures, experiences and world views are diverse.

Diversity is a fact of life within every culture. Within U.S. culture, diversity is a defining characteristic. The mix of cultural identities which characterizes U.S. cul-ture has contributed significantly to its unique national identity as a mosaic of many of the world's cultures. Nonetheless, we are all still products of the particular local, as well as national, cultures and subcultures of which we are a part. Our origins both form and limit our fundamental perceptions of reality and of one another.

When we enter into any interview, we bring with us our **world view,** that set of perceptions and beliefs about life and others that define how we see the world. Those perceptions act as a filter, or lens, through which we view—and judge—everyone we meet. It includes assumptions and judgments that affect all of our actions, interactions, and decisions in relation to others. It can, as is obvious in our opening interview, create real communication problems. It is vital, therefore, that we understand the filter through which we are communicating in order to make more accurate interpretations about the meanings, actions, and decisions of those we encounter in interview situations.

Mrs. Carrera, the social worker in the opening interview, made a number of false assumptions about Catandra Washington, based on a view of Catandra's cul-ture in which young women with children are assumed to be "unwed mothers," husbands are assumed to abandon their wives and children, and drugs and/or gangs are assumed to be what kills the males in the culture. In Catandra's situa-tion, all of these assumptions proved false, and Mrs. Carrera's use of them created real communication problems in the interview. When the world view and assumptions of one culture are applied to the experience of another, serious com-munication problems often result.

In this chapter we will define and briefly explore some of the basic elements and characteristics of culture—that thick web of ideas, assumptions, beliefs, and values in which all human beings reside. We will then examine how these ele-ments and characteristics affect us in interview situations, especially in regard to stereotyping. We will look at ways to guard against stereotyping in interviews and will examine the body of federal legislation that exists to protect individuals against discrimination in the workplace and elsewhere.

All interviews and interviewing situations are affected by human cultural diversity. In this chapter we will explore ways to respond and adapt to that diver-sity in the workplace and elsewhere. Angel and Barrera write: "The national inter-est in this issue cannot be overstated. By the turn of the century, one of every three American school children will be members of minority groups; within a few more decades minorities will constitute one-third of the United States' total population. Through the year 2000, minority workers are expected to compose one-third of net additions to the workplace."[2]

Defining Culture

The word *culture* is drawn from a Latin word meaning "to till." In a sense, we can begin by thinking of culture as the fertile soil out of which we grow. The concept of culture has been defined by those who study it in many ways. Samovar, Porter, and Jain offer this definition:

> *Formally defined, culture is the deposit of knowledge, experiences, beliefs, values, attitudes, meanings, hierarchies, religion, timing, roles, spatial relations, concepts of the universe, and material objects and possessions acquired by a large group of people in the course of generations through individual and group striving.* [3]

More simply, they describe culture as a "model for life."[4] Sarbaugh defined culture as "all one inherits from one's ancestors and acquires from those with whom one is in regular communication."[5] Berger offers this perspective:" . . . Culture can be thought of as a collection of codes [rules, norms or symbols] which shapes people's behavior."[6]

Maybe the simplest way to understand culture is in terms of its impact on how we perceive and understand reality. **Culture** is the world view or frame of reference of a human group, formed by a collective history, which defines and limits

Members of the Black and Hasidic communities argue over recent violence between the two groups.

its perceptions of reality. We've already referred to one way in which the impact of culture has been described; namely, with the concept of **world view** (i.e., the unique way of defining reality that grows out of our collective experiences).

Another term frequently used to describe the collective impact of culture is **frame of reference,** which describes the particular frame or focus that we bring to events. In a sense, culture operates much like a camera lens. The cumulative impact of our cultural experiences form the lens through which we perceive everyone and everything we encounter. Our cultural lenses sometimes distort what we see when we look out at "reality." We can see evidence of this tendency to distort in the false impressions which Mrs. Carrera brought to her interview with Mrs. Washington. Culture limits and selects what we focus on and thus "frames" our particular view of reality. A frame by its nature brings some elements of a person or event into focus and simultaneously excludes other elements.

In regard to perceptual frames of reference, for example, an individual from a culture that excludes women from positions of power may not "see" women as powerful when he or she meets them, even if they come to a job interview with clear evidence of their possession and exercise of power. We will see a clear example of this type of perceptual filter in the following example drawn from Saudi culture.

The Major Elements of Culture

As was stated earlier, culture includes such elements as one's language, values, and beliefs. The language with which a person is raised has a profound impact on how that person perceives and relates to other people. "In his introduction to *What is Called Thinking?* Vattimo suggests that language could be called `the house of being'. . . ."[7] In other words, language is the storehouse of a culture's definitions of reality.

For example, the English language does not include pronouns that distinguish class or status relationships between people. Thai language, by contrast, contains many pronouns that distinguish carefully between different ranks and classes of people.[8] It is easy to imagine that, simply by virtue of these language differences, a person raised speaking Thai would be more aware of status differences than would an American raised speaking English. In fact, linguist Benjamin Whorf and his colleague Edward Sapir developed the **Sapir-Whorf hypothesis** earlier in this century which suggests that, to a significant extent, language *determines* a culture's definitions of reality.[9]

Language differences often reflect value differences within and between cultures. We can assume, for example, that status differences are more fixed and formal in Thai culture because they are formalized in the language. Language and culture are so interdependent, in fact, with the structure of one influencing the structure of the other in various indefinable ways, that we cannot clearly separate the particular impact of language from the impact of other social and value elements of a culture.

The importance and impact of the values and beliefs of a culture extend both to the most fundamental beliefs, such as those found in religion and law, and to everyday beliefs and values, such as those which define standards of attractiveness within a culture. These standards cause inhabitants of a culture to decide who is ugly and who is beautiful. Cultural standards of attractiveness can have a powerful impact on the interview process, particularly in regard to employment selection interviews, as will be seen in a later section.

Another important element of culture is social organization. **Social organization** refers to the specific ways that a society is bound together by laws, relationships, and status differences. The social organization of U.S. culture, for example, places a heavy emphasis on individualism and personal freedom, as well as other important definitions of personal worth. Katz includes the following qualities as defining elements of white U.S. culture: individualism and personal control, competition and winning, mastery of nature, focus on the future, linear thinking, and Christian orientation.[10]

In interview situations, because of the cultural focus on the individual as the fundamental unit of social organization, a U.S. native is likely to perceive actions, decisions, and successes in terms of individual needs. Within Japanese culture, on the other hand, the individual is seen to be actively linked and responsible to the needs of society as a whole.[11] A Japanese interviewee might well make decisions in light of a sense of broader social responsibility. In the 1992 Winter Olympics, for example, Japanese figure skater Midori Ito offered a public apology to her nation after falling in her short program competition.

Other significant elements of social organization include the structure of workplaces and perceived relationships between owners and workers, women and men. Within Saudi Arabian culture, for example, women occupy roles separate from men and do not often sit at the same table with them, at work or at home.[12] Saudi businessmen coming to the U.S. to do business have been known to insist to U.S. companies that they will not engage in any business transactions if women are present. Within U.S. culture, where growing numbers of women occupy positions of authority in the workplace, real problems are likely to develop if a corporation seeking to do business in Saudi Arabia employs female executive officers whose participation is perceived to be essential to negotiation with the Saudis.

Likewise, the politics, laws, technology, and even the arts of a culture have a powerful impact on how the residents of that culture will perceive and define reality and the people who dwell in it. Our definitions of government, our beliefs about human rights as guaranteed by law, and our perceptions of what is useful or efficient, ugly or beautiful, valuable or worthless, are all influenced by the culture within which we were formed.

All of us bring all of these taken-for-granted perceptions of social order, right and wrong, and human relationships with us into every encounter we have with others. These perceptions, then, have obvious and important implications for interviewing. "The problem, therefore," Fiumara writes, "is that of creating sufficient silence to allow ourselves at least to hear the incessant rumbling of our cultural world. . . ."[13] Where do we get this "culture?" How do we receive it? Can we learn to see beyond the limits it imposes?

The Characteristics of Culture

Culture Is Learned

We are born into cultures, but we are not born with an innate knowledge of culture. From the time we're born, though, we are imbued with or taught our culture at the same time and in much the same way that we're given nourishment, comfort, and shelter. We learn culture from those who raise us, from the moment we first begin to perceive the world around us. We process and absorb the beliefs and values of our culture unknowingly through the language we're taught, the clothes we wear, what we hear about what is and is not appropriate for girls and boys to do, and so on. We learn by observing those around us about how human beings are supposed to behave in relation to one another. We learn whether and when we should touch, whom to call family, and whom to call friends. Consciously and unconsciously, directly and indirectly, we teach culture to our young and reinforce its meanings both by what we say and what we do.

Culture Is Dynamic

Culture is also dynamic; that is, continually undergoing change. Within U.S. culture, for example, we can find ongoing evidence of cultural influences being exchanged. For example, residents of the nation's Midwest decorate with Native American-influenced arts of the Southwest, and mainstream rock and pop musicians adapt to the influence of the rap music of urban minorities. On a broader scale, every human language contains words and meanings borrowed wholesale from other cultures, such as the French expression *le weekend* and the English description of *deja vu* experiences. Cultures are not static or fixed. The beliefs, values, and perceptions of reality within a culture evolve and change much as languages do, adapting to new realities and experiences.

With the advance of instantaneous global communication and rapid travel, nearly all of the world's cultural and subcultural groupings are now influenced by and adapting to other cultural realities. Nonetheless, there is an almost universal human tendency to believe in the greater value and truth of one's own culture above all others. According to sociologists Berger and Luckmann, culture as learned is perceived as "massively real," or as "reality par excellence."[14] From our earliest socialization, we do not just learn our culture's definitions of reality. We also adopt the ingrained attitude that our culture's definitions are superior to those of other cultures and that our own culture above all others has a "corner on the truth."

Culture Is Ethnocentric

This belief in the natural superiority of one's own culture is known as **ethnocentrism,** the literal meaning of which comes from the Greek word *ethno* which means *nation.* Ethnocentrism, literally, means "nation-centered," but ethnocentrism applies to more than just nationhood. We are just as likely to believe in the inherent superiority of our racial or ethnic group, our gender, our neighborhood, or our school as in our nation of origin. In whatever form it appears, in relation to whatever human grouping, ethnocentrism limits our ability to see and accept the reality and the value of the "other," that is, whoever stands outside the culture of which we are a part. Fiumara describes an ethnocentric attachment to the rationalist philosophy of the Western world, for example, in this way: "An unshaken faith in the validity of our own mother tongue—the rationalist tradition—prevents us from *seeing* any different logical tradition because it is believed that it cannot be `logical.' On the contrary it must be, for example, simply `magical' and, therefore, unworthy of being listened to. . . ."[15]

The dangerous limitations imposed by ethnocentric thinking are most obvious when we look at perceptions of people of different racial or ethnic backgrounds. The assumed superiority of one's own group inevitably gives way to **racism;** that is, systematic justifications for the assumed inferiority of the other. To the extent that we view other individuals from a superior stance, we inevitably view them through a set of filters that only allow us to perceive certain qualities—and these imperfectly—and this causes us to falsely judge the meaning or value of other qualities. "Racism," says Woolbright, "involves both prejudice against a group of people and the power to reinforce that prejudice."[16] Whenever an organization or group of individuals, in other words, is dominated by members of one subculture who hold racist views of others, the dominant subculture has the power to limit the actions and behavior of those against whom prejudice is maintained.

In interviewing, ethnocentric perceptions can seriously impede the accuracy and success of the interviewer's efforts. In our opening interview, for example, it appears to be part of Mrs. Carrera's ethnocentric view of Mrs. Washington's culture that women are "unwed mothers" and men abandon their offspring and die of drug abuse or gang violence. Until she could move past those limiting ethnocentric perceptions to see Mrs. Washington, Mrs. Carrera's responses were all inaccurately based on her sense of the inferiority and "difference" of Mrs. Washington's culture.

Cultural Stereotypes Limit Accurate Perceptions

Ethnocentrism is closely tied to **stereotyping,** which is the tendency to judge all of the people of a given culture or subculture on the basis of a fixed set of assumptions about their qualities. Stereotypes by their nature leave no room for an accurate assessment of a particular individual. Here is where the impact of culture in general and ethnocentrism in particular pose the greatest risk for interview participants. If we perceive the other inaccurately because of the blinders of stereotyping and other distortions, the success of the interview at obtaining accurate information is bound to be affected.

Cultures Contain Subcultures

We have referred several times to subcultures. A **subculture** is a group of persons within a culture who share in common (1) ethnic, social, gender or other experiences, (2) patterns of behavior, and/or (3) beliefs that exist apart from or in addition to other patterns of the larger culture. A subculture, in other words, is a culture within a culture. Hebdige perceives subcultures as those groups within a culture that express resistance to the structure and values of the dominant culture.[17] We will define subculture more broadly to characterize all groups within a culture that possess and express significant cultural differences. Urban African Americans, for example, are members of both the larger reality of U.S. culture and the urban and ethnic subculture of which they are a part. Homeless residents of Los Angeles, to the extent that they share a unique set of experiences and perceptions of life, are another example of subculture.

Subcultures can be geographic: city versus country dwellers, for example, or East Coast versus West Coast. Subcultures can be ethnic: Italian Americans, African Americans, and Russian Jews. Likewise, subcultures can be based on common experiences: Yale graduates, square dancers, highway construction workers, Vietnam veterans, Olympic skaters. In the broadest sense, males and females can even be considered different subcultures to the extent that the experience of being a male member of a culture is significantly different than the experience of a female member of the same culture.

All of us are simultaneously members of several subcultures within a larger culture. These memberships form overlapping frames of references which affect our perceptions and actions. We tend to be ethnocentric in relation to each of them, seeking out and liking those seemingly familiar persons who share one or more of our subcultures. Here again, we can easily see the risk these ethnocentric tendencies pose in interviewing situations. Women may struggle to be accepted within the subculture of male corporate executives, for example, while men may struggle to be accepted within the subculture of the nursing profession, which is dominated by women.

In a real sense, whenever we interview a person who does not share our cultural and subcultural experiences, we can benefit by approaching that interview with the understanding that we are speaking across cultures. And whenever we are communicating across cultures, we need to be aware and guard against cultural biases. Whatever the interviewing situation, we must be sure we are seeing the other person as clearly as possible. Ours is a culture which values diversity. As interviewers, we must work toward awareness and appreciation of diversity in our encounters with others.

Understanding one's own biases can aid in recognizing prejudice in the field of interviewing.

Understanding Our Own Cultural Biases

How can we guard against ethnocentrism and stereotyping in our roles as interviewers and interviewees? First, we must begin by understanding our own frames of reference—our own world views. We cannot develop ways to detect and protect against biases if we don't know ours. The more we understand about our culture of origin—its values, beliefs and standards—the better we can detect and protect against perceptual biases. Reading and study can aid understanding. Courses in communication, sociology, and anthropology can be especially useful.

Second, we need to develop the habit of asking others for their observations and feedback about how we interact with different kinds of people. Am I generally more critical of men than women? Do I express consistently negative opinions about persons from another culture or subculture? Do I place too much importance on how people are dressed and not enough on what they say or do? Those who know us well, if we listen without defensiveness while they speak honestly, can help us to perceive ourselves more accurately.

At the same time, especially as interviewers, we need to pay attention to our records of interviewing decisions to see what evidence they provide of patterns of biases. If we keep records and study them, we can see our own patterns over time. Are more younger applicants than older ones accepted, proportional to the pool of applicants for particular positions? Are harder questions asked of some people than others? Are more critical judgments recorded of dark-skinned than light-skinned persons? Is more attention paid to the complaints of one group of employees over another? Do men receive consistently higher grades than women? Just keeping records is not enough. Being willing to study our records periodically for patterns of response will help educate us concerning our individual and collective biases. It is difficult to know one's own biases. Inviting feedback from others and monitoring our personal records allows insights that are hard to obtain from direct self-observation.

Considerable research exists documenting patterns of bias in the field of interviewing, particularly in regard to selection interviewing in the United States. Research findings include, for example, that taller candidates are likely to be chosen over shorter ones and to earn higher salaries; that interviewers tend to select candidates who are most like themselves in gender, appearance, and attitudes;[18] and that applicants with noticeable ethnic and regional accents tend to be evaluated poorly and receive fewer job offers.[19] The more we do to become aware of typical patterns of bias within our culture and ourselves, the better prepared we will be to watch and guard against these tendencies.

Woolbright has developed a model for multicultural awareness competency that includes the following stages: (1) self-awareness, or knowledge of one's own culture; (2) awareness and acknowledgement of one's own racism; (3) developing acceptance of other cultures; (4) developing new attitudes and behaviors learned from intercultural contact; (5) confronting racist behaviors; (6) and integrating multicultural knowledge and responses through systematic action.[20] At the least, self-awareness and self-understanding are essential preparation for the kind of openness and action in interviews that foster good decision making in a diverse world.

Guarding Against Stereotyping In Interviews

Understanding our own cultural biases is the best advance preparation for preventing stereotyping and discrimination in our interactions with others. When it comes to specific interview situations, there are several additional steps we can take to assure that we are approaching the other person with the greatest possible openness. These steps include carefully defining the interview situation, being aware of the culture of the other, seeking clarifications of meaning from the other, and finding ways to utilize multiple interviews and interviewers in order to obtain more accurate assessments.

Defining the Interview

The clearer we are about our purpose and needs before the interview begins, the better able we are to look for specific information about or qualities in the persons we interview. If we approach an interview or series of interviews with a clear set of expectations, we are more likely to avoid being distracted by information or biases not relevant to our needs. Of course, we are also more likely to conduct effective interviews. An appraisal interviewer who limits the investigation to the specific elements of the job description and concrete evidence of fulfillment of job demands, for example, will be less likely to be affected by prejudices regarding the interviewee's ethnic or subcultural background.

Learning the Culture of the Other

Likewise, the more we know about the culture of the other persons in the interview, the better able we are to judge their actions and responses. If we know in advance, for example, that eye contact is avoided as a sign of politeness in another culture, we are less likely to assume that the person to whom we are speaking is untrustworthy or shy. If we are aware in advance of the cultural tendency for Asian persons to defer to authority, on the other hand, we can take care to refrain from making our own views clear before asking for input from an Asian immigrant. Knowledge is understanding.

Seeking Clarification of Meanings

Obviously, in certain kinds of interviews such as employment selection interviews, it may not be possible to know in advance about the culture of origin of applicants. In such cases, it is especially important for those involved in the interview to assume nothing about the other. Instead, carefully clarify the meanings of the statements and actions of the other person to make sure that meanings are shared. The use of paraphrasing, perception checking, and tactful probing questions are particularly essential when the shared cultural and subcultural experiences of interviewer and interviewee are limited.

Utilizing Multiple Assessments

Additionally, we can safeguard against biased or discriminatory judgments by testing our judgments against those of others. In U.S. business, for example, it is becoming increasingly common for selection interviews to be conducted by teams of employees who then share their various observations of each of the candidates. When we have multiple observations of this kind, even though there will be differences of opinion about each candidate, grossly inaccurate perceptions are more likely to be caught by the differing interpretations of others.

Another way to obtain multiple observations is for the same interviewer to interview the other party more than once. All of us have bad days, both as interviewers and as interviewees, and multiple contacts allow both sides the opportunity to obtain and offer different observations and experiences. Likewise, the interviewer may be afforded the opportunity to expand her/his awareness of the cultural background of an interviewee between interviews and approach the second interview, therefore, more knowledgeably.

There is no way to eliminate bias completely from our observations of any person or event. To some extent, each of our frames of reference is unique. But there is much we can do to assure that our minds are as open as possible and as free as possible from the kinds of distortions which ethnocentrism and stereotyping create. Ideally, everyone entering into an interview seeks to obtain and exchange the most accurate information possible. We cannot do so without understanding the obstacles that are likely to stand in the way of accurate perception and taking concrete steps to eliminate those obstacles.

Diversity and Bias in the Workplace

Nowhere have the questions of personal and cultural bias been more thoroughly and more heatedly explored than in the U.S. workplace. Here the broad cultural values that favor equality and diversity have been inconsistently enacted and hotly contested in the field of law. As a culture, we have become increasingly aware of the disparity between our values favoring equality and documented patterns of discrimination in hiring practices.

Over time, as a response to this discrimination, state and federal laws have been enacted as attempts to ensure that every person who seeks work will be judged on the basis of her/his qualifications for the job and nothing else. *At its simplest, the vast web of laws and constraints which govern those who interview in the workplace comes down to one central tenet: that every person who seeks work in this culture is entitled to be judged on the basis of her or his qualifications for the job and nothing more.* Because of a long history of discrimination in employment, additional legislation and executive orders have been created which demand affirmative actions to correct for past discriminatory practices.

Because these laws affect everyone, whether as interviewer or as interviewee, we will take time to briefly examine the federal laws that have developed to prevent discrimination in the workplace. It is important to remember, however, that most states have their own and sometimes different guidelines covering discrimination in employment. It is impossible to cover all of these variations in this textbook, but we urge you to be aware of the laws governing employment opportunities and discrimination in your own state. Figure 5.1 delineates the names and terms of the central federal laws governing employment. All of these laws have specific implications for selection and appraisal interviews in the workplace.

The Equal Pay Act of 1963 was the first significant piece of federal legislation governing employment. The act was passed in the face of clear evidence that women in the workplace were being paid less than men, even when doing essentially the same work. The legislation attempted to correct that existing gender inequality by insisting that women who do essentially the same jobs as men in the same workplace should be paid what men in that same job are paid. For example, female managers of clothing departments in a department store chain should be paid the same as male managers of clothing departments in the same chain. This

TITLE OF ACT	ENACTED	PROVIDES FOR OR PROHIBITS:
Equal Pay Act	1963	Provides for equal pay for men and women performing substantially the same work
Civil Rights Act (Title VII)	1964	Prohibits employment discrimination on basis of race, religion, color, sex, or national origin
Equal Employment Opportunity Act of	1972	Broadened coverage of Title VII of the Civil Rights Act of 1964 to include most employers of fifteen or more persons, all schools, state and local governments, employment agencies, labor unions, and certain apprenticeship programs
Executive Orders 11246 and 11375	1965 1967	Federal contractors and subcontractors must eliminate employment discrimination and correct prior discrimination through affirmative action.
Age Discrimination in Employment Act [amended]	1967 1978	Prohibits discrimination in compensation, terms, conditions, or privileges of employment on basis or age. Prohibits forced retirement except where age is *bona fide* occupational qualification.
Executive Order 11478	1969	Prohibits discrimination in Postal Service and various other governmental agencies on basis of race, religion, color, sex, national origin, handicap, or age.
Pregnancy Discrimination Act	1978	Prohibits discrimination against women affected by pregnancy, childbirth, and related medical conditions.
Vocational Rehabilitation Act, (amended by) Rehabilitation Act	1973 1974	Prohibits discrimination against handicapped persons by federal contractors of over $2,500
Vietnam-Era Veterans Readjustment Act	1974	Prohibits discrimination against Vietnam-era veterans by U.S. government federal contractors, requiring affirmative action
Americans with Disabilities Act	1990	Prohibits discrimination against persons with disabilities in employment, public services, and other public arenas; requires "reasonable accommodation" by employers to allow for broader employment opportunities for those with mental or physical disabilities
Civil Rights Act of 1991	1991	Amends existing legislation to provide right to jury trial, punitive and compensatory damages, and other safeguards

FIGURE 5.1 **Major Federal Legislation Related to Equal Employment Opportunity**

legislation does not prohibit pay differences for merit or seniority within a company, nor does it guarantee equal pay for jobs of "comparable worth."

Title VII of the Civil Rights Act of 1964 is the central piece of federal legislation governing employment because it prohibits discrimination on the basis of race, religion, color, sex, and national origin. The demographic categories referred to in the Act are those which historically have been most frequently the focus of stereotyping and discrimination. Once again, the legislation was enacted in response to existing problems within the culture—real and measurable disparities between the cultural value of equality and the unfair treatment of many members of subcultures on the basis of their race, religion, color, sex, or national origin. The most obvious implication of this law for interviewers in the workplace is that they must take care to ensure that questions of race, religion, color, sex, and national origin do not affect their decisions about hiring and firing individual applicants.

Later legislation and executive orders have been applied to these and other specific subcultures affected by discrimination. Executive Orders 11246 and 11375, the Vietnam-Era Veterans Readjustment Act, and the Vocational Rehabilitation Act (1973, 1974) each ordered that affirmative action in hiring was needed on the part of federal contractors and subcontractors and, in some cases, the federal government itself, to compensate for prior discrimination against those covered in Title VII, as well as Vietnam vets and those with disabilities. These affirmative action programs, for the most part, have been completed. Most present affirmative action programs are largely voluntary.

Many U.S. citizens in the workplace have been negatively affected by age; that is, forced into early retirement or laid off because a more youthful employee was desired. These individuals are aided by the Age Discrimination in Employment Act of 1967, revised in 1978. Pregnant women, who in the past were routinely fired, laid off, or replaced while on maternity leave are now protected by the Pregnancy Discrimination Act of 1978. In the years prior to the passage of this act, it was routine for employers to ask female applicants about their plans regarding marriage and childbearing and to refuse to hire women who expressed the intention to bear children at some future time. Now this and other legislation encourages interviewers to limit their questions and decisions to the individual's actual qualifications for the job, whether or not she intends to give birth to a child.

Prior to 1990, handicapped individuals were not protected from discrimination in any businesses not working under federal contract. Moreover, because physical space in businesses was often not flexible enough to accomodate handicapped persons, many disabled persons were not hired. The Americans with Disabilities Act of 1990 has greatly broadened access to employment for those who are disabled, as well as access to public services, public accomodations and services operated by private entities, and other areas of access for the disabled. The impact of this most recent legislation, in effect only since mid-1991 and not fully implemented until 1992, has yet to be felt. Changes in employment and appraisal practices will be made by individual employers and others in part in response to testing of the law in court. Figure 5.2 is the rationale and purpose for the Act as it is written in the law.

Americans with Disabilities Act
PUBLIC LAW 101-336
SEC.2 FINDINGS AND PURPOSES

FINDINGS—The Congress finds that—

(1) some 43,000,000 Americans have one or more physical or mental disabilities, and this number is increasing as the population as a whole is growing older;

(2) historically, society has tended to isolate and segregate individuals with disabilities, and, despite some improvements, such forms of discrimination against individuals with disabilities continue to be a serious and pervasive social problem;

(3) discrimination against individuals with disabilities persists in such critical areas as employment, housing, public accommodations, education, transportation, communication, recreation, institutionalization, health services, voting, and access to public services;

(4) unlike individuals who have experienced discrimination on the basis of race, color, sex, national origin, religion, or age, individuals who have experienced discrimination on the basis of disability have often had no legal recourse to redress such discrimination;

(5) individuals with disabilities continually encounter various forms of discrimination, including outright intentional exclusion, the discriminatory effects of architectural, transportation, and communication barriers, overprotective rules and policies, failure to make modifications to existing facilities and practices, exclusionary qualification standards and criteria, segregation, and relegation to lesser services, programs, activities, benefits, jobs, or other opportunities;

(6) census data, national polls, and other studies have documented that people with disabilities, as a group, occupy an inferior status in our society, and are severely disadvantaged socially, vocationally, economically, and educationally;

(7) individuals with disabilities are a discrete and insular minority who have been faced with restrictions and limitations, subjected to a history of purposeful unequal treatment, and relegated to a position of political powerlessness in our society, based on characteristics that are beyond the control of such individuals and resulting from stereotypic assumptions not truly indicative of the individual ability of such individuals to participate in, and contribute to, society;

(8) the Nation's proper goals regarding individuals with disabilities are to assure equality of opportunity, full participation, independent living, and economic self-sufficiency for such individuals; and

(9) the continuing existence of unfair and unnecessary discrimination and prejudice denies people with disabilities the opportunity to compete on an equal basis and to pursue those opportunities for which our free society is justifiably famous, and costs the United States billions of dollars in unnecessary expenses resulting from dependency and nonproductivity.

PURPOSE—It is the purpose of this Act—

(1) to provide a clear and comprehensive national mandate for the elimination of discrimination against individuals with disabilities;

(2) to provide clear, strong, consistent, enforceable standards addressing discrimination against individuals with disabilities;

(3) to ensure that the Federal Government plays a central role in enforcing the standards established in this Act on behalf of individuals with disabilities; and

(4) to invoke the sweep of congressional authority, including the power to enforce the fourteenth amendment and to regulate commerce, in order to address the major areas of discrimination faced day-to-day by people with disabilities.

FIGURE 5.2   Americans with Disabilities Act

This most recent employment opportunity law, with its specific applications, considerations, requirements, and areas of impact is a document of more than forty pages. The *Americans with Disabilities Handbook,* (October 1991) published by the Equal Employment Opportunity Commission and the U.S. Department of Justice, contains hundreds of pages of explanations and suggestions for implementation. The term *disability* is defined within this act as any "physical or mental impairment that substantially limits one or more of the major life activities of such individuals," as well as anyone with a record of impairment or regarded as being impaired.[21]

The area of the Americans with Disabilities Act of 1990 of greatest importance to interviewers in the workplace is Title I—Employment. This section of the law imposes strict guidelines on acceptable areas of inquiry in the hiring of persons with disabilities. An employer may ask if the applicant can perform job-related functions, for example, but is prohibited from asking if an applicant possesses a disability or the nature or severity of a disability, unless this information can be shown to be job related or tied to a business necessity. (The issues of job relatedness and business necessity will be discussed in a later section of this chapter.)

In addition, the law prohibits employers from denial of employment or patterns of discrimination in employment opportunities without making "reasonable accommodations" to individual disabilities. Reasonable accommodation is defined to include job restructuring or modified work schedules, acquisition or modification of equipment, training materials and policies, the provision of qualified readers or interpreters, "and other similar accommodations."[22]

At the very least, this act will result in increased physical access for handicapped persons to all businesses and premises which are available to other members of the populace, as well as to a much broader range of employment opportunities. As with all of these laws, however, the specific implications and limitations of the Americans with Disabilities Act of 1990 will evolve over time through testing in federal courts, where individual challenges by persons with specific disabilities will enable federal judges to dictate particular interpretations and applications of the law.

In November 1991, Congress passed the Civil Rights Act of 1991, which amends Title VII of the Civil Rights Act of 1964, the Age Discrimination in Employment Act of 1967, the Rehabilitation Act, and the Americans with Disabilities Act of 1990. The amendments to existing laws made by this act entitle plaintiffs in discrimination suits concerning these laws to a right to trial by jury, to compensatory and punitive damages, and to several other changes concerning burden of proof, statute of limitations, and other issues.[23] For example, under prior existing laws, only persons subjected to discrimination on the basis of race or ethnicity were entitled to punitive damages. Under the Civil Rights Act of 1991, compensatory and punitive damages for victims of age, sex, disability, and religious discrimination will also be allowed. One significant outcome of this most recent legislation is that employers who, in the interests of affirmative action, utilized lower acceptable test scores for minorities or other affected groups than for the rest of the employee population, may no longer do so.[24]

Each of these federal laws and orders prohibits discriminatory patterns in hiring and firing in U.S. workplaces. They protect different subcultures within the culture that have previously been unfairly treated by employers. In some cases, the laws have further legislated the need for positive steps, or preferential hiring, of qualified members of an affected group in order to compensate for past discrimination.

These laws are complex and varied. The information presented here in no way offers a complete understanding of them. As do cultures themselves, the laws of a culture evolve over time, through repeated testing and challenges in the workplace and in courts of law. In addition, there are various state and even local laws that also deal with discrimination in employment practices. An interviewer within the arena of U.S. business will need to become well-informed on these legal issues and to prepare carefully in order to function effectively within the constraints of employment discrimination law.

There are many specific ways which those seeking to enforce employment discrimination laws have developed in order to determine whether discrimination against a group or an individual has occurred. Three measures that are widely applied and are particularly important in employment interviewing are known as job relatedness, business necessity, and *bona fide* occupational qualifications.[25] These are measures whereby a business charged with discrimination can defend itself against such charges. They are not the only measures available or applied within the laws, but they are the measures most commonly used.

Job relatedness refers to a company's obligation to be able to demonstrate that the procedures it uses to select and place employees are related to and good predictors of an applicant's ability to be successful at that job. For example, a company cannot routinely ask applicants their overall academic GPA and make job decisions accordingly unless it can also present evidence that a person's chances of success at the job are related to possessing a certain GPA. Likewise, an interviewer seeking to hire a new employee must take care to employ questions that clearly pertain to the needs of the job for which the applicant is being considered. For example, an employer would have a difficult time proving that asking an applicant if she plays golf is a job-related question, unless she is an applicant for a position selling golf equipment or teaching golf.

Second, a company may counter charges of discrimination by demonstrating that its seemingly discriminatory actions are a business necessity. The concept of **business necessity** refers to concrete evidence that certain hiring patterns are necessary for the success of the business. For example, if a department store chain had evidence through consistent customer feedback that male clerks are overwhelmingly preferred when making mens' clothing purchases, it could give preference to male clerks applying for positions in mens' wear departments and justify that preference as a business necessity.

Third, by far the most familiar measure used to test for discrimination in employment practices is known as **bona fide occupational qualifications (BFOQs).** BFOQs are the specific qualifications a person needs in order to successfully do a job. This measure requires businesses to ensure that whatever qualifications they seek in applicants are directly related to the needs of that particular job. The Latin term *bona fide* literally means "good faith." Within the law, the term refers to authentic efforts made in good faith to obtain an end. Some examples of *bona fide* occupational qualifications include the need for bank tellers to be able to count money accurately, the need for firefighters to be able to carry heavy pieces of equipment used to put out fires, and even, in some cases, the need for employees to be of a specific sex, as in the case of female labor and delivery nurses in hospitals.[26] Interviewers in the workplace must be clearly informed as to the BFOQs for a given job and take care to frame interview questions that clearly pertain to those qualifications.

Often, when employment interviewing is discussed in other texts and courses, what is presented is phrased in terms of lawful or unlawful questions which can or cannot be used in hiring, appraisal, and termination interviews. Frequently, a specific list of "legal" and "illegal" questions is presented in relation to selection interviewing in particular.

There is good reason for this. The laws governing discrimination in the workplace are complex. They are decided and interpreted, furthermore, in court decision after court decision in which an employer who has been charged with discriminatory practices must defend herself or himself against the charges. In an effort on the part of employers and teachers alike to distill this maze of legislation into guidelines which employees can easily follow in the interviewing process, specific lists of questions and information have been compiled which either can or cannot easily be justified as being job-related, business necessities or BFOQs. An example of such a compilation is shown in Figure 5.3.

Such lists and guidelines are undeniably useful. However, when considering the relationship between these laws and the interviewing process, it is important to remember that the issue for the responsible employer is not whether or not the questions are legal, but whether the decisions were made on the basis of fairness and absence of discrimination. In general, federal laws do not specify particular questions that can or cannot be asked. The measure of the legality or illegality of specific questions is a secondary issue, because it is not the questions themselves so much as the use to which information gathered as a result of those questions is put. The responsible employer plans and participates in employment interviews in such a way that only job-related questions are asked.

When interviewing in the workplace, whether to select, to appraise, or to terminate an employee, care must be taken to assure that actions taken and decisions made are not discriminatory. Many employers and individuals tend to view this need as a "necessary evil" or an elaborate legal game that must be played in order to avoid expensive lawsuits. It is more accurate and more useful, however, to perceive the legislation concerning employment discrimination and the demands it makes upon businesses as a helpful, imperfect, and sometimes burdensome attempt by U.S. culture to make its fundamental value of equality into a practical reality. The greater diversity of persons in the workplace as a result of these efforts will in the long run benefit all. Existing laws are a safeguard and an encouragement to a long-standing cultural ideal.

SUBJECT AREA:	APPROPRIATE:	INAPPROPRIATE:
AGE	ONLY IF BFOQ	None but BFOQs
BIRTHPLACE	NONE	ALL
CITIZENSHIP	Permanent resident of U.S.? Prevented from employment because of visa or immigrant status?	Are you a U.S. citizen?
CRIMINAL RECORD	Ever convicted of felony that would affect ability to meet state bonding/ licensing requirements?	Ever been arrested?
EDUCATION	Schools attended? Relevant course work/experiences?	Social activities?
EXPERIENCE	Job-related or work experience? Military service and branch?	Type of discharge?
FAMILY	Relatives employed here or by competitors?	Do you have children? Do you have dependents? Do you need child care? Spouse occupation?
MARITAL STATUS	NONE	ALL
NAME	What is your name? Any name changes we need to know about to check work record and references?	Maiden name?
NATIONAL ORIGIN	What languages do you speak or write?	Where born? Where parents born? What kind of name is that?
ORGANIZATIONS	Professional or job-related only	ALL OTHERS
PHYSICAL CHARACTERISTICS	ONLY IF BFOQ	NONE BUT BFOQS
RACE	NONE	ALL
RELIGION	NONE	ALL
RESIDENCE	Current address? How long there? How long in this city or state?	With whom reside? Rent or own?

FIGURE 5.3   Sample Pre-employment Question Guide of Appropriate vs. Inappropriate Questions

Summary

Human diversity is an undisputed reality. We are products of the culture and sub-cultures of which we are a part. We also tend to prefer those most like ourselves (ethnocentrism) and to categorize and dismiss those who are different (stereotyping). As interviewers we can take several concrete steps to overcome ethnocentric and stereotyping tendencies by (1) developing an understanding of our culture of origin; (2) seeking feedback from others about the quality of our interactions with persons from other cultural or subcultural backgrounds; and (3) studying our own records of interviews in search of patterns of response to members of various cultural groupings.

Within the interviewing setting, we can work to prevent bias by (1) carefully defining the interview situation, (2) seeking information about the culture of the other, (3) arranging for multiple interviewers in order to obtain different observations, and (4) engaging in multiple interviews of the other person in order to have a broader base of information and observations on which to base our judgments.

The U.S. legislative branches have created laws that mandate employers to act in nondiscriminatory ways in employment-related interviews. Each of these laws, though differing in their particular applications, have in common a central tenet that individuals seeking or at work within the United States should be judged in relation to their work solely on the basis of their qualifications and their actual performance. The laws governing work employ three measures of appropriateness of employment practices: job relatedness, business necessity and *bona fide* occupational qualifications. An interviewer who frames their conduct of employment-related interviews with these measures will effectively assure fairness and nondiscrimination in employment practices.

We are seeking as a society for ways to accept, to encourage, and to live comfortably with the diversity of human beings in our midst and in the world at large. We cannot communicate effectively within interviews if our approach to the other person is based on our unscrutinized cultural biases. As interviewers, we must find ways to communicate across cultures and subcultures with acceptance rather than with bias if we are to be successful.

Discussion Questions

1. How would you describe the dominant beliefs and values of your culture of origin? How does your list compare with one or more of your classmates?

2. What changes in beliefs, values, or behaviors have you observed in your culture in your lifetime? Which of these changes seems most important, and why?

3. What are some positive and negative examples of ethnocentrism found in your culture at this time?

4. In how many subcultures can you currently claim membership? Rank them from most important to least important in terms of their impact on your world view or frame of reference.

5. Which of the various pieces of federal legislation do you think has had the greatest impact on U.S. culture, not just in the workplace, but elsewhere? Why?

Suggested Activities

1. As a group, create a list of subcultures that have an impact on the larger U.S. culture. Rank them from most to least important in influence on the larger culture.

2. With a group of your peers, generate a list of legally questionable or inappropriate questions you have been asked or know others have been asked in employment interviews. In each case, decide whether the question can be rewritten to make it appropriate or whether its content cannot appropriately be explored.

3. Using the same list of questionable or inappropriate questions created in the previous exercise, develop several suggested replies an interviewee could employ in response to each of the troublesome questions.

Related Readings

Berger, Arthur Asa. *Signs in Contemporary Culture.* Salem, WI: Sheffield Publishing Company, 1989.

Borden, George A. *Cultural Orientation.* Englewood Cliffs NJ: Prentice Hall, 1991.

Brislin, Richard W. *Cross-Cultural Encounters.* New York: Pergamon Press, 1981.

Dima, Nicholas. *Cross Cultural Communication.* Washington DC: Institute for the Study of Man, 1990.

Dodd, Carley H. *Perspectives on Cross-Cultural Communication.* Dubuque, IA: Kendall/Hunt Publishing Company, 1977.

Hebdige, Dick. *Subculture: The Meaning of Style.* London: Metheun, 1979.

Leach, Edmund. *Culture and Communication.* Cambridge: Cambridge University Press, 1976.

Lippard, Lucy R. *Mixed Blessings.* New York: Pantheon Books, 1990.

Samovar, Larry A., and Porter, Richard E. *Communication Between Cultures.* Belmont, CA: Wadsworth, 1991.

Samovar, Larry A. and Porter, Richard E., eds. *Intercultural Communication: A Reader,* 7th ed. Belmont, CA: Wadsworth, 1994.

Samovar, Larry A.; Porter, Richard E.; and Jain, Nemi C. *Understanding Intercultural Communication.* Belmont, CA: Wadsworth, 1981.

Sarbaugh, L.E. *Intercultural Communication.* Rochelle Park, NJ: Hayden Book Company, Inc., 1979.

Segall, Marshall H. *Cross-Cultural Psychology.* Monterey, CA: Brooks/Cole Publishing Company, 1979,

Thiederman, Sondra. *Bridging Cultural Barriers for Corporate Success: How to Manage the Multicultural Work Force.* Lexington, MA: Lexington Books, 1991.

Endnotes

1. Note: Traditionally, the word *race* has been used to refer to perceived physiological differences between human groups, while *ethnicity* has been used to describe one's national origins. We will use both words as though their meanings are fluid and to some degree interchangeable for several reasons. As long ago as 1954, in his classic text, *The Nature of Prejudice,*

Gordon Allport discussed our human fondness for tying our prejudices to the concept of race because it allows us to maintain the illusion that we can make visible distinctions between human groupings. The problem with racial identification is that we are a "mongrel" species and the number of human beings who are "pure" members of one race are few.

More recently, Lucy R. Lippard [Lippard, Lucy R., *Mixed Blessings* (New York: Pantheon Books, 1990), 5] makes this statement in which she quotes and affirms the scholar Henry Louis Gates, Jr. [Gates, Henry Louis, Jr., ed., "Race," *Writing and Difference* (Chicago: University of Chicago Press, 1986)] on the subject of race:

Race is still commonly used when culture is meant to connote, as Gates observes, some unspecific essence or feeling, the `ultimate, irreducible difference between cultures' . . . Although arbitrary and biologically unsupportable, it is carelessly used `in such a way as to *will* this sense of *natural* difference into our formulations. To do so is to engage in a pernicious act of difference, one which exacerbates the complex problem of cultural or ethnic difference, rather than to assuage or address it.' The word *racism,* alas, describes a social phenomenon that is less questionable.

2. Dan Angel and Adriana Barrera, eds., *Rekindling Minority Enrollment.* San Francisco: Jossey-Bass Inc., Publishers, Number 74, Summer 1991.

3. Larry A. Samovar, Richard E. Porter, and Nemi C. Jain, *Understanding Intercultural Communication* (Belmont, CA: Wadsworth, 1981), 24.

4. Samovar, et al. (1981), 25.

5. L. E. Sarbaugh, *Intercultural Communication* (Rochelle Park, NJ: Hayden, 1979), 143.

6. Arthur Asa Berger, *Signs in Contemporary Culture* (Salem, WI: Sheffield, 1989), 156.

7. Gemma Corradi Fiumara, *The Other Side of Language: A Philosophy of Listening,* translated by Charles Lambert. London: Routledge, 1990, 129.

8. Larry A. Samovar and Richard E. Porter, *Communication Between Cultures* (Belmont, CA: Wadsworth, 1991), 153–54.

9. Benjamin Whorf, *Language, Thought and Reality* (Cambridge, MA: MIT Press, 1956).

10. J. H. Katz, "The Sociopolitical Nature of Counseling," *The Counseling Psychologist* 13 (4), 618.

11. Derald Wing Sue and David Sue, *Counseling the Culturally Different,* 2nd ed. (New York: John Wiley & Sons, 1990), 197–99.

12. Samovar and Porter (1991), 81.

13. Fiumara (1990), 25.

14. Peter L. Berger, and Thomas Luckmann, *The Social Construction of Reality* (Garden City, NY: Doubleday Anchor, 1967) 21, 129–37.

15. Fiumara (1990), 25.

16. Cynthia Woolbright, ed., *Valuing Diversity on Campus: A Multicultural Approach.* (Bloomington, IN: Association of College Unions - International, 1989), 3.

17. Dick Hebdige, *Subculture: The Meaning of Style* (London: Methuen, 1979), 2–19.

18. Mark L. Hickson, and Don W. Stacks, *Nonverbal Communication,* 2nd ed. (Dubuque: William C. Brown, 1989), 286–90.

19. R. Gifford, C.F. Ng, and M. Wilkinson, "Nonverbal Cues in the Employment Interview: Links Between Applicant Qualities and Interviewer Judgments," *Journal of Applied Psychology* 70 (1985), 729–36.

20. Woolbright (1989), 68–69.

21. Public Law 101–336, July 26, 1990, Sec. 3. Definitions.

22. Public Law 101–336, July 26, 1990, Title I— Employment, Sec. 101. Definitions.

23. Niall A. Paul, "The Civil Rights Act of 1991: What does it really accomplish?" *Employee Relations Law Journal* 17 (4), 1992, 567–69.

24. Paul (1992), 575-76.

25. Randall S. Schuler, *Effective Personnel Management* (St. Paul: West Publishing Company, 1983) 157–66.

26. Schuler (1983), 162.

Part III

Information Interviews

Chapter 6

The Journalistic Interview

> *". . . I am a journalist because I believe that if all the world had all the facts about everything, it would be a better world. I understand that the facts and the truth are not always the same. It is my job to report the facts so that others can decide on the truth."*
> —Andy Rooney,
> Pieces of My Mind. (New York:
> Atheneum Press, 1984), 59–60.

Jonathan Kaile Ransom, environmental activist and editor of the student newspaper for the Midwest School of Scientific Research, has arranged for an interview with Kathleen Santini, public relations director of Industrial Waste Disposal Systems, a nationwide landfill management corporation with a large regional landfill not far from the campus of Ransom's school. At Santini's request, Ransom has agreed to meet her and conduct the interview at the local landfill. He has just arrived and Santini is waiting to meet him at the gate.

Santini: Mr. Ransom? I'm Kathleen Santini. Thanks for coming out here today. I'm looking forward to letting you see our operations firsthand so you can tell your readers that they have nothing to fear from IWDS.

Ransom: Well, I'm not sure that's what I'm going to tell them, Ms. Santini.

Santini: Please, call me Kathleen.

Ransom: Actually, my questions have to do with what happened here a week ago rather than with your company tour.

Santini: I'll be happy to hear your questions, Jonathan, but first let me show you our operations so you'll have the background information you need to do your story justice.

Ransom: Do you mind if I tape-record our interview?

Santini: Yes, I'm afraid I do. We have a company policy against having our employees' statements recorded except during company-scheduled press conferences.

Ransom: Like last week after the accident, for example.

Santini: There was no accident, Jonathan—a couple of our employees came down with the flu while at work; that was all. Now, how about you just hop in this golf cart with me, and I'll show you around. Then we'll go back to my office for questions afterward.

Ransom: Flu? You've got to be kidding. Three employees get sent into one of your fill areas to patch a leak and wound up at the hospital emergency room two hours later vomiting their guts out, and you say it's flu? Come on, Ms. Santini.

Santini: Mr. Ransom, is this supposed to be an interview or an inquisition? If you want to talk to me about our operations here and are willing to hear and report the *facts* to your readers, I'll be happy to let you see our operations and explain it to you. But if your mind is made up and all you're interested in is lodging unfounded accusations, then I have better things to do.

Ransom: What was the emergency room physician's diagnosis of the IWDS employees, Ms. Santini?

Santini: Our employees' medical conditions are their own business, Mr. Ransom.

Ransom: But you already told me they had the flu—all I'm asking is if the doctor's diagnosis confirmed or differed from your own. Which was it?

Santini: Mr. Ransom, I don't think a tour of our facilities would be of any use today. It is clear you have only one agenda here and your mind is made up about it. Perhaps another time you or another of your reporters would be more open to an objective look at our company.

Ransom: One of your employee's told me that two of your so-called flu victims are still being treated by a company physician at an undisclosed location and have not returned to work. Is that correct?

Santini: Who told you that?

Ransom: I'm not at liberty to divulge my sources, Ms. Santini, but—

Santini: Well, your unnamed source is misinformed, Mr. Ransom. All of the employees in question were back at work within two days. Now, if you'll excuse me.

Ransom: May I meet them?

Santini: No, sir, you may not. Now, if you'll excuse me, I need to get back to work. I'll have one of our security people walk you to your car.

Ransom: Back to work? I thought you had time to give me the whole company song-and-dance routine?

Santini: Good-bye, Mr. Ransom.

Chapter Goals

- To obtain a basic overview of the field of journalistic interviewing.
- To understand the interviewer's responsibilities for preparation, management, recording, and analysis of journalistic interviews.
- To recognize potential problems and special challenges faced by journalistic interviewers, including difficult interviewees, intercultural considerations, and ethical issues.
- To appreciate the journalistic interview from the interviewee's perspective, from preparation to participation and follow up.

Introduction

For most of us, no other form of interviewing is more familiar, or more deceiving, than journalistic interviews. We see snatches of journalistic interviews every night on the evening news. We read the results of them every day in newspapers and magazines. We see and hear more and more of them on television and radio. In most cases, what we see and hear is informative and well organized. Information flows from interviewer to interviewee and back again as if through a well-oiled machine, seemingly effortless and seamless. What we do not see or appreciate when we witness these mediated interviews are the hours of preparation and the years of experience that go into creating the best journalistic interviews and interviewers, not to mention the careful editing of hours of tape or notes to give the illusion of a perfect, seamless conversation.

Nor do we usually recognize that the skills of the journalistic interviewer are useful to people who will never work as professional journalists. Anyone who must talk to others to obtain needed information for reports, research, education, or analysis will need the skills of the journalistic interviewer. Additionally, all of us as journalistic audiences can benefit from understanding the journalistic interviewer's choices.

In this chapter we will look "behind the scenes" at the art and skill involved in journalistic interviewing, beginning with a brief overview of a variety of journalistic interviews currently in use and their purposes. Then, turning our attention to the journalistic interviewer's responsibilities, we will examine the necessity of preparation and planning prior to the interview itself. We will explore in detail the structure and format of typical journalistic interviews and questions. We will discuss methods of recording interviews and conducting post-interview analyses. We will look at potential problems and special challenges of journalistic interviewing, including listening considerations, difficult interviewees, intercultural issues, and ethical questions and concerns. Finally, we will examine the intervie-wee's role in preparation and participation in the journalistic interview.

The Varieties of Journalistic Interviews

What is a **journalistic interview?** Generally defined, it is an information-seeking interview in which the interviewer seeks information of interest for the purpose of capturing the attention of a particular audience. Journalistic audiences vary, from newspaper and magazine readers to television viewers and radio listeners. The journalist's responsibility is to use interviews to obtain information suitable for mediated presentation to an audience. A newspaper reporter assigned to a city news desk engages in numerous interviews daily, some of them brief and con-ducted over the phone, others in-depth and conducted face-to-face with persons who have information or opinions relevant to the story. A television news reporter may fly to the scene of a disaster seeking brief, video-recorded statements from persons affected by the disaster. A radio or television talk-show host such as Larry King invites guests who are currently in the news to engage in live, in-depth pro-file interviews for the edification and entertainment of his audience. While each of these interviewers has different approaches and purposes, all are involved in obtaining relevant information for their own specific audiences.

There are many forms of journalistic interviews currently in use.[1] **News inter-views** gather information to generate news stories for print or broadcast. They are usually based on questions that seek to discover answers to *who, what, when,* and *where* concerning the event in question. **News feature interviews** go beyond fact-finding to seek some understanding about the *how* and *why* of a story. In our open-ing interview, for example, the student reporter was hoping to discover not only what occurred, but also how the employees at the landfill became sick and why they were still being treated.

The use of interviews with a group of experts and others to present a diverse range of views on an issue is known as **round-up** or **roundtable interviewing.** Ted Koppel's *Nightline* news show is a good example of this type of interviewing. At a local newspaper, the round-up interview method might be employed to gauge public reaction to a proposed tax increase. Several people might be interviewed about the proposed increase and excerpts from their responses would be included in the final story. The goal of roundtable interviewing is to present diverse views on a subject.

Investigative interviews are news interviews that seek to explore an issue in depth for the purpose of coming to some conclusion or decision about it. An investigative journalist interviews many persons in order to explore an issue fully. In the opening interview, for example, the reporter might have continued his investigation by interviewing family members of the affected employees, other employees, emergency room personnel at the hospital where the employees were treated, and scientists or other "experts" who could speculate on the likely impact of the landfill accident on the persons directly involved as well as on the sur-rounding community.

A **profile interview,** on the other hand, is an in-depth look at one person. This is the kind of interview for which journalist Barbara Walters is well known. Profile interviews create for an audience a portrait or image of a person, how he or she thinks and feels, and what he or she believes. Popular magazines provide abun-dant examples of profile interviews, particularly of persons often in the news (e. g., movie stars, sports heroes, and political figures). On the other hand, local news-papers sometimes have regular features or columns that introduce to their read-ers members of the local community (e.g., a volunteer at a soup kitchen, a long-time baseball umpire for local teams, or a small business owner with a new product or service).

Less often, journalists also engage in **meet-the-press interviews** in which a key person is questioned by several journalists at the same time and place. A press conference is one example of this type of interview. Press conferences are usually controlled by the interviewee whose staff calls the press together and determines the place, time, length, and overall content of the interview. Politicians, particu-larly heads of state, conduct many interviews in the press or news conference form. One advantage of such interviews for journalists is that, because several journalists ask questions, unexpected knowledge or information may be obtained by all.[2] In a sense, each journalist at a press conference benefits from the research and skill of the others.

Each form of journalistic interview imposes unique needs and constraints on the interviewer. An investigative news reporter for a newspaper or magazine may conduct a series of telephone interviews as well as several face-to-face encounters with persons whose views are particularly important to a story. This interviewer selects the most revealing, interesting, or important statements made by the sources and eliminates the rest. Editing skill is vital to the effectiveness of the reporter's story. A live-broadcast roundtable interviewer, on the other hand, needs to be able to think quickly, to ask questions based on the immediate interactions, and to intervene as needed whenever problematic monologues or tangential responses develop in the course of the program.

The preparation and management of journalistic interviews will vary accord-ing to the specific type of interview being conducted, but some basic elements of interview preparation and management are the same for all. Traditionally, jour-nalistic interviews for print media were more common than those for broadcast media, but with the increasing popularity of live "talk" radio and television for-mats, more interviews are likely to be of the live-broadcast variety in the future.

Preparing for the Journalistic Interview

Even before it is scheduled, the journalistic interview begins with questions—not the specific questions the interviewer will develop in the interview guide, but the broader, larger questions that govern the entire information-seeking process. What is it the audience wants or needs to know about this person, issue, or event? What information must be obtained in order to satisfy the audience's wants or needs? Who can provide the information needed? What background information about the topic and interviewee(s) is needed in order to ask effective and intelligent questions? What preparations are necessary in order to be able to adapt effectively to unexpected responses or information? These are the questions with which the skilled journalistic interviewer will begin.

Suppose, for example, that an employee at an automotive assembly plant is asked by his supervisor to investigate a new team-assembly approach at the plant and to write an article for the company newsletter about how it is working. In response to the basic questions listed previously, the employee might decide that what the audience (employees at the plant) wants to know is how the team approach has affected production and morale. The information needed from interviews, therefore, should include specific figures on production rates before and after implementation of the team approach, as well as quotes from employees involved in the new procedure as to how they feel about the change.

In order to obtain the information needed, the employee may decide to interview the plant foreman to learn about the impact of the changes on production rates and to interview the members of two assembly teams in order to learn how employees feel about the change. To prepare for the interviews, the employee might observe the team-assembly approach in action as well as another line at the plant still operating under the older system, and read past company newsletters which introduced the team concept and explained why it was being adopted. Now the employee/interviewer is ready to begin to prepare the interview guide.

Audience Needs and Early Research

The needs of journalistic audiences vary according to the **medium,** or method of access to the audience (e.g., print, television, radio), through which the information will be disseminated. Newspaper and magazine audiences expect articles that convey answers to the standard questions of who, what, where, and when. Viewers of televisions news shows, on the other hand, expect brief capsule summaries of stories with pithy "sound bites," five to ten second edited quotes, that capture a response to a situation. Radio listeners have a different set of needs; they want to hear voices that convey information with sufficient intensity and brevity to hold their attention despite the lack of face-to-face contact.

The journalistic interviewer must consider both the questions that the audience is likely to have about the issue and the means by which that information will be conveyed. A journalist assigned a one-minute segment on the evening news, for example, will need to be much more selective in deciding what the audience needs to hear than a newspaper journalist with a two-column spread to fill.

The journalistic interviewer needs to know both how much and what kind of information is desired in order to conduct effective interviews. Once she or he understands how much and what kind of information is needed, the interviewer can begin researching the subject, including, if necessary, researching who would be the best interviewees on this subject for this audience.

Journalistic interviewers need to be knowledgeable about an issue before interviewing someone about it. Research provides that knowledge. The knowledge, in turn, allows the interviewer to ask effective questions of the most appropriate interviewees.

Background research for journalistic interviewing employs the same standard research tools as are employed in academic research—libraries, newspaper and periodical indices, electronic data bases, etc.[3] For example, a profile interview of an important civic leader would necessitate investigating past news coverage for information about what the public has already read or heard about this person. An investigative report on a local hazardous waste landfill might entail not only looking at previous local articles about the landfill, but also more general research and articles about environmental concerns. In addition, interviewers can ask knowledgeable persons about other appropriate interviewees. As we shall see, the journalistic interviewer's research continues even after the interviewees are selected.

Obtaining Appropriate Interviewees

The key questions a journalistic interviewer should keep in mind when seeking and selecting appropriate interviewees follow: Who has the needed information? Who is willing to share the needed information? Who is available at the necessary

Selecting appropriate interviewees is important to the credibility of the interview.

time(s)? Who will make the best interviewee? Background research and an understanding of the medium for which the interview is being conducted will help the journalistic interviewer begin to narrow the choices concerning appropriate interviewees.

The ideal journalistic interviewee will be articulate, reliable, willing to talk, accurate, and honest—in other words, credible.[4] Additionally, the interviewee may need to be reasonably telegenic for televised interviews and/or have a pleasant, resonant voice for TV and radio broadcasts. Obviously, a skilled interviewer will conduct sufficient research concerning the pool of potential interviewees in order to assess *in advance* which interviewee is most likely to meet all of the needs of the interview.

Once an interviewee is selected, the interviewer's next challenge is to obtain permission for the interview. MacDougall and Reid suggest that reporters should be brief and straightforward, quickly identifying themselves and their organization as well as the kind of information being sought.[5] Killenberg and Anderson suggest several additional strategies.[6] First, an interviewer should be realistic about her/his own status (or lack thereof) but not afraid to "aim high." A reporter for a small student newspaper may not be likely to get an interview with comedian Eddie Murphy, for example, but on the other hand, sometimes interviews are granted even when they seem unlikely. Likewise, the interviewer should be aware of the reputation of her/his organization and build on the credibility of the employer. Additionally, an interviewer should be willing to meet the interviewee briefly and in any setting, asking only for "time to ask a few questions" rather than a formal interview. In other words, the journalistic interviewer must be willing to adapt the need for an interview to the time and lifestyle constraints of the interviewee.[7] Interviewers should be persistent and ready to talk to persons close to the desired interviewee in order to have enough information to elicit the interviewee's interest and respect.

Biagi offers several suggestions for obtaining interviews. Agree to talk about what the individual is willing to discuss. Be creative in seeking ways to get through to the persons you want to interview, including calling or writing them at home or seeking to "run into" them in a public place where an interview can be requested. Appeal to a person's sense of pride or desire for attention, and her/his potential impact for the welfare of the community.[8]

From the point of first contact, the interviewer should create and maintain a solid rapport with the interviewee. Also, in order to be perceived credibly, the interviewer should dress and act professionally and be prepared for an immediate interview if the opportunity arises.[9] Then, once an interview is obtained—ideally, scheduled in advance—the interviewer can do as much additional research as time and circumstances allow on both the topic and the interviewee before preparing the interview guide.

Before the Interview

Before entering into an interview, the journalistic interviewer should be at least as informed on the subject as an intelligent layperson. The interviewer should have sufficient background information on the interviewee to be able to acknowledge her/his reputation and refer to her/his relevant experiences. This allows the interviewer to ask questions the interviewee is likely to be able to answer. For example, suppose an interviewer obtained an interview with an executive officer of a national sports team, but did not determine in advance the exact nature of the officer's duties. The unprepared interviewer might ask this person a series of questions about the financial affairs of the team which the interviewee, a public relations director, would not have the information to answer. The likely outcome of insufficient preparation will be embarrassment or discomfort for both interviewer and interviewee, as well as inefficient use of the interview time.

Different journalistic interviewers need different types of background knowledge. A profile interviewer, for example, needs to come to the interview with enough background information on the interviewee to be able to ask specific questions about that person's past experiences and future plans. An investigative journalist should come to the interview with a solid understanding of the basic facts of the issue under investigation as well as basic biographical information about the interviewee.

Once an interviewer has obtained as much background information about the interviewee and issue as possible, she or he should prepare a moderately scheduled interview guide, or at least a topic list. Ideally, the interviewer will begin with a tentative list of questions that address the broader questions with which the journalist began; namely, what does my audience want or need to know? What information is required in order to satisfy my audience's needs?

Advance preparation of questions adds to an interviewer's credibility, helps assure directional control over the interview, and provides a "safety net" of questions to fall back on in the event that the interview falters. Even interviewers with years of experience often bring specific written questions with them into their interviews. On many of Barbara Walter's televised interviews, for example, viewers can see that she refers to an interview guide on her lap.

Managing the Journalistic Interview

The assignment has been given, the research conducted, the interviewee selected, and the interview arranged. What happens now? Just as with other forms of interviews, journalistic interviews will have an opening, body, and closing, with concrete needs to be met in each of these phases. Additionally, the journalistic interviewer will need to guard against problem questions, make appropriate decisions about suitable methods for recording the interview, and effectively analyze the information obtained. Let's examine each of these aspects of interview management in turn.

Opening the Journalistic Interview

A journalistic interviewer begins with a self-introduction and agency or company affiliation: "Hello, Mr. Heller, I'm Gabrielle Marraro of the *Chicago Tribune*." The interviewee should clearly understand to whom he or she is speaking and for what purpose. It is unethical for a journalistic interviewer to obtain an interview under false pretenses, either by pretending the encounter is not an interview or by claiming false or misleading affiliations. For example, a political figure who has sponsored antigay legislation might well not grant an interview to a reporter from a gay activist magazine. Nonetheless, it would be unethical for that reporter to claim to be representing a different publication in order to obtain the interview.

The journalistic interviewer must also do everything possible to build rapport with the interviewee while setting a professional tone for the interview. In the first place, the interviewer should use a form of address with the interviewee that is appropriate to their relationship and maintains professionalism. In most situations, unless otherwise invited, the interviewer should address the interviewee using the appropriate title and surname: Ms. Wilson, Dr. Camaria, Mrs. Lavade. It would be a mistake to use an interviewee's first name as a way of creating a false sense of intimacy. If the interviewee took offense at the interviewer's informality, rapport would be lost and the interviewer's professional credibility would be damaged. In most cases, journalistic interviewers conduct their interviews with more formality than informality.

Once rapport is established, the interviewer should briefly explain the agenda for the interview and move directly to the first question. A businesslike approach to the interview will enhance the interviewer's professional credibility.

The Journalist's Questions

As mentioned previously, the journalistic interviewer benefits from following a moderately scheduled approach, with tentative questions that leave room for adaptation to the needs of the dialogue. A funnel sequence, which moves from broader to narrower questions, offers a logical question progression for information gathering, moving from general to specific information. Likewise, the parallel path sequence of organization lends itself readily to the journalistic interviewer's traditional who, what, when, where, why, and how questions. In any case, regardless of their organizational pattern, an interviewer's questions should be short, clear, and neutral.

Of key importance to journalistic interviewers is the skillful use of probes to amplify, clarify, and confront. In order to obtain the information needed, journalists need to ask tough questions that dig deeper and demand more from the interviewee. Amplification probes such as "Could you rephrase that for me?" or "Please tell me more" help the interviewer get better, more "quotable" statements and encourage reticent interviewees to say more about a subject. Clarification probes such as "Let me be sure I understand what you just said. . ." are essential to assuring the accuracy of information obtained.

Confrontational probes that challenge earlier responses are sometimes necessary in order to examine evasiveness and inconsistencies as well as to correct distortions. For example, an interviewer whose question was evaded might say, "Excuse me, Mr. Kallembach, but I don't believe you answered my earlier question. Were you aware that illegal deductions were being claimed against your company's travel expenses?" When an interviewee makes veiled accusations, on the other hand, the interviewer might probe further by asking, "Are you suggesting that Mr. Fontaine authorized this pattern of illegal business expense deductions?" Confrontational probes are essential, but they need not be hostile. A skilled interviewer confronts evasions, deceptions, or innuendos with firmness rather than anger. Journalistic interviewers need to continue to probe until they are sure, first of all, of the accuracy of their information and, second, that their questions have been answered completely.

Questions to Avoid

The perfect questions to ask—hard as they may be to predict in advance—are those which will provide the exact information the interviewer needs. But what about the other side of the coin? Are there certain questions that are unlikely to provide the journalistic interviewer with the desired information? The subject of problem questions common to all interviews was discussed at length in an earlier chapter. Additionally, there are certain types of questions that are particularly problematic for journalistic interviewers. The following includes some of these:

"How do you feel?" This is a question that is asked all too often of crisis survivors and athletic competition winners and losers, most often with painful or vacuous results.[10] A person who has suffered a loss or narrowly escaped a disaster is not likely to be coherent enough to be able to express feelings accurately. A more useful question for such persons would ask them to describe what they experienced or to report what exactly they witnessed.

Likewise, athletic winners or losers are better able to answer more specific questions: "What do you think was the turning point in this match?" "Tell me about that play against Esposito." "What would you change, if you could, about what happened here tonight?" Questions that ask for specific details aid both the interviewer and the interviewee in focusing clearly on the situation at hand.

"Don't you think . . . and don't you agree . . . ?" Leading questions are particularly problematic for the investigative interviewer because they can so easily bias the answers received, particularly in broadcast situations where some interviewees are reluctant to disagree openly. There is no room for leading the interviewee when accurate information is desired. Likewise, if the interviewer's bias is obvious, some interviewees are likely to match their responses to what they believe is being sought. On the other hand, if an interviewee believes the journalist's opinion is already fixed, as in our opening interview, he or she may become reluctant to answer at all. The journalistic interviewer must take every precaution, through advance planning and careful self-monitoring, to ask neutral questions that invite unbiased responses.

"What if you found yourself . . . ?" There is something creatively appealing about hypothetical questions: they allow the interviewer to seek responses to certain scenarios and invite the interviewee to offer specific responses to these possibilities. In certain settings, such as selection interviews, they can elicit useful information about how a person might respond to particular problems and people. However, hypothetical questions rarely serve such constructive purposes in jour-

nalistic interviews. Instead, they can serve as traps or potential pitfalls for unwitting interviewees. For example, the singer and activist Joan Baez wrote an extended fictional example of the misuse of hypothetical questions in her book *Daybreak*[11]:

"Okay. You're a pacifist. What would you do if someone were, say, attacking your grandmother . . .. Say he had a gun and he was about to shoot her. Would you shoot him first?"

"Do I have a gun?"

"Yes."

"No. I'm a pacifist. I don't have a gun."

"Well, say you do."

"All right. Am I a good shot?"

"Yes."

"I'd shoot the gun out of his hand."

"No, then you're not a good shot."

"I'd be afraid to shoot. Might kill Grandma."

More recently, then Vice President Dan Quayle, pro-life spokesman for the Bush administration, ran into trouble with his response to a hypothetical question on CNN's *Larry King Live.* King asked Quayle what he would do if his daughter came to him as an adult (she was then 13) with the news that she was pregnant. Quayle answered, "Well, it's a hypothetical situation, and I hope that I never have to deal with it. But obviously I would counsel her and talk to her and support her on whatever decision she made." As a result of his response, Quayle's subsequent 1992 campaign speeches on economic issues were drowned out by the uproar over his response to this hypothetical question.[12]

It is for just this reason that many political figures shy away from hypothetical questions as too risky.[13] Led by hypothetical questions, both interviewer and interviewee are soon discussing at length an event that has not occurred and is not likely to occur in the future. In general, journalistic interviewers are better off sticking with specific, reality-based questions.

Closing the Journalistic Interview

The closing of a journalistic interview offers the interviewer a final opportunity to assess the completeness and clarity of the information received, as well as to offer a sense of closure to the encounter. By summarizing aloud what has been heard and asking for corrections or clarifications, the interviewer is able to check perceptions for accuracy while at the same time rechecking notes or guide for missed or unclear information.

The closing also provides the interviewer with an opportunity to invite the interviewee to fill in any gaps in the information obtained. Sometimes, in the process of informational interviewing, important information gets missed because the question needed to solicit it was not asked. Fiumara writes: "Although it is certainly true that the answers are the material from which the edifice is built, the structure of the edifice is determined by the type of questions that were asked—in the sense that the answer collaborates with the question and produces everything that is demanded of it, and *nothing* else. The possibility, however, that the answer eludes the restrictive nature of the question remains."[14] An actor in a profile interview might fail to reveal a remarkable experience which led her into acting because the interviewer asked about her educational background but not about how her acting career began. A political candidate might be unable to talk about his qualifications for office because the interviewer asked only about future hopes and plans. If asked the right questions, an interviewee can often provide the interviewer with valuable insights into overlooked but relevant information.

After summarizing the interview, an interviewer can check for missing information in any of several ways: "On the basis of my summary, do you think there's any further information that's needed before I write this story?" "Is there anyone else I should talk to about this issue?" "What have I missed? Is there anything else you want me to know about you before we close?" Once such questions are asked, of course, the interviewee needs to be given the time to offer a response.

Finally, the interviewer should end the interview professionally, politely, and with a sense of closure, seeking permission to call back, if necessary, to correct or clarify details. Ideally, for the journalist, relationships with qualified sources are nurtured and maintained for the sake of potential future stories. Each journalistic interview, therefore, should end on a positive note if at all possible, so that a network of informed, willing, and experienced interviewees eventually will be developed.

Recording the Interview

Accuracy in detail is crucial for the journalistic interviewer. The importance of accuracy accentuates the need for good recording skills for journalistic interviewers. As with any interview, decisions about methods of recording must be made with a view to balancing the mutual concerns of accuracy and interviewee comfort. Additionally, however, the medium through which the journalistic interview will be conveyed obviously influences preferred methods of recording the interview. A newspaper reporter will not have the opportunity to show a video clip, nor will a radio broadcaster. A television interviewer, on the other hand, will want both sight and sound recording of the message. The variety of recording options discussed in chapter 2 are the same for journalistic interviewers as for others. Let's briefly reconsider these options—note taking, memorization, and electronic recording—as they pertain to the specific needs of the journalist.

Note Taking.   Note taking can be verbatim (word for word), a record of central ideas, or a category checklist prepared in advance. Verbatim note taking is only an option for persons with advanced shorthand skills, which would allow them to keep pace with the flow of the conversation. Most note takers, much like university students at lectures, make written notes that highlight central ideas. Journalistic interviewers also benefit from marking central ideas that need further probing and by occasionally writing out an interviewee's statement verbatim for purposes of direct quotation.

Note taking is portable and flexible. It can ensure some degree of accuracy in reporting. It allows the interviewer to jot down additional questions as they develop in the course of the interview and can save time during analysis because notes of central ideas are quick and easy to review. Additionally, note taking is widely accepted as a form of recording and does not usually meet with much interviewee resistance.

As to disadvantages, note taking can hurt an interviewer's concentration and listening, because it requires a "split focus," attending to both the ongoing dialogue and the need to record what is discussed. Often, it can also be hard to keep up with the pace of the spoken word, thus the flow of the interview is broken while the interviewer attempts to catch up. Note taking can also convey impressions about what the interviewer considers to be important information. This can result from an interviewee's sense that only what is written down is important. This perception, in turn, can affect the nature of the interview by influencing the interviewee's sense of what information is of interest.

For these reasons, some interviewers rely on delayed note taking; that is, waiting until immediately after the interview to write a record of what was said. However, delayed note taking poses inevitable risks in terms of information accuracy. There is considerable evidence that even concurrent note taking can be grossly inaccurate. A study of trial reporting in ten Canadian newspapers, for example, found that quotations recorded through on-the-scene note taking were significantly misreported at least 50 percent of the time.[15] Given the margin of error even in concurrent recording, clearly there is a risk that important details will be forgotten or inaccurately remembered if recording is delayed.

Memorization.   Accurate memorization, like advanced shorthand, is not a skill or tool available to most, and only someone very skilled at memorization would want to rely on memory alone as a means of recording an interview. For those who are able to memorize information quickly and accurately, however, memorization eliminates the "split focus" distraction, allows the interviewer to maintain better eye contact with the interviewee, and eliminates interviewee conjecture about what information is important.

Like perception itself, however, human memory is faulty. While memory can be enhanced with training and practice and through use of such devices as mental imagery and mnemonic devices, relying on memorization alone can lead to unintentional interviewer bias in what is remembered as well as what is lost. For the sake of accuracy, unless their memorization skills are excellent, journalists should use another form of recording their interviews.

Electronic Recording.   Because of its accuracy and relative ease of use, electronic recording is a very desirable recording method for journalists, particularly when used in conjunction with summary note taking.[16] Electronic recording offers an accurate, permanent, and complete record of the interview and thereby allows the interviewer to focus on the interviewee without concern for capturing information. Electronic taping also best allows for obtaining verbatim quotations.[17] For the journalistic interviewer, for whom accuracy and verifiability are vital, electronic recording is clearly the superior choice.

Regardless of the method of recording, an interviewer should explain to the interviewee the need to record for the sake of accuracy and to ask for permission. During the interview, the recording equipment should be employed as unobtrusively as possible, allowing both interviewer and interviewee to focus their attention on the interview itself.

Post-Interview Analysis

After the interview is over, the journalistic interviewer must examine the interview in light of the questions with which she or he began: Was the necessary information obtained from this interviewee? Is it the information my audience needs? What further information is needed?

In addition, the interviewer must verify the accuracy of the information obtained, whenever possible, by checking the details with other reliable sources. Some editors insist that reporters find at least two additional confirming sources of information before running a story.[18] Even persons who intend to communicate honestly can be inaccurate.

In order to analyze information effectively, the interviewer must also clearly recognize the difference between facts (i.e., verifiable observations) and inferences (i.e., conclusions based on observations). For the sake of accurate reporting, only supported or verified observations should be included.

For example, an interviewee might accuse a colleague of deliberate deceit. Unless the interviewer has or can obtain other evidence of deceit, the interviewee's accusation is not a fact but an inference—an opinion. The interviewer must sift the facts and inferences obtained in the interview and cull from them verifiable and accurate information. (Obviously, these are not the standards employed by tabloid journalists.)

The interviewer then must decide which, if any, of the verbatim quotations are the most newsworthy or capable of adding personal and dramatic emphasis to the story. Ideally, the quotations selected should convey a real sense of the personality and perspective of the person quoted, as well as provide an interesting or memorable capsulation of the story. Once both interview and analysis are complete, the interviewer is ready to prepare the information obtained in a suitable format for the audience.

Special Problems and Challenges

The journalistic interviewer faces some special challenges in the course of "getting the story." These are difficult interviewees whose input is necessary to the story;

an intensified need to listen for verifiable accuracy; the likelihood and challenges of intercultural encounters; and ethical issues unique to the field of journalistic interviewing which must be considered and understood. We will look at each of these special issues in turn.

Difficult Interviewees

It does not take a journalist or interviewer long to discover that all interviewees are *not* created equal. For whatever reasons, some interviewees are reticent, overly talkative, biased, emotional, hostile, evasive, or deceptive. If the person in question is the best source of needed information, the interviewer may not be at liberty to walk away. In such cases, how should a skilled journalistic interviewer respond in order to reap the best possible benefit from time spent with difficult interviewees?

Reticent Interviewees.   Whether from shyness, discomfort, or unwillingness to share their views, some interviewees are reluctant to speak. They answer in monosyllables or do not expand or provide details to their stories. For the journalist, interviewing such persons is like "pulling teeth"—ideas must almost be forcibly extracted because the interviewee will not volunteer them.

Faced with such an interviewee, the skilled interviewer has several options. Sensing reluctance or discomfort, the interviewer may decide, first of all, to spend more time building rapport with the interviewee before the real process of information-seeking and recording begins. During this time, the interviewer may attempt to allay the interviewee's fears by clarifying the desire to obtain a fair and accurate story. She or he may begin the interview with nonthreatening questions that ask for information the interviewee understands and can easily provide. The interviewer may reverse the typical order of questions and start with those that are narrow and specific, moving to the broader, more general questions as the interviewee becomes more relaxed and talkative. If other options exist, the interviewer may decide to interview someone who is more comfortable with the interview process.

Overly Talkative Interviewees.   At the other end of the spectrum there are those persons who have too much to say about any subject and who, for whatever reasons, lack the ability or desire to be succinct in their responses. These interviewees can undermine an interviewer's directional control by exerting so much informational control that the interviewer's power is damaged or lost. In response to early questions, they may talk for so long that the interviewer is left without time to ask essential questions.

The interviewer facing such an interviewee needs to listen carefully for even the smallest pauses or breaks in the interviewee's responses. Finding such a break, the interviewer should begin talking forcefully, interrupting and overriding the interviewee's monologue, if necessary. The interviewer should ask for more specific responses, using closed questions where possible and encourage the interviewee to move to the main point of the response. With these types of interviewees, it may be necessary to rely almost exclusively on narrowly focused questions, which by their nature discourage rambling responses.

Evasive or Deceptive Interviewees. Sometimes an interviewee may agree to an interview but nonetheless avoid giving complete and honest answers to some of the interviewer's questions. In these situations, the journalistic interviewer's competence and confidence to probe for clarification and accuracy are vital. The interviewer must note and return to areas where information was inconsistent or incomplete, responding with closed questions or confrontational and clarifying probes. If the interviewer detects what seems to be deception through inconsistencies, convoluted answers, or systematic evasion, the interviewer must press for details, asking for the facts on which the interviewee's judgments were based, verbalizing and questioning inconsistencies, and inviting the interviewee to respond to different statements made in the past.

For example, "Mr. Henderson, in an interview with the *Herald Star* last week, you were quoted as saying you had experimented with illegal drug usage in your youth. Are you now saying you did not in fact experiment with drugs at any time in your early years?" Of course, an interviewee intent on deception or evasion may refuse all attempts to probe or clarify, in which case the interviewer has the option of examining these inconsistencies and evasions in the finished story. "Confronted with the inconsistencies in his statements to the press, Henderson refused to answer or clarify them." The interviewer should be tactful but firm, refusing to allow the interviewee to evade the purpose or central issues of the interview.[19]

Biased or Emotional Interviewees. What about the interviewee who clearly has an emotional agenda in the interview, or who describes events and people with obvious bias, or whose responses are angry or upset? What are the journalist's options in these situations?

Biased interviewees are clearly not the best source for accurate information, but they may be useful as a source of dramatic interest or "color," particularly if the journalist's story about which there are sharp differences in opinion, as is the case with the question of legalized abortion in the United States. With emotional informants, the challenge for the interviewer is to select interviewee responses for publication or broadcast that clearly indicate that bias affects the judgments offered.

There are, of course, situations in which reporters are assigned to interview persons who are in highly emotional situations (e.g., the grieving parents of a murdered child, the survivors of earthquakes and airplane crashes, the widows and children of mineworkers killed in an underground explosion). Interviews with persons in pain may seem cruel at times, but, at the same time, recognition of the impact of events on real people is part of what makes audiences appreciate those events as newsworthy. For whatever reasons, readers are interested and moved by the traumas and tragedies of others; these stories "sell." The question the journalist faces is how to interview these persons in ways that neither manipulate nor add to their pain.

Killenberg and Anderson offer this advice: Begin with an expression of condolence: "I'm sorry you lost your son." Ask questions gently, probing for what the interviewee is able to express without being overcome by emotion. Be compassionate and nonjudgmental. Also, be careful to chose quotations that do not exploit an interviewee's loss of emotional control and that allow preservation of dignity.[20]

Hostile Interviewees.   What if an interviewer is faced with an interviewee who is overtly hostile in the course of the interview; who verbally attacks and challenges the interviewer's questions and comments? It is difficult to refrain from responding with hostility to hostility, but if the interviewer can remain calm and undefensive in the face of interviewee hostility, the interviewer can win the upper hand. The interviewer who remains calm in the face of hostility, particularly in TV or radio broadcast interviews, will appear stronger and more credible to viewers and may also influence the interviewee to temper behavior in order not to appear foolish or weak. In other circumstances, however, if an interviewee persists in being hostile, the interviewer may have no choice but to find a new source of information.

Listening for Accuracy

Implicit in the previous discussion of responses to difficult interviewees is the assumption (emphasized early in this text) that the interviewer must be an excellent listener by paying careful attention not only to what is being said, but also to what is being avoided or conveyed through other than the verbal content of the messages. A journalistic interviewer's need to listen, in most regards, is no different from any other interviewer's. However, there is one sense in which the journalist's listening responsibility should be emphasized; it is in the need to listen for ways to verify the accuracy of information essential to the story.

The journalist needs to listen in particular for the informational details which must be accurate in order for the story as a whole to be credible. These informational details include such things as dates, times, places, who was present or absent, and what transpired; namely, the "who," "what, "where," and "when" that is the essential "stuff" of informational interviewing. As a listener, the journalistic interviewer needs be able to make frequent "stops" in the course of the interview and to use amplification and clarification probes to check the accuracy of these details. "Was that Thursday or Friday when you made that appearance?" "Do you remember who else was in the room?" "What day was it when you first noticed the missing checks?" "Did you say you were twenty when this happened?"

Like an investigative officer probing a crime, journalistic interviewers must be willing to backtrack through a story until they are confident that it is complete in all its essential details. Perception checking and the careful use of probes are the journalist's primary tools for insuring accuracy. Additionally, the journalist who listens carefully and with an open mind is more likely to hear unknown informational details. In this way, the skilled journalistic interviewer may be led in unexpected directions and arrive at more interesting or accurate stories.

Intercultural Issues for the Journalistic Interviewer

Because of the role of news media as disseminators of information about cultural issues, the journalistic interviewer is likely to need information from persons of diverse cultural backgrounds both within and outside her/his own culture in the course of getting a story. Therefore, the interviewer must be attuned to the impact of cultural differences on the communication styles of individuals in order to understand the other's messages accurately.

The best preparation for intercultural interviewing for the journalistic interviewer is to research the interviewee's cultural background as a basic component of the broader research and preparation process. Such research should consist of reading about the interviewee's culture, as well as talking with other natives of that culture to obtain insights into how to approach the interview and what culturally specific behaviors to expect from the interviewee.

For example, suppose a newspaper journalist is assigned to a story about a Japanese entrepreneur who has purchased a business in a midwestern city. The journalist begins the research by reading both biographical material on the entre-

Questions asking for details enable both parties to focus on the situation at hand.

preneur and material about Japanese culture. One source is an article on Japanese communication styles, which provides her with the following information:[21]

1. Japanese use emotion less than Americans when they communicate.
2. Japanese are less likely to argue than Americans, tending to value harmony over controversy.
3. Japanese tend to be apprehensive in communication situations, more so even than other groups living in the Pacific Basin area.
4. Because of stronger identification with their social groups, Japanese tend to feel lonelier than Americans.
5. Japanese are less assertive and less responsive in their communication than Americans.

On the basis of information of this kind, obtained from a reputable source, the interviewer may decide to adapt the approach to the interview. For example, she or he might plan to offer more assurances, maintain a more formal social distance, and exercise more nonverbal restraint, attempting to adapt the communication style to the likely style of the interviewee. Likewise, the interviewer might try to monitor her/his own culturally based tendencies to assume that unemotional persons are cold or hostile and that quiet persons are shy or lack confidence.

Whenever there are known cultural or subcultural differences between interviewer and interviewee, the interviewer should seek to understand those known differences more fully prior to entering into the interview. However, even when there are no known or obvious cultural differences—a female American reporter interviewing a female American computer scientist, for example—the interviewer should be alerted to the possibility of cultural or subcultural differences and make a conscious effort to determine whether her own responses, perceptions, and judgments are being affected by prejudices or stereotypes about style rather than the actual intent or content of the other's messages. "For effective intercultural communication one's attitude is more important than one's knowledge and/or understanding."[22]

Ethical Guidelines for the Journalistic Interviewer

Accepted standards of ethical behavior for any occupation are not written in stone. Standards change as culture changes and as the nature of the work changes, and not always for the better or with the common consent of those involved. Journalistic interviewers are members of a profession that is undergoing continual redefinition as the media of television, radio, newspapers and magazines, and their audiences are refashioned and redefined.

In recent years, for example, the notion of the journalist as an objective reporter of facts has been gradually tempered or replaced by the idea of what radical journalist Hunter Thompson originally labelled "gonzo journalism,"[23] that is, the reporting of the journalist's point of view with emotions and biases acknowledged and intact. Moreover, the idea of the journalist as a mere conveyor of the news has been transmuted into an image of the journalist as entertainer, to the point where real-life journalists appeared playing themselves at a baby shower for the fictional TV sitcom journalist Murphy Brown. Local television newscasters devote a segment of the evening news to "prime time tie-ins" in which topics from the evening's entertainment shows are reported and discussed. Likewise, numerous "news format" television shows now cover entertainment subjects such as movies and movie stars, while "documentary style" television programming recreates events such as murders and other crimes with a mix of actors and real survivors of the events. Clearly, the line between "news" and "entertainment" has blurred in recent years.

All of these changes and blurring in the understanding of news and news reporters have ethical implications for the field of journalistic interviewing, the exact nature of which are unclear because the changes are ongoing. The following discussion of ethical standards for journalistic interviewers relies on previously accepted ideals or values governing the behavior of journalists as interviewers. Like all standards of ethics, these are a part of the ongoing debate over ethics among responsible professionals.

Ethical guidelines are standards or values that reflect what an individual or group believes is right and fair behavior. As in any group, but particularly a group undergoing redefinition and change, there will be broad individual differences in understanding and acceptance of ethical guidelines for the discipline. Nonetheless, the ethical guidelines of any group or profession can be seen as ". . . a common core of consistent and widely shared moral beliefs that save us from purely subjective preferences."[24] Journalists Klaidman and Beachamp define the underlying ethical guidelines or moral values of journalism as the freedom to seek and share information, the need to make ongoing moral judgments about information and how it is obtained, the goal of fairness in reporting, and the need for competence in one's craft, all in the pursuit of a reasonable standard of truth.[25]

On Accuracy and Fairness.   According to Frank McCulloch, editor of a discussion of ethical dilemmas of journalists, "The all-encompassing question, within which all others fall, is accuracy and fairness. If we proceed as reporters honestly, accurately, and fairly, there are no ethical questions left."[26] The first obligation of the journalistic interviewer, in other words, is to approach stories as impartially as possible and to strive for accuracy and fairness in the information presented. News commentator and author Andy Rooney offers these suggestions about how accuracy and fairness are attained in his *The Journalist's Code of Ethics.*

> . . . *I am a journalist because I believe that if all the world had all the facts about everything, it would be a better world. I understand that the facts and the truth are not always the same. It is my job to report the facts so that others can decide on the truth. I will try to tell people what they ought to know and avoid telling them what they want to hear, except when the two coincide, which isn't often. . . . No gift, including kind words, will be accepted when it is offered for the purpose of influencing my report. What I wish were the facts will not influence what investigation leads me to believe them to be. I will be suspicious of every self-interested piece of information. . .*

I will not use my profession to help or espouse any cause, nor alter my report for the benefit of any cause, no matter how worthy that cause may appear to be.[27]

On Lying.   There is a clear standard for honesty in the reporting of stories within the journalism profession. In 1981 the Pulitzer Prize-winning *Washington Post* reporter Janet Cooke was stripped of her 1980 award when it was discovered she had fabricated a story about an 8-year-old heroin addict. Cooke's lies, made public by the *Post* as soon as they were discovered, caused a widespread uproar in the journalistic community, where much was written and discussed about the relationship between accuracy in reporting and the public trust. There was no disagreement in the profession about the gravity or error of Cooke's falsifications.[28]

Where journalistic standards about lying are not clear, however, is in the area of telling lies to *obtain* a story. For example, a reporter might pretend to have evidence of criminal activity among police officers in order to get one police officer to admit that the activity is occurring. Then the reporter would proceed to interview other officers with the information thus obtained. In their discussion of this issue, Killenberg and Anderson recommend this ethical standard: lying should be used rarely, if ever, and journalists who lie should be certain that the end justifies the means.[29]

On Hidden or Withheld Identity.   In times past, it was not uncommon for newspaper reporters to obtain and use telephone interviews by claiming to be someone other than themselves. A Chicago police reporter named Harry Romanoff became renowned for his ability to obtain good stories by telephone through use of deceit.[30] Another Chicago reporter, Don Bishoff, formerly used the same tactic, routinely identifying himself as "Officer Fischer from the 35th Precinct.[31] While such habits may at one time have been considered ethically acceptable by some journalists, this is no longer the case in reputable news agencies.

In fairness to those they interview, journalists should clearly identify who they are and what agency they represent. While there may be certain situations in which reporters, like police, go undercover in order to discover the facts of a story, any interviewer who obtains information by deceiving the interviewee about her or his identity and purpose is abusing the trust of the other.

On Identification of Sources.   Journalistic interviewers need to be clear with interviewees, in advance of the interview, as to how the information obtained will later be used. Most journalists routinely plan to use whatever significant information they obtain in the course of an interview.[32] The journalistic profession, however, generally distinguishes these categories of information sources:

On the record: Everything the person says can be used by the interviewer and attributed to its source. Example: "Mayor Thomas Jenkins stated, `I will not run for office again in 1996; this is my last term.'"

Indirect quote: The information obtained can be shared and attributed to the source, but not quoted directly. Example: "Mayor Jenkins has indicated that he will not seek office again in 1996."

On background: The information obtained from the interview can be used as background to the story, but can only be attributed in a general way. Example: "According to a source at City Hall, Mayor Jenkins will not seek re-election in 1996."

Not for attribution: The information obtained can be referred to but cannot be attributed, even in a general way, to its source. Example: "According to information received by this station, Mayor Jenkins will not seek re-election."

Off-the-record: Information provided is confidential and cannot be used in any way unless obtained from another source. Sometimes interviewees will provide journalists with a story off-the-record and then insist that the journalist obtain the facts of the story elsewhere. Example: A reporter receives a confidential tip that Mayor Jenkins will not seek re-election. She then calls the mayor and several persons close to him in an attempt to get the information she has obtained off-the-record corroborated.[33]

Most journalists routinely refuse to grant off-the-record status to information shared by their interviewees. However, whatever agreement an interviewer makes about attribution with the interviewee should be honored exactly as agreed upon and used only for the purposes stated.

On Libel. Journalists are bound by laws concerning **libel,** the malicious (i.e., intending to harm) printing or broadcasting of false or injurious information about a person.[34] Libel laws vary from state to state and, like all laws, undergo continuous reinterpretation in the courts. In general, existing libel laws distinguish between public figures and private citizens. For libel to be proven against public figures, malicious intent on the part of the reporter must be proven, whereas private citizens can sue for libel on the basis of negligence, claiming that a reporter should have discovered that the information was false. To be libelous, the information in question generally must be proven to be (1) false, or (2) maliciously intended or negligently obtained, (3) communicated to a third party, (4) clearly identifying the person libeled, and (5) causing injury (e.g., lost wages, mental anguish, damage to the reputation, etc.) to the person libeled. [35] Journalistic interviewers need to become familiar with the laws governing libel in the states where they work.

In summary, the ethical issues and dilemmas faced by journalistic interviewers are as various as the situations themselves, and no simple set of guidelines will address them all. As a general rule, however, journalists should feel bound by an automatic preference for honesty and accuracy, not only in the information obtained, but also in the methods which are used to obtain it.

Being A Journalistic Interviewee

So far we have examined the arena of journalistic interviewing only from the point of view of the interviewer. Now, we will turn our attention to the person on the other side of the journalistic experience; namely, the person interviewed.

Certain individuals, because of the nature of their jobs, must speak regularly to reporters. Politicians and other public figures in a sense rely on journalists to keep their names in the public eye. Others—administrators of schools and agencies, union leaders or business representatives, and even prominent volunteers and community leaders—may not often seek the spotlight but will be called into it from time to time when a story affecting their organization is breaking. For all persons who are likely to encounter journalistic interviewers, some degree of training makes sense.

Roger Ailes, communication consultant to politicians and public figures, was once accused of being immoral for training people to meet the press when he was speaking at a journalism-school seminar. He responded, "We always advise our clients to tell the truth. But the thing that disturbs me most is that you are here in journalism school learning how to ask the questions, yet you would deny a person the right to learn how to answer those questions."[36] Given that training in advance of being interviewed is desirable for interviewees as well as interviewers, what kind of preparation or training is needed?

Before the Interview

The interviewee can prepare in advance of the interview, first of all, by verifying the credentials of the journalist seeking the interview. This can easily be accomplished by a call to the employer named by the interviewer to verify the journalist's employment and purpose.

Next, the interviewee should anticipate the questions the interviewer is likely to ask and decide in advance how to answer them. If the story being investigated is going to be printed or broadcast, the interviewee's statements are going to be seen or read by many people. The interviewee would want to represent herself or himself as accurately and well as possible. Ailes suggests that the interviewee should never be unprepared and furthermore should have a clear agenda of what needs to be communicated or accomplished in the course of the interview.[37]

During the Interview

During the course of the interview, the journalistic interviewee will want to pay particular attention to these two areas: answering questions well, and managing the impression. Let's look briefly at each of these in turn.

Answering Questions Well.   In order to answer questions well, the interviewee should make sure to listen closely to each question, being sure to understand it before attempting to answer. Also, the interviewee should not be afraid to take time to think about a response before answering.

The interviewee's answers should be concise and accurate. "The move will take place on August 22nd and we are confident all will go smoothly." The tougher the questions, the shorter and simpler the answers, providing the minimal information necessary before moving away from the topic. If, for example, a reporter asks, "Since you are the person who hired the teacher now accused of sexual harassment, don't you feel somewhat responsible?" an interviewee might answer, "I am concerned about what has happened and wish it could have been avoided."

If the interviewer asks a question that the interviewee cannot or does not wish to answer, it is better to answer minimally than to offer a "no comment" or similar response, which may be seen as defensive. For example, a reporter asks, "How many children now claim to have been harassed by this teacher?" and the interviewee responds, "I have been asked not to talk about the details of the case for legal reasons—I'm sure you understand."

Finally, the interviewee should look for ways to assure that her/his own agenda is met during the interview, even if that sometimes means including information in answer to questions for which the reporter may have had a different intent.

Manage Your Impression.   Finally, the interviewee should make every attempt to manage her/his overall impression in the interview. The interviewee should seek to appear as friendly, courteous, and cooperative as possible and to remain composed even if the reporter becomes aggressive or hostile. The interviewee who accomplishes this is likely to win the sympathies of the audience if the interview is broadcast.

Likewise, the interviewee will want to use nonverbal communication to express confidence and assurance. If the interviewee is speaking on behalf of an agency or organization, to a significant extent that agency will be judged by the interviewee's personal credibility. For example, an urban hospital in Fort Wayne, Indiana, built a new structure and announced its plans to move all of its patients via ambulance from one building to another in one day. The confidence of the hospital spokesperson who met the press was vital to the hospital's desire to assure the public that the hospital would provide safe care during the move. If that person had appeared harried or unsure, the public would have been less likely to make use of the hospital in the days preceding the move. Interviewees who represent the agencies they work for, like the journalists who interview them, need to be aware that they represent their agencies not only in the content of their messages, but also in their self-presentations as well.

Summary

The journalistic interview is an information-seeking interview conducted to obtain information of interest for a particular audience. Varied in form and methods of transmission, journalistic interviews require preparatory investigation to determine what information is needed for which audience and who will be the most effective interviewee. Before the interview, the journalistic interviewer should obtain as much information as possible about the topic and the interviewee and prepare a tentative guide to manage the interview.

Interview management includes beginning with professionalism, clarity of purpose, and efficient use of questions, especially probes, to clarify, amplify, and confront. The journalistic interviewer should avoid questions which ask, "How do you feel?" as well as leading and hypothetical questions. The interviewer should close the interview in a manner that allows checking for accuracy and gives the interviewee time to provide information that might otherwise have been missed.

Like other interviewers, the journalistic interviewer must make choices about methods of record keeping during the interview. Because of the importance of accuracy to journalistic interviews, electronic recording is beneficial; it is often used in conjunction with some form of notetaking. After the interview, the interviewer must examine the findings to determine if the information obtained is complete, accurate, and appropriate for the needs of the audience at which it is aimed.

The journalistic interviewer faces certain special problems and challenges, such as difficult interviewees, the need to listen for verifiable accuracy, and the need to interview effectively across cultures or subcultures. The journalistic interviewer also needs to understand and employ a set of ethical guidelines. Ethical guidelines governing accuracy and fairness, lying, hidden or withheld identity, identification of sources, and libel guide journalistic interviewers.

The role of the journalistic interviewee was also explored. The need for preparation in advance of the interview, as well as the need to manage the interview effectively, were discussed.

Discussion Questions

1. Looking back at the interview which began this chapter, try to pinpoint where problems developed and how the participants might have handled the situation differently. Discuss with another person how the interview could be rewritten, believably, in a way that might have resulted in a more successful outcome.

2. Which variety of journalistic interview do you think is most common today? Where is it most often seen, read, or heard? Which variety of interview seems most likely to become prevalent in the future? Why?

3. If you could interview any public figure, who would it be? Why? What would you want to ask the person? For which medium would you prefer the interview be prepared?

4. Suppose you were assigned to conduct an interview with your local mayor or a local

sports hero. How would you do background research on this person in advance of the interview?

5. With which of the ethical guidelines discussed in the chapter do you agree? With which do you disagree? Why? What other ethical issues do you think a journalistic interviewer might confront? What guidelines would you set regarding them?

Suggested Activities

1. Observe any journalistic interview on television. Write a three to four page paper in which you discuss and assess what type of interview was conducted, how successful both interviewer and interviewee seemed to be in covering their agendas, and what ethical issues, if any, arose in the course of the interview.

2. Individually or in small groups, decide on a person from history you would like to interview. Decide what background information is needed in order to prepare effectively for the interview. Conduct the necessary research and, on the basis of what is discovered, prepare a moderately scheduled interview guide for your historical figure.

3. As a class, select an ethical issue affecting journalists that is of interest to you. Develop some hypothetical examples of situations in which this issue might be important. Engage in a formal discussion with pros and cons on appropriate ethical responses to the hypothetical situations.

Related Readings

Ailes, Roger. *You Are the Message: Getting What You Want By Being Who You Are.* New York: Doubleday, 1988.

Biagi, Shirley. *Interviews That Work: A Practical Guide for Journalists,* 2nd ed. Belmont, CA: Wadsworth, 1992.

Brian, Denis. *Murderers and Other Friendly People: The Public and Private Worlds of Interviewers.* New York: McGraw Hill, 1973. This book is no longer in print, but it is available at libraries.

Hay, Vicky. *The Essential Feature: Writing for Magazines and Newspapers.* New York: Columbia University Press, 1990.

Hulteng, John L. *The Messenger's Motives: Ethical Problems of the News Media,* 2nd ed. Englewood Cliffs, NJ: Prentice Hall, 1985.

Killenberg, George M. and Anderson, Rob. *Before the Story: Communication Skills for Journalists.* New York: St. Martin's Press, 1989.

Klaidman, Stephen and Beauchamp, Tom L. *The Virtuous Journalist.* New York: Oxford University Press, 1987.

MacDougall, Curtis D. and Reid, Robert D. *Interpretive Reporting,* 9th ed. New York: Macmillan Publishing Company, 1987.

Metzler, Ken. *Creative Interviewing: The Writer's Guide to Gathering Information by Asking Questions,* 2nd ed. Englewood Cliffs, NJ: Prentice Hall, 1989, 117.

Endnotes

1. Shirley Biagi, *Interviews That Work* (Belmont, CA: Wadsworth Publishing Company, 1992), 3–6.

2. Curtis D. MacDougall and Robert D. Reid, *Interpretive Reporting,* 9th ed. (New York: Macmillan Publishing Company, 1987), 34.

3. For extensive information concerning research methods for interviewers, see Biagi (1992), 21–39.

4. Doug Newsom and James A. Wollert, *Media Writing: Preparing Information for the Mass Media,* 2nd ed. Belmont, CA: Wadsworth Publishing Company, 1988), 198–99. These authors suggest selecting interviewees on the basis of their accessibility, willingness, veracity, and quotability.

5. MacDougall and Reid (1987), 28.

6. George Killenberg and Rob Anderson, *Before the Story: Interviewing and Communication Skills for Journalists* (New York: St. Martin's Press, 1989), 17–22.

7. Vicki Hay, *The Essential Feature: Writing for Magazines and Newspapers* (New York: Columbia University Press, 1990), 50.

8. Biagi (1992), 59–64.

9. Hay (1990), 52.

10. Michael Arlen, *Living Room War* (New York: Random House, 1977); 69–70.

11. Joan Baez, *Daybreak* (New York: Avon, 1969), 158–59.

12. As reported in *The Journal Gazette,* Fort Wayne, Indiana, July 24, 1992, p. 2A.

13. Killenberg and Anderson (1989), 67–8.

14. Gemma Corradi Fiumara, *The Other Side of Language: A Philosophy of Listening,* translated by Charles Lambert (London: Routledge, 1990), 35.

15. Mark Fitzgerald, "Don't (Mis)quote Me on That!" *Editor and Publisher,* May 9, 1987, 114.

16. Hay (1990), 59.

17. Newsom and Wollert (1988), 201.

18. MacDougall and Reid (1987), 27.

19. MacDougall and Reid (1987), 30.

20. Killenberg and Anderson (1989), 149–53.

21. Donald W. Klopf, "Japanese Communication Practices: Recent Comparative Research," *Communication Quarterly 39,* (Spring 1991), 130–143.

22. George A. Borden, *Cultural Orientation: An Approach to Understanding Intercultural Communication* (Englewood Cliffs, NJ: Prentice Hall, 1991), xvi.

23. Dr. Hunter S. Thompson, *Songs of the Doomed* (New York: Pocket Books, 1990).

24. Stephen Klaidman and Tom L. Beauchamp. *The Virtuous Journalist* (New York: Oxford University Press, 1987), 4.

25. Klaidman and Beauchamp (1987), 3–56.

26. Frank McCulloch, ed. *Drawing the Line: How 31 Editors Solved Their Toughest Ethical Dilemmas* (Washington D.C.: American Society of Newspaper Editors Foundation, 1984). Quoted in Biagi (1992), 186.

27. Andy Rooney, *Pieces of My Mind* (New York: Atheneum Press, 1984), 59–60.

28. Klaidman and Beauchamp (1987), 173–77.

29. Killenberg and Anderson (1989), 198–99.

30. Ken Metzler, *Creative Interviewing: The Writer's Guide to Gathering Information by Asking Questions,* 2nd ed. (Englewood Cliffs, NJ: Prentice Hall, 1989), 117.

31. Metzler (1989), 191–92.

32. MacDougall and Reid (1987), 31.

33. William L. Rivers, *Free-Lancer and Staff Writer: Writing Magazine Articles* (Belmont, CA: Wadsworth, 1972) 177.

34. MacDougall and Reid (1987), 55.

35. Biagi 1992), 173.

36. Roger Ailes, *You are the Message: Getting What You Want By Being Who You Are* (New York: Doubleday, 1988), 201.

37. Ailes (1988), 186–87.

Information Gathering for Research

"The stumbling way in which even the ablest of scientists in every generation have had to fight through thickets of erroneous observations, misleading generalizations, inadequate formulations, and unconscious prejudices is rarely appreciated by those who obtain their scientific knowledge from textbooks."
—James Bryant Conant, Science and Common Sense, 1951, as quoted in John Bartlett's Familiar Quotations, 14th ed. (Boston: Little, Brown & Company, 1968), 1026b.

Elizabeth Young is a graduate student in social work, specializing in geriatric care. For her advanced degree in social work, Elizabeth is conducting research into the quality of care provided to residents of government-funded nursing homes. As part of her research, she is interviewing residents receiving various levels of care at three county homes in northern Arizona. The following is an excerpt from a transcript of a recorded interview with Irving Cassidy, an 82-year-old resident receiving moderate medical care.

Irving: This place is a morgue, you know.

Elizabeth: What do you mean, Irving?

Irving: I'm mean we're all sitting here waiting to die, and the people who work here act like we're dead already. They treat us like we're furniture.

Elizabeth: Can you give me an example of how they do that?

Irving: They talk about us like we're deaf and dumb! I'll be sitting in my room looking right at them and two of them will be standing at my door, and one will say, "Did Irving eat his breakfast this morning?" or "Has Irving gotten any exercise today?" And the other one will answer! I'm sitting there, not three feet away, looking them in the face. Why the hell don't they ask ME if I've eaten? Do they think I can't hear? Do they think I can't talk?

Elizabeth: I see what you mean. Is that kind of thing common? Do most of the staff talk about you instead of to you like that?

Irving: Yep. They sure as hell do. There's one little girl who cleans my room who's nice, though. I guess nobody's told her we're dead.

Elizabeth: Do you feel there's enough for you to do here? Are enough activities provided?

Irving: Ha! Activities! They think TV is an activity! Staring at a boob tube! Hell, they think bingo is a night on the town! Bingo! Now there's a game for the dead. And the things they pass off for prizes. Hell, I got enough lap quilts to carpet a barn, and I don't even use the damn things. Why can't they get a little band to play for us once in awhile on a weekend night? A little jazz band. Or how about poker? I used to play poker every Friday night. And how about a decent meal once in awhile—with candles on the table, and tablecloths, and a nice glass of wine? Bingo and TV, bingo and TV. Don't they think we had lives? Don't they think we have minds?

Elizabeth: What do you miss most from your life before moving here, Irving?

Irving: My car—my old automobubble, I called it. I still miss my car. And my dog. I had a great old mutt—Shepherd, I called him—Shep. I wish I had a dog. I wish we had dogs here. God, I'd love a dog.

Elizabeth: Irving, if you had the power to make one change in the quality of care here—just one—what would it be?

Irving: I'd put a sign on every door and around the necks of everyone here, every damned resident, even the poor old saps with Altzheimer's, and the ones dying in their beds. I'd put a sign on them. And you know what that sign would say?

Elizabeth: What would it say, Irving?

Irving: It would say, "Talk to me—I'm alive."

Chapter Goals

- To understand the nature and uses of research interviewing.
- To explore the goals and methods of qualitative interview research.
- To examine quantitative interview research, its goals and methods, preparation, and administration.
- To understand the nature of bias in qualitative and quantitative interview research.

Introduction

How do human beings learn about human life beyond what we learn by living our own lives? How do we discover how people live, the choices they make, and what they feel, believe, or desire? How do social scientists learn, market analysts probe, and pollsters predict? The answer in each case is that we learn by asking one another—in a variety of ways, through a variety of methods—and by collating and synthesizing what we are told in a form that makes sense. In other words, we use research interviewing.

Research interviewing is interviewing for the purpose of gathering information to test hypotheses or discover meanings. Research interviewing seeks to learn about human beings by asking them about themselves. Research interviewing is the primary tool whereby sociological and demographic information is collected, synthesized, interpreted, and shared.

Social science researchers use interviews to understand human needs, wants, beliefs, values, opinions, and concerns. The opening interview is an example of social science interview research. Research interviewing is also used by market analysts to learn how to sell products to particular audiences, as well as to discover whether past or current marketing strategies have been effective. Market researchers frequently send interviewers to places where people shop to conduct survey interviews. Pollsters such as Gallup, Harris, and major news agencies often use telephone interviews to ask citizens how they feel about candidates and political issues for the purpose of informed news reporting or for predicting election results. The research interview is a staple of modern life.

In general, research interviewing is divided into two types. **Qualitative research** or **depth interviews** seek to probe deeply into individual experiences by interviewing a few persons at great depth, to learn about the others' experiences in their own words, and to arrive at descriptive rather than numerical results. The word qualitative comes from the same root word as *quality* and refers to the goal of understanding the elements or qualities of the persons interviewed. The opening interview is an example of qualitative interview research.

Quantitative or **survey interviewing** seeks to reach representative samples of particular human populations to gather information that is quantifiable and can be subjected to statistical analysis. The word *quantitative,* from the same root word as *quantity,* refers to the use of large numbers of respondents to obtain information quantified and mathematically analyzed.

Occasionally, survey researchers engage in in-depth interviews with a few people from their targeted population in order to formulate and test questions for quantitative research, but each method of research interviewing can (and usually does) stand alone. As we shall see, there are advantages and disadvantages to both approaches. The fundamental goal of both qualitative and quantitative interview research is to obtain consistent and accurate information that can be generalized to other people in similar groups or situations. The nature of the information obtained from the two methods, however, is quite different and is used in different ways.

Two issues of concern to all researchers are the reliability and validity of the information their research yields. **Reliability** refers to consistency in procedures and techniques in one's research. Reliability is the likelihood that a particular interview question is asked of all interviewees in such a way that their responses can legitimately be compared to one another.[1] In order to be sure the answers obtained from interviewees are comparable, each interviewee needs the same basic understanding of the questions. For example, consider the question, "Are you pro-choice or pro-life?" If two interviewers with opposite views on this issue were asking this question of multiple interviewees, it is likely that their own perspectives would influence the way the question was asked (i.e., their inflection and tone of voice), thereby affecting the responses they obtained. The issue of reliability is an important one for interviewers because it has to do with the consistency with which interviewers present themselves and their questions to the interviewees.

In order to be sure that observed differences in responses reflect real differences between persons in populations, researchers seek consistency in interviewing procedures and techniques. For example, an interviewer who wants comparable responses from nursing home residents about their care will try to schedule and conduct all interviews so they are similar in length and setting and have comparable degrees of privacy. If some residents were interviewed in the nursing home's common area or lounge and others were interviewed in the privacy of their own rooms, their responses would not be comparable because we could not be sure that respondents interviewed with others present weren't influenced to respond differently than the residents who were interviewed privately. Any inconsistency in procedures or techniques can have an impact upon the reliability of the research findings.

Validity refers to the accuracy of a research procedure, technique, or question. Another way of phrasing the question of validity is to ask, "Does this question or procedure actually measure what I am seeking to measure?" For example, if a researcher wants to know what kind of care is provided to nursing home residents but asks only administrators of the homes, the information received will not be a valid measure of the quality of care. Likewise, if the interviewer interviewed only persons who had left nursing homes for other kinds of care, the validity of the findings would be lessened because the researcher only talked to people who had been dissatisfied with their care.

Question validity is the extent to which a specific question actually elicits the information sought. Interviewers must be sure that answers obtained accurately measure what the interviewer intended to measure. For example, a researcher interviewing respondents at a busy shopping mall asks each of fifty respondents, "Do you routinely engage in any bizarre sexual practices?" and all fifty of the respondents answer "No." Are these answers apt to be valid? No. Individuals are not likely to discuss their sexual preferences freely with strangers under most circumstances, especially sexual practices labelled "bizarre" at the outset. Furthermore, the setting in which this question was asked precluded the possibility of obtaining accurate information. Social pressure and setting combine to make it highly unlikely that the interviewer will receive valid answers to this question.

Or again, suppose an interviewer wants to know how many Americans believe that a controversial gun law should be enacted. The interviewer asks, "Are you in favor of gun control?" and, based on the findings, concludes that most Americans are in favor of the passage of the law in question. Has the interviewer obtained valid information? No. In order to obtain valid findings, the interviewer would need to describe the particular law in question clearly and accurately and then ask respondents if they were in favor of passing the law. Questions of validity and reliability are used at every stage of interview research to determine whether the researcher will, in fact, learn what he or she seeks to know.

In this chapter, we will examine both qualitative and quantitative interview research from the point of view of the interviewer. We will explore the goals and methods, the advantages and disadvantages of both forms of interviewing, and the questions of bias in both methods of research.

Qualitative Interview Research

Goals of Qualitative Research

In the opening interview, the social science researcher sought to learn about the quality of care given to residents of government-funded nursing homes in northern Arizona. To do it, she conducted qualitative interviews with a group of individuals receiving nursing home care. The purpose of her investigation was to learn about how residents of county nursing homes experience their care, as described in their own words. **Qualitative research interviews** explore the experiences and meanings of people in their own words and in-depth for the purpose of descriptive understanding.

Another word for qualitative research interviewing is ethnographic interviewing.[2] **Ethnology** is the descriptive study of contemporary cultural groupings. **Ethnography** is the collection of information about cultural groupings through interviews and/or observational research. In a sense, ethnographers paint verbal portraits of groups and individuals. Ethnographers are explorers and mappers of culture.

In general, ethnographers study how individuals communicate about themselves in their own words within the context in which they live. Frey, Botan, Friedman, and Kreps describe the difference between survey and ethnographic interviewing in this way: "Survey researchers usually dominate and control their interviews, channeling responses from subjects down desired tracks. In contrast, ethnographic interviewers want to empower respondents to speak freely, so they treat them more equally, often referring to them as *collaborators* or *consultants*."[3] A survey researcher seeking quantifiable results might ask, "How would you rate the overall quality of care you receive at this facility—very good, good, adequate, poor, or very poor?" This question channels the interviewees' responses into five clear, measurable categories. A qualitative or ethnographic researcher, on the other hand, might say, "Please tell me in your own words how you feel about the care you receive here at this facility." This statement allows interviewees to make autonomous decisions about the length, wording, and content of their responses. This basic and general difference between the two modes of research involves the use of interviewees as either "opinion givers," who respond to prepared information (survey research), or as the creators of personal narratives as information (ethnographic research). A **narrative** is a story told in the language and from the unique point of view of the teller of the tale.

Often ethnographers interview others to gather information for the purpose of generating hypotheses or theories. Sometimes they simply gather narrative descriptions from the persons in question. Qualitative researchers do not necessarily use the interview to test predetermined hypotheses. Our nursing home researcher's goal was to learn how nursing home residents perceived their quality of care. The interviewer may or may not have begun the research with an hypothesis concerning what respondents were likely to say.

An **hypothesis** is a proposition or idea to be tested. It is the prediction with which the researcher enters into the research. The nursing home researcher might have begun with the hypothesis that many nursing home residents are unhappy with the quality of care they receive. Her results would provide data to support or contradict her hypothesis.

Elliot Mishler uses the term *narrative analysis* to describe the qualitative interviewer's goal.[4] Mishler says: "In contrast to survey research, a well-worn tradition with widely agreed upon rules and procedures, in narrative analysis we find much diversity; different investigations bear a general family resemblance to one another but differ in theoretical orientation, in types of research questions formulated, and in method."[5] The domain of the qualitative interviewer, in other words, is more flexible in form than the survey researcher.

In general, the goals of the qualitative interview researcher are (1) to obtain unique narrative descriptions of their experiences (2) from a relatively small number of persons (3) through the use of lengthy interviews (4) that invite the respondents to speak in their own words. Next we will explore the methods through which the qualitative interviewer goes about meeting these goals.

Preparing for Qualitative Interview Research

The qualitative research interviewer begins with two basic questions: "What information do I need to obtain from this interview?" and "Whom do I need to interview in order to obtain that information?" The answer to the first question clarifies the specific informational goal of the interview research. The answer to the second question determines the **sample;** that is, the representative group of persons who will be interviewed. These two questions are closely related.

Let's look at an example of the impact of these two basic questions on the structure of the research. For her book, *Women in the Sanctuary Movement*, sociologist and anthropologist Robin Lorentzen sought to answer the question: "What is the role of women in the sanctuary movement?"[6] The sanctuary movement is a network of persons working to provide safe passage of political refugees who are not legal immigrants into new lives in the United States. To meet her goal, Lorentzen chose to interview at length "twenty-nine women who participated in the Chicago sanctuary movement between 1982 and 1987. . . . Using a snowball sample [asking each interviewee for the names of other persons to interview], I was recommended among acquaintances within a citywide network. . . ."[7] Lorentzen described the need to present herself as a trustworthy ally of the movement and its supporters in order to avoid being perceived as "a government agent."[8]

Lorentzen's question led her to interview women who worked within the sanctuary movement in ways that alleviated their anxieties about whether she was a government agent. Her approach allowed her respondents to describe in detail their involvement with this movement in interviews that lasted several hours each.[9] If her research question had been "What is the sanctuary movement?" Lorentzen might have interviewed a variety of persons with widely different points of view such as legal authorities, government agents, political refugees, and participants in the movement. The nature of the information she

The qualitative research interviewer must discover not only who has the needed information, but also aim for a representative population sample.

received would likely have differed substantially in its portraits of the sanctuary movement and its members. Lorentzen's research question led her to both her respondents and her methodology.

The qualitative research interviewer, like the journalistic interviewer, needs to discover who has the needed information and is willing and able to share it. "Rather than trying to interview a random sample of individuals from the group being studied, most ethnographers seek out a nonrandom *purposive* sample. . . . Sometimes they put out a call for interview volunteers; sometimes they go into the field and solicit the kinds of persons with whom they wish to talk; and sometimes they start out by interviewing people they already know and get from them referrals to others with similar experiences or characteristics."[10]

The qualitative research interviewer should aim for a representative interview sample so that generalizations about the group as a whole are possible. Jo Young Switzer conducted qualitative interview research with women in positions of power in the federal government.[11] In order to obtain a representative sample, she sought interviews with all women members of Congress, the Cabinet, and the Supreme Court. She spoke with women from a variety of geographical backgrounds, political parties, and liberal to conservative persuasions, seeking a sample that represented the full spectrum of women in national government.

With all interview research, the more nearly the sample of persons interviewed fairly represents the whole population from which they are drawn, the more accurate generalizations based on their responses will be. If our nursing home interviewer had interviewed only residents at one county nursing home, her findings would have been biased by the unique conditions at that particular residence. By interviewing a sampling of residents from several different homes, she is more likely to obtain information accurately descriptive of county homes in general.

Once the interviewer has clarified the research question and determined the nature of the interview sample, he or she is ready to prepare for the individual interviews themselves.

Conducting the Qualitative Research Interview

The Interview Guide.   The qualitative research interviewer often develops a moderately scheduled interview guide containing a tentative list of questions and possible probes. Most ethnographic research interviews are designed for maximum flexibility because they must allow the interviewee's responses to develop freely and to have an impact on the subsequent flow of information. The interviewer generally begins with a plan of inquiry—certain kinds of questions or topic areas—but does not have a set of standardized questions in rigid order.[12]

Because of the in-depth nature of qualitative interviewing, the interviewer needs to plan interviews that allow respondents the time and freedom to talk in detail about the subject. The interview guide will, therefore, outline in a general way a variety of questions or topics that probe the subject area. The interview guide of our nursing home researcher, for example, might have listed topic areas such as a typical day for residents, treatment by staff, problems with care, activities, and meals. The interviewer must be prepared to probe most deeply into topic areas that seem important to the individual interviewees.

Questions. The qualitative research interviewer relies primarily on open-ended questions that give the interviewee maximum freedom of response. Such questions also minimize interviewer bias. Open-ended questions allow interviewees to tell their stories in their own words, sometimes with brevity, sometimes in lengthy narratives. Open-ended questions invite descriptive responses. Lorentzen's standard questions in her sanctuary movement research included: "How did you first hear about sanctuary? How did you get involved? . . . How did you decide what to do? What was your experience? Are you still active?"[13] For the book, *Women's Ways of Knowing: The Development of Self, Voice, and Mind,* the researchers asked these and other open-ended questions: "Tell me something about what your life is like right now." "How would you describe yourself to yourself?" and "What does being a woman mean to you?"[14] Each of these open questions allowed interviewees "free rein" in regard to what and how much they would share.

If the open-ended question is not leading or biased, the interviewee has autonomy in the construction and content of the answers and in the language. In response to the question, "How would you describe a normal day?" one interviewee might answer, "Boring, uneventful" and another might launch into a detailed description of the day from the moment he awakens until he goes to bed. The interviewer not only needs to use probing questions to learn more details of the first respondent's experience, but also needs only to listen and respond empathetically to the second narrative. The success of the qualitative interview depends in large part on the skillful use of open questions and probes.

Likewise, the interviewer needs to listen carefully to the responses given in order to discover topic areas of importance to the respondent that may not have been a part of the interviewer's original plan or guide. For example, in the interviews with women in government mentioned earlier, Jo Young Switzer did not originally include questions about vocal pitch in her interview guide, but references to the importance of pitch by her first respondent led her to add this topic to later interviews.[15] The issue was significant to the interviewees.

Scheduling. The qualitative research interviewer usually conducts interviews of an hour or more in length. The exact length of the interview is determined in large part by the interviewee. In order to allow the interviewees the freedom to speak in their own words, the interviewer must take care to schedule a generous amount of time for the interviews.

Also, the interviewer should arrange in advance for a meeting place that is not tightly scheduled, so no pressure exists to end the interview too soon. The setting should be as free as possible from interruptions and distractions. However, because many qualitative researchers conduct interviews in the interviewee's home or workplace, they may not have control over distractions in the environment. Frey and colleagues write: "Interviews on-site are usually preferable, since the ethnographer can observe the context, and people are more likely to express themselves naturally on their `home turf.'"[16] However, as Lorentzen discovered in her sanctuary research, interviews in the homes of some of her respondents "averaged three to five hours, interrupted frequently by children, pets, visitors, phone calls, and meal preparations."[17]

Meeting in the interviewee's domain requires obvious flexibility and some surrender of control on the part of the interviewer. The interviewer needs to take the setting as it is and adapt to its limitations and demands as best as possible. When making arrangements for the interview, however, the interviewer can request certain conditions—a quiet place, privacy, a comfortable conversational area—and then be prepared to work within whatever constraints are found.

Depending on the subject, the "home turf" of interviewees could be their homes, their offices, or (as in the case of the homeless), some public setting. Most of Lorentzen's interviews with sanctuary workers took place in their homes, but a handful took place in restaurants and those with women in religious life most often took place in their offices. Lorentzen observed that the home interviews tended to be much longer and more wide ranging in topics covered than the office interviews with women in religious life.[18]

Ideally, the setting for the interview should be one that allows the interviewee to feel most comfortable and speak most freely. Whatever the setting, the interviewer needs to be alert to distractions and work to preserve confidentiality.

Recording. Because a primary goal of qualitative interview research is to allow interviewees to describe their experience in their own words, a method of recording the interviews that preserves personal narratives in their entirety is preferred. Audio taping is the least distracting method of preserving interviewee responses. It allows close textual analysis after the interview is completed, as well as the use of verbatim quotations in reporting the research which capture the unique voice of the interviewee.

As videotaping equipment becomes more commonplace, videotaping may replace audio taping as the standard recording tool of qualitative interviewing. It has the obvious advantage of capturing nonverbal as well as verbal content, but it is generally more intrusive. Also, unless a third party is present, the videocamera must be fixed at one angle of view that would limit the freedom of movement of the interview parties. A camera operator's presence would affect the interpersonal exchange.

There is a clear need for complete records of qualitative research interviews in order to use them for research. Mishler describes three approaches to analysis of narrative or depth interviews: (1) textual analysis, which examines narratives for their internal consistencies in language and structure; (2) ideational analysis, which explores content and meanings; and (3) interpersonal analysis, which seeks evidence of the relationship between the interview parties.[19] Each of these methods of analysis require close examination of the text of the interview. Cumbersome as it may be for the interviewer to carry equipment, assure it works, monitor it carefully, tape everything, and transcribe it afterward, there is no other way to obtain a record that does justice to the rich material obtained through qualitative research interviews.

Disadvantages and Advantages of Qualitative Interviewing

Qualitative research interviewing is not a standardized, easily categorized, nor easily manageable process. It is time consuming. Each interview takes several hours to conduct, especially since the interviewer often meets the interviewee where he or she is most at home. Recording complete interviews is cumbersome. Transcribing them is tedious. Much about the interview process is unpredictable. Interviewer flexibility is essential. The interviewees, because they are allowed to tell their stories in their own ways, exert pervasive influence and control on the process. And, in the end, when the interviews are complete, the interviewer is left with volumes of information through which to sift, seeking continuities, themes, and revelations that can be compared, synthesized, and shared in ways that enrich the understanding of others.

Why do it then? What is gained? In the first place, the interviewer benefits from the opportunity to delve deeply into the experiences and meanings of individuals and to engage in an exchange not governed by fixed assumptions or expectations. Approaching interviewees with open questions, the qualitative researcher can expect the unexpected in the form of new discoveries.

Ideally, if the relationship between interviewer and interviewee is synergistic (i.e., if both parties work together to their mutual advantage)[20], the interview will yield the opportunity to truly see an issue or experience from the point of view of another. A medical resident interviewing hospital patients might discover ways that hospital procedures rob individuals of their dignity. A social worker might discover simple changes in interactions and activities that could greatly enhance the lives of nursing home residents. Changed understanding changes individuals. At its best, qualitative research interviews offer the opportunity for such change. At the very least, qualitative research interviews offer interviewers the opportunity to engage in in-depth encounters with others and to explore with them subjects of mutual interest and concern.

Quantitative Interview Research

Goals of Quantitative Research Interviews

If qualitative research interviews are characterized by depth, then the word to characterize quantitative research interviews is breadth. The quantitative research interviewer seeks a broad base of information against which hypotheses can be tested and from which predictions, theories, or recommended actions can be drawn. Quantitative or survey interviews seek to reach representative samples of people and to gather information from them that can be statistically analyzed.

Whereas qualitative research interviews focus on the unique stories and experiences of individuals, quantitative research interviews seek ways to combine the responses of individuals for meaningful generalizations. Where qualitative research interviews seek narrative descriptions, quantitative research interviews seek information that can be summarized in terms of proportions, percentages, and categories of response.

Survey interviews, as they are also called, allow information from large numbers of respondents to be compared. For example, survey interviews of U.S. television audiences can estimate what percentage of the population watches certain shows or buys advertised products. Because survey interviews usually collect demographic information as well as attitudinal and behavioral responses, information can be further analyzed by categorizing it according to the sex, age, income levels, and so forth, of the respondents.

Survey interviews allow a broad range of data to be combined into comparative studies of populations. Certain research centers, such as the University of Michigan's Survey Research Center Institute for Social Research, for example, conduct research on the entire U.S. population for the use of researchers everywhere.[21] If the qualitative research interviewer is a portrait artist, the quantitative or survey interviewer is a landscape or vista artist, who seeks to portray whole populations on the basis of data collected from their samples.

An important difference between qualitative and quantitative interview research, which we will discuss in detail in another section, has to do with who conducts the actual interviews. It should be noted, however, that much survey research does not employ interviewers at all, but instead relies, like the U.S. Census Bureau, on the distribution of written questionnaires. Survey interviews use many of the same methods and strategies of questionnaire research, but employ persons to obtain the necessary information through face-to-face or telephone contact.

Decisions about whether to use telephone or face-to-face interview methods depend on cost factors (e.g., telephone is cheaper than travel), refusal rates (e.g., the percentage of persons who refuse to be interviewed), and other factors such as convenience, confidentiality, and the nature of the information being sought (e.g., information about certain sensitive subjects such as sexual practices may be more easily obtained through telephone contact than face-to-face).[22]

For most survey research purposes, no distinguishable difference in the populations tapped have been found when comparing telephone, face-to-face, and questionnaire survey results.[23] However, Fowler suggests some comparative advantages of face-to-face versus telephone interviewing.[24] For example, personal interviewing is more effective for obtaining interviewee cooperation and allows for collecting visual cues as well as verbal content information. Telephone interviewing is less costly, allows for the possibility of random-digit dialing (an effective random sampling method) for sampling purposes, is less time consuming, and it is generally easier to staff and manage because fewer people are needed.

The goals of the survey interviewer are (1) to obtain accurate information (2) from a representative sample of a population (3) through the use of standardized questions (4) that can be categorized and easily compared. Information obtained through quantitative research interviews is numerically tabulated and statistically analyzed for the purpose of testing hypotheses. Furthermore, survey research interviewers attempt to reduce the influence of factors other than the needs, values, and perceptions of the individual being interviewed through tightly controlled administration of the interviews.

Preparing for Quantitative Interview Research

Like the qualitative research interviewer, the survey interviewer begins with questions: "What do I want to know?" and "Whom must I interview in order to discover it?" The answer to the first question will determine the specific questions the interviewer will ask. The answer to the second question will determine the sample of the population under study. Together, these two questions outline the parameters of the interviewer's research.

In general, survey interviews require much more preparation than other kinds of interviews because of the number of different interviewers, the large numbers of interviewees, the standardization of questions, the training required, and the need for the data to be suitable for statistical analysis. Statistical analysis involves mathematical manipulations of data to predict or measure the degree to which a finding is statistically significant. In other words, statistical analysis determines whether information is more than a chance occurrence. Statistical analysis helps describe real differences between categories of people, responses, or events.

For example, recent research on organizational commitment involved statistical analysis of responses to questionnaires by 253 employees of various organizations. Statistical analysis of employee responses found significant correlations (relationships) between perceptions of freedom of speech in the workplace and the degree of organizational commitment of the employees.[25] Tests for statistical significance of findings employ mathematical procedures to determine that the differences or relationships discovered cannot be explained by chance, or random occurence.

The desire for statistical support both guides and restricts quantitative research interview preparation. The desire for statistically significant findings creates the need for random sampling and for standardization in interview questions and procedures. To conduct research that conforms to the standards of social science research, quantitative researchers follow certain set guidelines in the preparation of their questions and procedures.

Before conducting the interviews, the quantitative interview researcher develops and pretests survey questions, selects a representative sample of the population of interest, and trains the interviewers. We will look at each of these processes in turn.

Question Preparation and Response Bias. Unlike qualitative interview research, quantitative interviewing most often relies on closed format questions that can be answered in readily quantifiable form. A survey interviewer relies primarily on brief, closed questions that offer limited response choices and can be easily recorded and coded.

For example, a survey interviewer might say: "I'm going to read a list of top-ics having to do with current events. In response to each item on the list, please tell me if you consider yourself *very concerned* about this issue, *somewhat concerned, mildly concerned, not at all concerned*, or else say *I don't know* if you're not sure how you feel about a topic at this time. Okay, here's the first topic: urban violence. Would you say you are very concerned, somewhat concerned, mildly concerned, not at all concerned, or don't know. . . ?" The interviewer would continue through the list, each time seeking specific answers from the prescribed list of choices. Each answer option can be assigned a number, and the interviewer can easily record a respondent's answers as shown in Figure 7.1. In general, the survey inter-viewer's questions are designed not to elicit conversation but to gather specific answers as efficiently as possible.

For the survey researcher, good questions have the following set of character-istics. First, both the question and the answer options must be clearly under-standable. The language should be simple and the structure clear. For example, rather than asking, "Do you favor passage of House Bill #276–1?" a skilled researcher would say, "There is a bill in Congress right now which seeks to place new limits on the sale of handguns by imposing a seven-day waiting period before purchase. Are you in favor of such a law?"

	Very (5) Concerned	Somewhat (4) Concerned	Mildly (3) Concerned	Not (2) Concerned	DK (1)
Urban violence	(5)	4	3	2	1
Spread of AIDS	(5)	4	3	2	1
Decline of moral values	(5)	4	3	2	1
Teen promiscuity	(5)	4	3	2	1
Pollution	5	4	3	(2)	1
Drug usage	(5)	4	3	2	1
Abortion	(5)	4	3	2	1
Unemployment	5	4	(3)	2	1
Homelessness	5	4	3	(2)	1
Illegal aliens	5	(4)	3	2	1

FIGURE 7.1   Numerically Coded Responses of Interviewee A–17 to Questions about Social Concerns

Second, questions should be understood in the same way by each interviewee; in other words, the questions must demonstrate reliability. For example, rather than asking, "Do you favor gun control?" a more reliable question would state, "The proposal before Congress would impose a seven-day waiting period on sales of all handguns. Would you favor this proposal?" Likewise, the answer choices must be reliable (i.e., consistently understood to have the same general meaning).

In order to be reliable, questions and answers must be worded in such a way that all key terms are defined and the language used is appropriate for the people being interviewed. For example, while it might be appropriate to ask a sample of highly educated individuals if they "support regulatory control of the cultivation of *cannabis sattiva* for personal consumption," for most audiences this question should be reworded to ask, "Are you in favor of legal restrictions on the planting and harvesting of marijuana for one's own personal use?" For reliability and validity, research interview questions and answers should be worded simply, clearly, and appropriately. If questions are consistently understood (reliability), they are more likely to obtain accurate results (validity).

Nonetheless, not only the wording, but also the content of the questions and the answer options can affect the validity of the data generated because of response bias. **Response bias** refers to inaccurate answers from respondents. Any question that asks for information that is anxiety producing, for example, or about which there is an existing socially desirable response, is likely to obtain a "socially correct" answer that may not reflect the interviewee's real behaviors or attitudes.

For example, a question about drinking habits that asked, "Would you describe yourself as a non drinker, a social drinker, a moderate drinker, or a heavy drinker?" would be likely to obtain the answer of "social drinker" from most respondents, irrespective of their actual drinking habits because that choice is the socially desirable one. Likewise, questions about sexual habits, eating habits, and many other personal behaviors may elicit biased responses.

How does one then obtain accurate information about such things? With regard to the drinking question, for example, a better way to phrase the question would be to ask respondents to estimate the average number of drinks they consume per week. Doing so strips away the socially desirable language expressed in terms like "social drinker." Also, individual respondents are less likely to have a clear sense of the "socially correct" number of drinks that typifies a social drinker. However, with regard to alcohol consumption, alcoholic or problem drinkers are likely to under-report their consumption regardless of question form, so accuracy from such persons is unlikely.[26]

Accuracy of response to questions is also affected by the importance of the subject matter to the respondent. Studies reported by DeLameter found much higher levels of reliability in answers pertaining to **salient issues**; that is, issues of great relevance to the respondent or of high current social interest.[27] Additionally, interviewers can introduce response bias by offering answer options that do not include the actual choice preferences of the respondents. Respondents must not be forced to select an answer option that does not reflect their views accurately.

Answer options that allow for a full range of responses are essential in order to avoid response bias.

Fowler reports, "There are four basic reasons why respondents report events with less than perfect accuracy: (1) They do not know the information; (2) They cannot recall it, although they do know it; (3) They do not understand the question; (4) They do not want to report the answer in the interview context."[28] Fowler suggests that, in the first case, the wrong person is being interviewed. In the second case, researchers need to be aware of the reality of memory loss over time and not to ask for information the respondent is not likely to be able to recall accurately. The third problem can be resolved by explaining the question clearly. The fourth, pertaining to social desirability, can be tempered by carefully wording statements to eliminate judgmental language, by using self-administered questions, and by assuring confidentiality and anonymity. Fowler concludes, " . . . the limit of survey research is what people are willing to tell researchers under the conditions of data collection designed by the researcher."[29] In addition to response bias on the part of interviewees, there are also issues of interviewer bias that are vital to both qualitative and quantitative research that will be discussed in a later section.

Standard Answer Formats for Survey Interviewing.   In order to simplify the answers interviewees provide, to aid in the ease of recording responses, and to assure that answers obtained are reliable and accurate, survey researchers have developed and tested certain standard answer formats that attempt to increase reliability, validity, quantifiability, and ease of recording interviewee responses.

In order to be effective, answer options must be both **mutually exclusive** (i.e., there must be no overlap between options) and **fully inclusive** (i.e., there must be an acceptable answer option for every respondent).[30] For example, a researcher asks, "How would you describe your political affiliation?" and offers the following mutually exclusive answer options: Republican, Democrat, Independent, Other. If these four choices offer an acceptable response option for every interviewee, then they are fully inclusive as well.

Let's look briefly at some of the standard answer formats, known as **scales of measurement,** that are common in survey research:

1. **Nominal scales** seek to classify responses on the basis of assigned names; *nominal* means *as named*. So, for example, the classification scheme of Republican, Democrat, Independent, and Other is a nominal scale. Nominal scales place respondents or responses into discrete and equivalent categories for counting purposes. These scales do not employ a continuum or comparison of any kind. Nominal scales allow for descriptions of the sample: "In the sample interviewed, 53 of the respondents were male and 47 were female; 73 of the respondents described themselves as Democrats, 18 as Republicans, and 9 as Independent or Other." There are, in nominal scales, no comparisons of the discrete categories. Respondents are simply classified into a series of defining categories.

2. **Ordinal scales** ask respondents to rank information along a single dimension that compares the categories in some way; *ordinal* means *placing in order*. For

example, an interviewer might ask respondents to rank the following list of topics from most important (1) to least important (6) in their own lives: family, religious faith, career, security, health, and happiness. Ordinal scales do not imply that the distances between items on the scale are equal. For one respondent the topics of family, faith, and health might be very important while the other three categories are of minimal importance. For another, career and security might be highly and nearly equally important, while family and faith are of no importance. An ordinal scale does not specify and will not register relative distances along a scale.

One specific example of an ordinal response scale is the Bogardus Social Distance Scale, which measures changes in attitudes on issues depending on the relative closeness or distance of the issue from the respondents' own lives.[31] For example, a researcher might ask members of a university grounds crew: "The university is considering hiring mentally handicapped persons to work on its ground crews doing lawn care this summer. (a) Are you in favor of allowing mentally handicapped people to work at regular jobs if they can do the work? (b) Are you in favor of allowing mentally handicapped people to work at regular jobs in businesses you frequent if they can do the work? (c) Are you in favor of allowing mentally handicapped people to work at the university this summer if they can do the work? (d) Are you in favor of allowing mentally handicapped people to work on your grounds crew at the university this summer if they can do the work? (e) Are you willing to work closely with and supervise mentally handicapped people on your mowing crew this summer if they can do the work?"

Bogardus Social Distance Scales measure individual changes in attitudes about issues depending on whether or not they affect one's own life. Such scales seek to measure the difference between ideas in the abstract ("Do you believe that landfills for the disposal of toxic waste are a necessity?") and ideas as immediate reality ("Would you be willing to live within one mile of a toxic waste landfill?").

Some ordinal scales ask respondents to provide a judgment about an issue, object, or action on a scale that registers agreement or disagreement along a continuum. For example, the commonly used Likert scale uses a five-point continuum of agreement/disagreement with a mid-point (3) that registers a neutral response: (1) Strongly agree, (2) Agree, (3) Neither agree nor disagree, (4) Disagree, and (5) Strongly disagree. Likert scales are often used in standardized course evaluations, for example, in which the scale is explained (1 = strongly disagree, 2 = disagree, 3 = neither agree nor disagree, 4 = agree, 5 = strongly agree) and students respond by circling one of the answer options on the scale for each item:

My instructor was prepared for class. 1 2 3 4   5

My instructor challenged me to work. 1 2 3 4 5

My instructor gave clear instructions. 1 2 3 4 5

3. **Interval scales** are ordinal scales with a difference; the difference is that interval scales rank order items using categories or units of measure that are equal

and equidistant. Interval scales can be **numerical** that measure numbered differences as in the scale below: What is the combined annual income of the wage earners in your household? (1) $0–$15,000, (2) $15,001–$30,000, (3) $30,001–$45,000, (4) $45,000–$60,000, (5) $60,001–$75,000, (6) $75,001–$90,000, (7) Over $90,000. Each of these numerical intervals (except for the last, which is more broadly inclusive) are both equal and equidistant from one another.

Frequency intervals measure a number of occurrences per unit of time. For example, a dental care survey might ask respondents, "How often do you floss your teeth?" and offer an interval scale such as this one: (1) Don't floss, (2) 1–2 times per week, (3) 3–4 times per week, (4) 5–6 times per week, (5) more than 6 times per week. The respondents register the frequency of their actions on this interval continuum.

Research interview questions can be designed in a variety of closed and easily quantifiable forms. Several standardized formats exist, including nominal scales, ordinal scales (such as the Bogardus Social Distance Scale and Likert scales), and interval scales (such as numerical and frequency scales). The researcher's choices about question formats are decided on the basis of the research goal.

Preparing an Interview Opening.   The researcher must prepare an interview opening to be employed by all of the interviewers. The opening should be designed to describe the research project and elicit cooperation from the interviewees and should be developed and utilized during the pretest of the survey process.

The opening should include the interviewer's self-introduction and research project affiliation: "Hi, I'm Wanda Bolten from Marketing Research, Incorporated." Likewise, a general statement about the nature and purpose of the interview and the types of topics to be discussed should be included, along with an invitation to participate, obtaining either formal or informal consent as needed: "We're talking with people about their preferences in television viewing. Would you be willing to answer a few short questions about your favorite TV shows?"

Survey Pretesting.   Once a survey researcher has designed the **survey instrument,** the standardized schedule of questions to be used with every respondent, the researcher will pretest the instrument by using it with a limited number of respondents. **Pretesting** involves the administration of the entire survey interview, including the introduction, exactly as it will be administered to the sample, with a small group of respondents who are similar to those in the actual sample. Sometimes pretests are preceded by discussion of the survey instrument in **focus groups** of six to twelve persons, similar to the actual sample group demographically (two to four groups are recommended).[32] According to Fowler and Mangione, focus groups can identify problem concepts or terms, reveal the likely range of responses to a question, and improve the ability of researchers to design survey instruments that minimize interviewer and researcher bias.[33] These authors also suggest "think aloud" pretest interviews, in which interviewees are encouraged to voice all of their responses to the instrument, and a double pretest format in which each interviewee is led through the instrument twice, once to answer the questions and a second time to offer feedback about problems or concerns with the questions.[34]

The actual pretest involves experienced interviewers who conduct complete interviews with ten to twenty persons similar to those in the sample. Ideally, these pretest interviews are recorded so that the entire research team can listen for problems in the reading .or wording of the questions and make note of clarifications sought by respondents or questions that required repeated probing to obtain responses. A pretest provides valuable input concerning the range of answers interviewees are likely to provide.[35]

Pretests should be evaluated for (1) ease of understanding of the questions on the part of respondents, (2) the ease with which interviewers asked the questions, (3) the frequency of clarifications and probes needed, and (4) the degree to which respondents attempted to move beyond or clarify the choice of fixed responses they were offered. DeLameter suggests these additional problem areas to examine when evaluating pretest interviews: skipped, deleted or amended items or

Research samples must represent the population as a whole.

responses, and frequent "Don't know" responses.[36] Again, audio- or videotaped pretest interviews can be watched and analyzed for areas of awkwardness or apparent misunderstanding. On the basis of pretest results, researchers refine question and option choices to eliminate problems.

Determining Sample Populations.   Sampling is a frequently written about area of technical expertise. **Sampling** is a method of determining the views of a large group of people (e.g., a population) by surveying a smaller number, or sample, of the population. Research samples must be **representative** of the population as a whole. That is, the sample must be a demographic microcosm of the population, possessing the same relative proportions of men, women, age groups, income levels, and so forth, as the whole population.

Suppose a researcher wants to predict who will be elected governor of your state in the next election. How could this be done? If time and money were unlimited, the researcher could systematically contact all registered voters in the state and ask them for whom they will vote. For most researchers, however, time and money are not unlimited, and compiling data collected from millions of voters would be impossible.

Furthermore, repeated statistical studies of sample populations have discovered that, beyond a certain sample size for a given population, there are no gains in terms of the predictive accuracy of the information obtained. For example, repeated statistical analysis of samples of the entire U.S. population has determined that random samples of about 2,000 people are adequate for predictive accuracy because the reduction in error for larger sample numbers is minimal.[37]

In order to be able to generalize accurately about the population from which a sample is drawn, an appropriate sampling method must be employed. A sample size large enough for statistical analysis and generalizability to the population must be determined. Appropriate sampling involves careful assessment of these related questions: How will a representative sample for the given population be selected, and how large must the sample be for predictive accuracy?

Some researchers determine their sample size by relying on charts recommending sample sizes for given populations. Sudman offered one such chart (see Fig. 7.2) in his text on sampling. About sample size, Sudman says, "It may be seen that national studies, regardless of subject matter, typically have samples of 1,000 or more. Regional studies vary considerably. . . . sample size depends on how many population subgroups one wishes to study."[39] Sudman also cautions that tables such as he provides "are not intended to replace the formal procedures for sample size determination . . . but to give the inexperienced researcher some way of checking his judgments against those of others in the same field."[40]

Ultimately, the decision about the size of a sample is based on precise mathematical calculations to determine the exact sample size that will allow the researcher to make accurate statistical predictions. The ultimate concern with sample size is that the sample be large enough to yield useful and generalizable information. As shown in Figure 7.2, the more subgroups of the total population about which one seeks accurate information, the larger the sample size must be

Number of Subgroup Analyses	People or Households		Institutions	
	National	Regional/ Special	National	Regional/ Special
None or few	1,000–1,500	200–500	200–500	50–200
Average	1,500–2,000	500–1,000	500–1,000	200–500
Many	2,500+	1,000+	1,000+	500+

FIGURE 7.2   Typical Sample Sizes for Studies of Human and Institutional Populations

Source: Sudman, Seymour, *Applied Sampling* (New York: Academic Press, 1976), 87. Used with permission.

because there must be enough people in each subgroup to allow meaningful statistical analysis. The size of the sample must yield reliable information.

Once the population is determined and the sample size decided, the researcher must select a method for obtaining interviewees. Some standard sampling methods used for survey interview research are described.

In **simple random sampling,** each member of the population has an equal chance of being selected. This method can be employed by placing the names of all members of the population into a hat and drawing the needed number of names, or by assigning each member of the population a number and using a table of random numbers or a random number generator to identify the sample population.

Stratified random sampling allows the demographic characteristics of the population to be represented in the same proportions in the sample as they exist in the population. For example, if the student population of a university were 12 percent African American, 8 percent Hispanic American, 5 percent Asian American and 75 percent Caucasian American, the researcher would obtain a sample of students which had those same proportions. Likewise, the researcher might select representative proportions of freshmen, sophomores, juniors, and seniors in his sample. Within the demographic groups, members are selected randomly.

Skip interval random sampling selects sample members found at certain intervals of the total population. For example, a researcher surveying a city calls every 12th number of all available telephone numbers in the area. At one time, researchers were concerned that telephone surveys excluded the poor, but recent Census Bureau estimates are that 97 percent of all U.S. households have telephones, so this potential bias is no longer considered a concern.[41] (Homeless persons, however, would obviously be excluded from telephone samples.) Likewise, a researcher studying local businesses could seek interviews with owners or managers of every third business listed in the yellow pages of the local directory.

In **sample point random sampling,** several starting places within a geographic location are selected and then interviewers are told to interview a certain number of persons by moving outward in a set pattern from that starting point.

This sampling method is common in door-to-door interviewing. For example, an interviewer might be told to start at the corner of 12ᵗʰ St. and Vine and to move east on Vine seeking an interview at every fourth house on the south side of the street until ten persons have been interviewed.

Random sampling of some kind is necessary in order for sampling to be truly representative, but other sampling methods that are not random are nonetheless used for some research purposes. The **snowball sampling technique,** one such nonrandom method, involves being led to interviewees by persons known to the researcher; snowball sampling, while nonrandom, can nonetheless yield representative samples.

The **convenience sample** involves interviewing whoever is available and willing to take part. Convenience samples can consist of friends and acquaintances or of interviewing whoever walks by a certain location. Convenience samples are not likely to yield generalizable data unless one is conducting research on shopping mall customers through convenience sampling at a shopping mall.

In the final analysis, the important question with regard to sampling for interview research is, "Have enough representatives of this population been interviewed to be able to generalize to the population as a whole?" A mathematically derived sample of appropriate size and proportions will allow accurate generalizations about the population as a whole.

Interviewer Training.   Once the survey researcher has developed and pretested the interview instrument and has located a representative sample of the population, the researcher is ready to train the interviewers who will actually conduct the interviews. In some cases, with small samples, the researcher and the interviewer are one and the same; but for most survey analysis, where large samples are used, multiple interviewers are employed. To ensure reliability, the researcher trains all of the interviewers to administer the survey interviews in comparable ways.

Based on extensive studies of the effect of training and supervision on interviewers, Fowler and Mangione offer these observations about interviewer training: (1) Interviewers need actual interview practice, with supervision, in order to function adequately; training without first-hand practice is not enough. (2) Without first-hand supervised practice, interviewers handle the opening aspects of interviews well but do not do well with the question and answer process which is essential to the research. (3) Interviewers trained with supervised practice to use standardized procedures and reduce bias seem to generate higher quality data. (4) Probing skills in particular are improved by supervised practice training. (5) Video taping of practice interviews is a valuable teaching tool, especially when replayed for group discussion and shared insights. (6) Continued supervision while in the field is also important to interviewer success.[42]

Interviewer training frequently includes an interviewer's manual of instructions such as that provided by the Survey Research Center at the Institute for Social Research in Ann Arbor, Michigan.[43] The interviewer's manual explains the purposes of the study as well as step-by-step procedures for the entire interview process, from opening orientation to closing statements. Interviewers are given specific guidelines to govern their responses to problems that might arise, as well as concrete instruction about how to probe for more information in important areas.

The manual, in short, is a thorough guidebook to the entire interview process, including, as needed, maps to specific locations and lists of telephone numbers to be called. In addition, the manual provides thorough instruction about how to record the responses of interviewees. The purpose of the instructor's manual is not to replace supervised practice in interviewing, but to serve as a "field guide" to aid interviewers with situations as they develop in actual interviews. After training, careful use of the manual, along with ongoing performance evaluation, will help ensure uniformity and skill in the interview process and, ultimately, will result in greater accuracy of information.

Conducting the Quantitative Research Interview

The primary responsibility of the quantitative research interviewer is to conduct the interview from start to finish as it has been designed and tested by the researcher. The need for precision and uniformity is fundamental to the researcher's goal to obtain comparable data. To obtain such data, the effects of different interviewers conducting the interviews must be minimized. The first step in this process involves having every interviewer conduct the opening phase of the interview in such a way that the interviewee's cooperation is obtained. This combined need for impersonal uniformity and friendly rapport-building skill poses a clear challenge to the survey interviewer.

Eliciting Interviewee Participation. Obtaining an agreement to be interviewed is a chronic and growing problem for interview researchers. Goyder reports that, since the end of the 1960s, numerous researchers in the United States and in Europe have documented a decline in **response rate,** or agreement to be interviewed, by as much as 20 percent for face-to-face interview studies.[44] Goyder also contends that the salience or relative interest of the topic to the interviewee is crucial to obtaining agreement and that issues of privacy are central to nonresponse. "Researcher's technique, or a citizen's assessments of the merits of a survey, is often sufficient to outweigh qualms about privacy invasion."[45] Nonetheless, Goyder maintains that nonresponse rates of 20–40 percent are standard, whether conducted face-to-face or via telephone.[46]

The interviewer must begin by successfully eliciting cooperation from the interviewees. To this end, there is evidence that flexibility in addressing the respondent's questions and concerns at the outset of the interview improves response rates.[47] The interviewer must follow the opening format as designed and tested but, where flexibility is allowed, can utilize interpersonal skills to allay concerns at the outset. This can be accomplished through expressions of interest in the interviewee, empathy for the interviewee's concerns and circumstances, and other similar behaviors.

Conducting the Question-Answer Phase.   Once the interviewee's cooperation has been obtained, the interviewer follows the interview guide exactly as it was designed and tested, asking each question as worded, in the order indicated. Typically, for ease of recording and coding, questions will be closed and the interviewer will clearly explain the available answer options. If open questions are included, the interviewer will proceed as trained to record responses and probe for clarifications and details as needed.

The use of probes is essential to obtain accurate and complete information, but, at the same time, probes should be used in fairly standard ways that do not unduly bias the findings. Sometimes researchers will instruct interviewers to choose from a given narrow range of probes when more information is needed. Fowler and Mangione recommend training interviewers to use only three probing questions, each of which is nondirective, easy to remember, and not likely to bias or contaminate the data: (1) How do you mean that? (2) Tell me more about that, and (3) Anything else?[48]

The Survey Research Center at Ann Arbor recommends the use of these and other probes when seeking clarifications or responses: "Would you tell me what you have in mind?" "Why do you feel that way?" "Which would be closer to the way you feel?" Additionally, the Center recommends repeating the question, pausing, and repeating the interviewee's response as ways to elicit clarified or corrected responses.[49] Probes must be neutral and used in standard ways across interviews in order not to bias the data.

Recording the Data.   Techniques for recording data are decided by the researcher who trains the interviewers in their use. Usually, a set of standard abbreviations are employed for recording certain standard responses, such as *DK* for don't know, *RQ* for repeat the question, and so forth. In general, in response to closed questions, the answer options are printed after each question and the interviewer needs only mark the selected response. If questions are open, verbatim hand-recording of the responses is usually required. All interviewers are trained in the same recording methods to reduce the possibility of recording errors and to ease the process of compiling data after the interviews are complete.

Closing the Interview.   Just prior to the close, the interviewer should quickly scan the entire survey to make sure no questions have been missed. In general, the close of a quantitative research interview is very brief; it consists of an opportunity for the interviewee to add something to what has been covered and for the interviewer to thank the respondent for cooperating.

When the interviews are complete, the researcher compiles the data in numerical form, employing a statistical computer program for that purpose, and submits the data to appropriate statistical tests. From these findings, then, generalizations are made and hypotheses are supported or not supported.

In order for the findings to be as accurate as possible, researchers seek to eliminate bias from the instrument, the methods of collection, and the handling of the data. We have discussed some of these sources of error in other sections. However, the interviewer as a source of bias is of special concern in both qualitative and quantitative interviewing and merits focused examination.

Interviewer Bias in Qualitative and Survey Research

Human beings differ in how they respond to one another. No two people will encounter a research interviewer the same. One may find the interviewer warm and charming, while the other will find that same person cold and manipulating. **Bias,** a feeling for or against someone, is inevitable in human encounters. **Interviewer bias,** sometimes called *interviewer error,* refers to an impact on the interview by the interviewer, which is so strong that it alters the outcome of the interview by affecting the responses offered by the interviewee.

Let's look at an example of interviewer bias. Suppose an interviewer is hired who is muscular, tall, speaks loudly, and tends to stand close to people when he talks to them. Some people would be intimidated by such a person and would refuse to talk to him. His pool of interviewees, as a result, would be contaminated by interviewer bias, because only those who were brave enough to face this intimidating person would agree to be interviewed. This pattern of nonresponse would have been triggered by interviewer error. This imbalance in the interviewee sample—only brave people were interviewed by this particular interviewer—could affect the results.

Most cases of interviewer bias, however, are not so obvious. Consider this example: A respondent opens her/his apartment door one afternoon and finds a very attractive interviewer about the same age standing there. The respondent agrees to the interview because he or she finds the interviewer appealing and proceeds to answer every question not as truly believed but with what she or he hopes are answers the interviewer will approve of and find appealing. Through no fault of the interviewer, this interviewer has had a biasing effect on the data collected. Skilled interviewers, aware of subtle indications that interviewees are responding too strongly to them, will make observations to that effect on the interview-recording sheet to alert the researcher to the possibility of bias.

Sources of interviewer bias include: personal characteristics of the interviewers, differences in handling of the interview by different interviewers working on the same research project, interview assignments that are so demanding (i.e., too many to conduct in one day) that they result in recording and other errors, and interview formats that leave too much room for individual discretion in the eliciting of information.

Interviewer bias or error can be minimized through careful training and supervision. In addition, various researchers have found that the following behaviors help to minimize excessive interviewer influence on the responses of interviewees: (1) reading questions as worded, without paraphrasing; (2) nondirective and nonjudgmental probing; (3) standardized methods of recording responses; (4) neutral, nonjudgmental relationships with interviewees; (5) consistent pacing of interviews; (6) consistent instructions to interviewees before and during the interviews, including consistently requesting interviewee commitment to a specific degree of performance (i.e., "Please answer each question as honestly as possible, choosing the one answer choice which most closely reflects your feelings or beliefs.").[50]

Interviewer bias can never be completely eliminated. It is impossible to remove "the human factor" of interpersonal influence from human encounters. In fact, some researchers, such as Mishler and Goyder, argue that elimination of the individual impact of the interviewer is neither possible nor desirable. Mishler writes, "The interviewer's presence as a coparticipant is an unavoidable and essential component of the discourse, and an interviewer's mode of questioning influences a story's production. Differences in whether and how an interviewer encourages, acknowledges, facilitates, or interrupts a respondent's flow of talk have marked effects on the story that appears." [51]

Mishler further argues that interviewer-interviewee relationships are integral to all research and cannot be "minimized," that these relationships should be freed from a forced "asymmetry of power"[52] (i.e., the interviewer's standardized control over interview structure and content) and should be considered and analyzed along with every other aspect of the context of the interview. Goyder, too, discusses the inherent inequality of the interviewer-interviewee relationship. Both of these authors suggest that interviewer-interviewee relationships that strengthen the ability of interviewees to influence the course of the interview would also strengthen the findings of the research.[53] Issues relating to the inevitable influence of the interviewer on the results obtained continue to be discussed and researched by both qualitative and quantitative researchers.

The issue of bias in research—whether that bias is located in the structure of the project, the wording of questions, the influence of the interviewer, or the analysis of data—is not one that can be eliminated or definitively resolved. At best, researchers and interviewers can do no more than to be aware of the potential for bias at every stage of their research and to minimize its impact on their findings by eliminating its sources where possible and acknowledging its presence in their analyses of findings. Interviewers must be aware of their power to influence the other in the interview and strive to build relationships with their interviewees that are nonjudgmental and nondirective.

Summary

Research interviewing is conducted for the purpose of gathering information to test hypotheses and/or to discover meanings. Qualitative research or depth interviews probe deeply into individual experiences, interviewing fewer people at greater depth to learn about their experiences, beliefs, and feelings in their own words, and to arrive at descriptive or narrative results. Quantitative or survey interviewing seeks representative samples of populations and gathers information from them in ways that are quantifiable and can be tested for statistical significance. In all interview research, the issues of reliability (consistency) and validity (accuracy) are a primary concern.

A summary chart depicting the general differences between qualitative and quantitative research interviewing is provided (see Figure 7.3). Keep in mind as you review this chart that the described differences between the two approaches are not fixed and absolute. There is great variation in the actual choices made by researchers using either approach, but, in this chapter and in Figure 7.3, we have attempted to depict the major differences in these forms of research as they are most often conducted.

In both forms of research interviewing, interviewer bias or error—the influence of the interviewer's personality or procedures on the outcome of the inter-

Type of Research	Qualitative	Quantitative
Also called	Depth, narrative, ethnographic	Survey, market
Goals	Narrative descriptions in interviewee's own words	Quantifiable responses from representative sample
Number of Interviewees	Generally few (under 50)	Usually many (statistical sampling)
Type of sampling	Nonrandom, purposive	Random for population
Length of Interviews	Usually lengthy (1–3 hours)	Usually brief (under 1 hour)
Who Interviews	The researcher(s)	Trained interviewers
Interviewer Style	Relational, flexible, conversational	Consistent, methodical, standardized
Type of Guide	Moderately scheduled, flexible	Highly scheduled, standardized
Type of Contact	Usually face-to-face	Face-to-face or telephone
Settings	Varied, often in interviewee's "home turf"	Varied, often in public settings
Locus of Control	Resides with the interviewee	Resides with the interviewer
Methods of Recording	Usually taped	Usually hand-recorded on standardized response sheet
Advantages	Relational contact, unexpected responses, unique voice of other, depth of understanding	Comparability, statistical analysis, breadth of knowledge
Disadvantages	Time-consuming, data unwieldy, categorization & comparisons difficult	Eliminates individual voices of respondents, closed questions limit discoveries

FIGURE 7.3   Summary Comparison of Qualitative and Quantitative Research Interviews

view—is an issue of ongoing concern. While some steps can be taken to minimize interviewer bias, the impact of the interviewer-interviewee relationship on research cannot be eliminated or ignored.

Discussion Questions

1. What are some issues or topics about which you might be interested in conducting research? What questions do you have about the topic?

2. Have you ever participated in a research interview? Was it qualitative or quantitative research? How did you feel about your participation and about the questions you were asked?

3. Which method of research, qualitative or quantitative, would you propose using to answer these questions, and why:

   a. What effects, if any, does heavy television viewing have on young children?

   b. How does winning the Nobel Peace Prize affect the lives of the winners?

   c. Which tastes better: Pepsi™ or Coke™?

   d. What is the impact of childhood abuse on adult survivors of abusive families?

4. How would you design a research project that attempted to incorporate the advantages or strengths of both methods of interview research?

5. Where do you think bias is most likely to occur in the design and implementation of an interview research project? What safeguards against bias in that area do you think would

Suggested Activities

1. Analyze the opening interview for this chapter. Consider the potential for bias in the questions asked, the interviewer's relationship with the interviewee, and the design of the research project. In order to evaluate the responses of this interviewee, what more would you want to know about him? What other questions would you want to ask? On the basis of his recorded responses, what, if any, questions would you consider adding to later interviews?

2. Design a qualitative or quantitative research interview guide on a topic of your choice. What is your goal? Do you have a hypothesis? Whom would you interview? What would you ask?

3. With a group of classmates, design a simple research project to test the impact of inter-

viewer bias. Devise a brief interview guide and have each group member administer the interview to a willing volunteer while deliberately engaging in behaviors designed to influence the interviewee's response. Tape record these interviews and compare them, discussing apparent differences in responses obtained.

4. Your assigned topic is the question of whether individuals who are terminally ill should be able to choose when and how they will die. Design five questions, either open or closed, to elicit respondent feelings or beliefs about this issue. Compare and analyze your questions with those of several colleagues, selecting the best three questions from those compared. Justify your choice of those three questions.

Related Readings

Babbie, Earl. *The Practice of Social Research*, 6ᵗʰ ed. Belmont, CA: Wadsworth, 1992.

Dijkstra, W., and Van der Zouwen, J., eds. *Response Behaviour in the Survey Interview*. London: Academic Press, 1982.

Fink, Arlene, and Kosecoff, Jacqueline. *How to Conduct Surveys: A Step-by-Step Guide*. Beverly Hills: Sage Publications, 1985.

Fowler, Floyd J., Jr. *Survey Research Methods*, rev. ed. Newbury Park, CA: Sage Publications, 1988.

Fowler, Floyd J., Jr., and Mangione, Thomas W., *Standardized Survey Interviewing: Minimizing Interviewer-Related Error*. Newbury Park, CA: Sage Publications, 1990.

Frey, Lawrence R., Botan, Carl H., Friedman, Paul G., and Kreps, Gary L. *Interpreting Communication Research: A Case Study Approach*. Englewood Cliffs, NJ: Prentice Hall, 1992.

Goyder, John. *The Silent Minority: Nonrespondents on Sample Surveys*. Boulder, CO: Westview Press, 1987.

Lavrakas, Paul J. *Telephone Survey Methods: Sampling, Selection, and Supervision*. Newbury Park, CA: Sage Publications, 1987.

Mishler, Eliot G. *Research Interviewing: Context and Narrative*. Cambridge, MA: Harvard University Press, 1986.

Sudman, Seymour. *Applied Sampling*. New York: Academic Press, 1976.

Endnotes

1. Earl Babbie, *The Practice of Social Research*, 6ᵗʰ ed. (Belmont, CA: Wadsworth Publishing Company, 1992), 129.
2. For an excellent introduction to ethnographic interview research, see L.R. Frey, C.H. Botan, P.G. Friedman, and G.L. Kreps, *Interpreting Communication Research: A Case Study Approach* (Englewood Cliffs, NJ: Prentice Hall, 1992), 247–50, 285–311.
3. Frey, *et.al.* (1992), 286.
4. Elliot G. Mishler, *Research Interviewing: Context and Narrative* (Cambridge, MA: Harvard University Press, 1986). See especially pages 73–116.
5. Mishler (1986), 76.
6. Robin Lorentzen, *Women in the Sanctuary Movement* (Philadelphia: Temple University Press, 1991).
7. Here the author cites Ann Oakley, "Interviewing Women: A Contradiction in Terms," Helen Roberts, ed., *Doing Feminist Research* (London: Routledge and Kegan Paul, 1981), 30–61.
8. Lorentzen (1991), 203–06.
9. Lorentzen (1991), 204.
10. Frey, *et al.* (1992), 286.
11. Jo Young Switzer, "Political Women Speak: Communicative Adaptations in a `Man's World.'" Paper presented at Central States Communication Association Conference, Chicago, 1991.
12. Earl Babbie, *The Practice of Social Research*, 6ᵗʰ ed. (Belmont, CA: Wadsworth, 1992), 293–95.
13. Lorentzen (1991), 206.
14. Mary Field Belenky, Blythe McVicker Clinchy, Nancy Rule Goldberger, and Jill Mattuck Tarule, *Women's Ways of Knowing: The Development of Self, Voice, and Mind* (New York: Basic Books, Inc., Publishers, 1986), 231–32.
15. Switzer (1991).
16. Frey, *et.al.* (1992), 288.
17. Lorentzen (1991), 207.
18. Lorentzen (1991), 207.
19. Mishler (1986), 77.
20. Michael Osborn and Suzanne Osborn, *Alliance for a Better Public Voice* (Dayton: National Issues Forum Institute, 1991), 32–35.
21. *Interviewer's Manual*, rev. ed. (Ann Arbor, MI: University of Michigan, 1976), p. iii.

22. Babbie (1992), 275.
23. Floyd J. Fowler, Jr., *Survey Research Methods*, rev. ed. (Newbury Park, CA: 1988), 65.
24. Fowler (1988), 70–71.
25. William I. Gorden, and Donimic A. Infante, "Test of a Communication Model of Organizational Commitment,"*Communication Quarterly,* vol. 39, no. 2, (Spring 1991,) 144–55.
26. John DeLameter, "Response-effects of Question Content," in W. Dijkstra and J. Van der Zouwen, eds., *Response Behaviour in the Survey Interview* (London: Academic Press, 1982), 17. See also Fowler (1988), 94.
27. DeLameter (1982), 21–22.
28. Fowler (1988), 91.
29. Fowler (1988), 95.
30. Donald S. Tull and Gerald S. Albaum, *Survey Research: A Decisional Approach* (New York: Intext Educational Publishers, 1973), 84.
31. Babbie (1992), 182–83.
32. Floyd J. Fowler and Thomas W. Mangione, *Standardized Survey Interviewing: Minimizing Interviewer-Related Error* (Newbury Park, CA: Sage Publications, 1990), 136–7.
33. Fowler and Mangione (1990), 92.
34. Fowler and Mangione (1990), 92–93.

35. Fowler (1988), 104–05. See also Fowler and Mangione (1990), 92–94 and 136–37.
36. DeLameter (1982), 39.
37. Frey, *et.al.* (1992), 89.
38. Seymour Sudman, *Applied Sampling* (New York: Academic Press, 1976), 87.
39. Sudman (1976), 87.
40. Sudman (1976), 86.
41. Babbie (1992), 275.
42. Fowler and Mangione (1990), 106–119.
43. *Interviewer's Manual* (1976).
44. John Goyder, *The Silent Minority: Nonrespondents on Sample Surveys* (Boulder, CO: Westview Press, 1987), 61–67.
45. Goyder (1987), 79.
46. Goyder (1987), 188.
47. Goyder (1987), 189.
48. Fowler and Mangione (1990), 42.
49. *Interviewer's Manual* (1976), 15–16.
50. See, for example, Dijkstra and VanderZouwen (1982), 139–40, and Fowler and Mangione (1990).
51. Mishler (1986), 105.
52. Mishler (1986), 117–170.
53. See Goyder (1987), especially 1–35 and 181–190. See also Mishler (1986), 105–170.

Chapter *8*

Selection Interviewing Preparation

> *"Preparation is essential because whenever you speak to other people they must have absolute confidence that you know what you're talking about. That doesn't mean you need to be the world's leading authority on the subject. But your listener should feel that you know more about the subject than they do and that you've done some preparation for addressing them—either formally or informally."*
> —Roger Ailes, You Are the Message: Getting What You Want by Being Who You Are (New York: Doubleday, 1988), 64.

Joseph Campano has just been hired as personnel manager of the Kendall-Jameson Employment Agency, which provides skilled temporary employees to businesses in the Seattle area. In order to familiarize himself with the agency and its employment needs, he has decided to interview some employees who have been with the agency for two years or more. His first interview is with Staci Munoz, the agency's most experienced office temporary, who has been with Kendall-Jameson for six years. When Campano called, she readily agreed to talk with him about office temporary employment.

Campano: Staci? Hi, I'm Joe Campano. Thanks for coming in to talk with me today.

Munoz: Nice to meet you, Mr. Campano. I'm glad to help.

Campano: Please, call me Joe. Kathryn Kendall told me you are Kendall-Jameson's best employee, so I knew you'd be the best person to help me understand what I should look for in any new office temporaries I hire. Ideally, we'd like to have our whole agency consist of first-rate, long-timers like yourself.

Munoz: Thanks. I love this work and I've always felt that Kendall-Jameson takes good care of its people. I'm glad to help.

Campano: Well, I know you have a lot to teach me, so why don't we begin? What would you say are the most important qualities that I should look for in our employees?

Munoz: Well, honestly, I think there are a lot of them. To go into unfamiliar offices and businesses takes adaptability, first of all, and a real interest in learning new . systems and procedures. And then being a quick learner goes along with that— the company doesn't want to spend two weeks getting you up to speed for a one-month placement.

Campano: So, adaptability, curiosity, and the ability to learn quickly—that's good. This is just the kind of information I need. Please go on.

Munoz: Well, the other part of what's needed in order to do well in new work-places is a real interest in people and a pretty high degree of acceptance, too.

Campano: What do you mean by acceptance?

Munoz: Well, as you know, you meet all kinds wherever you go and some of them are going to be pleasant, interesting, and fun; and others are going to be shy, hostile, or opinionated and pushy. And you've just got to be able to say to yourself, "These people were here before I was and will be here when I'm gone, and it's my job just to live with them the way they are until the job is done."

Campano: Don't you meet some people you just can't stand to be around, though?

Munoz: Yeah, sometimes I do. Once I even asked to be removed from a job that was supposed to last six months because I knew I'd be either homicidal or suicidal if I stayed. (She laughs.) But mostly, I just think, "Hey, this poor person has to live with himself for the rest of his life; I guess I can put up with him for two more weeks."

Campano: That's a great attitude to have. What else can you tell me about what I should be looking for in our employees?

Munoz: Well, this may sound silly, but I think you need to find people who read maps well, have a good sense of direction, and have a sense of adventure. Almost every job I've had has taken me into parts of the city I've never seen before— sometimes not the most attractive parts, either—and I think it would be hard to enjoy this work if you were uncomfortable with exploring new places.

Campano: That's an interesting idea and one I would never have thought of myself. Anything else?

Munoz: Well, yeah. Maybe this goes without saying, but I think office temporary work as a career takes a certain kind of person, one who likes being independent, calling the shots, being able to decide from one day to the next or one week to the next if she wants to work and where she wants to be, someone who prefers variety to security. Most of the people who come into temporary work see it as something to do until they get a real job, but for me, it's the best and most real job there is. This kind of job lets me feel that I'm in control of my own destiny—that I own my days and don't owe my soul to anyone. You know what I mean?

Campano: Yes, I think I do. Thank you, Staci. You've given me some good ideas about what kind of person to seek for our work here. I sure hope we find some more like you.

Munoz: Thanks, Joe. Nice meeting you.

Chapter Goals

- To understand the importance of preparation to the success of selection interviewing for both the interviewer and the interviewee.
- To appreciate the general and specific preparations an interviewer must make in order to conduct successful job search interviews.
- To recognize the preparation necessary for the interviewee to be able to secure and participate effectively in selection interviews.

Introduction

The groundwork for the success or failure of selection interviews is laid long before any interviews take place. In the days and weeks before the interviewing process actually begins, the skilled interviewer begins gathering information and designing the structure of the interviews themselves. Likewise the successful interviewee begins preparations for selection interviewing long before an interview is scheduled, using a variety of research, networking, and material preparation and planning skills.

The most successful interviews are those for which both parties have carefully engaged in a series of strategic preparations. Our purpose in this chapter is to lead you through those necessary preparations, first from the point of view of an interviewer and then from the perspective of one who seeks employment. For both parties, preparation is the key to interview effectiveness.

A report published by the Northwestern University Placement Center in 1988 described the most frequent interviewer complaints about applicants seeking employment.[1] The complaints included were poor appearance and careless dress, lack of goals or knowledge of interests, inability to express self well, lack of information about the organization, inability to ask intelligent questions, and lack of preparation for the interview. Each of the complaints can be explained by the last complaint—lack of preparation for the interview.

Earlier research by Downs in 1969 found that typical complaints by employers about job applicants included perceptions that applicants had vague goals and interests and low levels of information about the companies with whom they were interviewing.[2] Both of these complaints also indicate a lack of preparation on the part of interviewees.

While documentation of the lack of preparation of interviewers is less readily available, research indicates that interviewer effectiveness is related to the perceived clarity, coherence, organization, and relevance of the interviewer's questions and comments.[3] Likewise, several recent court decisions involving discrimination in hiring practices (*Gilber v. City of Little Rock*, 1986; *EEOC v. American National Bank*, 1979; *Green v. USX Corporation*, 1988; and *Bailey v. Southeastern Apprenticeship Committee*, 1983) have faulted lack of interviewer training as a contributing factor in discriminatory practices.[4]

Certainly, most of us have experienced at least one selection interview for which the interviewer seemed unprepared and ineffective. If an interviewer is obviously uncomfortable; fumbles for words or questions; is unclear about purpose, company policies, procedures, or follow-up plans; or does most of the talking and very little actual listening, we can safely assume that too little preparation preceded the interview.

In this chapter we will examine issues and strategies involved in the preparation for selection interviewing from the perspective of both parties in the process. First, with regard to interviewers, we will explore the preliminary preparation issues of learning about the company, the specific position, laws governing the pre-employment selection process, and methods for creating a climate conducive to effective interviewing. Next, we will examine the specific preparation needed for individual interview sessions, including job descriptions and postings, preparation of materials, planning of the interviews, decisions about evaluation criteria, and the choice of questions to be asked. Turning our focus to interviewee preparation, we will investigate strategies for researching companies, developing job search networks, preparing effective resumes, and preparing questions to ask and answers to offer in the course of the interview.

Interviewer Preparation

Preliminary Preparation

An interviewer's first task is to obtain the necessary information about the company, the needs of the position for which applicant selection is sought, the laws governing the pre-employment selection process, and ways to plan a successful interviewing climate. We will look at each of these stages of preliminary preparation in turn.

Knowledge of the Company.   Most of the time, when we consider the role of the interviewer in job searches, we think of the interviewer as the person who seeks and chooses from among the pool of available candidates for the position, and this is certainly an important part of an interviewer's job. At the same time, though, the interviewer is also the person whose presentation of the company and whose role as a representative of the company will influence the interviewee's decision about whether to work for the company.

To do both of these jobs well, an interviewer needs to know as much as possible about the company for which the hiring is being done. Knowledge of the organization is crucial for several reasons. First, the interviewer must be well informed in order to choose candidates whose skills and philosophy of work are compatible with the company's needs and vision of the future. If a company planning to reorganize its factory into self-managing employee teams is seeking a plant manager, the interviewer will seek applicants familiar with the team concept, willing to initiate and adapt to change, and capable of letting go of traditional managerial control. An interviewer without this knowledge of the company's future plans might otherwise select an authoritarian candidate who would resist employee self-governance. Knowing a company's values, philosophy, and future plans is essential to choosing candidates well.

An equally important responsibility of the interviewer is to "sell" the company to applicants. Research conducted by Schmitt and Coyle indicates that the adequacy of the information provided by interviewers, along with their perceived personalities and delivery skills, influences applicant evaluations of both interviewer and company as well as the likelihood of job acceptance.[5] Selling the employer to job applicants requires being able to answer applicant questions about the company, the position, benefits, and opportunities for education and advancement. An interviewer who cannot answer applicant questions or who does not know where to get the requested information will create confusion and a negative impression of the company in the minds of applicants.

Additionally, the interviewer needs to represent the company in such a way that applicants are encouraged to view it as a desirable place to work. At the same time, honest representation of the company is a necessity. Traditionally, employers have assumed that effective selling of a workplace requires emphasizing what the institution and the job at their best have to offer, much as job applicants attempt to represent themselves at their best. Certainly, no skilled selection interviewer would focus exclusively on a company's failings and problems unless specifically seeking to hire a person trained to deal with problems. However, in order to avoid the quick loss of employees who were lured to a job by unrealistically glowing job previews, clear identification of job negatives that cannot be corrected should be included in the information the selection interviewer presents.[6] **Realistic job previews** provide job applicants with balanced information about both the strengths and the weaknesses of the job and the company. An analysis of fifteen separate experiments with realistic job previews involving thousands of subjects found that realistic job previews reduce employee turnover on average by 9 percent.[7]

How does an interviewer learn about the company before hiring? Becoming familiar with available written materials containing information about company policies and practices, benefits packages, and financial status is a good place to start, while paying particular attention to aspects of the company such as benefit packages that are likely to be of interest to applicants.

The skilled interviewer also talks with those people in the company who are knowledgeable about the company's philosophies, policies, and visions. If, for example, the business in question has a new chief executive officer (CEO), the selection interviewer would want to know what plans the new leader has for change in the business. Likewise, an interviewer would want to talk with union representatives about policies and procedures when seeking a candidate for a union shop. Who the interviewer needs to talk with within the company depends on the position available, the current company climate, and the kinds of information likely to be needed or desired by the applicant.

Additional and valuable sources of information for selection interviewers are exit interviews conducted earlier with departing employees. **Exit interviews** are planned interviews conducted with employees who are leaving or have left a company. The purpose of exit interviews is to learn about the strengths and weaknesses of a company from individuals who are free to speak candidly because they have nothing to lose by doing so.

Often, exit interviews are conducted only with employees who have left a company voluntarily because it is assumed that those who have been dismissed will be so negatively biased that their comments would have little constructive value beyond offering the exemployee the opportunity to vent feelings.

Typically, exit interviews are conducted during an employee's last day on the job. Effective exit interviews are conducted by someone other than the employee's immediate supervisor. Because a departing employee is not likely to speak freely unless sure the interview will not hurt evaluations or letters of recommendation for future jobs, the confidentiality of the employee's responses must be assured.

Exit interviewers ask about the strengths and the weaknesses of the company, including its organizational climate, policies, and salary issues. They are also useful for obtaining uncensored information about supervisors for whom an employee has worked, as well as specific feedback about the particular job(s) an employee held with the firm. In addition, exit interviews provide an opportunity to discuss issues such as severance pay, benefits, and outplacement services when appropriate.[8] A list of typical exit interview questions and concerns is provided in Figure 8.1. The value of exit interviews for departing employees includes the potential opportunity to have an impact on the company and to obtain some closure on their employment experience.

Information obtained from exit interviews should be summarized and compiled so that the identity of the respondent is protected. This information can be helpful in revising job descriptions and in understanding the qualities or skills necessary to perform the job effectively. Likewise, exit interviews allow selection interviewers to obtain information about the strengths, weaknesses, and needs of the company.

1. Reasons for departure:

   Voluntary or involuntary?
   New position or prospects?
   Problems with salary, company, or supervisors?
   Other?

2. Evaluation of position employee is leaving:

   What did you enjoy about this job?
   What did you not enjoy?
   What frustrations, if any, did you experience?
   How clear were your assignments and responsibilities?
   Did your job description match your actual duties?
   What would you change about the job description?
   What would you change about the job?
   What training do you think is needed for this job?
   What qualities do you think are needed in a person who holds this kind of job?

3. Evaluation of supervision employee received:

   Describe the strengths of your immediate supervisor.
   What would you say were her/his weaknesses?
   What would you tell a new employee coming into this job about the skills or qualities
        needed in order to work effectively with this supervisor?
   What kind of supervisor is needed for this job?

4. Evaluation of the company:

   What would you say are the strengths of this company?
   How would you describe its weaknesses?
   How would you evaluate this company's commitment to its employees?
   How would you evaluate the benefit programs of this company?
   How would you evaluate the training and advancement programs offered by this com-
        pany?
   How would you describe communication in this company?
   What would you do to improve communication in this company?
   In a different job or under different circumstances, would you work for this company
        again?

5. What else do you think this company should know about your experience here?
   What do you think your supervisor here should know about the quality of her/his super-
        vision?
   What do you think the person replacing you should know?

FIGURE 8.1 Typical Exit Interview Issues and Questions

In order to help the interview process, the interviewer can obtain information about the position from the other employees.

Knowledge of the Job.   In addition to input from exit interviews, the selection interviewer obtains additional information about the position from other employees, including those working in similar jobs, those who will work closely with the new hire, and the immediate supervisor for the position. Information received about the nature of the job and its relationship to other positions helps the interviewer decide who needs to be involved in the interview process and whether interviews should be conducted by a team of interviewers.

In larger companies, initial interviews are sometimes conducted by interviewers in the company's Personnel or Human Resource Department, while final selections are made from a select pool of applicants by the supervisor or team with whom the candidate will work. Before the interview process can begin, a selection interviewer needs a clear understanding of the job and its place within the larger matrix of the company. From this information, a job description is prepared that will accurately represent the position to applicants.

Knowledge of Legal Considerations.   That discrimination in employment practices continues to be a widespread problem has been amply documented, but the interview itself has been an issue in less than 1 percent of the more than 8,000 cases occurring between 1979–1987.[9] Nonetheless, an important aspect of the preparation necessary to selection interviewing involves careful review of the legal constraints that affect employment in order to avoid potentially discriminatory actions.

Many companies provide their interviewers with pre-employment interview guides that offer specific suggestions concerning permissible questions and questions to be avoided in selection interviews. An example of a pre-employment inquiry guide and an introduction to federal employment laws was provided in chapter 5.

As a rule, questions should be limited to BFOQ's (*bona fide* occupational qualifications). No questions should be asked that seek information that could be used to discriminate on the basis of age, race, ethnic origin, religion, sex, veteran status, or handicap. Likewise, job descriptions must be nondiscriminatory. Also, the selection interviewer must remind all who participate in the interview process about EEOC legislation and about appropriate and inappropriate areas of inquiry.

The interviewer should be familiar with specific local, state, and federal laws that pertain to the workplace and the job. On the basis of a review of discrimination decisions in the courts, Campion and Arvey offer these recommendations for guarding against discrimination in the interview: (1) develop and use job descriptions as interview guides; (2) select and train interviewers, preferably tapping individuals from diverse racial, ethnic, and gender backgrounds; (3) assure the job relevance of all questions and ask the same questions of all applicants; (4) use multiple interviewers or panel interviews to introduce review of decisions; (5) keep detailed records of procedures and processes; and (6) monitor decisions for evidence of discriminatory impact on protected classes.[10]

Specific Preparation for the Interview

Preparation and Posting the Job Description.   **A job description** is a formal written document that describes the title, duties and responsibilities, place in the organization, and requirements of a particular position. The purpose of a job description is to provide all interested parties (e.g., applicants, supervisors, interviewers and employees) with a clear understanding of the job.

A job description should be dated in order for all involved to know when it was last revised. This also allows employees and applicants to know whether it is current. It should identify the job by title, indicate the hours and wage status of the position, and specify by title to whom the job holder reports, as well as who reports (by title) to the holder of the position. The job should be described in summary form. This should be followed by a detailed list of duties and responsibilities and clearly stated academic, experiential, and competency requirements for the job. The potential for advancement from the position described is also often included.[11] Finally, a job description should provide interested parties with information about where to direct inquiries and applications. A sample job description based on the chapter's opening interview is found in Figure 8.2.

A clear job description guides the entire selection process. On the basis of the job description, the interviewer determines the skills and qualities needed to per-

---

JOB POSTING: 11/7/93 Kendall-Jameson Employment Agency

JOB TITLE: Skilled Office Temporary

JOB STATUS: Full or part-time (hours dependent on employee and placement location needs). Starting wage for skilled employee: $5.25 per hour

SUPERVISION
RECEIVED: Varies with placement. Agency provides ongoing evaluation and supervision of placements.

SUPERVISION
PROVIDED: Varies with placement

JOB SUMMARY: Challenging position for a skilled office worker with diverse clerical skills. The position involves placements of several days to several months with a variety of large and small businesses in the Seattle metropolitan area. The Kendall–Jameson employee will select from among offered placements in available firms, conform to company needs and expectations, deliver high quality temporary service, and fullfill a wide variety of clerical tasks, including typing, word processing, filing, reception, etc. Complete job and company descriptions will be provided in advance of placements.

DUTIES AND RESPONSIBILITIES:

1. The employee will represent the Kendall-Jameson Employment Agency with high-quality work, a positive company image, and efficient adaptability to the needs of the assigned workplace.

2. The employee will accept and perform office and clerical duties as specified in job descriptions provided in advance by firms being served. Additional duties not specified in job descriptions may be accepted upon mutual agreement of employee and employee's supervisor at the Kendall-Jameson Agency.

3. The employee will accept placements for their duration. In the event of placement problems, the employee will notify her/his Kendall-Jameson supervisor, who will take appropriate action. The employee has discretion in the acceptance or refusal of placements offered by the Kendall-Jameson Agency.

4. The employee will arrive at work promptly, dress appropriately, perform required tasks in a timely and efficient manner, and maintain high standards of ethical integrity at all times.

5. The employee will make regular reports concerning her/his placement experiences and will complete a Placement Evaluation Survey at the end of each assignment.

POSITION REQUIREMENTS: Excellent office skills, including typing, word processing, filing and reception skills. Strong organizational skills. Adaptability and flexibility, willingness to learn and ability to learn quickly. Strong interpersonal skills. High school diploma or GED equivalency. Excellent references required.

FIGURE 8.2   Sample Job Description

form the job. With the description as a guide, the interviewer decides who to interview and what questions to ask in order to find the best person for the job. This is why careful research into the needs of the job must precede the creation of the job description and why selection interviewers must be sure the job description is accurate and up-to-date before beginning the actual selection interviews.

Once prepared, the job description must be announced, advertised, and posted both within and outside the company so that information about the position is available to all qualified candidates. **Job posting** is a method of making employees within a company aware of job vacancies by listing the jobs available in central locations or through an in-house computer network, and by indicating application deadline dates.[12] Job postings are essential for internal recruiting in companies. In some firms, job posting is computerized and accessible to all employees at their terminals.[13] In at least one firm, computer software further aids employees at matching their own skills to available jobs.[14]

Externally, jobs are advertised through classified ads in newspapers and appropriate trade publications. University teaching positions, for example, are usually advertised in *The Chronicle of Higher Education.* Legally, in order to avoid

Many companies computerize their job listings, allowing employees access to the information through their terminals.

discrimination in hiring, jobs must be announced in ways that give equal access to all qualified candidates.

Preparation of Application Forms and Other Materials.   In many cases, these written materials are uniform within a company and do not require interviewer preparation. However, interviewers still must collect appropriate materials and make sure they are current. Application forms must be nondiscriminatory, asking only for information related to BFOQ's and other necessary information such as applicant address, phone number, and so forth. Likewise, interview evaluation forms to be used during interviews should be legally appropriate, recording only information pertinent to the job.

The more clearly interview materials focus on the needs of the specific job, the more effective they will be. For example, the interviewer may want to develop a candidate evaluation checklist that corresponds to the duties of the position being filled. Such a form allows the interviewer to easily determine which applicants best meet the requirements and needs of the job. Sometimes applicant evaluation checklists, such as the one shown in Figure 8.3, incorporate a scoring system to allow participants in the interview process to rate the applicants interviewed. A sample applicant checklist appropriate to the job description provided in Figure 8.2 is shown in Figure 8.4.

Planning for the Interview Process.   Based on research information obtained, the interviewer next decides who to involve in the interview process. Will the interviewer be the sole interviewer for the initial screening? Will there be a team interview with relevant current employees? Who should be involved? Will a second interview be necessary? These and related questions are usually decided in consultation with other relevant personnel.

Once decisions about interview participants have been made, the interviewer decides when interviews will be held, how long they will last, and where and how they will be conducted. A quiet and comfortable location for the interviews is desirable. If more than one interviewer is involved, decisions need to be made about who will meet and greet the applicant and how movement from one stage or facet of the interview process to another will be accomplished.

Next, decisions are necessary concerning the handling of relevant paperwork. How will application materials be assembled and distributed prior to the interviews? How will they be checked for completeness? What verification procedures will be used with the applications, resumes, and references of all applicants? The *Columbus* (Ohio) *Dispatch* reported a 1987 study which revealed that up to 67 percent of job applicants falsify or misrepresent information on their resumes.[15] What procedures will be employed to assure that information obtained is accurate?

How will applicants to be interviewed be selected and how will they be informed of that invitation? Once the interviews are complete, how will the selection decision be made? Who will be involved in the decision-making process and how will the best applicant be chosen? Last, how will applicants (hired or not) be informed of the decision?

Applicant Name _____

Evaluator Name _____

Rank the applicant on the following characteristics by circling the appropriate number:

> 1 = not apparent or not assessable
> 2 = poor
> 3 = fair
> 4 = good
> 5 = excellent

Knowledge of the company	1	2	3	4	5
Understanding of the job	1	2	3	4	5
Relevant skills	1	2	3	4	5
Relevant work experiences	1	2	3	4	5
Leadership ability	1	2	3	4	5
Oral communication skill	1	2	3	4	5
Written communication skill	1	2	3	4	5
Career commitment	1	2	3	4	5
Listening skills	1	2	3	4	5
Asked pertinent questions	1	2	3	4	5

Total score: _____

Evaluator's overall assessment of the candidate's ability to do the job:

1	2	3	4	5

Recommendation for hire: YES   NO

Comments:

FIGURE 8.3   Sample Applicant Evaluation & Scoring Form

All of these details are important to complete the interviewing process successfully. The interviewer wants procedures clarified and a consistent and efficient system for handling the interviews in place before the actual interviews begin.

Preparation of Interview Questions.   Keeping in mind the goal of hiring the best possible person for the job, the effective interviewer will create an inter-

---

APPLICANT NAME_____

EVALUATOR NAME_____

QUALIFICATIONS OF APPLICANT:

1. Office skills:

    Typing test score: _____ words per minute

    Filing test score: _____ items misfiled

    Telephone skills test score: _____ errors

    Word processing knowledge:

    Supervision experience:

2. Evidence offered of

    Organizational skills:

    Adaptability/flexibility:

    Willingness to learn:

    Quick learning:

    Strong interpersonal skills:

    Diploma or GED:

    Professionalism:

    Interest in and commitment to office temporary work:

    Interest in K–J:

3. References provided?

    Contacted?   Responses attached?

FIGURE 8.4   Sample Applicant Evaluation Checklist

view guide to be consistently employed with each of the applicants. The guide will include suggested opening remarks and a list of specific questions to be asked of all candidates. In addition, the interviewer may want to prepare certain questions that pertain to individual applicants, such as questions about education in progress or areas where information provided in resumes or applications was unclear. Specific questions let the applicant know that the interviewer has done her/his homework. They also let interviewees know that they are recognized as individuals. All questions must conform to the legal requirement of applicability to the job in question.

Finally, if more than one interviewer is involved, decisions about who will ask which questions must be made. Sometimes when there are multiple interviewers, they will divide the questions into topic areas and each will be responsible for a certain set of questions. Other team or panel interviewers will rotate questions arbitrarily. More extensive information about specific interview questions will be provided in chapter 9.

It is clear by now that effective selection interviews take a great deal of preparation on the part of the interviewer. Likewise, careful preparation is vital to interviewees who want to successfully negotiate the interviewing process. A summary checklist of the preparations necessary for the effective interviewer is shown in Figure 8.5.

Interviewee Preparation

How many interviews have you had thus far in your life? And how many total hours would you estimate you have spent in preparation for those interviews? By conservative estimates, the average undergraduate college student spends more than 4,000 hours in course work and study preparing for a chosen career. Yet, for the selection interviews that will determine the student's options to use those hours of training, the average interviewee probably spends less than an hour or two preparing for the interview—and most of that time is probably spent on deciding what to wear! Many interviewees have never considered how to prepare themselves for a job interview.

Preparation is essential in order to interview effectively. For the interviewee, preparation begins with research, requires the creation of effective resumes and cover letters, and involves careful preparation of both questions to ask and answers to anticipated interviewer questions. Then, as a final step, the interviewee must consider dress and other issues related to self-presentation for the selection interview.

Researching Personal Goals and Direction

Too often, job applicants start their job search with an underlying attitude that their goal is "to get a job" and, by implication, that almost any job will do. Certainly, there are times in our lives when we need immediate income more than the job of our dreams, and we take what is available in order to support ourselves. Often, however, this "any job at any cost" attitude causes people to jump at jobs unsuitable to their needs and that they will soon want to leave.

While it is sometimes necessary to accept employment that is less than ideal, an applicant should begin a job search by considering these two simple questions: "What do I want from a job? What goals do I have for my future?" Addressing these questions thoughtfully and answering them honestly is the best place to begin the process of looking for work. The better job seekers understand their own

PRELIMINARY PREPARATION:

    1.   Knowledge of the company:
        _____ Review company documents
        _____ Talk with relevant employees
        _____ Gather information from exit interviews

    2.   Knowledge of the job:
        _____ Examine relevant exit interviews
        _____ Interview employees in similar jobs
        _____ Interview immediate supervisor for position

    3.   Knowledge of legal considerations:
        _____ Review preemployment guides
        _____ Review relevant legislation
        _____ Remind all involved employees about legal constraints

SPECIFIC PREPARATION:

    1.   Prepare and post job description:
        _____ Date
        _____ Title
        _____ Hours and wage status
        _____ Summary description
        _____ Duties and responsibilities
        _____ Applicant requirements
        _____ Applications and inquiries to
        _____ Posting for equitable access

    2.   Prepare application forms and other materials:
        _____ Application forms
        _____ Evaluation forms
        _____ Other necessary materials

    3.   Plan for interview process:
        _____ Who will interview?
        _____ How many interviews?
        _____ When?
        _____ Where?
        _____ Format?
        _____ How will paperwork be handled?
        _____ How will applicant materials be verified?
        _____ How will decision be made?
        _____ How will applicants be informed?

    4.   Prepare interview guide:
        _____ Opening
        _____ Questions for all applicants
        _____ Questions for individual applicants
        _____ Who will ask which questions?

FIGURE 8.5   Interviewer Preparation Checklist

expectations about work and career ambitions, the better able they will be to decide what kind of organization they want to work for and what kind of job they want to hold.

The well-known book *What Color is Your Parachute?* by Richard Bolles, now in its 25th annual edition, helps readers to decide their own skills, needs, goals, and expectations, as well as offering many concrete suggestions about job hunting. Bolles recommends conducting job-hunting research based on these four questions: (1) "What are the names of jobs that would use my strongest and most enjoyable skills and fields of knowledge? (2) What kinds of organizations have such jobs? (3) What are the names of the organizations that I particularly like, among those uncovered in Question #2? (4) What needs do they have or what outcomes are they trying to produce that my skills could help with?"[16]

Researching Companies

How does one begin to learn about what kinds of companies and jobs are available? There are several sources for this information; namely, library research, campus placement offices, information interviews, and networking. Each offers different levels of information to expand the applicant's understanding and employment options.

Before setting out in search of these resources, however, the applicant should consider what information will be helpful to know about businesses and the jobs within them. A job-seeker's self-assessment should lead to essential questions to ask about each company. If, for example, an applicant is a female with definite long-range and upwardly mobile career ambitions and a family with young children, she may seek a company with a strong record of promotion of women to executive positions and solid company support for families, including on-site child care. The questions, "What is this company's record with regard to the promotion of its female employees?" and "What support does this company offer for employees with children?" may be the central questions by which this prospective employee judges the companies she researches. Meanwhile, for a male applicant with no children, these questions may be of no interest.

Each individual's information-seeking questions about organizations will vary according to individual needs. The best questions to ask will be those that pertain directly to one's own needs, expectations, and goals. Some examples of questions an applicant might ask include:

For Those Seeking Job Stability:

How old is this organization?

How stable is the demand for its products and services?

What is its financial record?

How secure is its stock-ownership base from takeovers?

What is the rate of employee turnover?

For Those Seeking a Socially Responsible Company:

What is this organization's safety record?

What is its history and philosophy regarding environmental pollution?

What are its involvement in and contributions to the local community?

What is its promotion record with regard to ethnic minorities and other protected classes?

Are this company's products compatible with current ecological concerns?

For Those Seeking Companies with Strong Employee Involvement:

Is this company employee-owned?

Is employee involvement in innovation and decision making encouraged?

How are decisions made here?

Is a team concept utilized in day-to-day operations?

What actions does this company engage in to recruit and keep active, involved personnel?

For Those Inquiring About a Specific Job:

Why did the last person who occupied this position leave?

How much decision-making autonomy does a person in this position have?

What are the toughest aspects of this job?

What opportunities for professional growth exist for someone in this job?

How good is the match between my skills and needs and the demands and benefits of this position?

Once applicants have decided what they need to know about the companies and positions being considered, based on what they know about themselves, they are ready to seek the best positions available to meet their skills and needs.

Library Research

The reference section of your public or university library contains many valuable books about existing businesses. Particularly, for those just out of college who are looking for their first career jobs, these reference works can broaden awareness about the options available. Some common library resources are listed that a job-seeker should explore:

American Almanac of Jobs and Salaries
Bernard Klein's Guide to American Directories
Best Companies for Women
Career Guide: Dun's Employment Opportunities Directory

College Placement Annual
Contacts Influential: Commerce and Industry Directory
Directory of Directories
Directory of Occupational Titles
Directory of Professional and Trade Organizations
Dun & Bradstreet's Million Dollar Directory
Encyclopedia of Associations
Encyclopedia of Business Information Sources
Encyclopedia of Careers & Vocational Guidance
Jobs Rated Almanac
Moody's Industrial Manual
New York Times Index
Occupational Outlook Handbook
Standard and Poor's Register of Corporations, Directors and Executives
Thomas' Register of American Manufacturers
Wall Street Journal Index
Ward's Business Directory
Worldwide Chamber of Commerce Directory

Campus Placement Offices

There are over 3,000 colleges and universities in the United States and most of them offer some form of placement service.[17] Most placement services offer a variety of assistance for the job hunter, including aptitude testing, preference testing, local job listings, and occupational counseling. Some services are also linked to computerized national job listings. Any college student who has access to a college placement service should make use of its resources. Some of these services also offer placement assistance for their graduates and other university employees.

Information Interviews.   In addition to conducting library and placement service research, job applicants should consider who to interview for helpful employment information. Ideal persons to interview for this purpose are individuals already employed in the type of job being sought in the applicant's company of choice, but there are other helpful possibilities as well. For example, a student graduating with a degree in communication might ask each of her professors for suggestions on types of jobs to seek and industries to explore. Another job seeker might schedule interviews with four persons in the chosen field of physical therapy, asking each for information about their jobs and workplaces. Another person might interview individuals employed in various specializations of a chosen field, such as corporate, small-business, and tax accounting, in order to obtain information about the advantages and disadvantages of each.

Applicants should use informational interviews to ask for names of specific persons in business or industry who might be useful contacts or information sources, thereby expanding the network of individuals the candidate can ask for leads. A job seeker who asks for names of contacts should also ask for permission to use the name of the person interviewed when making contact with those named. Because information interviews of this kind essentially ask for assistance without offering much in return, they should be well-planned, brief, and specific in order not to waste the time of the individual being interviewed.

   Networking.   Networking is a fairly new term to describe a very old phenomenon, well-expressed in the adage that "it's who you know." **Networking** is the deliberate effort on the part of job-seekers and others to expand their "who you know" list in order to have contacts and potential links to information, job recommendations, and other career advantages. A network is not a formal structure; it's an informal web of friends, family, coworkers, classmates, and acquaintances who together have contacts and links to job-related information. For many people, membership in professional organizations is another method of creating and maintaining networks of colleagues and peers.

   The reason for networking is fundamentally clear—personal contacts and personal introductions make a difference. Many jobs are filled without being advertised.[18] According to Bolles, recent research by an outplacement firm indicated that between 1981–1987, 68 percent of its candidates found their new jobs through personal contacts.[19] Networking is an important job search avenue that the skillful applicant will want to explore.

Preparing Effective Resumes

A **resume** is a formal, one-to-two page summary of the academic, work, and professional experiences of an applicant. The word *resumé* comes from the French verb *resumer*, which means *to summarize*. A resume is the document most often used by applicants seeking employment and by interviewers for the screening of applicants. While the resume is a document with certain traditional requirements and conservative standards, it should be at the same time a unique, individual statement about relevant skills, training, and experiences pertinent to a particular job.

   Contrary to the thinking of inexperienced job seekers, a resume is not a document to be created once, duplicated indefinitely, and sent in the same form to all prospective employers. The best resumes are revised and recreated, time and again, to conform to the demands of particular positions being sought. The skilled job applicant will create a basic resume that summarizes relevant skills and experiences accurately, and then will revise and adapt the resume as needed for specific positions sought. Fortunately, with the aid of a computer, this is now easy to do.

   The purpose of the resume, again, is to introduce an applicant and to represent in summary form what that person has done and can do. The resume *is not* a job application or even, used alone, an effective job search tool. Bolles claims that only 1 in every 1,470 resumes submitted to companies results in a job.[20] Bolles also claims that only 2 to 5 of every 100 resumes submitted to companies survive the most preliminary screening.[21] Another writer claims that the average length of time spent looking at a resume by individual employers and interviewers is fifteen seconds.[22] The resume alone has little power to secure a job for an individual.

Frequently, resumes are requested in job postings or advertisements for available positions. Often, resumes and their accompanying cover letters are used by interviewers for an initial screening of applicants. While jobs are seldom obtained by resumes alone, many opportunities to be interviewed have been lost because of resumes that were flawed, uninteresting, vague, cluttered, or unclear. A survey of staff at 170 corporations found that most hiring personnel respond negatively to resumes with poor grammar or spelling, poor organization, or which conveyed a sense of exaggerating what an applicant could do.[23] As an introduction, a resume should create a positive first impression of the individual it represents, and it should do so as succinctly and clearly as possible.

In general, a resume should possess three essential qualities. First, it should be an accurate and positive summary of the individual's experiences, accomplishments, and skills. Second, a resume should be targeted to specific jobs and specific company needs rather than prepared and printed in a standard, unchanging form. Third, a resume should be attractive, brief, clean, clear, and error free. The specific information that should (and should not) be included in a resume is listed in Figure 8.6. Some general recommendations regarding resume form, representing the best information culled from cited sources and others, are listed in Figure 8.7.

Most writers of resume handbooks recommend a conservative approach to resume creation,[24] avoiding, for example, the use of bright-colored papers and the use of unusual design or typeface features. Other writers, recognizing the current competitive realities of the job market, recommend more innovative approaches.[25] The key to resume creation, however, lies not in one certain style or look, but in targeting the document to the intended audience. A bold and creative resume might be just what is needed to get the attention of an advertising executive, while a stark, plain resume on heavy white paper may be what appeals to the president of an established law firm. Overall, the question of who will receive the resume should dictate answers to questions of format and design. Sample resumes in traditional and untraditional formats, geared for different hypothetical audiences, are shown in Figures 8.8 and 8.9.

Books containing advice and samples of resumes abound. The Public and American Library Associations' *The Guide To Basic Resume Writing* lists thirty other resume guides.[26] At a small local bookstore, the authors found eighteen resume handbooks in stock. (By contrast, only two books on job interviewing were available.) In addition, most university placement offices provide resume writing assistance.

Keeping in mind the recommendations made here, job applicants should consult one or more of these resources and then proceed to create resumes that accurately and effectively introduce themselves to specific organizations. The less that is known about the employer, the more careful the applicant should be to err on the side of traditional, conservative resume organization and style. Above all, applicants should keep in mind that their success in the employment market will depend, not on the resume alone, but on the combined, skillful use of resumes, cover letters, research, networking, and interviewing skill.

Name
Address
Phone Number

Relevant skills
Relevant work experience, paid and voluntary
Work history should note accomplishments
Education
Specialized training, including relevant licenses

Other options sometimes recommended:

Statement of career objective: Do not include unless it is specific, unique, strongly worded, and
 geared toward this company's needs.

References available upon request: This statement has traditionally appeared at the bottom of
 all resumes. As a result, nobody reads it. Don't bother. Instead, mention references in
 cover letter or list names on separate sheet to provide at interview.

Personal information: Omit. It has the potential for being used in a discriminatory manner.

Photo: Omit unless related to BFOQ

Salary requirements: Omit. This limits both applicant and interviewers.

FIGURE 8.6   What a Resume Should Include

Preparing Cover Letters

Like resumes, effective cover letters must be targeted specifically to individual employers, based on the best available information about the company and the job. A **cover letter** is a letter of introduction to a prospective employer, usually accompanied by a resume, in which a job applicant expresses an interest in working for a company.

A cover letter should be brief and well written, using strong, positive language. It should clearly identify the applicant and the recipient. Cover letters should *always* be addressed to a specific person. If an applicant doesn't know who in the company should receive the letter, then research is needed to find out.

The first paragraphs of the cover letter should positively identify the applicant's best skills and accomplishments and the way they match the organization's needs. Connections between the experience of the applicant and the needs of the company build a bond with the employer and demonstrate that the applicant has done her/his homework. If interested in a specific position, the applicant should name the position.

RESUME ORGANIZATION:

Chronological: This is the traditional, and still preferred, method. Usually, the resume is divided into two sections, education and work experiences. Information in each section is listed in reverse chronological order, from most recent to least recent.

Functional: This format organizes achievements and experiences around specific skills and talents and is often recommended for persons with unusual or interrupted work histories.

Combination: Utilizes a combination of both of the above, sometimes beginning with a skills summary and followed by a chronological history.

OTHER FORMAT RECOMMENDATIONS:

Length: 1–2 pages. Leave spaces between sections. Use phrases, not sentences. Edit, don't crowd.

Type: Readable, 12 pt. type. Use boldface to emphasize the **individual applicant—name, job titles, degrees, accomplishments.** Don't overuse fancy type choices.

Margins: At least 1″ on all sides, leaving a clean look and room for the interviewer to write in the margins.

Also:

1. **Use asterisks (*) or bullets (•)** to mark divisions or highlight achievements.

2. **Proofread** repeatedly, and have others do the same, to insure that there are **no** typographical, spelling, or grammatical errors.

3. Arrange categories (degrees, work experiences, etc.) so that **the individual's title, degree,** or **accomplishment is listed first** (i.e., closest to the left-hand margin). The interviewer should be able to skim down the left-hand side of the page and obtain a listing of applicant's degrees, titles, etc.

4. Use **high-quality typewriter or printer,** not dot-matrix.

5. Unless there is a good reason to do otherwise, stick with **white paper and black type** for the cleanest, sharpest look.

6. **Be consistent** with spacing, punctuation, organization, use of boldface, etc.

FIGURE 8.7   Recommendations for Resume Format

SHAMA CHABRHA
1813 Atlanta Ave.
Coldwater, MI 49036
(313) 555–0303

EDUCATION:

Bachelor of Science in Business: Accounting Major.
Indiana University–Purdue University,
Fort Wayne, IN. May, 1993.

* **GPA: 6.0/6.0**
* **Dean's List** every semester for four years.
* **President,** Accounting Honor Society, 1992–93.
* **Treasurer,** International Student Organization, 1991–93.

EMPLOYMENT EXPERIENCES:

Bookkeeper: Karen's Corner Market, Fort Wayne, IN, 1990–93.
            Part-time.

* **Developed** computerized inventory system.
* **Managed** all accounts receivable, accounts payable, and payroll.
* **Increased** profit margin by 6% in 3 years through inventory controls and perishables loss reduction.

Mathematics Tutor: Mathematics Department, Indiana
            University – Purdue University,
            Fort Wayne, 1991–93. Part-time.

* **Tutored** in algebra, calculus, and basic math areas.
* **Chosen** Math Tutor of the Year, 1991–92 and 1992–93.
* **Successfully assured** that all 24 tutored students passed with grades of C and above.

COMPUTER SKILLS:

* Pascal	* Cobol	* IBM
* Lotus 123	* Basic	* Apple

FIGURE 8.8   Sample Chronological Resume (Response to job posting for entry-level accountant at local branch of a conservative national accounting firm)

Jonathan J. Thompson
2611 Shipley
DeKalb, IL 60115
(815) 555–7716

CREATIVITY:

* **Created** "Dog (Meat) Days" cartoon strip for
  University News; Ran daily, 9/92–6/93.

* **Developed** innovative ad campaign for candidate for student body
  president, 5/92.

* **Conceived and developed** aluminum can and paper recycling
  program for University Towers residence halls, 9/91–6/92.

LEADERSHIP:

* **President,** East Tower, University Towers residence halls, 9/91–6/92.

* **Residence Hall Assistant,** University Towers residence halls, 9/92–6/93.

* **Business Manager,** University News, 9/90–6/92.

COMMUNICATION SKILLS:

* **Bachelor of Arts Degree in Communication,** Northern Illinois University, Dekalb,
  IL, 6/93.

* **Minors in English and Journalism.**

* **Advertising Sales,** University News, 8/90–6/92.

* **First Place in Extemporaneous Speaking,** Illinois State High School Speech
  Sectionals, 3/89.

COMMITMENT:

College degree 100% self-financed.

* **Involved** in student newspaper operations and residence hall maintenance and gov–
  ernment since 9/90.

* **Completed** Bachelor's degree in three years through continuous full-time enroll–
  ment, summers included.

FIGURE 8.9 **Sample Functional Resume (Response to ad for creative, committed communicator and leader for entry-level position in advertising business)**

A specific statement about career goals and the names of references, with an open invitation to contact them, may also be included. Never include the names of persons as references without first obtaining their permission to be used as references. Also, each time the names of references are used, they should be notified and provided with the name of the employer who might be contacting them.

Even the most perfect resume, if accompanied by a poorly written cover letter, will most likely never be seen, because the interviewer will not be motivated to turn the page to find accompanying documents. Like the resume, cover letters create first impressions; there is no room for errors. Two sample cover letters are provided in Figures 8.10 and 8.11.

Preparing to Answer Interviewer Questions

Many job applicants walk into interview after interview without having once considered in advance what questions they might be asked or how to answer them. Apparently many applicants believe that since they cannot know exactly what they will be asked, preparation is impossible. In fact, many job-related questions that interviewers ask are standard in form and content, so much so that numerous texts and trade publications contain lists of typical questions.

Strasser and Sena, for example, list twenty questions most frequently asked at job interviews, including such questions as, "What are your major strengths?" and "What are your major weaknesses?"[27] Anthony and Roe list "50 Questions Asked by Employers" and include such standard questions as "Tell me about yourself" and "Why should we hire you?"[28] Bostwick lists eighty-two questions, including twenty described as the "twenty most embarrassing questions," among which he lists "Tell me about yourself" and "Tell me about your most important achievements."[29] Bolles, too, lists some common questions, but goes on to report that "beneath these dozens of possible questions there are really only four."[30] He describes the four underlying questions as these: (1) Why did you choose to come to this organization in search of a job? (2) What special skills and knowledge do you possess? (3) What kind of persons are you willing to work with? And (4) what do you need and want for a salary?

The point of all these lists of questions is not to encourage job applicants to prepare specific answers to each of them. Such a task would be anxiety-producing, if not overwhelming, for most people. Rather, the most effective preparation for selection interviewees is to consider what kinds of information the interviewer is most likely to want, as well as what information the applicant wants to be sure the interviewer receives. During the days before the interview, the applicant can consider possible answers to possible questions. Practicing answers aloud provides the opportunity to actually hear how they sound and to adapt wording accordingly. The following questions found in Figure 8.12 can help organize the interviewee's thoughts about what information it is important to share.

Hamilton and Parker report research that suggests that successful job applicants answer interviewer questions with relevant technical jargon; namely, "active, positive and concrete language," specific examples and illustrations,

May 1, 1993

Ms. Jennifer Taylor
Small Business Accounts Advisor
Latham & Jones
10 West Main Street
Fort Wayne, IN 46802

Dear Ms. Taylor,

I was pleased to obtain your posting for an entry-level accounting position in Small Business Accounts at Latham & Jones through my academic advisor, Dr. Charles DeWald at Indiana-Purdue, Fort Wayne. It has long been my personal goal to obtain employment with your organization upon graduation, and now that time has come. I am eager to be considered for this position and confident that I possess the skills and qualities you seek.

I am an accomplished accounting student and leader who has supported herself for three years through employment as the bookkeeper for a small local business. As a result, I know through first-hand experience the needs, concerns and problems of small-business owners as well as the best and most current accounting skills and practices.

My employer, Karen Magnusen of Karen's Corner Market, has offered to talk with you, at your request, about my skills and accomplishments as her employee. Her address and phone number are listed below. My resume, which summarizes both academic achievements and employment experiences, is attached. I will be sitting for the CPA exam on May 10.

The opportunity to be a part of Latham & Jones, offering optimum service to Fort Wayne area small businesses, would be the perfect realization of my first career ambition. At the same time, I could offer you a level of expertise and commitment to service which matches perfectly your company's stated vision and goals.

I look forward to talking with you about this opportunity.

Sincerely,

Shama Chabrha
1813 Atlanta Avenue
Coldwater MI 49036
(313) 555–03037

        Employer: Karen Magnusen, 1099 Pemberton,
        Fort Wayne, IN 46802. Phone: (219) 555–9947

FIGURE 8.10   Sample Cover Letter

June 12, 1993

Tom Petrovsky
President
Media Management, Inc.
263 Solfisburg
Aurora, IL 60136

Dear Mr. Petrovsky,

I am the person you need for the expansion of your business. I have seen samples of your work in *The Beacon Journal* and on Channel 10 and am greatly impressed by their strong innovative edge. I am eager to explore the possibility of joining your firm as advertising assistant.

In your job posting with the placement office at NIU, you requested applicants who are creative, committed leaders and strong communicators. I am all of these and more. My three years of work experience with the university newspaper have given me valuable experience in every aspect of advertising for the print media. My academic experience in the Department of Communication Studies included numerous hands-on experiences with the media of television and radio as well.

Mr. Petrovsky, I know I can provide Media Management, Inc. with a level of industriousness and innovation that will help it grow into the needs and markets of the 21st century. I can both lead and follow. I can listen well, as well as speak. See for yourself: call me. My resume is attached.

Let me help you grow.

Sincerely,

Jonathan J. Thompson
2611 Shipley
DeKalb, IL 60115
(815) 555–7716

FIGURE 8.11   Sample Cover Letter

humor as appropriate, and positive approaches to weaknesses and handicaps.[31] In all cases, and in response to all questions, the interviewee should keep these three needs in mind: (1) the need to present one's self in the best possible light, (2) the need to be honest and accurate in one's presentation of self, and (3) the need to demonstrate genuine interest in the company.

1. **Who are you?** What are your talents, skills and accomplishments? What have you done that you're proud of? What do you most want the interviewer to know about you? (Interviewers want to know who you are at your best.)

2. **Where are you headed?** What are your goals, ambitions, plans? What do you want to accomplish? What do you think you can accomplish in this job, with this company? (Interviewers want to know whether this job and this company are right for you and if it will be able to take you where you want to go.)

3. **What are your limitations, failings or weaknesses?** What are you doing about them? (When they ask these questions, interviewers want to be assured that you are aware of your weaknesses as well as your stengths.)

4. **Will you be happy here?** Have you done your homework? Do you know enough about this company and this job to be fairly sure it is right for you? Are you clear about what you can earn here, and is it enough for you? (The interviewer wants to be assured that you have clear reasons for being there and that you are informed about the company, the job, and the rewards.)

5. **What can you do for this company?** Here again, research into the company is needed in order to be able to tell the interviewer what particular insights and abilities you would bring to this place at this time. (Interviewers want to believe you have the company's needs and interests in mind.)

6. **How do you want this person to remember you?** What can you say about yourself that will make you stand out in this person's memory? People remember stories. What story can you tell about yourself which describes you at your best and will help the interviewer to remember you? (The interviewer wants to be sure you are the best person for the job; help her/him to remember you positively.)

7. **Be specific.** Give concrete examples. The more concrete your examples , the more con–vincing and memorable you will be.

8. **Be brief and concise.** Demonstrate through your responses that you express yourself well and do not waste other people's time.

FIGURE 8.12   Questions and Considerations for Applicants Preparing for Selection Interviews

Preparing Questions to Ask

Nearly every interviewing book, guide, and chapter insists that interviewees in selection interviews *must* ask some questions of the interviewer. Why? Isn't it the interviewer who is trying to obtain decisive information? If interviewees have done their homework about the job and the company, shouldn't all their questions already be answered? What is the purpose of interviewee questions anyway?

Questions do more than obtain information. They also communicate information about the questioner, such as how much is known already about the company or job. Applicant questions can reveal what aspects of the company and job are of the greatest interest to them. Furthermore, questions indicate involvement, interest, assertiveness, and awareness of the reciprocal nature of communication. Good questions are an indication of an active, intelligent mind. Questions also provide job seekers with the opportunity to demonstrate their listening skills. In other words, questions serve many purposes and communicate much more than their verbal content. For all of these reasons, it is important for interviewees to prepare useful, intelligent questions that convey both knowledge and the desire to know more.

Here again, many texts and guides offer lists of suggested questions for applicants. Often, these lists include questions about training programs, professional growth or continuing education opportunities, advancement opportunities, and the structure and day-to-day operations of the organization; and these are all reasonable questions and concerns.

Fundamentally, however, an interviewee's questions should pertain to what she or he really wants to know about the company and/or the position, beyond what was learned from library research, informational interviewing, and networking sources. The applicant might learn, for example, that the company has a mentoring program and want to ask how the program works. An applicant who plans to continue an education will want to know if the company encourages and supports employee education.

Einhorn found that the questions of successful applicants were specific, focused, and covered a wide range of subjects, including questions about company policies and the interviewers' backgrounds.[32] Research by Babbitt and Jablin, on the other hand, found that unsuccessful applicants asked more general or miscellaneous questions, as well as more questions about the expectations and structure of the interview process as opposed to questions about the organization and the job.[33]

As a general rule, there are certain cautions that interviewees should keep in mind as they consider what questions they want to ask. First, questions about salary and benefits are usually best left to the interview in which a concrete job offer is made, unless the interviewer initiates a salary discussion. Interviewees should avoid communicating only selfish interests and concerns through their questions. Salary and benefits questions can suggest a "What can this company do for me?" mentality. Effective applicants ask questions that allow them to reveal ways they can meet the needs of the organization.

Salary needs are real, however, and applicants should discover the salary range for a position before being interviewed, if possible, for two reasons. First, they should be sure before the interview that the salary for the job in question will meet their financial needs. Second, in order to offer reasonable answers to interviewer questions about salary desired, they should have a clear sense of what the company is able and willing to pay.

More broadly, applicants should develop several questions that together indicate genuine interest in the organization and reasonable concerns about one's own career. Additionally, applicants should note and ask questions arising from the interview in response to information the interviewer provides. These spontaneous questions convey an applicant's listening skills and create a genuine sense of dia-

1. _____   Assess personal goals and direction

2. _____   Research companies

    _____ Library research
    _____ Campus placement office
    _____ Information interviews
    _____ Networking

3. _____   Prepare effective resume

    _____ Insure accuracy
    _____ Adapt to specific company and position
    _____ Include all relevant information
    _____ Format appropriately
    _____ Proofread carefully

4. _____   Prepare effective cover letter

    _____ Highlight skills and background
    _____ Demonstrate how these match company needs

5. _____   Prepare answers to anticipated questions

6. _____   Prepare questions to ask of interviewer

FIGURE 8.13   Interviewee Preparation Checklist

logue with the interviewer. Obviously, all interviewee questions should be tactful, nonjudgmental, and clear.

When the anticipation and preparation of questions is complete, the interviewee's preparation for the job hunt is complete as well. In the next chapter, we will consider specific preparations for individual interviews, including appearance, timeliness, and other nonverbal issues. An advance preparation checklist for selection interviewees is provided in Figure 8.13.

Summary

For both interviewer and interviewee, preparation for selection interviewing involves many stages. The interviewer must know both the organization and the specific job for which interviews are being conducted and be informed about all pertinent legal considerations pertaining to selection interviewing and the job in question. Before the actual interviews begin, the interviewer must prepare a job description, advertise and post the position, prepare application forms and other necessary materials, plan the interview process, and prepare an interview guide.

Likewise, interviewee preparation begins with research. The interviewer should learn about the company and the job through library research, informational interviews, campus placement offices, and networking. Interviewees should prepare resumes that are concise, accurate, positive, and that effectively summarize skills, abilities, and accomplishments. Likewise, individualized cover letters, which present a positive first impression and indicate a match between applicant and job, are important. Finally, as part of preliminary preparation, interviewees should prepare and practice answers to anticipated interviewer questions and questions to ask the interviewer. Preliminary preparations by both interviewer and interviewee form the groundwork for the actual interviews, which will be discussed in the next chapter.

Discussion Questions

1. How could a selection interviewer look for the applicant qualities that Staci Munoz recommended in the opening interview of this chapter? What kinds of questions would help an interviewer discover whether a candidate possessed those qualities?

2. As a prospective applicant for employment in an organization, what kinds of information would you want your interviewer to possess and to share with you about the organization and the job?

3. If you were to write a realistic job preview of your current or last job held, what do you feel it would be important for applicants to know? Are there aspects of the job that would seem to make it undesirable to most people?

4. Would you rather be interviewed by an individual or a team? Why?

5. What are the five most desirable qualities of your ideal workplace? Why? Compare with others.

6. What do you think is the purpose of the interviewer question, "Tell me about yourself"? How would you answer it?

Suggested Activities

1. Using what you have learned about office temporary work from the opening interview, the sample job description (Figure 8.2) and the sample applicant evaluation checklist (Figure 8.4), work together with a group of your classmates to create a team-interviewing process designed to find the best candidate for office temporary work. Develop an interview guide to be used in seeking the best candidate for such a job.

2. Choose the name of a national organization or business that interests you as a workplace, but about which you know little. Conduct research into this organization, using the following sources of information: (1) Obtain information about the organization from at least five reference works at a local library. (2) Visit your campus placement office and ask for any information available about the organization. (3) Conduct one information interview, either by phone or in person, with an individual who works for the organization. (4) Check with your network (people you know), asking for names or information about persons who work for the organization of interest. Write a three to five page paper describing your research, what you discovered, and whether the information obtained has strengthened or weakened your interest in the organization.

3. Harry Kaplan is forty-five and has just been laid off after twenty-two years of work at the Camden Motor Corporation. Harry is a high school graduate who went to work for Camden at a time when a college degree was not required for advancement. Over the years, he worked himself up through the ranks of the business, from the factory floor through the drafting department and eventually into plant supervision, first as a floor supervisor and finally as plant manager. Now Camden is closing its plant in Detroit where Harry works, and because Harry has no degree, the company will not transfer him to another of its plants.

   Harry needs a job. For four years, he has been attending school part-time to obtain a degree in manufacturing engineering technology, but he is still nine credits short of an asso-ciate's (two-year) degree. Harry has developed many skills in many facets of the motor business in his years at Camden, but he lacks the academic training to identity himself as either a draftsman, a manufacturing engineer, or a mechanical engineer.

   Harry has come to you for advice on how to look for work. As an individual placement counselor or as a placement team, advise Harry on how to structure his resume, including what to include and where and how to look for work. Give him whatever suggestions you can on how to present himself, what to emphasize, who to contact, and how to do research. When you have finished, compare your advice with other placement counselors or teams and talk about why you made your choices.

Related Readings

Allen, Jeffrey G. *Jeff Allen's Best: The Resume.* New York: John Wiley & Sons, 1990.

Anthony, Rebecca Jesperson, and Roe, Gerald. *Over 40 and Looking for Work?* Holbrook, MA: Bob Adams, Inc., 1991.

Beatty, Richard. *The Resume Kit.* New York: John Wiley & Sons, 1984.

Bolles, Richard N. *What Color is Your Parachute?* Berkeley, CA: Ten Speed Press. New editions are issued annually. Look for the most recent edition.

Bostwick, Burdett E. *111 Techniques and Strategies for Getting the Job Interview.* New York: John Wiley & Sons, 1981.

Dahl, Dan, and Sykes, Randolph. *Charting Your Goals.* New York: Harper & Row, 1988.

Dayhoff, Signe A. *Get the Job You Want.* Acton, MA: Brick House Publishing, 1990.

Einhorn, Lois; Bradley, Patricia Hayes; and Baird, John, E., Jr. *Effective Employment Interviewing: Unlocking Human Potential.* Glenview, IL: Scott, Foresman, and Company, 1982. [This book is no longer in print, but is available in many libraries.]

Fry, Ronald W. *Your First Resume,* 2nd ed. Hawthorne, NJ: Career Press, 1989.

The Guide to Basic Resume Writing. A publication of the Job and Career Information Services Committee of the Adult Lifelong Learning Section, Public Library and American Library Associations. Lincolnwood, IL: VGM Career Horizons, 1991.

Jackson, Tom. *The Perfect Resume.* New York: Doubleday, 1990.

Johnson, Willis L., ed. *Directory of Special Programs for Minority Group Members.* Garrett Park, MD: Garrett Park Press, 1990.

King, Julie Adair, and Shelson, Betsy. *The Smart Woman's Guide to Resumes and Job Hunting.* Hawthorne, NJ: The Career Press, 1991.

Lathrop, Richard. *Who's Hiring Who?* 12th ed. Berkeley, CA: Ten Speed Press, 1989.

Nivens, Beatryce. *The Black Woman's Career Guide.* New York: Doubleday, 1987.

Parker, Yana. *The Damn Good Resume Guide.* Berkeley, CA: Ten Speed Press, 1986.

Parker, Yana. *The Resume Catalog.* Berkeley, CA: Ten Speed Press, 1988.

Strasser, Stephen, and Sena, John. *From Campus to Corporations.* Hawthorne, NJ: The Career Press, 1990.

Tepper, Ron. *Power Resumes.* 2nd ed. New York: John Wiley & Sons, 1992.

Wegmann, Robert, and Chapman, Robert. *The Right Place at the Right Time: Finding a Job in the 1990s,* rev. ed. Berkeley, CA: Ten Speed Press, 1990.

Endnotes

1. Victor Lindquist, "The Northwestern Lindquist-Endicott Report," Evanston, IL: The Northwestern University Placement Center, 1988.

2. Calvin Downs, "Perceptions of the Selection Interview," *Personnel Administration 32* (1969).

3. Richard L. Street, "Interaction Processes and Outcomes in Interviews," *Communication Yearbook* 1985, 217.

4. James E. Campion, and Richard D. Arvey, "Unfair Discrimination in the Employment Interview," Robert W. Eder, and Gerald R. Ferris, eds., *The Employment Interview: Theory, Research and Practice* (Newbury Park: Sage Publications, 1988), 217.

5. As reported in Richard D. Arvey, and James E. Campion, "The Employment Interview: A Summary and Review of Recent Research," *Personnel Psychology 35,* (1982), 308.

6. Bruce Horovitz, "Cut the Baloney Out of Job Previews," *Industry Week,* (October 31, 1983), 66.

7. G.M. McEvoy, and Wayne F. Cascio, "Strategies for Reducing Employee Turnover: A Meta-Analysis," *Journal of Applied Psychology,* (May, 1985), 342–53. As reported in John M. Ivancevich, *Human Resource Management: Foundations of Personnel,* 5th ed. (Homewood, IL: Irwin, 1992), 229.

8. John M. Ivancevich, *Human Resource Management: Foundations of Personnel,* 5th ed. (Homewood, IL: Irwin, 1992), 782–3.

9. James E. Campion, and Richard D. Arvey, (1988), 62.

10. James E. Campion, and Richard D. Arvey, (1988), 66–67.

11. Judith A. DeLapa, "Job Descriptions that Work," *Personnel Journal,* (June 1989), 156. As reported in Lloyd L. Byars, and Leslie W. Rue, *Human Resource Management,* 3rd ed. (Homewood, IL: Irwin, 1991), 91.

12. Ivancevich (1992), A25. See also Byars and Rue (1991), 527 and Randall S. Schuler, *Effective Personnel Management* (St. Paul: West Publishing Company, 1983), G–7.

13. David Jamieson, and Julie O'Mara, *Managing Workforce 2000: Gaining the Diversity Advantage* (San Francisco: Jossey-Bass Publishers, 1991), 49–50.

14. John M. Ivancevich, (1992), 221.

15. Stephen Strasser, and John Sena, *From Campus to Corporations* (Hawthorne, NJ: The Career Press, 1990), 45.

16. Richard Nelson Bolles, *The 1992 What Color Is Your Parachute? A Practical Manual for Job-Hunters & Career-Changers* (Berkeley, CA: Ten Speed Press, 1992), 129.

17. Bolles (1992), 31.

18. Lois Bradley Einhorn, Patricia Hayes, and John E. Baird, Jr. *Effective Employment Interviewing: Unlocking Human Potential* (Glenview, IL: Scott, Foresman and Company, 1982), 34.

19. Bolles (1992), 41.

20. Bolles (1992), 15.

21. Bolles (1992), 17.

22. David Swanson, *The Resume Solution* (Indianapolis: JIST Works Inc., 1991), 4.

23. Edward Rogers, "Elements of Efficient Job Hunting," *Journal of College Placement 40,* (Fall, 1979), 55–58.

24. See, for example, Ronald W. Fry, *Your 1st Resume,* 2nd ed. (Hawthorne, NJ: Career Press, 1989), Richard Beatty, *The Resume Kit* (New York: John Wiley & Sons, 1984) and *The Guide to Basic Resume Writing* (Lincolnwood, IL: VGM Career Horizons, 1991), a publication of the Job and Career Information Services

Committee of the Adult Lifelong Learning Section, Public Library and American Library Associations.

25. See, for example, Ron Tepper, *Power Resumes,* 2nd ed. (New York: John Wiley & Sons, 1992) and Bolles (1992), 173–181.

26. *The Guide to Basic Resume Writing* (1991), 61–64.

27. Strasser and Sena (1990), 50–59.

28. Rebecca Jesperson Anthony, and Gerald Roe, *Over 40 and Looking for Work?* (Holbrook, MA: Bob Adams, Inc., 1991), 149–151.

29. Burdette E. Bostwick, *111 Techniques and Strategies for Getting the Job Interview* (New York: John Wiley & Sons, 1990), 246–251.

30. Bolles (1992), 188–89.

31. Cheryl Hamilton, with Cordell Parker, *Communicating for Results: A Guide for Business and the Professions,* 3rd ed. (Belmont, CA: Wadsworth Publishing Company, 1990), 237.

32. Lois Einhorn, "An Inner View of the Job Interview: An Investigation of Successful Communicative Behaviors," *Communication Education 30,* (July, 1981), 223–4.

33. Laurie V. Babbitt, and Fredric M. Jablin, "Characteristics of Applicants' Questions and Employment Screening Interview Outcomes," *Human Communication Research 11,* No. 4, (Summer 1985), 529.

Chapter 9

The Selection Interview

*"Hire people who are better than you are, then leave
them to get on with it. . . . Look for people who will aim
for the remarkable, who will not settle for the routine."*
—David Ogilvy as quoted in William
Safire and Leonard Safir, Leadership
(New York: Simon & Schuster, 1990), 111.

Kenneth Cliborn arrived at the offices of Canterbury School, a parochial elementary school in Evanston, Illinois, at 2:00 P.M. on June 2. Kenneth had an appointment with Dr. Malachi Nash, the principal, to be interviewed for a position as science teacher for the upper grades. Kenneth had submitted a resume in response to a newspaper ad the week before and was called by Dr. Nash's secretary, who scheduled the appointment. Kenneth was dressed in a business suit and carried a briefcase. Dr. Nash stepped out of his inner office to greet Kenneth.

Cliborn: Dr. Nash? Hi, I'm Kenneth Cliborn.

Nash: Hello. Welcome. Please come in and have a seat. Make yourself comfortable.

Cliborn: Thanks.

(Kenneth seats himself in a chair in front of Dr. Nash's desk. Nash takes his seat behind the desk.)

Nash: So, Mr. Cliborn, what interests you about our little school?

Cliborn: Well, sir, to tell you the truth, I don't know much about it, other than what was in the ad in the paper. It looks nice, though, from what I can see.

Nash: And what is it that appeals to you about teaching science here?

Cliborn: Well, science was my major, of course—actually, physical science, but I took a lot of other things, too—you know, chemistry, physics, biology, microbiology. And I like to teach.

Nash: Do you have teaching experience?

Cliborn: Uh, yes. Did you get my resume?

Nash: Yes, I did, but I don't believe in hiring from resumes. I like to hear people talk about their experiences firsthand.

Cliborn: Oh. Well. I've got plenty of teaching experience, that's for sure.

Nash: Tell me about it.

Cliborn: Well, I taught at Custer Military Academy for four years right out of college—that's in South Dakota. Then I went to the St. Charles Boys' School for six years, and then to a place called Shriver Academy in Galena, Illinois. I was there for two and one-half years.

Nash: Are you currently employed?

Cliborn: Well, since January I've been selling science equipment to schools in the Midwest, but I'm hoping to get back into teaching again.

Nash: Can you tell me something about why you left Shriver mid-year? That is what happened, isn't it?

Cliborn: (nodding) Well, sir, in all honesty, I was let go.

Nash: Was there a problem with your work there that would be a concern related to your working here?

Cliborn: No, sir, I don't think so. To be truthful, the principal and I did not see eye to eye, and it got so I didn't feel I could really teach the kids there as I thought I should.

Nash: Tell me more about it.

Cliborn: Well, you see, sir, I think that to really teach science to kids, you have to make it alive for them. You know what I mean? I mean, I like taking kids into the lab or out in the field most days and giving them experiments to run, ideas to test, problems to solve—that kind of thing. I don't think kids appreciate science, what it means, the scientific method and all that, unless they can dive right in and test it for themselves. Then, when they're done with the hands-on stuff, I have them write up their findings and compare them, and we talk together about what we learned.

Nash: What you describe is very much like our preferred approach to learning here at Canterbury.

Cliborn: Is it really? I'm glad to hear that. I mean, I was hoping I'd find a place that understood my problem at Shriver. And my philosophy.

Nash: Please finish your story.

Cliborn: Well, Mr. Ditmer couldn't understand what we were doing outside all the time, or making explosions in the lab, you know. He had this idea that effective learning has to be quiet, with kids sitting in neat rows and with the teacher doing all the talking. So he'd come by my classroom and see what looked to him like chaos when it was just the messy excitement of scientific discovery. And I kept pushing for a bigger budget so we could do more in the lab and take field trips and stuff, and he wouldn't support me because he didn't think I was really working.

Nash: So you left then?

Cliborn: Well, as I said, he let me go—sent me packing, in fact. But it was my fault, really. I wanted to approach the board for money to take my eighth-graders to Kettle-Moraine State Park in Wisconsin, you know, to see first-hand how receding glaciers rolled some valleys into the earth. There was a meeting coming up, and I wanted to ask for money to take the kids on a camping field trip there in the spring. He wouldn't support me—in fact, he told me I couldn't go to the meeting. So I lost my temper and yelled some things, said he was standing in the way of learning, stuff like that. . . . He fired me, right there on the spot. It was my fault. So now I'm selling the equipment I couldn't get him to buy—I miss teaching, though.

Nash: Well, Mr. Cliborn, we don't have a lot of money here, but we do invite the spirit of discovery. Maybe you'd like to see our lab?

Cliborn: I sure would!

(The two men stood to leave the office.)

Cliborn: I hope what I've told you about Shriver doesn't ruin my chance of being considered for a job here.

Nash: Well, Mr. Cliborn, I'd have to say that, while I admire your candor, as a principal I'm not too keen on having my teachers losing their tempers and yelling at me.

Cliborn: Oh.

Nash: On the other hand, I confess I've lost my temper and done some yelling myself on more than one occasion—most recently at our departing science teacher.

Cliborn: Why? Did he want more money?

Nash: No, that wasn't it. It was because he wouldn't take the kids outside or into the lab. All he wanted to do was lecture at them all day.

(Cliborn smiled broadly.)

Cliborn: Well, sir, I assure you, you wouldn't have that problem with me!

Chapter Goals

- To explore the elements of selection interviewing from the points of view of interviewers and interviewees.
- To understand the preparation needed for the selection interview and the behavior required of interviewers during the selection interview.
- To appreciate the participatory responsibilities and desirable behaviors of interviewees in the selection interview process.

Introduction

Hiring—and being hired—is risky business. For both interviewers and interviewees, important, potentially long-term, and costly decisions are involved. If the interview process is successful and a match takes place, then the many hours of preparation, advertising and interviewing will have been well spent. If the process is unsuccessful, however, a great deal of time and money will be lost in the process of hiring, training, losing or firing, and hiring again. A study of employee turnover at J.C. Penney, for example, found that a program reducing employee turnover by 429 persons saved the company $6,000,000, not including the costs of training and recruitment. A program of interviewer training at Penney's reduced employee turnover by 19.3 percent.[1]

In the meantime, when employees leave, important positions are left unfilled. As a result, the productivity of the business can be seriously affected. The "interview [is] the most widely used method of evaluating job candidates despite a long history of research findings suggesting it is among the least reliable and valid predictors of job behavior."[2] Clearly, there are benefits to be gained through training and careful preparation.

For interviewees, too, selection interviewing is risky and costly. Hours of preparation and planning are involved, as well as travel and numerous expenses, including postage, printing of resumes, and clothing purchases. In addition, selection interviewing is emotionally and psychologically taxing, because the odds of being refused for a job are higher than those for being hired. According to Richard Bolles, author Tom Jackson created this accurate visual depiction of the odds of rejection in job hunting:[3]

> *NO NO NO NO NO NO NO NO NO NO NO NO NO NO*
> *NO NO NO NO NO NO NO NO NO NO NO NO NO NO*
> *NO NO NO NO NO NO NO NO NO NO NO NO NO NO*
> *NO NO NO NO NO NO NO NO NO NO NO NO NO YES*

For most people, rejection is a difficult experience under any circumstances. It makes sense that the rejections involved in job hunting are particularly painful, both because so much is at stake and because the persons experiencing the rejection have presumably presented themselves at their best.

Because the process of selection interviewing is risky and costly for both parties, it is even more important for both parties to learn to do it well. Those who do not, whether interviewer or interviewee, stand to lose either the best applicants to other jobs or the best jobs to other applicants. In either case, they compound their costs and risks tremendously.

In this chapter, we will engage in a step-by-step exploration of the selection interview, first from the point of view of the interviewer and then from the point of view of the applicant, or interviewee. Beginning with a discussion of goals for selection interviews, we will examine the final preparations of the interviewer and the factors involved in conducting the interview, including questions to ask and to avoid and useful probes. We will explore team interviewing, the interview closing, and the process of evaluation and notification of candidates after the interview is done.

Turning our attention to interviewees in selection interviews, we will discuss nonverbal communication and the importance of impression management. We will consider the verbal communication skills involved in answering interviewer questions and in asking one's own questions of the interviewer. Last, we will recommend closing and follow-up strategies for the interviewee.

Goals of Selection Interviews

What can be said about the goals of selection interviews? Isn't it obvious? The interviewer wants to fill a job, and the interviewee wants to find one. Certainly, these are the primary goals of interviewer and interviewee in the selection interviewing process.

In their synthesis and history of employment interview research, Eder, Kacmar and Ferris define the selection interview in this way: "The employment interview is defined as a face-to-face exchange of job-relevant information between organizational representatives and a job applicant with the overall organizational goal of attracting, selecting, and retaining a highly competent workforce." We would add to this one-sided definition the goal of the applicant to find a suitable job and an organization. Clearly, these are the dominant goals of the selection interview exchange.

But both parties to the process have secondary goals as well. For example, interviewers also seek to sell their companies to those outside. Ideally, they want even those who are not hired to perceive the organization positively. In fact, the entire category of recruitment interviews, as they are typically conducted at colleges and universities, exist more for the purpose of selling the company than for actually screening applicants.[5] Likewise, applicants often participate in selection interviews to learn about the company and/or as a means of honing their interviewing skills, in addition to or instead of actually pursuing a particular job at that moment in time.

In any case, however, both parties are involved in an elaborate process of impression management wherein they seek to present themselves (and, for interviewers, their companies as well) in the best possible light. It is possible to describe the interview itself as having goals conforming to a standard cultural norm, or script, of how a selection interview should unfold. A **script** can be defined as any fixed set or sequence of events that come to be expected in certain interpersonal encounters.[6]

For example, in encounters between customers and servers in a restaurant, there are scripted expectations that the server will take the customers' orders, bring the food and drink to their tables, and bring the check without much actual involvement or participation in the customers' meal. It would not be acceptable within this standard script for a server to pull up a chair and join the customers at the table. Likewise, the customer/server script requires the customer to be seated, look at a menu, place an order, eat a meal, pay the tab, and leave the restaurant. It would be a violation of this script for the customer to go into the kitchen to find out why the food is taking so long to prepare (however tempting it may sometimes be to do so) or to get up and bring water to another table.

The selection interview can also be described as a highly scripted encounter because expectations on both sides about what should happen in the interview and in what order are fairly standard. Tullar summarizes the selection interview script in scenes, or stages, with certain expected behaviors for both parties in each scene, as shown in Figure 9.1. In every scene of the selection interview, both par-

Scene	Applicant Actions	Interviewer Actions
Before the interview	Check appearance Arrive promptly Review notes	Review resume and interview guide Prepare setting
Interview opening	Shake hands Sit when invited Manage initial impression	Shake hands Invite applicant to sit Establish rapport with small talk
Interview body	Give academic background Give work history Discuss skills and abilities Show enthusiasm for the job	Ask academic background Ask for relevant work history Seek skills and abilities Explore applicant's motivation to work
Interview closing	Ask relevant questions Emphasize strengths Wait for cues to close Stand and shake hands Exit	Answer questions Represent company well Introduce closure Explain follow up Stand and shake hands Show the way out

FIGURE 9.1   Selection Interview: Standard Script

Adapted from: Tullar, William L., "The Employment Interview as a Cognitive Performing Script," in Eder, Robert W. and Ferris, Gerald R., eds., *The Employment Interview: Theory, Research, and Practice* (Newbury Park, CA: Sage Publications, 1988), 239. Used with permission.

A successful interview contributes to both parties meeting goals.

ties have certain goals, the attainment of which will lead to the successful completion of the interview.

The various goals of interviewer and interviewee involve mutual persuasion by both parties. The interviewer seeks to persuade applicants of the desirability of the organization and the job. The applicant seeks to persuade the interviewer of her/his suitability for the position in question. In both cases, the parties do more than just exchange information—each wants to exercise some influence over the other's perceptions.

The measure of the success of a selection interview is not as clear-cut as it seems. There is a tendency to view only those interviews that result in a hire as successful interviews, or better still, only those interviews that result in the interviewer finding the ideal applicant at the same time that the applicant finds an ideal place to work. If this were the only measure, there would be few successful interviews.

A successful interview, however, could be one in which an applicant discovers, before taking a job, that it is not at all the kind of work or company desired. The interview has successfully clarified for the applicant that he or she does not want the job and has therefore spared the interviewer the costs and difficulties associated with hiring someone who will not stay. Alternatively, a successful interview might be one in which an interviewer discovers that an applicant whose paper credentials seemed ideal is unsuited for the work in question or has misrepresented her/his training and experience.

Finding the best candidate or the best job involves ruling out poorly matched candidates and jobs. A successful interview, therefore, is one that contributes to the process of either party meeting goals. The better prepared the parties to a selection interview are, the greater the likelihood that one or both parties will obtain the information needed in order to make the best possible decision about the applicant, company, or job.

The Interviewer in the Selection Interview

Final Preparations

Why begin the interview fully prepared? The reasons are compelling. In the first place, abundant research exists that the reliability and validity of the interview as a predictor of job success is quite low, but that both reliability and validity are higher when an interview is structured; that is, prepared, planned and somewhat standardized in form.[7] Dreher, Ash, and Hancock write, "Generations of managers and staffing specialists have been confronted with pessimistic evidence regarding the validity of the employment interview, and yet the use of the interview persists."[8] These authors go on to suggest that there are wide ability and rating differences between interviewers and that research is needed to examine and account for these differences.[9] Careful preparation can ensure that selection interviews are successful.

Goodale states, "There can be little doubt that unstructured interviews are doomed to failure. Many contributors . . . have cited evidence that unstructured employment interviews produce low reliability and validity. In addition, [unstructured interviews] enable interviewers to confirm their own biases, stereotypes, and first impressions . . . and are therefore subject to charges of unfair discrimination."[10] Goodale also describes the interviewing problems "consistently raised" by even trained, experienced interviewers: (1) lack of clarity about information needed and how to ask for it, especially without violating EEO requirements; (2) how to see past one's own biases; (3) uncertainty about how to question and/or respond to certain types of applicants and applicant responses; and (4) lack of clarity about how to reach a hiring decision.[11]

Each of the problems mentioned above can be eased by careful preparation. For example, there is evidence that selection interviewers who rate candidates on specific job-related characteristics can accurately distinguish between more qualified and less qualified persons, with greater agreement among interviewers.[12] Additionally, interview effectiveness increases with the interviewer's knowledge and understanding of the job being filled, which is a clear indication of the desirability of interviewer preparedness.[13] Evidence also suggests that interviewers prepared sufficiently to offer adequate information improve the likelihood that applicants will perceive companies favorably and accept employment with them.[14]

Another research effort found that agreement among multiple interviewers increases when interviews are structured and that panel or team interviews produce more reliable results.[15] Perhaps the increased reliability of multiple interviewer approaches stems from the ability of multiple perceptions to rule out the most skewed or biased perceptions, as some authors suggest.[16] It is also possible, however, that the use of panel or team interviews results in more careful structuring of the interviews.

In addition to the kind of long-range interviewer preparation discussed in the last chapter, the successful interviewer will engage in essential final preparations in advance of each specific applicant interview. These preparations include reviewing the job description, making decisions about how a candidate's written application and resume will be evaluated, and making decisions about controllable nonverbal aspects of the interview. Let's look at each of these specific final preparations in turn.

Reviewing the Job Description. A careful review of the job description prior to beginning actual interviews benefits the interviewer in several ways. First, the interviewer can refresh and clarify an understanding of the job in order to be able to answer applicant questions accurately. Second, the interviewer can recheck the prepared interview guide in relation to the job description in order to insure the accuracy, suitability, sufficiency, and job relatedness of the prepared questions. Also, the clearer the understanding of the specific needs and characteristics of the job, the greater the likelihood that the best candidate will be selected.[17]

Reviewing Candidate Applications and Resumes. The issue of prior assessment of applications and resumes raises difficult questions for the interviewer. Review of applicant credentials and development of interview questions based on them are standard procedures in selection interviews. Often applicant credentials are reviewed twice, once as a means to decide who will be interviewed and a second time to become familiar with applicant backgrounds and frame relevant questions. Abundant evidence exists, however, that impressions formed by prior examination of written materials exert a strong biasing effect on interviewer judgments of applicants.

According to Eder, Kacmar, and Ferris, mental judgments formed by interviewers after examining applicant resumes and application materials seem to "predetermine" the outcome of selection interviews.[18] In a comparative study of the relative impact of verbal behavior, nonverbal behavior, and resume credentials on selection interview outcomes, Rasmussen found that resume credentials had the greatest impact.[19] Research by Dipboye, Stramler, and Fontenelle found that initial interviewer impressions of poorly written credentials resulted in subsequent recall of fewer favorable characteristics of applicants during interviews.

These authors also found that negative impressions of credentials led to negative judgments of applicant performance in answering interviewer questions.[20] Macan and Dipboye found that the questions interviewers asked of applicants with poor credentials were more negatively biased than those asked of other applicants.[21] In yet another experiment, Dipboye, Fontenelle, and Garner found that interviewers who did not preview paper credentials of applicants made more reliable assessments of applicant fit to job and applicant performance in the interview, while interviewers who previewed credentials increased the amount of accurate additional information obtained.[22]

Clearly, though there are benefits to prior examination of interviewee credentials, the risk of interviewer bias as a result of prior review is substantial. Interviewer impressions of applicants based on paper credentials tend to bias assessment in actual interviews. Interviewers tend to see and hear in the interview what they have already decided is true about the applicant. Some researchers further speculate that these impressions become self-fulfilling prophecies for applicants, who proceed to perform "up or down" to interviewer expectations.[23] At the least, as one researcher put it, "whatever information occurs first has a disproportionate influence on the final outcome of interviews."[24]

At the same time, prior review of credentials seems to have some value to the information-gathering process. In any case it is standard procedure for most selection interviewers. Dipboye, Stramler, and Fontenelle conclude their study of preinterview bias in this way: "One obvious solution, which professional interviewers are likely to resist, is to interview candidates and evaluate their performance in the interview before examining paper credentials. A more realistic solution, which should be assessed in future research, is to train interviewers to form hypotheses on the basis of paper credentials and use the interview to test these hypotheses."[25] In other words, interviewers should acknowledge their judgments based on paper credentials and use them as ideas to be tested in the interview, rather than as impressions solidly formed.

In the face of research evidence about preinterview bias, what should an interviewer do? There are no absolute answers to this question. However, on the basis of existing research, it is possible to offer several specific recommendations for interviewers to consider.

First, interviewers should be aware of the reality of preinterview bias based on examination of paper credentials and strive for conscious awareness of their impressions, keeping in mind that they are impressions only and not proven truths about the person. Also, interviewers should be aware of interview bias based on ideal stereotpyes. Several research studies have found that interviewers possess stereotypical "ideal images" of successful applicants against which they measure and evaluate the real applicants they interview.[26] The more idealized and unrealistic the stereotype, the harder it is to accurately assess applicant suitability. Interviewers must be aware of their "ideal applicant images" and be willing to set them aside in face of the real candidates they encounter.

Second, interviewers should strive to frame their impressions as questions to address in the interview, thereby testing them for accuracy. The very act of framing impressions or judgments as questions moves them from the realm of fixed assessments into the more tentative realm of ideas to be examined. The interviewer needs to make every possible effort to remain tentative in judgments until all available information, including the interview itself, has been obtained.

Third, the interviewer should compare an applicant's credentials to the exact needs of the job description, looking for specific areas of fit as well as gaps in desired experience or knowledge. Does the applicant meet the stated requirements for the job? If not, what equivalent experience or training may make her/him suitable? The degree of "match" between stated requirements and actual applicant qualifications should be noted on the candidate evaluation forms used to rate applicants when the interviews are complete.

Fourth, interviewers can consider ways to distance themselves from preinterview bias based on paper credentials by distancing themselves from the credentials themselves. For example, if time permits, an interviewer could examine application materials several days before the interviews are scheduled to be conducted and develop specific, nonjudgmental questions for each applicant on the basis of information provided. Furthermore, the interviewer should bring only credentials-based questions, and not the credentials themselves, to the interviews. Distancing themselves from the paper credentials of applicants may allow interviewers to ask about important substantive matters without being unduly influenced by other impressions of the credentials.

Awareness of the reality of preinterview bias, testing of one's judgments, assessment of credentials through comparison to actual job descriptions, and creating some distance between credentials review and the actual interview process may help interviewers to make effective use of application materials in advance of the interviews themselves.

Evaluating Candidate Applications and Resumes. What methods should interviewers employ in order to evaluate credentials fairly and accurately? First, the interviewer should carefully compare the information provided on the application materials with the needs of the job as expressed in the job description. Does the candidate meet the stated requirements for the job in terms of education, years of experience, types of experience, and so forth? Does the candidate appear to possess the technical and other skills necessary to do the job well? If the candidate does not meet certain requirements, what specific questions can be asked to determine whether he or she has equivalent training or experience which would satisfy the job requirements in other ways? With the job description in hand, the interviewer should examine all available applicant information with the goal of answering this basic question: Does this individual have the knowledge, skills, and experience necessary to do the job? A simple checklist of job requirements and degree of match (see Figure 9.2) can be created and completed for each applicant. If certain tests or licenses are required for the position, the interviewer can check at this point to be sure all such requirements have been met.

Next, the interviewer should study available credentials for information that gives rise to job-related concerns about the applicant. For example, does the

Position being filled: Plant Manager, Schneider Electrical Systems

Applicant name: Jeanette Klein

Degree of match scoring: 3 = Exact Match
2 = Acceptable match
1 = Possible or questionable match
0 = Poor or no match

Job requirements:	Applicant Match:	Score:
B.S., Engineering or related degree	B.S., Manufacturing Systems Technology	2
Five years managerial experience	2 yrs. plant mgr. 2 yrs. shift foreman	1
Same or related field	Appliance motors	1
Union shop: Int'l Brotherhood of Electrical Workers	Yes: International Union of Electronic. . . (IUE)	2
Just-in-time inventory control system experience	Yes: similar system	3
Industrial robotics experience	Yes: Robotic assembly of electrical controls	3

Total match score: 12/18

Scores of other applicants
to be interviewed for the position: 10, 12, 12, 15

FIGURE 9.2   Sample Checklist for Matching Job Description to Applicant Credentials

resume indicate a job history that includes numerous jobs held for less than six months? Such a record may give rise to realistic concerns about whether this individual will stay with a job long enough to justify the costs of training. Observing such a work history, the interviewer may decide to ask: "I noticed on your resume that you haven't held a job for longer than six months in the last three years. Is there anything about this employment pattern that should be of concern to me as I consider whether to hire you?"

Likewise, if application materials are vague or confusing about dates and places of work, the interviewer should note areas of concern and ask for specific clarifications during the interview. If an applicant lists two places of work with overlapping time periods, the interviewer might ask: "According to your resume, you worked at both Lakeview Ranch and at Kustom Kitchen during 1990–92. Tell me how that worked."

Third, the interviewer should contact each of the references provided. In order to do so, the interviewer must be aware of the legal aspects of reference checking and should have a clear plan for handling reference checks. **Reference checking** is the systematic process of contacting former employers and/or other references whose names are provided by the applicant for the purposes of verifying employment records and obtaining job-related information about the applicant's work or academic history.

In recent years, reference checking has been made more complicated by the passage of various state and federal laws pertaining to the rights to privacy of individuals. At the federal level, the chief privacy laws that affect reference checking are the Fair Credit Reporting Act, the Privacy Act of 1974, the Family Education Rights and Privacy Act (also known as the Buckley Amendment), and the Freedom of Information Act.[27] While most of these federal laws do not pertain directly to private businesses and organizations, various court decisions regarding these laws, as well as various state laws, have extended legal concerns about violation of privacy into the private sector. For example, a Supreme Court decision in 1977, *Whalen v. Roe,* emphasized that the Constitution protects ". . . the individual interest in avoiding disclosure of personal matters. . . ."[28]

With regard to state laws, the degree of protection afforded to individuals differs greatly. According to Marshall, limitations on employers checking applicant backgrounds vary widely from states such as Colorado, for example, in which private companies amass information from an eleven-state area for employers to access, to Virginia, where notarized consent from applicants is required, to California, which allows no searches for California employers.[29] Marshall suggests that legal notions of privacy are still in the process of being defined.

A chart, indicating the number of states having privacy laws governing employment information as of 1988, is provided in Figure 9.3.

As a result of increased legal protection of personal privacy and because of the variety and disparity of state laws, many employers, especially those with offices in several states, have developed fixed policies limiting the information their employees can reveal in reference checks. Many times, former employers will share only such information as dates of prior employment.

Nonetheless, the responsibility of the interviewer preparing to interview an applicant is to engage in a careful check of the references and job histories provided, obtaining whatever job-related information is available. Interviewers should become informed about all relevant state and federal laws affecting reference checks, as well as company guidelines concerning what to ask and/or to reveal. Interviewers should obtain written consent from applicants giving permission to check with references or former employers. References provided by applicants on resumes or application forms do not require additional written consent.

Many reference checks are conducted by phone. However, due to the existing climate of legal concern about privacy issues, preparation and use of a standard-

State	Laws Protecting Employment Records	Laws Concerning Testing in Employment
Alabama		x
Alaska		x
Arizona		x
Arkansas		x
California	x	x
Colorado		x
Connecticut	x	x
Delaware	x	
Dist. Columbia	x	
Florida	x	
Hawaii	x	
Illinois	x	
Iowa	x	x
Maine	x	
Maryland	x	
Massachusetts	x	
Michigan	x	
Minnesota		x
Montana		x
Nevada	x	
New Hampshire	x	
New York	x	
North Carolina	x	
Ohio	x	
Oregon	x	x
Pennsylvania	x	
Rhode Island	x	x
South Dakota	x	
Tennessee	x	
Utah	x	x
Vermont	x	x
Washington	x	
Wisconsin	x	

FIGURE 9.3 States Having Privacy Laws Governing Employment Records as of 1988

Adapted from: Smith, Robert Ellis, *Compilation of State and Federal Privacy Laws*, 1988, p. 2. As reported and reprinted in Marshall, Patrick G., "Your Right to Privacy," *Editorial Research Reports 1* (January 20, 1989), No. 3, pp. 30–42, reprinted in *Social Issues Research Series: Privacy* (Boca Raton, FL) Vol. 4, Article 21. Used with permission.

ized reference check form that includes the signature of the applicant is more likely to obtain detailed information if time permits. A sample of such a reference form is found in Figure 9.4.

Interviewers should ask former employers only job-related questions or questions to verify informational details provided by applicants. For example, most employers are willing to verify dates of employment, job titles, and time in positions. In addition, promotions, attendance record, and reason for termination may also be provided. Again, however, what information a former employer will provide varies according to company guidelines and the way in which the information is requested.

Conducting the Selection Interview

Finally, the interviewer is ready to conduct individual candidate interviews. In the course of these interviews, the interviewer must manage nonverbal considerations, especially during the opening phase of the interview; ask questions to obtain necessary information; probe for completeness and accuracy of information; protect the applicants' civil rights; coordinate the team interview process if one is used; close the interview effectively; and evaluate the applicant's suitability for the position.

Attending to Nonverbal Considerations in the Interview.   Ensuring a private, distraction-free, and comfortable setting for the interview is essential. Relevant nonverbal issues with regard to setting should be decided in advance, following guidelines recommended in earlier chapters.

In addition to the environmental aspects of the interview setting, the interviewer should be aware of the importance of nonverbal communication to the actual conduct of the interview. A warm handshake and a smile, paralanguage that is sincere and expressive, and sustained and affirming eye contact will do much to help the applicant to feel at ease. Interviewers who gesture, nod, maintain eye contact, and smile frequently are perceived more favorably by interviewees and encourage positive interviewee behaviors.[31] Also, as indicated earlier, the interviewer's performance in the interview affects applicant perceptions of the company.

Likewise, the interviewer should be aware of the possible impact of an applicant's nonverbal cues, including dress and other nonverbal messages, on the assessment of the individual's abilities. Some authors suggest that interviewers tend to hire "in their own image," looking for candidates who resemble themselves in appearance and dress.[32] If this is so, candidates who differ from the interviewer in gender, race, ethnicity, or style are at a distinct disadvantage. Interviewers must take care to guard against bias and to seek the best match for the position, regardless of whether the applicant is a visual or nonverbal mirror image of themselves.

TO:

Name of Former Employer or Reference

Address

     I,   <u>Name of Applicant</u>, give my permission to

           <u>Name of Interviewer</u>

           <u>Name of Company</u>

           <u>Phone Number of Company</u>

           <u>Address of Company</u>

to use the attached reference verification form in order to obtain necessary job-related information about my skills and experiences. Please cooperate with this company and its representative by providing the information requested below. I waive my right to privacy regarding the job-related information requested below.

        _____

        Signature of Applicant

        Address of Applicant

        Phone Number of Applicant

        Date: _____

Please provide the following information about the individual whose consent is indicated above.

1. Dates of employment: From   To

2. Job titles during employment and time held in each position:

    Title: Dates:

    Title: Dates:

    Title: Dates:

3. Please underline any of the above positions which were obtained as a result of a promotion.

4. How would you evaluate the attendance record of this individual while he or she was in your employ: (circle one)

    Excellent   Very Good   Good   Fair   Poor

5. What additional job-related information can you provide about this individual which might be helpful to us in our search for the best candidate for the position of _____?
(Use the back of this form or attach a separate sheet if more room is needed for your reply.)

Thank you for your assistance. Please return this form in the attached envelope to the company address provided above.

FIGURE 9.4 Sample Reference and Former Employer Verification Form

Asking Questions to Obtain Necessary Information.   An information classification system developed by Hellervik categorizes interview information into four categories: (1) objective verifiable credentials, (2) descriptions by applicants of duties, skill areas, and responsibilities, (3) opinions, including responses to hypothetical questions and self-perceptions, and (4) detailed descriptions by the applicant of actual past behaviors.[33] While much objective verifiable information comes from applicant written credentials, the other types of information must be obtained through the interview.

Most of the questions asked by selection interviewers rest on two fundamental premises: first, that an applicant's past performance and behavior is predictive of future performance; and, second, that an applicant's performance in a selection interview is predictive of performance in the workplace.[34] To predict applicant success accurately on the basis of the interview, the interviewer asks questions designed to obtain information not available in written materials that will indicate past, current, and future performance.

Interviewing texts abound with lists of questions asked by employers. Here are some examples of the kinds of questions often included in these lists:

Tell me about yourself.

What are your strengths/weaknesses?

Tell me about an important past accomplishment.

What are your career goals?

Why do you want to work for us?

What do you know about our company?

How have past work experiences prepared you for this job?

Typical question areas usually include work and academic experiences, specialized training, career goals, knowledge of the job and the organization, strengths and weaknesses, and salary history or salary needs.

Always, the interviewer's questions must be job related. Questions asked must have a defensible connection to the job for which the applicant is applying. Not all of these connections may be direct or obvious to applicants. For example, a student might ask, "What does my GPA have to do with whether or not I'll be a good child care aide?" The answer is tied to the first premise; namely, that past performance is predictive of future success. A student with a high GPA is thought likely to have worked hard to attain it and may also be thought to possess discipline and organization in her/his approach to work. In interviewing as in other fields of knowledge, predictions of the future tend to rest on records of past occurrences. In the case of selection interviews, research supports the predictive value of past performance.[35]

The interviewer's task is to ask questions that test the assumptions or predictions arising from the candidate's paper credentials, as well as to measure the degree of fit between the applicant's skills and experiences and the specific needs of the job. To this end, the interviewer should ask a broad range of questions that seek to know not only *what*, but also *how* the interviewee will answer.

For example, an interviewer might ask an applicant, "Tell about a time when you failed to accomplish a goal. What did you do about it?" The interviewer's purpose in asking this question would not be so much to learn the details of an applicant's failure (*what*), but rather to learn *how* that individual responds to failure. Does the applicant blame the failure on others or take responsibility for it? Did he or she learn from the failure or dismiss it as an isolated event and walk away? Did he or she take steps to correct the failure? The applicant's answer to this question provides the interviewer with clues as to how this individual might handle future frustrations, failures, and disappointments.

Likewise, an interviewer can employ hypothetical questions to assess an applicant's likely responses to problems. **Hypothetical questions** offer realistic descriptions of job-related incidents or problems and ask the applicant to describe how he or she would respond. Many hypothetical questions begin with the phrase, "What would you do if . . .?" For example, an interviewer might ask an applicant for a supervisory position, "What would you do if one of your employees consistently arrived at work ten to fifteen minutes late?"

One particular method of selection interviewing that employs hypothetical questions systematically is known as situational interviewing. **Situational interviewing** seeks to predict an employee's future performance by presenting a series of job-related hypothetical situations that ask applicants how they would respond to given circumstances.[36] Situational interviewing is a specific form of selection interviewing based on careful job analyses which identify important likely job situations or problems. These identified "critical incidents" are then developed into "What would you do if. . ." scenarios to which the applicant responds.[37]

If an applicant were interviewing for a position at a customer service desk, a situational interview might include questions to gauge applicant responses to predictable customer service scenarios, such as: "What would you do if a customer returned an item that had clearly been worn and that they insisted had just been received as a gift and didn't fit?" "What would you do if two customers waiting for service got into a loud disagreement over who should be helped next?" "What would you do if you encountered a customer who insisted on an immediate cash refund even though company policy prohibits cash refunds?" In order to obtain trustworthy results, hypothetical questions must be worded so that the applicant cannot discern a "right answer."

In situational interviewing, interviewers also develop scoring guides for anticipating and rating possible responses to the hypothetical situations. A summary analysis of ten studies of structured situational interviews found that properly developed situational interviews are generally valid and reliable, bias-free, and useful. This same research analysis also indicated that the greatest problem area affecting the validity of situational interviewing appears to be tied to scoring guides that are not truly representative of typical applicant responses.[38]

A second method of selection interviewing that utilizes set question formats is known as **patterned behavior description interviewing**. This interviewing method seeks to predict future performance on the basis of specific descriptions of past behaviors. Applicants are asked to describe in detail specific choices made or actions taken in the past.[39] For example, the interviewer might ask an applicant to describe a situation in which he or she had a strong difference of opinion with a supervisor. In order to be effective, behavior description questions must be followed by careful probing for complete details of the situation and the applicant's actions. A 1985 study by Orpen found significantly higher predictive validities for patterned behavior description interviews than for unstructured interviews.[40]

Probing for Better Information.   Probes are particularly important to interviewers seeking detailed behavior descriptions, but they are important to all selection interviewers as a means of obtaining complete information. Let's look at some examples of the effective use of probes:

To Obtain More Detailed Answers:

Employer: How do your ten years of work at the retirement home make you a good candidate for us?

Applicant: Well, I've got a lot of experience.

Employer: Tell me how that experience makes you a good candidate for us. (Probe)

To Clarify Inconsistencies:

Employer: Your application says you left Jayco for a job that paid better.

Applicant: That's right.

Employer: But when we called your Jayco reference, he said they cut staff. So which is the reason you left Jayco—better pay, or staff cuts? (Probe)

To Check Applicant's Knowledge:

Employer: This job requires skilled word processing.

Applicant: That's great. I love word processing.

Employer: What word processing programs have your used?

Applicant: Oh, a lot of them. In my vocational training, I had two courses on word processing.

Employer: What word processing programs did you use there? (Probe)

Probes aid interviewers in pinning down unclear, inconsistent, or insufficient responses to important questions. Without the effective use of probes, many interviewers would be left with insufficient information about applicants' skills and abilities when the interview was done.

Listening and Responding Appropriately.   As in all interview situations, an applicant's responses to questions is influenced by the degree to which he or she believes the interviewer is interested in the answers. Research suggests that an applicant's answers to interviewer questions are shorter when the interviewer does not sustain eye contact.[41] Additional research has found that approving non-verbal behaviors by interviewers resulted in more relaxed interviews and better interviewee impression management.[42] Authors Arvey and Campion suggest that ". . . interviewers must become more aware of their impact on job applicants."[43]

The reciprocal nature of interview interaction demands that interviewers take care to indicate responsiveness to employee answers and that this responsiveness be as affirming and encouraging as possible. Responsiveness includes listening intently, paraphrasing applicant answers to assure they have been understood, probing deeper into information the applicant provides, and maintaining a level of attentive nonverbal involvement through eye contact and posture. Too often, interviewers get into the habit of simply saying "Good" in response to every applicant answer; such wooden response patterns do nothing to encourage the applicant to answer carefully.

Avoiding Questions that may Violate Applicants' Civil Rights.   The various federal laws that protect the civil rights of job applicants were described in chapter 5. These rights are not regulated by specific lists of questions that can or cannot be asked, but by protections accorded to areas of applicant lives which are not relevant to the ability to meet the *bona fide occupational qualifications* for the job. Despite the existence of federal and state legislation to protect individuals against discrimination in these areas, persistent evidence exists that interviewers continue to ask applicants questions that elicit information about protected areas, the discriminatory use of which violates civil rights. A study of 157 organizations in Wisconsin found that 96 percent of the interviewers for those organizations would or might ask questions of a potentially discriminatory nature in their selection interviews.[44]

Wall Street Journal columnist Arthur Eliot Berkeley found continuing and persistent use of discriminatory questions by interviewers, particularly in the area of the childbearing intentions and childcare needs of female applicants. Berkeley told of company strategies such as having a low-level employee ask an applicant about her choice of insurance plans or having the interviewer casually bring up the subject of children in an informal setting at a restaurant. The author also found that many female applicants lie in response to illegal inquiries and feel justified in doing so.[45]

Questions to be avoided in employment interviews are those that seek information about protected areas of an applicant's personal life, unless that information can be shown to be a BFOQ. Let's look at some potentially troublesome employment interview questions:

May I have a photo of you for our files? Because photos can be used to make inferences about a person's race or ethnicity for discriminatory purposes, this is not an acceptable question or practice unless physical appearance is a BFOQ, as in the case of fashion models, for example.

Do you have children? This is not a permissible question, even if asked of both male and female candidates, because of persistent evidence that employers tend to assume women are primarily responsible for the childcare needs of offspring and are more likely to miss work because of them. Another way of asking this question involves asking applicants if they are interested in making use of childcare facilities. It is hard to imagine a circumstance under which questions about one's children would relate to a BFOQ, except perhaps in the case of applicants for a beauty pageant open only to single women without children.

Do you have any objection to working closely with people of different races or ethnicity? This question is acceptable if working with diverse people is a BFOQ, a qualification necessary to the successful performance of the job. This might be the case in a position in international business involving worldwide travel, for example. It would *not* be acceptable to ask this question only of white, working-class men or women with noticeable southern drawls, for example, or only of white Americans about African Americans; the question, if related to a BFOQ, must be asked of all applicants. As in all areas of hiring practices, the potential for discrimination exists both in what is done with the information obtained and in whether some information is only required of certain types of applicants.

Are you a U.S. citizen? This question is acceptable if citizenship is a BFOQ, as in the case of those applying for positions within the U.S. justice system, for example, or in various federal, state, or municipal organizations. The question is not acceptable unless citizenship is a BFOQ, but an employer may ask if an applicant is legally entitled to work in the United States, because employers are prohibited from hiring those without work status approval.

How old are you? This inquiry is unacceptable except when age is a BFOQ. Even then, as in the case of bartenders, for example, who must be of legal drinking age, the question should be phrased in such a way as to obtain only the information necessary: "As you know, bartenders in this state must be at least 21 years of age. Do you meet that occupational requirement?"

What is your native language? This is not an acceptable inquiry. It is acceptable, however, to ask an applicant what foreign languages she or he speaks, reads, or writes fluently if these abilities relate directly to the job.

Do you have any handicaps? This question is unacceptable as written here. However, it is lawful to ask an applicant about any handicaps that would prevent performing the job sought. For example, if a job requires heavy lifting, it would be acceptable for an interviewer to ask applicants if they are able to lift heavy weights.

Have you ever been arrested? This is not an acceptable inquiry, but it is acceptable to ask applicants if they have ever been convicted of a crime which has bearing on the job for which they are applying. For example, it is acceptable to ask applicants for positions at childcare centers if they have ever been convicted of crimes involving the physical or sexual abuse of children. Likewise, it is acceptable to ask applicants for the position of bank teller if they have ever been convicted of theft, fraud, forgery, or other relevant crimes. Questions about arrests that did not result in convictions are never appropriate.

Appealing as it is for interviewers to want clear-cut lists of questions to avoid in selection interviews, the legal issues involved in hiring practices are not that simple. However, interviewers who confine their questions to areas of qualifications, skills, duties, and experiences as specified in the job description are on safe legal ground.

Conducting Team Interviews.   The use of teams as the central organizational structure of the modern workplace is a significant trend in recent years. Executive consultant and organizational advocate Tom Peters, author of the influential *Thriving on Chaos: Handbook for a Management Revolution*, encouraged the widespread use of multifunction work teams to facilitate organizational service, growth, and product development. In his 1987 book, *Thriving on Chaos*, Peters cited numerous examples of U.S. industries that had converted to team product development, team management, and team organization of work.[46] Influenced by Peters and others, major U.S. businesses such as General Electric, Ford Motor Company, and others have eliminated traditional layers of managerial hierarchy and created in their place multifunction, multispecialization work teams. In a chapter of "Second Thoughts" added to a 1988 edition of *Thriving*, Peters affirmed and strengthened his advocacy of and evidence for the "destruction of hierarchy (and its replacement by fully empowered, continuously reeducated work teams)."[47]

In the face of this radical alteration of the structure of many businesses, it is important to recognize the likelihood that team interviewing will become the selection interview method of choice for the future, at least in large industries. Many businesses are turning to some form of *team panel* (i.e., several interviewers at a time conducting interviews with individual applicants) or *sequential* (i.e., multiple individual interviews) interviewing as the preferred method of involving employees affected by a new hire in the selection interviewing process. Both of these methods of team involvement in selection interviewing usually include a structured team evaluation process for selecting the best applicant.

To date, little research has focused on testing the validity and value of team interviewing. However, a review of existing interview research by Dreher and Maurer reported the following findings that have bearing on the potential benefits of team interviewing:[48]

1. *Several different research studies found evidence of substantial and consistent differences in interviewer ratings of applicants.* Team interviews have the potential benefit of helping individual interviewers to learn about their own rating tendencies through comparative examination. Over time, they also allow businesses to determine which interviewers consistently make accurate predictions of job success.

2. *Several studies found supportive evidence for the superiority of consensus ratings of applicants.* A likely benefit of team interviewing would be more accurate ratings.

Additional research has also found that interviewers who were accountable for their decisions (i.e., had to justify them to others) and felt responsible for the decision made (i.e., knew their judgments would affect the final decisions) provided ratings that more accurately matched applicant characteristics.[49] Arvey and Campion concluded their review of research about team interviews with the suggestion that panel interviews appear "promising" as a method of improving reliability and validity in interviews.[50]

Clearly, more research on the effectiveness of team interviewing is needed. In the meantime, the need for training, planning, preparation, and systematic evaluation affect team interviewers as all others. In fact, team interviews may require *more* careful planning and preparation than individually conducted interviews in order to effectively integrate the contributions of the various team members.

At the very least, specific steps must be taken in the conduct of team interviews to coordinate the rapport, questioning, and closing phases of the interview among the various team members. When interviews are conducted by multifunction teams, it makes sense for the team members with the most relevant technical knowledge to ask specific technical questions of the applicants and for the remaining interview tasks to be distributed more or less evenly among the other team members. Additional suggestions about team interviewing were provided in chapter 8.

Closing the Interview.   When all relevant information has been gathered and recorded, it is time to bring the interview to a close. The closing of a selection interview should include the following important steps: (1) allowing the interviewee to ask additional questions, (2) explaining what will happen next, (3) and providing a clear sense of closure to the interview.

Hopefully, the interviewer has left room throughout the interview process for the applicant to ask questions as they arise. Additionally, though, interviewers should invite applicant questions at the end of the interview. The purpose of these questions is twofold: to allow the interviewee to ask for additional information about the company or the position, and to hear and assess the applicant's questions in terms of how they reflect the applicant's abilities, interest, and research about the company. For example, an applicant who asks, "I read in yesterday's *Journal* that your company is currently exploring a joint business venture with China—is it possible there will be opportunities to work on such a venture if I were to take this position?" indicates both knowledge of the company and interest in its future direction. Interviewee questions can also offer indications about the personal concerns and interests of the applicant. The interviewer should attend to interviewee questions, answer them as completely and carefully as possible, and make note of whatever relevant observations they can infer from the questions asked.

When the applicant has no further questions, the interviewer should clarify as concretely and accurately as possible what the applicant can expect in the future. For example, "We will be conducting interviews for the next two weeks and will plan to make our final decision by July 15. We will call you early next week to let you know whether you have been selected to return for a second interview. What would be a good time of day to call?" Often, interviewers also explain the next phase of the interviewing process if there is one. Finally, the interviewer should thank the interviewee for her/his time and signal the end of the interview with appropriate nonverbal behaviors such as standing, shaking hands, and walking the applicant to the door.

Evaluating Applicants.   In the end, after all the preparing, considering, and conducting of the interview, the most important task remains to be performed. When all is said and done, how does one decide which of the applicants encountered is best suited to the job? Who is most likely to succeed? On what basis can such a judgment be made? As one frustrated older interviewing student—herself experienced in employment interviews—once asked, "How do you really know?" The act of assessment and the need to choose remains the hardest task of all.

How do you really know? You don't. However, if the preparations have been exhaustive and the necessary information has been obtained, if the interviewing process was thorough and careful observations were made and recorded, and if a reliable system of comparing the applicants on the basis of job-related criteria has been employed, interviewers can make an informed and educated guess as to which of these "examined strangers" most nearly matches the needs of the company and the job.

The final decision should be made only when the entire process is complete—when all of the interviews are over, when all of the necessary information has been obtained, when all of the relevant persons have had the opportunity to examine and compare the information and to render their own judgments in some systematic way. Where team or multiple interviews have been conducted, the various interviewers should aim for consensus, complete agreement, in their decision. Where there is doubt, attempts to obtain more information should be made. Where time permits, the decision should not be hurried; instead, the interviewers should allow a brief interval to pass, to test their perceptions, to assess the candidates on various measures, and to seek clarity of thought.

Then, once the decision is made, the interviewer should approach the selected person with confidence to welcome her/him to accept the job. Ultimately, the success or failure of an individual in a position is not settled at the moment of hire. As we have seen, there are predictive measures that "improve the odds" of a good match, but individuals, jobs, and companies change, and even the best prediction is no guarantee.

As soon as the selected applicant has accepted the position, the remaining applicants should be notified that the decision has been made. Usually, the notification of nonhires is made in writing. Sometimes, applicants will call to ask for feedback as to why they did not get the job. Interviewers should handle such inquiries with tact and honesty, recognizing the continuing impact of their messages on applicant perceptions of the company.

A skilled interviewer will follow the careers of those hired, seeking evidence over time of the strength or weakness of her/his predictive and evaluative skills.

Did the applicants stay? Do they seem satisfied with the company and job? Are their superiors happy with their work? Have they continued to grow in the job? Companies, too, should track this information in order to discover their best interviewers and to make more extensive use of those who make selection decisions most effectively.

No interviewing process is complete until the interviewers have assessed the strengths and weaknesses of the process and made decisions about what changes are needed when the process begins again. Just as the selection interviewer's work begins long before the interviews themselves are conducted, it ends long after the interviews are done.

The Interviewee in the Selection Interview

The initial contact with an employer has been successfully negotiated: a phone call made, a professional resume sent along with an effective cover letter, references notified, and application forms completed. The applicant has been called for an interview and given an appointment.

The applicant has done some homework by researching the company, obtaining and studying a job description; and considering what questions might be asked, how to answer them, and what questions to ask in order to learn more about the company and to demonstrate her curiosity, preparedness, and interests. The preparation process is complete; it is the day of the interview.

The applicant's responsibilities in the conducting of the selection interview are many. The applicant must take steps to create a positive first impression through careful management of nonverbal communication skills, negotiating the crucial opening phase of the interview successfully. She or he must answer questions accurately and positively, responding with precision and care even to questions about weaknesses and those which probe into protected areas of personal life. She or he must ask good questions well, moving through the closing phase of the interview with grace. Finally, the applicant must follow up the interview with appropriate responses and careful assessment of what was learned in the interview process.

Creating a Positive First Impression

"First impressions are important." How many times have you heard this truism? Those first few moments in human encounters appear to be vital, having the potential power to influence both the perceptions that follow and the decisions that will be made on the basis of them. Are first impressions fixed and unalterable? No. Many times people decide later that their first impressions of another person were inaccurate. Nonetheless, research in the field of selection interviewing has found that negative first impressions tend to be powerful and have lasting effects.[51] It is of obvious importance, therefore, to manage the opening phase of the job interview successfully.

For the interviewee, the process of managing first impressions in the selection interview begins not at the interviewer's office door but at the interviewee's home, where elements of appropriate dress and grooming are decided. It continues with the applicant's prompt arrival at the interviewer's office and her/his successful management of the opening phase of the interview.

Attending to Personal Appearance.   In recent years, the idea that "clothes make the person" has had such popularity that it has spawned a series of books and notions about "dressing for success."[52] Many people cringe at the idea that our judgments about one another are made on the basis of such superficial information as what cloth is wrapped around our bodies. And, in truth, most long-term decisions and judgments do not rely solely on these superficial criteria.

Nonetheless, we do make judgments and form expectations about one another on the basis of these and other overtly observable information in the opening minutes of interviews. Various researchers have found that personal appearance, being appropriately dressed for the interview, is one of the most significant nonverbal cues in the selection interviews.

Watson and Smeltzer found that interviewers judge first impressions to be very important and that the two most important nonverbal behaviors interviewers consider are the applicant's personal appearance and eye contact.[53] In other research, Bovee and Thill found poor personal appearance to be the most important factor leading to rejection in employment interviews.[54] Because these superficial criteria matter, whether we want them to or not, job applicants must use them to advantage if they wish to be successful at obtaining the work they desire.

Professional personal appearance includes not only appropriate clothing (conservative business suits or dresses), but also good grooming and minimal, tasteful jewelry and adornments. Research by Forsythe and others found that female applicants were more favorably evaluated when their dress was a tailored suit, somewhat masculine in style.[55] Some writers suggest that applicants should visit the workplace at which they will be interviewing prior to the interview in order to observe the informal dress codes of that environment. However, there are many businesses that have adopted casual everyday dress codes for their employees, while the scripted expectations for applicant dress in selection interviews demand that applicants appear for interviews in their best professional dress.

Managing Other Aspects of Nonverbal First Impressions.   The first impression, formed at the greeting between interviewer(s) and interviewee, includes not only personal appearance but also the applicant's handshake, promptness, eye contact, and smile. Applicants should take care to be courteous and attentive in the impressions they are creating even with secretaries, receptionists, and others, because any of these other persons may be asked for their perceptions as part of the decision-making process.

Nonverbal researchers Hickson and Stacks contend that communication in the workplace is primarily concerned with status and power. They recommend, therefore, that job applicants have a strong, firm handshake, a warm smile, and sustained eye contact, and that they arrive on time, citing evidence that prompt persons are perceived as more credible and that people who smile more are perceived as more intelligent.[56]

Nonverbal impressions continue to have impact throughout the interview. McGovern and Tinsley conducted research with fifty-two personnel specialists who watched videotapes of interviews and evaluated applicants. Applicants who employed sustained eye contact, energy and facial expressiveness, vocal variety, and fluent speech were rated significantly higher by the personnel specialists.[57] In a review of multiple research efforts on interviewee behavior and interview outcomes, Street reported the following compilation of characteristics found in applicants who were favorably evaluated: physical attractiveness, professional appearance, "standard or prestigious accents," and energy and enthusiasm in eye contact, gestures, posture, smiles, forward leaning, vocal variety, and nodding.[58]

Effectively Responding to Questions

Which is more important to the success of an interview in the long run—the nonverbal or the verbal communication of the applicant? Opinions on the subject differ. Street cites several authors who argue nonverbal messages carry more weight in the selection interview and several others who insist that the strength of verbal content is primary.[59] Street concludes that nonverbal and verbal communication by the applicant in the interview are equally important.[60] In support of this notion, research by Riggio and Throckmorton found that applicant verbal behaviors and appearance were the two strongest influences on evaluations received.[61] Also, Rasmussen found that high levels of applicant nonverbal animation had a positive impact on interviewee evaluations only when their verbal content was also strong.[62]

The verbal communication behaviors found by Einhorn to have the most positive outcomes for applicants included: the expression of specific, consistent career goals; a clearly expressed desire to work for the company at which the interview occurred; verbal evidence of research into the company; verbal responsiveness to and support for interviewer comments; the consistent, effective use of supporting evidence in the form of factual and hypothetical illustrations, testimony from others, comparisons, etc.; and the use of relevant, appropriate humor.[63] Compiling findings from various researchers, Street included support for opinions, good grammar, well-organized comments, good questions, and appropriate content as the verbal communication skills of successful interviewees.[64]

Obviously, first impressions created by the applicant, however positive they may be, do not by themselves carry an interviewee successfully through to a favorable evaluation. The content and organization of applicant response to questions is at least equally vital to success in the interview. This is why preparation in handling interviewer questions is so important. Now let's look at some specific suggestions regarding applicant answers to interviewer questions.

Listen Carefully.   An answer can only be as good as one's understanding of the question. Interviewees must listen closely and ask for clarifications about questions as needed before answering. For example, in the response to the question, "What is your game plan?" an applicant might ask, "Do you mean what are my short-term goals if I obtain this position, or are you more interested in knowing my long-term career ambitions?"

Make Answers Succinct, Organized and Specific.   Emphasize specific skills and accomplishments with brief, clear supporting evidence. For example, in response to the question, "Tell me about your accomplishments," an applicant might respond, "Academically, I have been on the dean's list for the past two semesters; my GPA is 3.4 overall and 4.0 for the past two semesters. I was awarded an academic scholarship which paid for my senior year of college. In the workplace, I've successfully completed two cooperative internships with local accounting firms and received the highest possible rating from both of my supervisors."

Frame Answers Positively, Emphasizing Strengths.   The interviewee's responsibility in the interview is to present her/himself in the best possible light. This does *not* mean being dishonest. It does mean applicants should know how to express their strengths effectively, choosing language carefully and using words that have connotations of strength. For example, instead of saying, "I work hard," an applicant might describe her/himself as "diligent and determined." Instead of saying, "I stay with tasks until they're done," an applicant might say she or he is "tenacious and thorough."

Discuss Weaknesses Honestly.   If the applicant's job is to emphasize the positive, what can be done with the inevitable questions about weaknesses or failings? First, all questions should be answered honestly, but without dwelling on the negatives. "I can be impatient and demanding at times, both with myself and others. This makes me a very hard worker, but it means that at times I need to be reminded to go easy on myself and others." "I'm a procrastinator at times, but I am attentive to deadlines and have learned to impose tight deadlines on myself in order to compensate for my tendency to put things off." The applicant should *not* deny having weaknesses ("I can't think of any") or attempt to pass off what she or he really considers a positive quality as negative ("I'm a perfectionist.").

When asked about previous failings, the interviewee should briefly describe one and go on to say what was learned from the experience. For example, in a videotaped classroom interview, a student was asked to explain why he had spent only one year at a major state university before leaving school for a year and then returning to an extension campus near his home. He answered, "When I went away to school, I was immature and inexperienced. I had a great time, but then the university gave me the grades I deserved, along with the opportunity to take a year off to learn what it was I really wanted from my life. I came back to school having learned my lesson and have maintained good grades ever since."

This student's honesty enhanced his credibility, while at the same time he managed to describe flunking out as an opportunity from which he learned. He was also careful not to blame his failing on anyone but himself. Honesty, assessment of what was learned from failure, and taking full responsibility for one's own actions—these are essential elements of effective verbal communication for job applicants.

Respond Appropriately to Potentially Discriminatory Questions.   As discussed earlier, there are still many interviewers who find ways to seek information about protected areas of an applicant's personal life. In the face of this reality, how are applicants to respond when they are faced with questions which invade nonjob-related areas of their lives?

Interviewees should be attentive even to questions posed by persons other than the interviewer (secretaries, other employees) that seek information pertaining to protected areas. When asked questions directly about such areas, applicants must decide how to respond on the basis of their own assessments of the risks involved; namely, how important is it to obtain this job? Would it be better to answer and risk discrimination, or to refuse to answer and risk rejection due to lack of cooperation? Both options involve risks, and only the individual applicant can choose which risks to take.

Suppose, for example, that an applicant is asked about her childbearing plans despite the clearly discriminatory nature of the question. What are her options?

> *She can answer the question:* "I have no immediate plans to have children, but if and when I do, that decision will not in any way interfere with my dedication to my work and pursuit of my career ambitions."

> *She can refuse to answer:* "My family plans have no bearing on my ability to be a first-rate employee if hired for this position."

> *She can respond to the implied question that underlies the question:* "If you are concerned about my commitment to my work and my ability to work conscientiously, I assure you I will remain conscientious no matter what changes occur in my personal life."

> *She can end the interview and report the interviewer to the appropriate federal and state agencies:* "This question is clearly discriminatory in nature and I have no interest in continuing this interview."

Any applicant faced with potentially discriminatory questions, whatever immediate decision made about how to respond, should make note of the questions asked, the circumstances, the dates and the times so that the option of reporting the violation after the fact remains open. This is particularly valuable if the applicant is not offered the position and the troublesome questions seem to have been a factor in the decision.

Ask Questions Well.   As was discussed in the previous chapter, the interviewee should come to the interview with prepared questions designed to communicate knowledge of the company, long-range goals, and/or curiosity and eagerness to know more about the work. Interviewees should take care not to ask "canned," generic questions such as those that are often suggested in popular get a job publications, questions such as, "Are there opportunities for advancement?" or "Are there company training programs available?" Rather, the applicant's questions should be self-designed and specific to the mutual needs of company and individual.

As a general rule, applicants should think in terms of asking at least three questions, one of which indicates an informed interest in the future of the business ("Will the company's plans to expand its international markets include efforts to establish offices in Latin America?"), one of which indicates the applicant's long-range ambitions ("If I were to take this position, would there be opportunities to develop leadership skills through supervisory responsibilities within the next few years?"), and one which asks, "What happens now?" ("Will there be a second interview for the best applicants for this position?") Again, applicants should not ask these questions but rather questions tailored to their own unique circumstances.

Additionally, the applicant should plan to ask questions when appropriate throughout the interview process. The interviewee should seek to learn as much as possible about the nature of the job and the philosophy and plans of the larger organization.

End the Interview Effectively.   It is the interviewer's responsibility to indicate that the interview is at an end and to provide the appropriate nonverbal signals of closure. The interviewee should wait for the appropriate signals—stand-

Appropriate nonverbal signals will help to end an interview effectively.

ing, handshakes, moving toward the door—and respond to them promptly, gracefully, and confidently.

The applicant should thank the interviewer for the interview, express a genuine interest (if honest and appropriate) in the position, and perhaps offer a brief summary comment about her/himself. For example, an applicant might say, "As you review your records concerning my application, I hope what you will remember most about me is my enthusiasm for the values this company represents and my eagerness to join this team." Immediately after the interview, the applicant should write a brief letter to the interviewers, thanking them for the opportunity to be considered and briefly re-emphasizing the qualities he or she possesses which match the needs of the organization.

Evaluate the Interview.   Just as with the interviewer, the interview process is not complete for the interviewee until he or she has thoughtfully reviewed and assessed the process. After the interview, the applicant should realistically assess whether the job and company are a good match and opportunity for her/his particular talents and goals. Likewise, the applicant should assess the interview itself, considering which questions were handled well and which were not. This allows real improvement to take place so that the next interview, wherever and whenever it occurs, will not include the same mistakes. Finally, the applicant should consider what, if any, additional follow-up information or action is needed. Every interview, even those which are utterly unsuccessful, should be viewed as opportunities to learn more about oneself and about the art of interviewing.

Summary

Both interviewer and interviewee have multiple responsibilities in the conduct of selection interviews. For the interviewer, the actual conduct of the interview involves final preparations, opening the interview effectively, questioning and probing well until all of the necessary information is obtained, using team interviews as needed, closing the interview effectively, and completing the evaluation process and notifying of candidates. For the interviewee, the actual interview requires careful attention to impression management, answering and asking questions well, and completing the interview process with appropriate follow up and evaluation. For both parties, successful completion of the interview involves having obtained the information necessary in order to make the best decision.

Discussion Questions

1. What are the three most important things you want in a job? In a company? Rank your personal needs and compare them with your peers.

2. What was the worst job interview you've ever had? What made it so bad? Did you get the job?

3. What are the toughest job interview questions you have ever been asked? What are the

toughest questions you've heard or read about? What makes these questions tough? How would you answer them?

4. Develop a hypothetical question based on a problem or conflict you have experienced. How would you answer the question differently now from how you actually handled the problem at the time?

5. Think of yourself in the role of interviewer. Would your tendency be to rate applicants too harshly or too gently? Of what nonverbal

aspects of the applicants' self-presentations would you be most aware? What conclusions would you draw from them?

6. What are your nonverbal and verbal nervous habits? How could you consciously manage them in a job interview situation?

7. What are your weaknesses? How might you talk about them in a selection interview? What could you honestly say about what steps you've taken to respond to them or what you have learned from them?

Suggested Activities

1. What more would you want to know about Mr. Cliborn, in the opening interview of the chapter, before you decided to hire him? How would you find out what you wanted to know? Specifically, what further questions would you want to ask? Would you want to check references? Which? What would you ask? What other steps would you want to take in order to assess his teaching ability? Develop a two to three page plan for continuing this interview and evaluation with Mr. Cliborn.

2. Select one of the two sample resumes provided in chapter 8. Quickly jot down your assumptions, judgments, and questions about this person. Now develop a moderately scheduled interview guide with which to interview this person. Include in your guide several hypothetical questions and behavior description questions, including two or three questions you consider to be tough or challenging. Compare your assumptions, judgments, and guides with one other person who selected the same resume.

3. Consider the previous activity. Now assume that you as the interviewer have discovered

that your applicant is wheelchair-bound. What adaptations would you make in your interview with this applicant? Would you acknowledge the individual's disability? What questions, if any, would you ask about it? What changes would you make in the interview setting? Critically consider and discuss with others what differences there might be in your perceptions of this person on the basis of her/his disability. Consider whether and why the nature of this person's disability might realistically or honestly affect your decision to hire.

4. Now go through the same thought process as suggested in the previous activity, only this time assume that the individual you are interviewing has severe cerebral palsy, which results in somewhat slurred speech, continuous erratic hand and body motions, and difficulty with many "small motor" activities such as drinking from plastic cups, handwriting, and carrying small objects. How would these behaviors affect your perceptions? What questions would you ask to ascertain their impact on this individual's ability to do the job?

Related Readings

Chastain, Sherry. *Winning the Salary Game*. New York: John Wiley and Sons, 1990.

Eder, Robert W., and Ferris, Gerald R., eds. *The*

Employment Interview: Theory, Research, and Practice. Newbury Park, CA: Sage Publications, 1989.

Haldane, Bernard. *Career Satisfaction and Success: How to Know and Manage Your Strengths.* Seattle: Wellness Behavior, 1988.

Krannich, Caryl Rae, and Ronald L. *Interview for Success.* Woodbridge, VA: Impact Publications, 1990.

Krannich, Ronald L., and Caryl Rae. *Salary Success.* Woodbridge, VA: Impact Publications, 1990.

LeFevre, John L. *How You Really Get Fired.* New York: Simon and Schuster, 1989.

Jamieson, David, and O'Mara, Julie. *Managing Workforce 2000: Gaining the Diversity Advantage.* San Francisco: Jossey-Bass Publishers, 1991.

Strasser, Stephen, and Sena, John. *From Campus to Corporations.* Hawthorne, NJ: The Career Press, 1990.

Endnotes

1. Jeffrey W. Daum, "Interviewer Training: The Key to an Innovative Selection Process that Works," *Training 20,* (December, 1983), 63.

2. James E. Campion and Richard D. Arvey, "Unfair Discrimination in the Employment Interview," Robert W. Eder, and Gerald R. Ferris, eds., *The Employment Interview: Theory, Research, and Practice* (Newbury Park, CA: Sage Publications, 1988), 61.

3. Richard Nelson Bolles, *The 1992 What Color Is Your Parachute? A Practical Manual for Job-Hunters & Career-Changers* (Berkeley, CA: Ten Speed Press, 1992), 12. Bolles' source is Tom Jackson, *Guerilla Tactics in the Job Market,* rev. ed. (New York: Bantam Books, 1980).

4. Robert W. Eder, K. Michele Kacmar, and Gerald R. Ferris, "Employment Interview Research: History and Synthesis," in Eder and Ferris (1988), 18.

5. Eder, *et al.,* (1988), 18.

6. William L. Tullar, "The Employment Interview as a Cognitive Performing Script," Eder and Ferris (1988), 233–34.

7. Richard D. Arvey, and James E. Campion, "The Employment Interview: A Summary and Review of Recent Research," *Personnel Psychology 35* (1982), 285–94.

8. George F. Dreher, Ronald A. Ash, and Priscilla Hancock, "The Role of Traditional Research Design in Underestimating the Validity of the Employment Interview," *Personnel Psychology 41* (1988), 322.

9. Dreher, *et al.,* (1988), 323–24.

10. James G. Goodale, "Effective Employment Interviewing," Eder and Ferris (1988), 311.

11. Goodale (1988), 308–09.

12. Robert Bloom and Erich P. Prien, "A Guide to Job-related Employment Interviewing," *Personnel Administrator,* (October, 1983), 81–2.

13. Arvey and Campion (1982), 287.

14. N. Schmitt and B.W. Coyle, "Applicant decisions in the employment interview," *Journal of Applied Psychology 61,* 1976, 184–92.

15. Arvey and Campion (1982), 285–93.

16. Arvey and Campion (1982), 293.

17. Bloom and Prien (1983), 81–2.

18. Eder, *et al.,* (1988), 28.

19. Keith G. Rasmussen, Jr., "Nonverbal Behavior, Verbal Behavior, Resume Credentials, and Selection Interview Outcomes," *Journal of Applied Psychology 69,* 1984, 551–56.

20. Robert L. Dipboye, Carla S. Stramler, and Gail A. Fontenelle, "The Effects of the Application on Recall of Information from the Interview," *Academy of Management Journal 27* (1984), no. 3, 561–575.

21. Therese H. Macan, and Robert L. Dipboye, "The Effects of Interviewers' Initial Impressions on Information Gathering," *Organizational Behavior and Human Decision Processes 42,* 1988, 364–387.

22. Robert L. Dipboye, Gail A. Fontenelle, and Kathleen Garner, "Effects of Previewing the Application on Interview Process and Outcomes," *Journal of Applied Psychology 69* (1984), no. 1, 118–128.

23. Sara L. Rynes, "The Employment Interview as a Recruitment Device," Eder and Ferris (1988), 133.

24. M. D. Hakel, "Employment interviewing," (1982) as reported in Dipboye (1988), 52.

25. Dipboye, *et al.* (1984), 572.

26. Arvey and Campion (1982), 287.

27. Sources consulted on relevant privacy laws include: Patrick G. Marshall, "Your Right to Privacy," *Editorial Research Reports 1* (January 20, 1989) no. 3, 30–42, reprinted in *Social Issues Research Series: Privacy,* (Boca Raton, FL) vol. 4, article 21. Also, Randall S. Schuler, *Effective Personnel Management* (St. Paul: West Publishing Company, 1983), 254–55.

28. Marshall (1989), Article 21.

29. Marshall (1989), Article 21.

30. Robert Ellis Smith, *Compilation of State and Federal Privacy Laws,* 1988, 2. As reported and reprinted in Marshall (1989), Article 21.

31. Richard L. Street, "Interaction Processes and Outcomes in Interviews," *Communication Yearbook 9* (1985), 240. 9, 1985, 240.

32. Mark L. Hickson, III, and Don W. Stacks, *Nonverbal Communication: Studies and Applications,* 2nd ed. (Dubuque, IA: William C. Brown Publishing, 1989), 289.

33. As reported in Tom Janz, "The Patterned Behavior Description Interview: The Best Prophet of the Future is the Past," Eder and Ferris (1989), 159.

34. See, for example, Janz (1989), 159, and Hubert S. Feild, and Robert D. Gatewood, "Development of a Selection Interview: A Job Content Strategy," 145, also Eder and Ferris (1989).

35. J.E. Hunter, and R.F. Hunter, "Validity and Utility of Alternative Predictors of Job Performance," *Psychological Bulletin, 96,* 72–98. As reported in Tom Janz, (1989), 159.

36. Gary P. Latham, "The Reliability, Validity, and Practicality of the Situational Interview," Eder and Ferris (1989), 171.

37. Latham (1989), 169–182.

38. Latham (1989), 179.

39. Janz (1989), 159–160.

40. As reported in George F. Dreher and Steven D. Maurer, "Assessing the Employment Interview: Deficiencies Associated with the Existing Domain of Validity Coefficients," Eder and Ferris (1989), 255.

41. As reported in Robert C. Liden and Charles K. Parsons, "Understanding Interpersonal Behavior in the Employment Interview," Eder and Ferris (1989), 219.

42. Arvey and Campion (1982), 308.

43. Arvey and Campion (1982), 307–308.

44. Jeffrey Springston and Joann Keyton, "Defining and Quantifying Potentially Discriminatory Questions in Employment Interviewing." Unpublished Paper, Speech Communication Association, San Francisco, 1989.

45. Arthur Eliot Berkeley, "Job Interviewers' Dirty Little Secret," *Wall Street Journal,* (March 20, 1989), A14.

46. Tom Peters, *Thriving on Chaos: Handbook for a Management Revolution* (New York: Harper & Row, 1987). See especially 256–67 and 637–41.

47. Peters (1987), 637.

48. Dreher and Maurer (1989), 252–256.

49. Eder, "Contextual Effects on Interview Decisions," Eder and Ferris (1989), 123.

50. Arvey and Capion (1982), 293.

51. Hickson and Stacks (1989), 289.

52. John T. Molloy, *Dress for Success* (New York: Warner Books, 1975) and *The Woman's Dress for Success Book* (Chicago: Follett, 1977).

53. As reported in Hickson and Stacks (1989), 290.

54. As reported in Hickson and Stacks (1989), 290.

55. Sandra Forsythe, Mary Frances Drake, and Charles E. Cox, "Influence of Applicant's Dress on Interviewer's Selection Decisions," *Journal of Applied Psychology 70,* 1985, 374–78.

56. Hickson and Stacks (1989), 273–292.

57. T.V. McGovern and H.E. Tinsley, "Interviewer Evaluations of Interviewee Nonverbal Behavior," *Journal of Vocational Behavior 13* (1978), 163–71.

58. Street (1985), 217.

59. Street (1985), 218.

60. Street (1985), 241–42.

61. Ronald E. Riggio, and Barbara Throckmorton, "The Relative Effects of Verbal and Nonverbal Behavior, Appearance, and Social Skills on Evaluations Made in Hiring Interviews," *Journal of Applied Social Psychology 18,* 1988, 331–48.

62. Rasmussen (1984), 551–56.

63. Lois J. Einhorn, "An Inner View of the Job Interview: An Investigation of Successful Communicative Behaviors," *Communication Education 30* (1981), 220–25.

64. Street (1985), 217–18.

Chapter *10*

Employment Interviews: Performance Appraisal

"Fear cannot be banished, but it can be calm and without panic; and it can be mitigated by reason and evaluation."
—Vannevar Bush, Modern Arms and
Free Men (1949), conclusion.

Mickie LaMar has invited Carol Mishra, the new receptionist in the five physician cardiology office, into her office for an appraisal review. Carol has been working for the cardiologists for six weeks. This initial six weeks' appraisal is standard for all new employees. After this initial review, Carol will be reviewed twice each year.

Mickie: Come on in and sit down, Carol. (Carol sits down tentatively.) How is your son doing? Is he feeling better?

Carol: Yes, he's really doing great now. The antibiotics took care of it right away. He gets bronchitis every year, so we've been through this before, I'm afraid. But he's okay now.

Mickie: I'm glad to hear it. It's really tough for kids to have to miss school. What is he, a second grader?

Carol: Yes. Hard to believe.

Mickie: Isn't that the truth? They really grow up fast! (Looks down at papers.) But now, let's talk about you. (Carol laughs nervously.) The main point I want to get across today is that appraisal interviews happen all the time here. The doctors think that all employees should get lots of feedback about how they're doing, so we have them twice a year. The reason yours has come so soon is that we always talk to new people six weeks after they start. So you've been here six weeks, and here we are!

Carol: That's a relief. I thought I was in trouble.

Mickie: No! (Laughing) Not at all. We keep trying to let people know that we do these all the time and *definitely* not just when you're in trouble. But I guess the word doesn't get around.

Carol: Okay. I'll try to relax. (Laughing)

Mickie: Sorry if you'd been worrying. Trust me, you're not in trouble. (Laughing) Okay, (looking at papers) let's get started.

Carol: Okay.

Mickie: One of the things we hired you for was your ability to handle multiple telephone lines. I've watched you and so has Nancy, and we both think you've done a great job of learning our system. Nancy told me the second week you were here that you had learned the system faster than any other receptionist we've had. So I think that's going great.

Carol: Good!

Mickie: We also try to monitor how quickly the receptionist gets the patients' records forwarded to the nurses after they sign in. We check that by looking at the sign in times and comparing them to the times that the nurses have what they need to take patients back to the examining rooms. When you started, it took you about nine minutes to get the patients' records to the nurses' box. Now, it takes you a little less than six minutes. That's a big improvement. We'd like you to keep working at this so you can get it down to four. Otherwise, the patients spend a lot of time waiting. And I don't have to tell you that they don't like it.

Carol: I know they don't because they gripe to me! I know I need to do it quicker. I just asked Nancy to help me learn to use the computer system to get their file codes quicker. I think that will help.

Mickie: Good. If you think of other ways to speed that up, it's an important area to work on. We're not unhappy with your progress. We're just always looking for ways to make the patients more comfortable.

Carol: Yeah, I know. I'll keep working on it.

Mickie: Great. One last area: working with the elderly patients. One problem that I hope you will work on especially is how you talk to the very elderly patients. Lots of them are hard of hearing, and several have complained that they can't hear you when you tell them about the check-in procedures. I have noticed this problem, too. Actually, I think it will be pretty easy to solve. When you have a person who is elderly, or anyone who seems hard of hearing, please speak very slowly and much louder. If you enunciate clearly and really speak up, I think the patients will be able to understand you much better.

Carol: I didn't even know I did that.

Mickie: Well, it's not a terrible problem; but it is an area that I think you would want to work on.

Carol: No kidding. I didn't realize they couldn't hear me.

Mickie: So you'll try to speak up more?

Carol: Definitely. I really am glad you told me because I'm trying to do a good job, and if they can't hear me, I'm not doing a good job. I'll definitely make sure I speak louder to the older people.

Mickie: Well, I can't ask more than that! So, let me summarize the things I wanted to talk about. First, you're doing a great job with the phones. Second, you're speeding up on the processing time. Just keep getting quicker. Third, you're going to work to speak so that the people who are hearing impaired can hear you better. Okay. Now, tell me what you'd like to add.

Carol: Nothing really. Maybe when I have my six months meeting, I'll have more ideas about how I can improve the desk. Right now, I feel like I'm still learning the ropes. I appreciate that you and Nancy understand that a new person can't learn everything at once.

Mickie: Well, we're really glad you're on the team here. We thought we made a good choice when we hired you, and we think that even more now. I'll write up a summary of this meeting because that's what we do with all appraisal reviews. Then I'll give you a copy to sign to indicate that you received it, and it will go in your file. Okay?

Carol: That'll be fine. Thanks for your time. (Carol stands up.)

Mickie: Thank you for your openness. See you later. (Carol leaves.)

Chapter Goals

- To define appraisal interview.
- To identify reasons why appraisal interviews are difficult.
- To propose a reconceptualization of appraisal interviews which suggests that both parties have active roles.
- To suggest ways that appraisal interviewers can plan for, execute, and evaluate their interviews.
- To offer ways interviewees can prepare for and participate in appraisal interviews.
- To provide information about appropriate follow up to appraisal interviews.

Introduction

In the workforce, employers hire workers each day. These workers represent an enormous range of abilities and motivations. Some workers arrive at work on time, and others arrive late every day. Some greet customers respectfully, and others use foul language when they get upset with customers. Some do their jobs well; others do not. Supervisors have the responsibility to evaluate this work. Evaluation usually includes a performance **appraisal interview,** which is an interview based on carefully collected data that allows organizations and workers to assess worker performance so that they can work together to set goals and improve effectiveness. The appraisal process is a pervasive part of work in the United States. Over 90 percent of U.S. organizations use appraisal interviews with their employees.[1]

Performance appraisal helps both the individual workers and the organization itself to be more effective. The functions of regular, consistent, and constructive appraisal are many:

- To assess workers' performance on the job.
- To give workers feedback about their work performance.
- To help workers find ways to improve work performance.
- To set work goals.
- To set compensation sometimes.
- To act on personnel changes like promotions sometimes.[2]

Like hiring, these functions must be achieved within particular legal constraints. At times, the appraisal process causes certain personnel actions to occur. For example, in some organizations workers who receive three negative evaluations in a row are automatically terminated from their jobs. When appraisal is causally related to terms of employment, the same legal guidelines that ensure nondiscriminatory treatment of employees in the selection process must guide the appraisal process. The basic guideline is based on Title VII (Section 703, as amended) of the Civil Rights Act of 1964:

> *It shall be an unlawful employment practice for an employer: 1) to fail or refuse to hire or to discharge any individual or otherwise to discriminate against an individual with respect to his compensation, terms, conditions, or privileges of employment because of the individual's race, color, religion, sex or national origin . . . .*

All aspects of the appraisal process—record keeping, assessment, the appraisal interview, and resulting personnel decisions—must be grounded in data about the worker's work performance, *not* her/his race, color, religion, sex, national origin, or handicap.

Despite the fact that appraisal interviews are a part of almost all jobs, many supervisors and workers find them stressful, unpleasant, time-consuming, and discouraging. In this chapter, we will examine reasons for the negative impression of appraisal interviews and will offer techniques for making appraisal a more constructive part of work life. Because appraisal interviews have potential to improve employee work life and productivity in general, improving them will benefit workers, supervisors, and organizations.

What has led to such a negative impression of appraisal interviews by supervisors (i.e., people who conduct them) and workers (i.e., those who are appraised)? Three powerful factors make appraisal interviews difficult for the different participants. First, they are difficult for interviewers because they are a demanding and often frustrating part of their workload. The opening interview suggests that the supervisor conducts many appraisal interviews in the course of a year. Supervisors must give large amounts of time to prepare, conduct, and follow up on appraisal interviews. Likewise, supervisors must devote considerable time and effort to keep accurate and complete records about attendance, production rates, relations with coworkers, disciplinary problems, customer relations, and licensing. All these tasks take time away from other tasks that many supervisors may find more urgent. Moreover, appraisal interviews force the interviewer to act simultaneously as an evaluator, a motivator, a counselor, and a supervisor,[3] which is an almost impossible combination of roles. In addition, supervisors often need to give negative feedback to workers as part of the appraisal process. Managers report that giving negative feedback to their direct subordinates is one of the hardest and most unpleasant jobs they have.[4] In fact, some managers report that they avoid giving negative feedback because of the likelihood that it will strain productive, ongoing working relationships with their subordinates.[5] The possibility that appraisal will strain interpersonal relations between supervisors and workers is real, and the appraisal interview sits at the center of this threat.

A second factor that makes performance appraisal a difficult process is that interviewees are often defensive about the process. As Gibb's research has demonstrated, people become defensive and guarded when they believe they are being evaluated.[6] Workers often perceive the job performance appraisal to be particularly unpleasant. They perceive appraisal as a top-down event, required by management, scheduled by management, conducted by management, and controlled by management. This perception, whether it is accurate or not, leads to defensiveness because it contains managerial messages of evaluation, control, dogmatism, and superiority, all of which are behaviors that generate defensiveness on the part of the worker.[7] Workers also get defensive because the appraisal interview threatens their reputations. Goffman suggests that human beings are concerned with maintaining their "faces,"[8] that is, their socially approved identities. In an appraisal interview, a worker wants to maintain a socially approved identity, a positive self-presentation; but the interviewer may point out behaviors that conflict with that image. For example, a health care worker may believe and want others to believe that she or he works well with people. In the appraisal interview, the supervisor might discuss a series of specific problems that the worker has had with patient interaction. The fact that the interviewer points out these weaknesses may cause the worker to lose face. Losing face is a frightening and threatening event. Stamp, Vangelisti, and Daly note that losing face increases defensiveness:

"Defensiveness is a response to threat-evoking communication which attacks and identifies a flaw within the other."[9] As people become defensive, accurate communication becomes more and more difficult. Moreover, workers who anticipate that appraisal interviews will dwell on their weaknesses rather than on their strengths will enter those interviews defensively. Gibb suggests that " . . . Arousing defensiveness interferes with communication and thus makes it difficult—and sometimes impossible—for anyone to convey ideas clearly and to move effectively toward the solution of . . . managerial problems."[10]

A third difficulty with appraisal interviews involves both parties; namely, interviewees and interviewers often bring significantly different perceptions about worker performance to the interview. Interviewers tend to believe that interviewees can solve most of their work performance problems. For example, a nursing supervisor may believe that slow responses to patient calls for assistance result from the nurse's lack of motivation to respond promptly to each call. The supervisor may envision that the nurse is engaging in social conversation or drinking coffee instead of attending to patient needs. Interviewees, on the other hand, frequently attribute work performance problems to situational factors. For example, nurses whose supervisors think they are not responding quickly enough to patient buzzers may believe the problem is understaffing. The nurses may believe that they respond as promptly as possible to each call, but that the hospital has not hired enough nurses to answer each call when it comes into the nursing station. A study of subordinates and managers found that managers often believed that work performance was much more a function of workers' personal characteristics than the workers did.[11] The researchers found that workers thought that external variables like machinery quality, coworkers, job duties, and so forth had a much larger impact on the work performance than their supervisors did.

In summary, three problems make appraisal interviews particularly challenging. First, they are time-consuming work for interviewers. Second, interviewees get defensive; and as a result, communication is difficult. Third, the two parties often have different perceptions of the reasons for problems with worker performance. It is apparent, then, that appraisal interviews are often unpleasant and hard. Even more alarming is research that suggests that appraisals done poorly can actually become counterproductive;[12] that is, they can hurt employee morale and lower productivity rather than improving it. Despite these problems, performance appraisal interviews can be constructive. The following section of this chapter suggests a reconceptualization of the appraisal interview, one that empowers both parties and minimizes defensiveness.

Reconceiving the Appraisal Interview

Performance appraisal, particularly the interview, can enhance productivity. A basic change in how participants think about an appraisal interview can bring about this change.

Appraisal as a Team Effort

To work effectively, an appraisal interview must involve *two* active parties. The definition of appraisal interviews at the beginning of this chapter is based on the assumption that the best appraisal involves input from both the interviewer and interviewee. That definition describes the appraisal interview as being "based on carefully collected data that allows organizations *and* workers to assess worker performance so that they (i.e., interviewers and interviewees) can work together to set goals and improve effectiveness." Such a definition represents a new notion of the appraisal process as a team effort, not just a tradition required by management. In a team effort, both the interviewer and interviewee cooperate to assess accurately and to plan effectively. Such a team effort can very quickly improve worker cooperation in the appraisal process. Burke, Weitzel, and Weir have found that worker satisfaction with the appraisal interview is directly correlated with the degree of worker participation in the appraisal process.[13] Workers who have received realistic job previews before they were hired and who have collaborated with their supervisors about measurable work goals generally find more satisfaction with the appraisal process. Not only does mutual participation lead to worker satisfaction, but it can also affect the interview in other ways.

Understanding that defensiveness is also an *interactive process* adds to the attractiveness of a team approach to appraisal interviewing. While most people believe that interviewer messages create defensiveness, a more accurate understanding of defensiveness is that both parties can create or lessen it. "Defensiveness is dyadic: both people involved in the interaction are integral to creating defensiveness."[14] Defensiveness results from a combination of the interviewer's messages and the interviewee's predisposition to become guarded. Obviously, both parties can choose to reduce specific behaviors that create defensiveness. The interviewer can send messages that are oriented to description, provisionalism, and problem solving. The interviewee can enter the interview with a resolve to keep defensiveness as low as possible.

The team effort can include yet another activity that will increase the success of the appraisal; that is, *mutual goal setting.* Goal setting that uses suggestions and information from both the supervisor and worker is identified as a key to effective appraisal. In fact, goal setting is the only current variable in appraisal that has been identified as having a beneficial impact on work performance in 90 percent of the reported studies.[15] For example, improvements in workers' performances in specific organizations correlated with the degree to which the appraisal interview included job-related activities like mutual goal setting.[16] The opening interview demonstrated that Mickie and Carol agreed upon certain areas for improvement. While Mickie suggested a goal for Carol, she also invited Carol's reaction to it. She asked for Carol's input about how to achieve the goal. As the research suggests, when workers help to set goals, they both report a desire to improve and then actually show improvement on the job.

Creating a team effort by (1) involving the workers in appraisal, (2) understanding that both parties can reduce defensiveness, and (3) incorporating mutual goal setting into the interview will result in a revitalized appraisal interview.

The Interviewer and Appraisal

Preparation

Assessment. The first step in the appraisal interview process is the actual appraisal of performance. **Appraisal** is the assessment, or evaluation, of an employee's work performance. A supervisor who has direct knowledge and contact with the person being evaluated usually conducts the assessment. The evaluation also may include self-assessment; namely, the worker's own evaluation of her/his work performance. The assessment process begins long before the appraisal interview and provides the information that eventually becomes the basis for that interview. Good assessment is consistent, valid, and complete.

Evaluations of employee work performance should use *consistent measures and criteria* for all employees. Many workers know the frustration of different standards being applied to different employees. Some examples include the boss's daughter who gets raises that better workers do not get, the worker who is rewarded with the best work schedule because he flirts with the office manager, the golfing buddy of the crew leader who gets an early promotion. Supervisors need to be sure that their assessment is fair and equitable for all employees. They need to be particularly careful that the evaluation does not include judgments formed on the basis of the race, sex, age, ethnic background, or handicapped status of the interviewee.

To ensure consistency, supervisors need to be sure that their evaluations do not have an adverse impact on any particular group of employees. For example, they should not evaluate workers negatively who miss optional weekly breakfasts when it is clear that those who do not attend are all women who have responsibilities for young children before they come to work. Evaluations about work performance need to focus solely on work-related issues and should not negatively impact one segment of the workforce, in this case, the women, more than any other. Assessment of work performance should focus on work performance and nothing else.

Valid measures of work performance are also essential for fair assessment. Such measures will be discussed more specifically in the next part of this chapter. The primary question is: Is this information about the employee's work gathered in such a way that it measures what it purports to measure? To increase validity of work performance measures, standardized methods of data collection should be used consistently for all employees. Moreover, supervisors who have personal knowledge and contact with the persons being evaluated can provide more valid data than supervisors who are not directly familiar with the workers' performance.

Assessment also works best when it includes a *complete* picture of the employee's work performance. Too many times, appraisal interviews are based on a tiny sample of the employee's work that may not be representative. For example, an education professor evaluated a student teacher's performance in a high school English class. When the students in the class realized that their student teacher was being evaluated, they behaved differently. They listened attentively, participated enthusiastically, wrote down assignments, and even laughed at all her jokes. The student teacher had struggled with mixed success all semester to get the students to listen, to ask questions, and to write down assignments. When the professor and the student teacher met for the appraisal interview, the professor gave her excellent marks in all areas. He said he had never seen such a productive, participatory class. Although the student teacher was pleased at the positive appraisal, she knew that it was based on incomplete information. Fifty minutes of observation did not provide a comprehensive picture of her overall effectiveness with the class. To be constructive and to help the worker improve, assessment should be based on a comprehensive sample of all the supervisor can possibly learn about the employee's work performance.

Too often, supervisors rely only on measures of outcome for assessment. They may assess "bottom-line" productivity and nothing else. For example, a sales rep-

Employee involvement in the appraisal process will result in a cooperative and revitalized appraisal interview.

resentative for a medical supply firm may be evaluated solely on the basis of quantity of sales. Other important measures of work performance are lost by supervisors who look only at sales numbers. If the sales representative is spending time visiting hospitals that have not purchased from this firm, but that are now giving serious attention to its products, even though a sale has not been finalized, important and potentially profitable work is going on. The supervisor should note all activities that relate to work performance. A study of managers and workers by Carson, Carby, and Dobbins found that too many supervisors relied only on measures of outcome (such as productivity) to measure worker performance.[17] The authors concluded that many raters took nothing but outcome into account in their evaluations. They suggest that fair appraisals factor everything that affects work performance, including situational factors, into the assessment process. All aspects of performance can then be discussed in the appraisal interview (see Figure 10.1).

Methods for Assessing Worker Performance. The best way to make assessment consistent, valid, and complete is to gather information prior to the interview carefully and systematically. We will describe several of the most common methods for assessment in the section that follows. Most supervisors use a combination of these methods adapted to their organization's workers in order to evaluate fairly and constructively. More detailed explanations of these methods appear in the books listed at the end of this chapter.

1. Category rating systems

   —Graphic rating scale

   —Checklist

   —Behaviorally anchored rating scales (BARS)

2. Comparative rating systems

3. Written evaluation systems

   —Critical incident method

   —Essays

4. Management by objectives

5. Self-assessment

FIGURE 10.1   Common Methods for Conducting Appraisals

1. Category rating systems. Category rating systems are those in which the supervisor rates an employee's level of performance in a series of predetermined categories. Most of us have been evaluated with this system at some time in our jobs because it is a common assessment tool. The most common kinds of category rating include the **graphic rating scale** which uses a Likert scale to judge work performance. A Likert scale includes a single statement followed by a scale, usually with five to seven levels, which allow the rater to express degrees of agreement or disagreement. On a continuum of numbers, the supervisor assesses the employee's work in a particular area. A sample graphic rating scale follows:

Worker Completes Work on Time

1	2	3	4	5
(Poor)		(Satisfactory)		(Outstanding)

Although the graphic rating scale is commonly used, it has several weaknesses. For example, if the job duty being evaluated is described vaguely or contains more than one activity, it may be difficult for the worker to know precisely about what she or he is doing well or badly. For example, if the job duty says "acts professional on the job," a worker who receives a poor rating may not know what needs to be changed. Another problem in organizations where multiple supervisors use the same graphic rating system is that they may not interpret the evaluative words the same way. What one supervisor might rate as "outstanding" might be rated only a "satisfactory" by a different supervisor. This poses problems with fairness if evaluation across different departments is connected with promotions and salary decisions.

A second category rating system is the **checklist,** which is a rating method where the interviewer checks a statement that best describes the employee's work from a given list of statements. This allows a more comprehensive evaluation than the graphic rating approach by giving a more thorough description of the worker. A checklist might include a statement like this one:

(Check the one statement that best describes this worker.)

——Sees work that needs to be done without asking and does it

——Does work immediately when asked

——Needs to be asked more than once to attend to work

——Does not follow work orders

A checklist approach should also be used cautiously because words can mean different things to different raters. Moreover, all the items in a checklist may not be of equal importance, so a poor rating in a vital task area may not stand out on paper as much as it stands out in importance. For example, a factory worker's appraisal might refer to work behaviors such as attendance, safety, thoroughness, and sense of cooperation. Although the items all appear equal in importance, a negative rating on safety should be considered much more seriously than poor ratings in other areas.

A third set of category rating systems are **behaviorally anchored rating scales (BARS),** which individually design scales for specific jobs in specific organizations. These scales include short statements that describe particular behaviors related to a specific position. All statements that the supervisor uses for evaluation describe behaviors related to actual dimensions of the specific job being evaluated. Evaluators read the statements and evaluate the worker's performance with a numerical rating. BARS are particularly useful when supervisors have to evaluate many different employees who do basically the same kind of job. For example, a restaurant with many servers might use BARS to assess their work performance. In advance of the appraisal process, the evaluator prepares a series of short statements describing behaviors related to various aspects of the job. These statements are called *anchors* that reflect important job dimensions. Specifically, the restaurant supervisor might expect the servers, among other things, to (1) deliver food effectively to the tables, and (2) work well with dissatisfied customers. BARS anchors reflecting these two dimensions might look like this:

Anchor 1: The server can carry trays with up to five entrees with balance and poise.

1 (excellent)	—
2 (good)	—
3 (satisfactory)	—
4 (fair)	—
5 (poor)	—

Anchor 2: The server consistently returns to dissatisfied customers with corrected orders, an offer for a free dessert, and a respectful demeanor.

1 (excellent)	—
2 (good)	—
3 (satisfactory)	—
4 (fair)	—
5 (poor)	—

Evaluators simply mark each of the anchor statements numerically to demonstrate how effective each worker is in each of the important job-related behaviors.

BARS are very promising as standardized measures for performance because once they are developed, they are easy to administer and gather a rich impression of the worker's performance. The extensive effort needed to develop a good BARS tailored to a specific organizational position, however, is their biggest drawback. They are time consuming to create. Each job being evaluated requires an individualized BARS designed for that specific position. Once developed, however, these are effective measures of performance.

2. Comparative rating systems. Evaluators use comparative rating systems when they want to compare the relative performance of different workers. The most common form of comparative rating is the **ranking system,** which asks the evaluator to rank employees from best to worst in terms of performance. A principal of a school, for example, might be required to rank the work performance of all department chairs. The principal would have to indicate, in numerical order, who was the most effective chair, second most effective, and so on through the least effective chair.

Ranking poses important problems. A significant weakness with the ranking method is that the size of the increment (i.e., degree of difference) between employees appears equal when it might not be equal at all. The two best employees in a department might be nearly identical in their performance with a major gap between them and the rest of the workers, but the ranking system will not show this difference. Moreover, ranking does not give workers feedback about why they got their ratings. All it does is indicate where they rank in relation to their coworkers. Finally, ranking places more emphasis on the results than on the process of evaluation. Constructive change results from both parties' active participation in appraisal. Such participation and dialogue is missing from ranking methods of evaluation when they are used alone.

3. Written method. Various written methods can be effective forms for assessment. A common form is the **critical incident method** in which a supervisor keeps a written record of each employee's most effective and least effective work experiences throughout the entire period of evaluation. This method requires that the supervisor make written notes about specific examples of the worker's best and poorest performances. Often used in conjunction with more standardized methods of record keeping and assessment, the critical incident method provides a rich, reality based picture of how the worker handles job problems. An example of directions for a critical incident file follows in Figure 10.2.

The critical incident method of assessment can, if done well, create a comprehensive picture of the employee's performance and demonstrate the employee's strengths and weaknesses. Its liabilities are that it takes supervisor time and skill for record keeping, depends heavily on the supervisor's writing ability, reflects a subjective impression from the evaluator, and makes comparisons among workers difficult.

A less structured method for written evaluation is the **essay method,** which asks the supervisors to write brief essays describing each worker's performance. The organization usually suggests several categories that need to be addressed in the essays. In most universities, for example, administrators use essays for faculty evaluation, including evaluation of the faculty member's teaching, research, and service to the university and community. The administrative evaluator needs to refer to each of the relevant work areas so that the essay provides an acceptable and comprehensive evaluation.

Essays are also problematic because they rely so heavily on the supervisor's writing skill. Because they are very time consuming, they are impractical where

Knowledge of the job
Example of outstanding work:

Example of poor job performance:

Responsiveness to customer needs
Example of outstanding work:

Example of poor job performance:

Ability to solve difficult customer relations problems
Example of outstanding work:

Example of poor job performance:

Cooperation with departmental coworkers
Example of outstanding work:

Example of poor job performance:

Other
Example of outstanding work:

Example of poor job performance:

FIGURE 10.2   Critical Incident Method. Directions to supervisor: Give a specific example of the employee's outstanding and poor work performance for each of the following areas. Your example should represent typical job performance behaviors.

large numbers of employees are affected. They are not useful in comparing employees if the comparison needs to be highly systematic. Essay assessments are generally used in combination with other forms of evaluation.

4. Management by objectives (MBO). Management by objectives, the **MBO** approach to assessment, combines goal setting with performance appraisal and invites employees and supervisors to work together in the process. This assessment invites and uses information from the supervisor and employee so that it is a kind of guided self-appraisal.[18] In an MBO appraisal system, the worker and manager identify reasonable, measurable goals for the worker to achieve within a specific period of time. The process has four stages and all of them are done collaboratively in a series of appraisal interviews: (1) job review in which the manager and worker discuss and agree upon the duties of the job; (2) establishment of performance standards by the worker and manager; (3) goal setting by both parties; and (4) follow-up interviews to discuss whether the worker is moving toward or has achieved the previously established goals.

Using MBO provides distinct benefits for workers, supervisors, and organizations. These benefits are grounded in the requirement that MBO assessment includes dialogue between workers and their supervisors. This dialogue increases the likelihood that both parties will have an accurate understanding of the job itself and the criteria by which performance will be evaluated. Since the focus of assessment is improvement, this process is likely to generate higher productivity and morale because both the workers and their supervisors understand why particular goals are being implemented and why they are being measured with particular standards. Finally, in the MBO approach, the employee can usually predict the outcome of appraisal interviews on the basis of prior meetings; hence, it is less threatening. Because the method requires collaboration throughout the process, employees can anticipate both the areas for evaluation during the appraisal interviews and the conclusions that are likely to be reached.

These benefits do not come without costs. One major drawback to MBO is that not all job requirements are flexible enough for it to work. Many repetitive tasks, such as those in factory assembly lines or fast food, do not have enough flexibility to allow workers to have meaningful input on goals. A second problem is that at times the personal goals of workers and the organization's goals will conflict. For example, a worker may want a goal about spending more time on research at a time when the organization wants more time to be spent on sales. Finally, MBO will not work unless the organization and its management team are committed to worker participation in the appraisal system. If the manager does not genuinely want worker input, an integral part of the MBO system, it will not work.

5. Self-assessment. Self-assessment invites workers to evaluate themselves and share that evaluation with the supervisor so that a fuller picture of the employee's work performance is available. Self-assessments can use all of the evaluative methods that have been described to this point; namely, category rating systems, comparative rating, written forms, and MBO. Supervisors who invite self-assessment as a part of their appraisal process need to consider two important cautions: (1) self-assessment can be inflated, and (2) self-assessment norms vary according to the cultural backgrounds of the employees. Let us look at those two issues separately.

Research in business and higher education has identified a tendency for individuals to rate their own performance significantly higher than other people rate the same performance. This inflation of self-assessment was apparent, for example, in a research project that included an analysis of independent samples of self-assessments by workers. When these workers' self-ratings were compared to ratings by supervisors, Harris and Schaubroeck found that the self-ratings were one-half of one standard deviation higher than the supervisors' ratings for the same people.[19] Studies of university professors found the same pattern of inflation of self-evaluations. Two different studies found that university faculty members consistently rated their own teaching higher than their students rated it.[20] Self-assessments enhance the evaluation process, but a tendency for persons to give themselves positive ratings needs to be considered when incorporating self-assessments into the appraisal process.

A second caution for persons using self-evaluations in appraisal is to realize that persons from different cultures may have different norms in conducting self-appraisal. For example, Farh, Dobbins, and Cheng found that Chinese (Taiwanese) subordinates rated their own work performance significantly lower than did their supervisors.[21] Contrary to studies in the United States where worker self-ratings were very high, the Chinese self-ratings were consistently low. Multinational corporations or firms employing persons from different cultures need to be aware of such cultural patterns as the Chinese "modesty bias"[22] when they compare different employees' self-evaluations.

In summary, different approaches to assessment of worker performance can provide a valuable foundation of valid information on which to base the appraisal interview. Most supervisors use a combination of methods to gather consistent, valid, and comprehensive information about each worker. Using some combination of category rating, comparative rating, written evaluation, MBO, and worker self-assessment can provide a strong base of information that will make a constructive appraisal interview possible.

Increasing Accuracy in Assessment.   Good assessment is hard to do. Even with sophisticated techniques, the conclusions of experienced assessors can be unreliable. For example, Ryan, Barbera, and Sackett found that highly experienced evaluators gave such different written assessments about the same three workers that outside evaluators were unable to identify the workers as being the same individuals.[23] These findings suggest that it is imperative that supervisors use multiple reliable and valid measuring instruments, such as those described in the previous section to counteract the tendency for inconsistent evaluation. Moreover, assessors should verify by discussion or written materials that the interviewer and interviewee are basing their conclusions on the same information.

Training for appraisal interviewers is essential so the appraisal process is rigorous and fair. Ivancevich found that a one-day training program for team leaders led to significant improvements in their workers' perceptions of the fairness, accuracy, and clarity of appraisal interviews, especially when the evaluators had received training in goal setting.[24] The U.S. Department of Labor has developed an initiative designed to counteract the "glass ceiling" that many women and minorities in management encounter. The **glass ceiling** refers to the invisible barrier that many women and minorities encounter when they get to the top of mid-level management and are unable to break through to the highest levels of management. The Department of Labor suggests that any managers who make promotion decisions receive training in appraisal so that all workers are treated fairly. In this training, supervisors should learn to establish objective guidelines and clear criteria for evaluation.[25]

Finally, when the organization has found a reliable and valid method of assessment, it is important that the organization continue to use it. Repeated use of a system of evaluation leads to familiarity, and familiarity reduces the anxiety related to uncertainty and increases the skill and knowledge of both parties. Consistent use of an evaluation procedure also insures that data can be compared over time.

Conducting the Appraisal Interview

Interviewers who have conducted thorough and fair assessments of their workers have a strong foundation to use in the actual appraisal interviews. Certain other procedures and behaviors will also contribute to an interview appraisal process which is constructive for the organization and its workers.

Regularity.   Effective organizations build regular appraisal into the work schedules of their employees, because when appraisal is universal and regularly scheduled, workers are less likely to associate it with punishment. When appraisal interviews occur periodically, workers associate them less with disciplinary problems and more with the normal work-related activities that their supervisors coordinate. Regular and frequent appraisal assures that appraisal occurs even when nothing is wrong.

Organizations wanting to make appraisal a more constructive part of the life of their workers will schedule the first appraisal interview early in a worker's time with the organization. Early appraisal can reduce stress-producing ambiguity about initial performance for new employees.[26] Employees, especially newcomers, are eager to get a sense of how supervisors view their work. Conducting early and regular appraisals helps reduce newcomer uncertainty and increase comfort with the job. Even if the appraisal includes negative feedback, it gives new employees an early opportunity to correct their efforts, if they choose.

Although the appraisal process is time consuming, a growing number of organizations try to conduct quarterly reviews (four times during each work year). However, annual reviews are still most common.[27] Quarterly appraisals are particularly valuable for the newer and less experienced workers. Frequent appraisals encourage constant attention to improvement in less experienced employees.[28] Moreover, workers who participate in appraisal interviews at least once a year or more view the evaluation process as being fairer and more accurate than workers who participate in it less frequently.[29]

Scheduling appraisal interviews frequently and regularly makes it less likely that workers believe they are being punished for mistakes they have made. Regular appraisal sends the message that appraisal is important and normal.

Clarifying Interview Goals.   Appraisal interviewers use specific interview goals to guide their work in the interviews. Appraisal interviewers often adopt goals such as the following:

- To improve employee performance for the next appraisal period.
- To improve employee performance over a long time period.
- To assess the employee's work performance accurately and completely.
- To work with the employee to set work goals for the next six months.
- To get employee input into organizational and departmental goals.

Most appraisal is designed to motivate workers to improve their work performance.

Appraisal interviews function best if they are separate from interviews about salary review.[30] Combining salary review and appraisal forces the interviewer to function simultaneously as a motivator and a judge. These contradictory roles diminish the effectiveness of each individual role.[31] If a supervisor wants to motivate a worker, the supervisor raises different issues than those which might pertain to a discussion about salary increases. Salary increases should be conducted separately after the appraisal process is complete.

Inviting the Employee to Prepare.   Supervisors who understand the value of active employee participation in the appraisal process invite interviewees to prepare for the interview. This invitation demonstrates the supervisor's interest in collaborative appraisal. It also encourages worker involvement and commitment to the process. Researchers have found that workers who gave thought to the appraisal interview before they participated in it described the interview as a more positive experience than those who did not.[32]

Some organizations ask their employees to (1) complete a brief form before the interview, (2) read the supervisor's written review before the interview to encourage thoughtful reaction and suggestions, and (3) evaluate their own performance using the same forms that the supervisor uses.[33] The supervisor can also ask the worker to consider several simple questions before coming to the interview. The questions might be:

1. What job related activities have I performed best since my last appraisal interview?
2. What areas of my work could I improve in?
3. What resources do I need to help me do my job better?
4. What is the most challenging part of my job? How do I usually approach that part?
5. What should my manager know about my job that she or he might not already know?

These questions acknowledge that work performance is related both to the employee's skill and motivation *and* to situational factors. Realizing that work performance is a consequence of a combination of internal and external factors allows the appraiser to have a more comprehensive understanding of the reasons for the performance.

Creating a Positive Climate for Communication. **Communication climate**, the atmosphere of a communication event, is described by Gibb as being supportive or defensive. A good climate for appraisal is a supportive one; it is a climate that reduces defensiveness and allows exchange of potentially distressing information. Such a climate goes beyond superficial praise and encouragement. The climate, set largely by the behaviors of the supervisor, should be one in which the worker senses that she or he is valued by the supervisor and the organization.

Gibbs' classic work about communication climate identified six specific behaviors which, when expressed verbally or nonverbally, often lead to increased defensiveness. He identified six counterpart behaviors that create supportive climates. Any specific communication interaction like an appraisal interview is seldom completely defensive or supportive. Instead, an interview climate rests along a continuum between a defensive and supportive one. A supervisor conducting appraisals has the responsibility to create as much supportiveness as possible for effective communication to occur. What are the dimensions of defensive and supportive climates? (See Figure 10.3.)

Let us look at the behaviors that affect communication climate in appraisal interviews. First, people become defensive when they perceive *evaluation*. Being judged by others is threatening. Defensiveness, in turn, impedes performance. An example of this is common to most people. Imagine yourself at a keyboard and typing a paper. You are typing fairly quickly and without many errors. Then someone comes, stands behind you, and watches you type. Suddenly you make a lot of errors. Why? Most of us believe, accurately or not, that the person watching is evaluating our work. When we were not evaluated, we performed fine. When we believed an evaluator was judging our work, we suddenly became more tense and less accurate. In more significant professional settings, the impact is powerful. Bosses who enter employee work spaces and say, "just pretend I'm not here" should

Defensive Climate	Supportive Climate
1. Evaluation	1. Description
2. Control	2. Problem orientation
3. Strategy	3. Spontaneity
4. Neutrality	4. Empathy
5. Superiority	5. Equality
6. Certainty	6. Provisionalism

FIGURE 10.3   Communication Climate[45]

Used with Permission of Oxford University Press.

know that such pretending is impossible. If the boss is present, most people get more defensive because they sense that the boss is judging their performance. Research by Kay, Meyer, and French found that subordinates whose managers had used appraisal interviews to evaluate a weakness and point out a need for improvement believed that the managers were threatening to their self-esteem.[34] Moreover, the greater the threat the subordinates perceived, the more negatively they felt toward the entire appraisal system. Even more important, greater perceived threat actually led to less constructive improvement in job performance.

Appraisal interviews are inherently evaluative. Thus, by their nature, they generate some defensiveness. Although evaluation cannot be removed from the appraisal process, the appraisal interviewer can adopt what Gibb suggested was a counterpart behavior that leads to a more supportive climate; that is using description instead of evaluation.

Supervisors who want to create a more supportive climate use *description* rather than evaluative comments whenever possible. They spend much of the appraisal interview describing work behaviors rather than judging. One of the primary triggers for defensiveness is a sense of being attacked. To lessen this sense of attack that comes in appraisal, the interviewer can word statements descriptively.[35] For example, the supervisor might say, "Your payroll spreadsheets came in late three different weeks since our last appraisal in May. This means they were late three out of twelve weeks, 25 percent of the time. We need to talk about how to improve this." A supervisor whose climate is defensive might say, "You're really wasting time down there. Your personal procrastination meant that payroll came in late 25 percent of the time since our last meeting. This is totally irresponsible on your part." The first supervisor demonstrates description, and the second shows evaluation. Most workers prefer hearing information descriptively and drawing their own evaluations. They also become less defensive and are better able to work toward good solutions.

The second behavior that increases defensiveness is *control,* or domination. Most people do not like to be told exactly what they have to do. In fact, many adults, if they are ordered to do something a particular way, revert to a child-like response and refuse to cooperate at all. In appraisal, a supervisor who does assessment without employee input, provides feedback about performance without inviting comment, and then imposes a set of work performance goals on the worker exhibits control. Such an approach *rarely* motivates improvement.

An alternative and more supportive approach is what Gibb calls the *problem orientation* in which the supervisor and the employee work together to solve the problems in work performance and then collaboratively set goals for the period of time before the next appraisal. Research with 270 health care personnel found that the more the employees had participated actively in the interview, the more they felt their supervisors were helpful and constructive.[36] Joining with the employee in a problem orientation allows the supervisor to give feedback, receive feedback, and work collaboratively toward a solution that the worker can genuinely endorse.

A third defensiveness producing behavior is *strategy,* which is a behavior that leads an individual to believe that the other is trying to manipulate the situation.

Workers become guarded when they believe their supervisors are trying to manipulate them. In appraisal interviews, for example, some supervisors believe they should be cheerleaders for their workers by cheering them to better productivity by focusing only and superficially on their good work. Such "cheerleading" supervisors do not have much credibility with employees after a while because the workers quickly sense what the supervisor is up to. This leads to defensiveness because workers do not believe that the supervisor is being honest with them. The counterpart behavior that leads to a more supportive appraisal climate is *spontaneity*, or honesty and candor. Although at times the truth is less pleasant than a cheerful and superficial "you're doing great," if a worker needs to improve, the supervisor needs to say it tactfully and truthfully. Being straightforward about the worker's strengths and weaknesses is a constructive alternative to appearing manipulative and having a hidden agenda.

A fourth defensive behavior is what Gibb calls *neutrality*, or indifference. The meaning of neutrality in Gibb's categories is not fair-mindedness or objectivity, but rather a message that says "I won't treat you differently from anyone else—you're just another employee to me." Employees want to believe that they are more than social security numbers to their supervisors. They want supervisors who demonstrate *empathy* with them. Expressions of empathy show the workers that supervisors understand the demands of their jobs and their lives. Such empathy increases the supportiveness of the communication climate.

Fifth, workers become defensive when their supervisors demonstrate blatant *superiority*. Obviously, supervisors are higher on the organizational chart than their subordinates. They usually make more money, assume more responsibilities, and often have more training and experience. Despite these characteristics, they do not necessarily know everything about the job, the worker, and the organization. People with "know-it -all" attitudes demonstrate the kind of superiority that Gibb believes increases defensiveness.

People, regardless of their standing in the organization, want to hear expressions of *equality*. All workers are valuable in their professional roles. Without the custodian who unlocks the building in the morning, the chief executive officer cannot get into the office. Without the vice-president for finance, no one receives a paycheck. Without the security guard, the judge cannot begin the trial. In appraisal interviews, workers want to hear that they are important in the organization, regardless of where they stand on the organizational chart.

Last, persons who are rigidly certain in their ideas create defensiveness in those with whom they work. *Certainty* refers to behaviors that demonstrate that persons will not listen or consider any views that are different from theirs. Obviously, this kind of closed mindedness does not help in appraisal interviews. A more supportive behavior includes what Gibb describes as *provisionalism*, which is an attitude of openness and receptivity to ideas and information. For an appraisal interview to reflect a collaborative effort between the worker and the supervisor, both need to exhibit provisional behaviors and be open to the other's ideas and reactions.

Working to create a supportive climate is an important responsibility for the appraisal interviewer. Such a climate does more than create good feelings—it creates a good working environment for appraisal. Since defensiveness leads to less accurate understanding of messages, more distortion, and lower ability to perceive the sender accurately, supervisors should do all in their power to create supportive rather than defensive climates for the interview.

Giving Criticism Constructively.   Constructive criticism involves information, both positive and negative, given in a way that follows certain principles for effective feedback. Effective feedback, as Figure 10.4 shows, is focused on work behaviors. It is specific, descriptive, problem solving, limited, and appropriately timed.

---

1. Focus on work behaviors, not the employee's personality.

   Example: You listened carefully to Ms. Solski's complaint, and your report really showed it You had all the details right. Versus: You're a great person!

2. Provide evidence about the conclusions by referring to specific behaviors, not general inferences about the worker.

   Example: In the meeting yesterday, you did not hear what your team members proposed. You couldn't even answer the question that Mathers asked about what they had just said. Versus: You are really distracted.

3. When possible, describe worker behaviors rather than evaluate them.

   Example: Your accident with the fork lift last week caused over $3,000 damage to the lift and $1,000 to the pump. Versus: You're so irresponsible with equipment that we'll never be able to afford your recklessness.

4. Focus on mutual problem-solving rather than giving large amounts of advice.

   Example: I've gotten four calls from suppliers about late payments from your office. We've got a real problem with this. Let's talk about what is causing it and try to come up with a solution that will really work. Versus: Four suppliers have called about late payments. I want you to have the checks for each week on my desk by Thursday noon. No exceptions.

5. Limit the amount of information given to the worker to what is manageable, usually two to four areas for improvement.

   Example: There are always lots of areas we can all improve, but I'd like you to focus on two— reducing your numbers of errors in data entry and coordinating the data entry with the other department better. VERSUS I have a list of 25 suggested areas I want you to work on between now and next week.

6. Give information in a time and place so that difficult issues can be discussed appropriately.

   Example: I'd like to schedule an hour on Friday in my office so we can look at the assessment, talk about areas for improvement, and hear any ideas you have. I think an hour will be enough, but if it's not we can schedule another meeting. VERSUS Got a minute? I know you've got to sit here by the phone, but let me just run through your annual assessment.

FIGURE 10.4   Effective Feedback in Appraisal Interviews

Giving feedback constructively is an art. Persons who receive constructive feedback during appraisal, even if it identifies their weaknesses, are less angry, happier, and more inclined to view the appraisal process as fair than those who receive destructive feedback.[37] Destructive criticism, criticism that violates the basic guidelines for effective feedback, has consequences that linger far beyond the actual appraisal interview in which the criticism is shared. Such negative criticism often has (a) a tone that is inconsiderate and threatening, (b) attributions of internal reasons for poor performance, and (c) general rather than specific complaints.[38] Its consequences are severe. It generates stronger anger and tension in those who receive it, increases the tendency for the worker to use ineffective techniques (such as excuses) to deal with poor performance, intensifies conflict with the supervisor, and reduces both parties' commitment to work goals.[39] All these results are counterproductive to the goal of appaisal.

Constructive feedback is sensitive to the worker's need to save face. Effective appraisers realize that workers need to protect their images, and the appraisers will respond appropriately. Applegate and Woods found that persons with higher levels of awareness and concern for others face needs used more behaviors that allowed others to save face by offering them options that gave them autonomy.[39] Effective supervisors give feedback carefully and constructively.

Inviting the Worker to Share in Goal Setting. Persons are more likely to work toward goals when they have helped create them. Workers who perceive that they have input and control over goals are more likely to support them than when they believe they are externally imposed.[41] Including the worker in the goal setting can be done in various ways: inviting worker self-assessment, using MBO method of appraisal, setting aside time during the interview to hear the worker's ideas about appropriate goals, and requiring that all work performance goals be mutually established. By its very nature, mutual goal setting increases worker participation in the appraisal interview.

Listening Well. Good listening is a vital skill for an appraisal interviewer.[42] Good listening gathers valuable information and conveys to the workers the sense that their ideas are important to their supervisors. Although the traditional view of the appraisal interview is one in which the supervisor does most of the talking, the reconceptualization of the appraisal interview as one with two active parties means that the supervisor needs to listen frequently and well. Chapter 2 provided extensive information about ways to improve listening in interviews.

Closing the Interview

The supervisor assumes responsibility for ending the interview. This should not be done before the worker has had a chance to share information about job performance and react to the evaluation itself. Often, an organization has an official assessment form that needs to be signed before the interview concludes.

Generally, the employees' signatures on the forms means that the employees have read the form, not that they necessarily agree with it. The interviewee may not have to sign the form immediately. Supervisors often give the employees the opportunity to attach a written response before signing, if they choose.

Two brief, additional activities help increase the power of the interview to improve worker performance. First, the supervisor should restate the goals that have been mutually agreed upon. If possible, the supervisor can also highlight the organizational resources that will be available to the worker to achieve those goals. In the interview at the beginning of the chapter, the supervisor explicitly summarized her three main areas for evaluation. This summary reminded the worker about what the supervisor believed the important areas were.

Second, the supervisor should end the interview with a statement that suggests that the interview was important and valuable. Rather than say, "Well, I guess we're done with this for another six months," an interview can end with: "I really appreciated the chance to talk with you about your work here. I know this hour was really helpful to me in getting a sense for what you're doing out there, and I hope it was valuable for you too. I look forward to doing this again in another six months. In the meantime, I hope the goals you set for yourself work out." The explicit reference to appraisal as helpful and important increases the sense that it is a constructive process.

Following Up After the Interview

Many organizations miss the opportunity to follow up on information obtained in appraisal interviews. Often, workers volunteer information about machinery problems, broken vehicles, unclear policies, or scheduling problems during the interviews. An easy way to boost worker morale and demonstrate that supervisors really listened during appraisal interviews is to solve some of those problems in the days immediately after the interview. Many times the solutions are inexpensive and workable. In fact, for many situations, the only reason the problems had not been solved earlier was because the supervisor did not know about them.

Effective follow up to appraisal interviews can also take the form of spoken comments about the appraisal ("Hey, I really appreciated talking with you yesterday") or solving problems that the workers had raised during the interview. Both suggest that the supervisor considered the interview important.

Appraisal and the Worker

Preparing for the Interview

Active participation in the appraisal process means that the worker has more to do than attend the appraisal interview. Preparation for the appraisal interviews begins from the first day on the job.

From the time of recruiting interviews through the first several weeks on the job, workers can gain an understanding of the requirements for the job. All workers should have a clear understanding about the standards for their job performances. Some organizations share copies of the evaluation forms with the employees at the outset of employment. In organizations that do not do this, workers may request these evaluation forms to become aware of the criteria that will be used to assess their work.

An employee is wise to keep a record of information about her/his own work performance. Many workers actually keep a file of information about procedures, memos, special recognition, disciplinary warnings, notes of compliment, copies of past appraisals, and productivity records. All of this information can provide a good basis for appraisal or, if necessary, to dispute a supervisor's appraisal.

Preparation for an actual appraisal interview is more focused. Workers should anticipate the interview by preparing a list of issues and concerns that they want to discuss during the interview. The interview is an excellent opportunity to educate the supervisor about aspects of the job that may not be obvious to her/him. If certain facilities, machinery, software, coworkers, or facility arrangements impair productivity, the appraisal interview is a good opportunity for the worker to inform the supervisor of the problems. An appraisal interview is a two-way interaction. Interviewee preparation helps ensure that the discussion goes both ways.

Participating in the Interview

Some supervisors make active participation for workers easier than others. The effective appraisal interview affords employees a valuable resource; namely, it's a time to advance their own ideas for change and improvement and develop workable objectives for the future.

Reduce Defensiveness. As mentioned earlier, defensiveness is affected by two factors—the supervisor's messages and the employee's tendency to become defensive. Workers who enter into appraisal interviews assuming that they are "flawed" automatically heighten their defensiveness.[43] Reminding themselves that appraisal is a process with two active participants helps workers lessen this sense of threat. As much as it is possible, workers who try to participate less defensively are able to send and receive the messages more clearly, accurately, and with less distortion.

Listen Carefully. One way to ensure reduced defensiveness is to listen carefully. When feedback is negative, it is difficult to hear it without distortion and defensiveness. Some employees even find it difficult to listen to positive feedback because they find it embarrassing. Hearing a supervisor's feedback, positive or negative, can help make an employee a better worker. In the opening interview, the receptionist listened carefully to her supervisor's concerns about older patients not hearing her instructions. Her responses indicated that she accepted the suggestion and made plans to change. Even when there are differences of opinion, listening to the feedback is valuable. It opens the door for change or for discussion.

Ask for Information and Materials. Employees are entitled to know the standards of performance review, to discuss issues that are not clear, to dispute evaluations that seem unfair or untrue, to have input in goal setting, and to know how the appraisal information will be used.[44] Several of these rights become particularly relevant to the ways the employee participates in the interview. For example, if a supervisor gives general, evaluative comments like "you really need to improve your attitude," workers can ask for specific behaviors that the supervisor believes reflect this "attitude." They can also ask for specific suggestions about change. Workers who know the specific behaviors for the basis of appraisal, both positive and negative, can continue to perform the good ones and stop the bad ones.

A worker can also use the appraisal interview to seek the supervisor's counsel about professional development. If the worker wants to move up in the organization or eventually move to another type of organization, the supervisor can be a good source of information and training. Seeking the supervisor's advice about improvement and career advancement lets the supervisor know about the employee's professional goals. It also allows the supervisor to function in a positive mentoring role to the employee, which may help reduce a supervisor's defensiveness. In addition, it opens the door for supervisor assistance to the employee over the long term in reaching those professional goals.

State Disagreement Tactfully. A worker who disagrees with the appraisal should also voice that disagreement during the interview. Using factual information to subtantiate the points of disagreement will help the worker communicate clearly about the difference of opinion. For example, a teacher was evaluated negatively by her principal for having "too low of expectations for a college preparatory class" after his brief observation of her teaching. In the appraisal interview, the teacher stated that she disagreed with his evaluation because he had not observed a college preparatory class. He had confused his schedule and visited a class of low-functioning students. Because his evaluation was based on misinformation and was consequently wrong, she expressed her disagreement with it. Her tactful correction prompted a new observation and evaluation.

When the disagreement is less obvious, employees who base their disapproval on facts will be more persuasive with the supervisors and, if necessary, in subsequent grievance meetings. When evaluations are unfair, most organizations have a grievance procedure through which workers can appeal an earlier evaluation. The worker needs to ask the supervisor or the appropriate organizational or union representative for information about the grievance guidelines. Many grievance procedures have short deadlines, so employees should check into such procedures very quickly after having received what they believe to be unfair evaluations.

Learning After the Interview

Constructive feedback should not be a once a year or quarterly event; it should be part of the daily work experience. Workers should take advantage of any suitable times to ask their supervisors for additional feedback. If a worker senses that productivity is suffering, it is perfectly acceptable and very wise to ask a supervisor for suggestions, even if it is not the scheduled time for formal appraisal.

Summary

Although appraisal interviews are often seen as negative and unpleasant communication exchanges, they are a pervasive part of work in the United States. Workers who view appraisal interviews as a team effort between workers and supervisors find them more motivating. Working to lower defensiveness and to create mutual goals helps build this team effort.

Interviewers must plan for, conduct, and follow up on appraisal interviews carefully. Preparation includes consistent, valid, and complete assessment of the workers' performances. Common methods for assessment of performance include category rating systems (e.g., graphic rating scales, checklists, and BARS); comparative rating systems; written evaluation systems (e.g., critical incident method, essays); MBO (management by objectives); and self-assessment. Individual and cultural differences need to be considered in all forms of assessment. Training helps ensure that assessment is valid and consistent. The appraisal interview should be conducted regularly. Interviewers should prepare clear goals for the interview, invite the employee to prepare for the interview, create a supportive communication climate, give constructive feedback, invite the worker to participate in goal setting, and listen well. Appropriate follow up after the interview is also the responsibility of the supervisor.

The workers (i.e., interviewees) can also prepare for appraisal interviews by educating themselves about evaluation procedures, keeping a record of pertinent information, and listing issues to be discussed. Workers can enhance the interviews by reducing their own defensiveness, listening carefully, asking for information, stating disagreement tactfully, and participating actively.

Appraisal interviews work best for employees and organizations when both parties assume their appropriate responsibilities in the appraisal process.

Discussion Questions

1. What behaviors did the supervisor exhibit that helped to create a supportive climate in the interview at the opening of the chapter?
2. In what ways did the opening interview demonstrate reasons that workers and supervisors often find appraisal interviews unpleasant, negative experiences?
3. Discuss why workers rate their own work more highly than others rate it. Consider ways that supervisors can talk to workers about this issue.

4. Why does involving the worker in goal setting in an interview make the experience a more constructive one for the worker and the organization?

5. From your own experiences, discuss the reasons why workers can listen to constructive feedback better than destructive feedback. Look at the characteristics of each in discussing these reasons.

Suggested Activities

1. In groups of three or four, discuss a problem you have experienced in the university food service, bursar's office, or registrar's office. Recall how the worker in that situation handled your concern. Then imagine that you are that worker's supervisor conducting an appraisal interview. Prepare an interview goal and several suggestions for the worker's improvement. Role play the interview, referring to the specific problem that actually occurred as you attempt to motivate the worker to improve.

2. If you have participated in appraisal interviews, prepare a verbatim transcript of the last one in which you participated. After preparing and re-reading the transcript, identify the interviewer's goal, the areas of focus for improvement, and the type of communication climate. Support your ideas with references to specific behaviors. Write a two to four page paper in which you discuss these areas and make suggestions for the supervisor's improvement.

3. In groups of three, role play the following appraisal interview. Have one person act as observer. The interviewer is the maintenance supervisor for the evening shift at an elementary school. The worker (i.e., interviewee) is a custodian who has worked for six months. This is the first regular appraisal interview for the custodian who has been late at least twice each week. In addition to the problem with tardiness, teachers have complained that their floors have not been swept well, trash has not been removed, and sticky materials have been ignored on desktops. The supervisor knows it is hard to find good custodians. The custodian likes the job. Conduct a ten minute interview. Discuss.

Related Readings

Andrews, Patricia Hayes, and Baird, John E. *Communication for Business and the Professions*, 5th ed. Madison, WI: Brown and Benchmark, 1992.

Byard, Loyd L., and Rue, Leslie W. *Human Resource Management*, 3rd ed. Homewood, Illinois: Irwin, 1991.

Cleveland, Jeannette N., Murphy, Kevin R., and Williams, Richard E. "Multiple uses of performance appraisal: Prevalence and corre-lates," *Journal of Applied Psychology* (1989), 130–135.

Gibb, Jack R. "Defensive communication", *Journal of Communication* 11 (1961), 141–48.

Ivancevich, John M. *Human Resource Management: Foundations of Personnel*, 5th ed. Homewood, Illinois: Irwin, 1992.

Mathis, Robert L., and Jackson, John H. *Personnel: Human Resources Management*, 5th ed. St Paul, Minn.: West Publishing Company, 1988.

Endnotes

1. B. S. Moskal, "Employee Ratings: Objective or Objectionable?" *Industry Week* (February 8, 1982), 51.
2. Lloyd H. Goodall, Jr., Gerald L. Wilson, and Christopher Waagen, "The Performance Appraisal Interview: An Interpretive Assessment," *Quarterly Journal of Speech 72* (1986), 74–87.
3. A. S. Grove, "Performance Appraisal: Manager as Judge and Jury," *Research Management* (Nov.-Dec., 1983), 32.
4. J. F. Veiga, "Face Your Problem Subordinates Now!" *Academy of Management Executive 2* (1988), 145–52.
5. J. R. Larson Jr., "The Dynamic Interplay Between Employees' Feedback-seeking Strategies and Supervisors' Delivery of Performance Feedback," *Academy of Management Review* 14 (1989), 408–22.
6. Jack R. Gibb, "Defensive Communication," *Journal of Communication 11* (1961), 143.
7. Jack R Gibb, (1961), 141–48.
8. Goffman Erving, *The Presentation of Self in Everyday Life* (Garden City, N.J.: Doubleday & Co., Inc., 1959).
9. Glen H. Stamp, Anita L. Vangelisti, and John A. Daly, "The Creation of Defensiveness in Social Interaction," *Communication Quarterly* 4 (Spring, 1992), 1980.
10. Jack R. Gibb, (1961), 148.
11. Kenneth P. Carson, Robert L. Cardy, and Gregory H. Dobbins, "Performance Appraisal as Effective Management of Deadly Management Disease," *Group and Organization Studies* 16 (June 1991), 143–59.
12. Kay Loraine, "How Effective are Work Evaluations?" *Supervision* 45 (1983), 7–8; Mary Zippo and Marc Miller, "Performance Appraisal: Current Practices and Techniques," *Personnel* 61 (1984), 57–59.
13. Ronald J. Burke, William Weitzel, and Tamara Weir, "Characteristics of Effective Employment Performance Review and Development Interviews: Replication and extension," *Personnel Psychology* 31 (1978), 903–919.
14. Glen H. Stamp, Anita L. Vangelisti, and John A. Daly, (1992), 185.
15. E. A. Locke, K. N. Shaw, L. M. Saari, and G. P. Latham, "Goal Setting and Task Performance," *Psychological Bulletin* 90 (1981), 125–52.
16. Ronald J. Burke, William Weitzel, and Tamara Weir, (1978), 915.
17. Kenneth P. Carson, Robert L. Cardy and Gregory H. Dobbins, (1991), 153.
18. Robert L. Mathis and John H. Jackson, *Personnel: Human Resource Management*, 5th ed. (New York: West Publishing, 1988), 353.
19. M. M. Harris and J. Schaubroeck, "A Meta-analysis of Self-supervisor, Self-peer, and Peer-supervisor Ratings," *Personnel Psychology* 41 (1988), 43–62.
20. J. A. Centra, "Self-rating of College Teachers: A Comparison with Student Ratings," *Journal of Educational Measurement* 10 (1973), 287–95; M. J. Clark and R. T. Blackburn, "Faculty Performance Under Stress," In A. Sockloff (Ed.) *Faculty Effectiveness as Evaluated by Students* (Philadelphia: Temple University Press, 1973).
21. Jiing-Lih Farh,, Gregory H. Dobbins, and Bor-Shiuan Cheng, "Cultural Relativity in Action: A Comparison of Self-ratings Made by Chinese and American Workers," *Personnel Psychology* 4 (1991), 129–47.
22. Jiing-Lih Farh, Gregory H. Dobbins, and Bor-Shiuan Cheng, (1991), 141.
23. Ann Marie Ryan, Karen M. Barbera, and Paul R. Sackett, "Strategic Individual Assessment: Issues in Providing Reliable Descriptions," *Human Resources Management* 29 (1990), 280.

24. John M. Ivancevich, "Subordinates' Reactions to Performance Appraisal Interviews: A Test of Feedback and Goal-setting Techniques," *Journal of Applied Psychology* 67 (1982), 581–87.

25. Peter J. Gunas III, "The Department of Labor's 'Glass Ceiling' Initiative," *Employment Relations Today* 17 (Winter 1990-91), 279–80.

26. David E. Switzer and Jo Young Switzer, "Strategies for Managerial and Employee Intervention in the Idealization-Frustration-Demoralization Cycle," *Management Communication Quarterly* 3 (1989), 256.

27. George S. Odiorne, "The Trend Toward the Quarterly Performance Review," *Business Horizons* (July-August 1990), 38–41.

28. George S. Odiorne, (1990), 38–41.

29. F. J. Landy, J.L. Barnes, and K. R. Murphy, "Correlates of Perceived Fairness and Accuracy in Performance Evaluation," *Journal of Applied Psychology* 63 (1978), 751–43.

30. H. H. Meyer, "A Solution to the Performance Appraisal Feedback Dilemma," *Academy of Management Executive* (February 1991), 68–76.

31. H. H. Meyer, E. Kay, and J. P. French , "Split Roles in Performance Appraisal," *Harvard Business Review* 43 (1976), 123–29.

32. Ronald J.Burke, William Weitzel, and Tamara Weir. (1978), 917.

33. Ronald J. Burke, William Weitzel, and Tamara Weir, (1978), 917.

34. Emanuel Kay, Herbert H. Meyer, and John R. P. French Jr., "Effects of Threat in a Performance Appraisal Interview," *Journal of Applied Psychology* 49 (1965), 313–315.

35. Glen H. Stamp, Anita L. Vengelisti, and John A. Daly, (1992), 187.

36. Ronald J. Burke, William Weitzel, and Tamara Weir, (1978), 910.

37. R. A. Baron, "Countering the Effects of Destructive Criticism," *Journal of Applied Psychology* 75 (1990), 235–45.

38. R. A. Baron, (1990), 235.

39. R. A. Baron, "Negative Effects of Destructive Criticism: Impact on Conflict, Self-efficacy, and Task Performance," *Journal of Applied Psychology* 73 (1988), 199–207.

40. James L. Applegate and Ed Woods, "Construct System Development and Attention to Face Wants in Persuasive Situations," *The Southern Communication Journal* 56 (1991), 203.

41. Erez Miriam and Frederick H. Kanfer, "The Role of Goal Acceptance in Goal Setting and Task Performance," *Academy of Management Review* 8 (1983), 455.

42. John F. Kikoski and Joseph A. Litterer, "Effective Communication in the Performance Appraisal Interview," *Public Personnel Management* 12 (1983), 33–42.

43. Glen H. Stamp, Anita L. Vangelisti, and John A. Daly, (1992), 185 & 187.

44. Patricia Hayes Andrews and John E. Baird, *Communication for Business and the Professions*, 4th ed., (Dubuque, Iowa: William C. Brown, 1989), 195.

45. Jack R. Gibb, (1961), 143.

Chapter *11*

Persuasion in Interviews

> *"To be persuasive, we must be believable.*
> *To be believable, we must be credible.*
> *To be credible, we must be truthful."*
> —Edward R. Murrow
> Bob Woolf, Friendly Persuasion:
> My Life as a Negotiator (New
> York: G. P. Putnam's Sons, 1990), 19.

Two young door-to-door salespersons knock at the door of a young mother and housewife, Kathy Magaña. Kathy answers their knock.

Kathy: Yes?

Brian: Hi, I'm Brian and this is Joe, my associate. Can we come in? (The two push forward.)

Kathy: I'd rather stand here.

Brian: Okay, so I'm Brian and this is Joe. He's quiet. What's your name?

Kathy: Are you selling something?

Brian: No, I just need you to vote for me.

Kathy: Vote for what?

Brian: I need you to vote for me according to my personality. How am I doing so far?

Kathy: What is it you want?

Brian: I'll explain that to you in a minute. First, I need to know, do you work?

Kathy: Yes, I do.

Brian: Where?

Kathy: I'm losing my patience here. What is it you want?

Brian: I'm trying to win a trip to London, Paris, or Acapulco, and I need to get the most votes from people like you to do it. All I need is your vote. Will you do it?

Kathy: How do I vote?

Brian: All you need to do is to buy some of these magazines here. (He pulls out a descriptive sheet and shows her.) And I get votes for every sale. So will you buy some to help me get the votes I need?

Kathy: I can't afford any magazines right now.

Brian: Are you married?

Kathy: What?

Brian: Are you married? If you're not, maybe I'll take you with me if I win a trip.

Kathy: You know, you're never going to sell anything with this approach of yours. Even if I had the money, I wouldn't buy anything from you.

Brian: I've already sold a lot in your neighborhood.

Kathy: Well, you won't sell anything here. (Kathy starts to close the door.)

Joe: I'm nice. Will you buy from me?

Kathy: No. (She closes the door.)[1]

Chapter Goals

- •To examine the nature of persuasion.
- •To distinguish persuasion from coercion and manipulation.
- •To recognize the persuasive interview as a distinct form of interviewing.
- •To delineate guidelines and strategies for persuasive interviewing.
- •To explore the ethical issues involved in persuasive interviewing.

Introduction

All interviews have a persuasive component. Journalistic interviewers use persuasion to obtain the information they need for the stories being investigated. Research interviewers persuade respondents to participate in the interviewing process. Most employment interviews involve mutual persuasion; namely, the interviewer seeks to "sell" the company and the job, and the interviewee seeks to persuade the employer that he or she is the best candidate for the job. Likewise, appraisal and disciplinary interviews involve persuasion on the part of one or both parties. As we shall see in later chapters, persuasion is also an element in employee intervention interviews, diagnostic interviews, and counseling.

In addition to the persuasive element in other forms of interviewing, there are interviewing situations that are distinctly persuasive in nature and do not fit into other standard interview categories. **Persuasive interviews** are those in which an interviewer seeks to influence the actions or attitudes of the interviewee(s) through the use of questions, rational arguments, and emotional appeals. These questions, arguments, and appeals use verbal and nonverbal communication.

Rational arguments use facts, reason, and supporting evidence to win acceptance of an idea or action. An HIV counselor seeks to persuade individuals to be cautious and use protection in their sexual relationships by citing the growing numbers of HIV-infected individuals in the nation and the evidence that transmission HIV can be prevented through the use of condoms. **Emotional appeals** seek to persuade or influence another by involving their feelings and emotional attachments in the decision-making process. The HIV counselor might also seek to persuade the persons to use condoms by describing in painful detail the stages of disease in those who die from AIDS. Both rational and emotional appeals are effective persuasive tools provided they are used with accuracy and respect for the other.

Persuasive interviews include, of course, **sales interviews,** in which interviewers seek to persuade interviewees to purchase some commodity or service. In the sales interview, one individual (i.e., the interviewer) seeks to make money by persuading another (i.e., the interviewee) to spend some. Young people, as we have just seen in the opening interview, try to sell magazines door to door. Insurance agents persuade individuals to buy policies that provide financial protection for their homes, cars, and so forth. Realtors persuade us to buy or build homes. Almost every time we make a purchase of a large item such as a car or appliance, we enter into persuasive interviews.

Not all persuasive interviews, however, are sales interviews. Often persuasive interviews occur in other contexts, such as a child seeking to persuade her parents to let her begin dating, an employee trying to persuade his boss to let him handle a new design project on his own, and a teacher seeking to persuade a student to develop a more cooperative attitude. Whether or not we work in sales, all of us at times employ persuasive strategies in interview contexts to obtain outcomes we desire. We will categorize as **persuasive interviews** all interviews in which effective persuasion of the interviewee toward some desired end is the primary goal of the interviewer.

In this chapter, we will explore the nature of persuasive interviewing. We will begin by understanding the nature of persuasion and recognizing the difference between persuasion and coercion or manipulation. We will briefly explore some of the many settings and situations in which persuasive interviews commonly occur. We will develop some guidelines and strategies for persuasive interviewing and, finally, we will explore ethical issues involved in persuasive interviews.

The Nature of Persuasion

Woodward and Denton define persuasion as a *communicative process* involving five elements or dimensions: (1) preparing and delivering (2) nonverbal and verbal messages (3) to independent individuals capable of free choice (4) in order to change or bolster (5) their beliefs, actions, or attitudes.[2] **Persuasion,** in other words, is a process of seeking to influence the thoughts or choices of an independent person through communication. The word *independent* suggests that the interviewee must be able to decide freely what to think or do.

Simons describes persuasion as a co-active process in which one party employs communication to influence another in the hope that the second party will move toward acceptance of the first party's views. "Persuasion begins from the perception of differences—differences between where we stand on a given issue and where others stand, or differences between their covert actions and how we as persuaders would have them act. . . . Persuasion may thus be conceived of as a process of *bridging* differences . . . so as to secure preferred outcomes."[3] Simply put, persuasion is a process of seeking to win agreement between two parties on some specific issue or plan. In the opening interview, the two salespeople were trying to win Kathy's agreement that she should purchase magazines.

Where does persuasion end and coercion or manipulation begin? How do we draw the line? Lee and Lee write: "The line separating strategy from deception, audience adaptation from manipulation, and the hard sell from coercive persuasion is often difficult to recognize. The moral challenge for the advocate [interviewer] is to argue both persuasively and responsibly."[4]

Coercion is the act of compelling another to act or change through the use of power, threats, or intimidation.[5] Coercion implies force, although not necessarily physical force. The parties being influenced are denied free choice when coercion is employed. Lee and Lee suggest that coercion is present whenever the advocates or persuaders "wish only to force their will on the audience."[6] The key element in separating persuasion from coercion, then, is the autonomy, or independent right to choose, of the person(s) over whom influence is sought. Let's look at an example that will help distinguish between persuasion and coercion.

American political prisoners in Beirut in the early part of this decade were occasionally interviewed on videotape by their captors. These videotapes were then distributed to the international press and shown widely on television throughout the world. In these interviews, the prisoners often were critical of their own governments for not cooperating with the captors. Often they spoke as if they were in agreement with their captors' views.

When these prisoners were eventually freed, their stories were quite different. They explained that during the videotaping processes, they often had guns aimed at them to make them make the statements that their captors wanted them to. They were forced to answer as their captors wanted or put themselves at risk. They did not have free choice in the kinds of responses they could give. Once they were free, when they again had choices, their answers were different. These interviewees' videotaped answers exemplified coercion, because the prisoners had few choices but to answer as instructed.

Cooper puts it this way: "When advocates do not recognize the capacity of choice in the audience and thereby dismiss the notion that the audience is autonomous, they are . . . manipulating, coercing, or engaging in propaganda."[7] **Manipulation** involves an attempt on the part of the persuader to bring the audience to agreement or action through less than honest or forthright means. Cooper suggests that failure on the part of the persuader to offer sufficient information, concealment of information, or employment of half-truths or exaggerations are evidence of manipulation. Any such actions have a negative effect on the free and informed choice of the one being persuaded. Lee and Lee write: "The manipulative advocate views the listeners as objects."[8] Our sales agents in the opening segment of this chapter were attempting to persuade through manipulation by using half-truths and revealing disinterest in the needs of their audience. They did not treat their customer as an autonomous person but as an object to be manipulated.

To be persuasive, an interviewer must seek to ascertain and respond to the needs and concerns of the interviewee, employing arguments and appeals that respect the interviewee's choices. An effective persuasive public speaker employs extensive audience analysis in order to know the audience and develop arguments that appeal to its needs. An effective persuasive interviewer employs questions to determine the needs, beliefs, and attitudes of the interviewees in order to frame arguments that address and respond to those needs, attitudes, and beliefs. "If the saleswoman operates according only to her own agenda, her customers will probably feel neglected and she will probably not make a sale. On the other hand, if she recognizes that both parties in the exchange have a stake in the outcome, her talk will deal with the concerns of the customers and she will more likely make the sale."[9] The goal of the persuasive interviewer is to win agreement for a plan, idea, or action without resorting to coercion or manipulation.

Persuasive Interview Settings and Situations

Sales interviews are the most obvious and the most common form of persuasive interviews. In retail businesses, in our workplaces, on our telephones, and even at the doors of our homes, we encounter salespersons seeking to persuade us of our need or willingness to purchase a product they have for sale. However, many of these sales encounters are not really interviews but packaged presentations that are delivered in the same manner and with the same messages no matter who comes to the store, telephone, or door. A presentation that does not adapt to the needs of the other party is *not* an interview.

A sales encounter is only a **sales interview** if the interviewer/salesperson employs questions to ascertain the needs of the interviewee and presents persuasive arguments based on the answers to those questions that respond to the needs the interviewee has expressed. A sales interviewer works with interviewees in a co-active process to arrive at a mutually agreeable solution.

A sales interview can and does occur anywhere—in our homes, on the street, over the telephone, and in retail establishments. Unlike many other specific forms of interviewing, the creation and maintenance of a particular type of setting does

The salesperson (interviewer) employs questions to ascertain the needs of the customers (interviewees).

not seem to be as important to the success of the sales interview, although it may be that different individual interviewees are more amenable to sales interviews in certain settings than in others. Most sales interviews occur in nonprivate settings with a relatively high degree of noise, such as the noise of piped-in music on the open floor of a retail establishment. Certain retail establishments, however, such as car dealerships and some expensive clothing stores, create semiprivate settings such as a table and chairs in a corner of the sales floor or a closed sitting room in which the customer views and selects from the merchandise. Apparently, an effective sales interview can happen almost anywhere, depending on what is being sold, the needs of the interviewee, and the skills of the sales interviewer.

Other interview situations that have persuasion as their primary goal are harder to distinguish and classify and, perhaps, are less likely to be formalized. Nonetheless, persuasive interviews are a frequent occurence in everyday life. A college speech teacher has a bright, capable student whose presentations are all flawed by grammatical errors that affect her credibility. The professor asks the student to come for an interview and seeks to persuade her through the use of careful questioning about her needs and goals to make use of the university's special tutoring labs to correct her difficulties with grammatical forms. An assistant editor at a small publishing firm has just learned about a new software package that would allow him to track the status and progress of every book in process at the firm. He asks for an interview with the publisher with the goal of persuading her through the use of questions about the needs of her firm that the purchase of this package will streamline many aspects of the firm's operations, thus justifying its high cost.

Sometimes persons whose primary interview goals are other than persuasion—a physician who primarily uses interviews to obtain diagnoses, for example, or a journalist who primarily employs interviews to investigate—may need to employ persuasive interviews. A seventy-two-year-old woman diagnosed with a recurrence of cancer has decided she will not submit to further surgery in order to stop the cancer's spread. Her physician conducts a persuasive interview in order to understand and allay her fears and to convince her that with surgery she might have many more years of a rich life. A journalist writing a story on the reasons for and extent of unreported rapes has met a woman who acknowledged that she was raped and did not report it but refused to talk about it further. The journalist asks for an interview to explore the woman's reluctance to tell her story and to offer assurances that the story will protect her confidentiality and possibly aid others who have had the same experience. In each case, what distinguishes these as persuasive interviews is both the element of persuasion and the use of questions to determine the needs, concerns, and feelings toward which persuasion will be directed.

Persuasive Interviewing Guidelines and Strategies

Winning Trust: Opening the Persuasive Interview

The opening phase of a persuasive interview involves demonstrating the personal trustworthiness of the interviewer and respect for the interviewee. This personal trustworthiness, the interviewer's credibility, has been the focus of considerable study in communication. Interviewers are considered credible when interviewees perceive them to be knowledgeable about their products, have good character (integrity), and demonstrate enthusiasm for their ideas and products.[10]

Interviewers can send a variety of messages during the opening of the interview that enhance, or damage, their own credibility. Aristotle argued that if an audience perceives the speaker as credible, the audience will be predisposed to be persuaded by the speaker's messages.[11] Early credibility building is important for the interviewer.

For example, persuasive interviewers need to demonstrate that they know what they are talking about, and that they have expertise about their product. Someone selling wholesale groceries to owners of food stores and restaurants, for example, might begin a persuasive interview by demonstrating knowledge of the products already being carried by the purchaser. From the outset of the interview, the interviewer needs to demonstrate expertise.

Moreover, interviewers need to demonstrate personal character or trustworthiness. They can do this by giving the interviewee the sense that they are looking out for the interviewee's needs and desires. An interviewer can assure the interviewee, for example, that the primary concern is the interviewee's ability to use products purchased profitably.

Finally, the interviewer's enthusiasm for the product affects credibility. In a classic study by Berlo, Lemert, and Mertz, dimension of credibility—dynamism—worked as a persuasive element in how people responded.[12] Interviewers who are excited about their products will find that their excitement in itself is persuasive to those they interview.

All three dimensions of credibility—knowledge, character, and dynamism—rest in the perceptions of the interviewee. That is, interviewers cannot insist that others perceive them as credible. Interviewers can and should, however, make careful choices to establish their credibility, especially in the opening phase of the interview.

In those opening minutes, the interviewer must seek to assure the interviewee of genuine interest in the interviewee as an autonomous individual and of the importance of identifying the interviewee's needs in order to respond to them. This challenge is increased by the fact that most individuals have already experienced many persuasive situations in which their own needs, concerns, and autonomy were not considered. As a result, establishing trust in such encounters is a major challenge for the interviewer.

Unless the parties are already known to one another, the opening will begin, of course, with introductions. The interviewers introduce themselves and ask the name of the interviewee. Depending on the situation, the interviewees may or may not be willing to offer their names. Customers at an appliance store, for example, may be leery of "hard pitch" salespersons and reluctant to establish any kind of relationship with the salesperson. In any case, the interviewer's self-identification is a simple form of self-disclosure that begins the process of building trust.

Once the self-introduction is made, the interviewer provides an orientation to the interview that offers the assurance of trustworthiness. For example, an ad campaign by a major appliance store chain offers repeated assurances that the salespersons in the chain are no longer paid commissions and are not under pressure to make sales. This campaign seems designed to assure customers that they can trust the salespeople not to pressure them into unwanted purchases. Sales interviewers working at such a chain might explain in the opening about the no-commission policy, express interest in providing assistance and service, and suggest that they would like to begin by determining what it is the customer needs to determine what products might match those needs.

A doctor seeking to persuade his patient to have surgery, on the other hand, might begin by assuring the patient that the purpose of the interview is to understand concerns, allay fears, and offer reasons why surgery is a good option. Simultaneously, the physician can state that he recognizes and respects the right of the patient to make her own decision about this important matter. Trust is won by sincerely assuring the interviewees that their own needs are paramount and that the right to their own informed and independent decision making is respected. The opening phase of persuasive interviews, then, involves rapport-building that establishes interviewer credibility and provides orientation that recognizes the autonomy of the interviewee.

Assessing Needs: The Question Phase

In order to be open to persuasion, and in order to be motivated to act, an individual must have some need that can be met by action. "A concept basic to the study of motivation is that of need. *Need*, or in its less extreme form, *desire*, produces instability in the relationship between a person and the environment. It is this instability which is presumed to have motivational properties, that is, properties that can be brought into play to reduce need or needs, and thereby restore stability or equilibrium."[13] Need, in other words, is some perceived imbalance in the interviewee's life that the purchase or acceptance of some change is thought to rectify.

The successful persuasive interviewer employs questions to assess the needs of the interviewees in order to persuade them that proposed actions will meet those needs. "People respond according to their needs, not yours. This is an essential rule of successful selling. . . . The only way to find out where people are coming from and what their needs are is through a planned process of questioning and active listening."[14] The persuasive interviewer uses a planned structure of questions and careful listening to determine what needs exist before developing a persuasive strategy. Let's look at an extended example of how questions aid the persuasive interviewer in meeting the needs of the interviewee.

A young couple walks into a car dealership and explains that they are "thinking about buying a new car." The salesperson begins by asking them what kind of car they now drive, its age, if they are having problems with it, and how long they expect it will be before the car will have to be replaced. The answers to these questions help the interviewer determine the immediacy of the interviewees' need for a new car and the likely trade-in value of the vehicle they now own.

Next, the sales interviewer asks what the couple will want or need in a car when they are ready to buy. Is safety a major concern? How much space will they need? Do they have or will they have children for whom a four-door vehicle or minivan might be appropriate? How will the car be used primarily—for short trips to work and to the store, or for lengthier travel? How important are gas mileage and other issues of economy? The answers to these questions will help the interviewer to determine what kinds of vehicles will best meet the interviewees' needs.

Once some level of trust has been established, the interviewer will seek to discover what kind of financial resources the couple has available for a new car, how much they are willing and able to spend, and what they will need in the way of financing and payment plans. With these questions answered, the interviewer will have the necessary information to steer the customers toward car options that will meet their needs and be affordable to them.

The ultimate decision about whether to buy and what car to choose will reside with the interviewees as they assess for themselves which of their needs are predominant and which vehicle pleases their tastes. In order to persuade them effectively, the interviewer must identify these needs and preferences accurately. With the information provided in response to these questions, the interviewer may learn that the couple has two young children, is very concerned about safety issues, travels often to their home state which is three hundred miles away, and will be loaned the money to purchase this, their first new car, by their parents. On the basis of this information about their needs, the interviewer recommends that the couple consider either a six-passenger minivan with built-in child safety seats and good gas mileage or a four-door sedan with dual air bags and anti-lock brakes, which has more comfortable seats for long trips. The couple will be able to make an informed choice on the basis of their own priorities.

The use of questions to assess interviewee needs is the heart of the persuasive interview. The skilled interviewer will use a planned sequence of questions to obtain as complete an understanding as possible of the pertinent concerns, needs, and desires of the interviewees before ever proposing solutions to those needs.

In order for the use of questions to be authentically mutual, interviewers must remain open to the possibility that meeting the needs of the interviewee may not necessarily meet their own persuasive agendas. For example, the car salesperson in the previous example, in order to attend to the autonomy of the interviewees, must be open to the possibility that this young couple cannot afford a new car at this time. Likewise, the physician seeking to persuade the patient to have surgery must be open to discovering that, in fact, this person has little pleasure in her life, has lost her loved ones, and is really ready to die. The use of information obtained from questions, in other words, must not be used for manipulative or coercive purposes. Interviewers must be willing to adapt or abandon their tentative persuasive agenda on the basis of what is discovered in the question phase.

Proposing Solutions: The Information and Options Phase

The persuasive interviewer must be knowledgeable about the subject matter, whether that subject matter is cars or medical procedures. Having the necessary information about all of the options available is a vital part of the preparation process for the interviewer. Persuasive arguments that are not grounded in complete and accurate information will deny the interviewee the opportunity to make accurate and informed choices.

The car saleperson must know the stock of cars available and the options available for each. The physician must have an accurate understanding of the nature of the recommended surgery, as well as the rehabilitative and recuperative demands the surgery will place upon the patient. The assistant editor must have a thorough understanding of the tracking and scheduling needs of the publishing company, as well as the specifications and abilities of the software package in order to persuade the publisher to buy it. Whatever the nature of the persuasive interview situation, the interviewee is entitled to accurate and complete information about the options available.

Furthermore, wherever possible, the interviewer should present whatever solutions are available as clear options, each with their own advantages and disadvantages, even if the interviewer has a clear preference for one. For example, the physician may believe that one type of surgery is the best treatment available for the patient's cancer. He would say so, and say why, presenting the most complete information possible in terms the patient can understand. At the same time, however, in order to truly assure the patient of autonomy in the decision-making process, the physician will talk about other options—laser treatment, chemotherapy, and so forth—and why the surgery seems to be the best option available. Not all options need to be presented as equal, but each option must be presented as fairly as possible in order to guarantee the interviewee's right to make a free choice. It is the interviewer's responsibility to have the necessary information about options before the interview takes place.

Allowing Free Choice: The "Quiet Space" Phase

The interviewer and interviewee have met and trust has been established. Through careful questioning and listening, the interviewer has obtained an understanding of the needs of the interviewee. Options appropriate to those needs have been clearly presented to the interviewee with assurances that the choice belongs to the interviewee, and it will be respected. At this point the persuasive interview differs sharply from other forms of interviewing, because the effective persuasive interviewer will provide the interviewee with the time and space to consider the options and reach a decision. In other words, a scheduled break in the interview process is usual and recommended in order to allow the interviewee to choose without feeling pressured.

The car salesperson provides the young couple with the two best car options to meet their needs—the minivan and the four-door sedan. After a test drive in each vehicle, the interviewer leaves them alone to discuss their preferences and make a decision. The physician offers the patient the information about surgery and other options and then suggests that the interviewee take time to discuss the options with family. If desired, obtaining a second opinion might be recommended, in order to allow the interviewee to come to a decision about what choice is preferred. The assistant editor leaves the publisher with the necessary information and expresses willingness to wait for a response.

Offering the interviewee this time and space to decide is an important part of the persuasive interviewing process. Anyone who has ever tried to work when another person was watching them closely knows that often the mere presence of the other person creates internal pressures—fear that we're working too slowly, that our work is being judged negatively, or that the observer wants some action or response. Distancing oneself from the situation assures the interviewees that their autonomy is truly respected.

This "quiet space" phase may be a temporary break in an ongoing interview, as at the car dealership, or it may signal the end of the interview, as when a physician sends a patient home to consider her options. In either case, the interviewer should make clear before providing the quiet space what will happen next. For example, the car salesperson might say, "I'm going to leave you two alone now to consider your options. I'll come back in about five minutes to see how you're doing, but if you want me sooner than that, just step into my office over there and tell me you're ready for me." The physician might say, "Let's schedule a time for you to come in early next week and tell me what you've decided, but if you want to talk again before then, just call and I'll be glad to answer any other questions you might have, talk to your children, or hear what decision you've reached." In each case, a clear follow-up contact is specified.

Accepting Outcomes: The Closing Phase

Suppose, after investing an hour or more with that young couple at the dealership, the salesperson leaves them alone and returns a few minutes later only to be told that they have decided to wait until the new car models are out before making a purchase. The salesperson who still wants to build on the investment already made will accept the couple's decision willingly, encourage them to return and ask for him when they are ready to buy, provide a business card to help them remember, and express willingness to introduce them to the new car options when the cars are available and the couple is ready. The closing phase of a persuasive interview involves acceptance of the choice made by the interviewee and the provision for future contacts.

Interviewer acceptance of the decision rendered is the ultimate test of the interviewer's respect for the autonomy of the interviewee. The physician who responds, "Then find someone else to treat you!" when the patient opts for chemotherapy over surgery has effectively robbed the patient of the free choice offered previously . Now, it is no longer a free choice but a choice made at great cost, the loss of the physician's services. The lesson for the persuasive interviewer is to offer only options that can be met with acceptance, including the right of the interviewee to refuse. The physician's ultimate refusal to accept the patient's decision makes it unlikely that the patient will be open to future persuasive efforts from that physician.

Closure of the persuasive interview varies according to the decision reached. If the couple buys a car, the salesperson will help them complete the details of the purchase and explain warranty information, and so forth. If the patient chooses surgery, the physician will call to schedule it and make sure the patient knows what to bring, when to arrive, and what to expect from the preoperative and postoperative process. Closure of the persuasive interview, in other words, will involve making whatever necessary arrangements are required by the choice the interviewee has made.

Persuasive Interviews Involve Ethical Choices

"Potential ethical issues are inherent in any instance of communication between humans to the degree that the communication involves possible influence on other humans and to the degree that the communicator consciously chooses specific ends sought and communicative means used to achieve those ends."[15]

Wherever persons communicate, there are ethical choices and implications in that communication. By now the ethical questions and guidelines relevant to persuasive interviewing should be somewhat evident from our earlier discussions, but let us summarize them here for the sake of clarity. Based on the issues and concerns already discussed, we can express the following recommended ethical guidelines for persuasive interviewers:

1. *Persuasion should not include coercion.* Coercion involves the use of real or implied force or intimidation in order to obtain a desired decision or end. In seeking to persuade, interviewers, whatever their relative status or power, should not use that status or power to force compliance with their agendas. Interviewees should be considered equal to the interviewer in the persuasive interview.

2. *Persuasion should not involve manipulation.* Manipulation involves the use of less than forthright means, incomplete and inaccurate information, and lack of respect for the right of the interviewee to make a free and independent decision. Persuasive interviewers should take care to assure that interviewees have the most accurate and complete information available in order to decide.

3. *The logical and emotional appeals employed by persuasive interviewers should speak to the strengths rather than the weaknesses of the interviewees.* In order to avoid manipulating interviewees, interviewers must not play upon or abuse the fears or logical misunderstandings of the interviewees.

4. *The capacity for choice and the right to choose of the interviewee(s) should be recognized and respected.* This is the fundamental premise underlying persuasive interviews. Without respect for the right of the individual to choose, questions designed to assess and respond to the needs of the interviewees would not be necessary, coercion and manipulation would be acceptable, and strategies that eliminated choices would be appropriate. The recognition of the interviewee's right to choose is the cornerstone of the persuasive interview's purpose and structure.

5. *Persuasive interviews should be mutual.* Together, the interviewer and interviewee work to clarify the needs of the interviewee and explore possible options. A persuasive interview does not consist of an interviewer who tells the interviewee what choice or action must be taken. Instead, it involves mutual information sharing, negotiation, and problem solving.

6. *Persuasive interviews should be based on trust.* The interviewer should trust the capacity of the interviewee to choose. Interviewees should be able to trust the interviewer to present accurate information and options.

7. *The persuasive interviewer's agenda should be geared toward and adapted to the needs of the interviewee.* Interviewers need to be willing to surrender their own agendas or goals to the legitimate needs of interviewees.

8. *The persuasive interviewer should provide the most complete and accurate information possible.* It is the interviewer's responsibility to be informed about the subject before the interview begins.

9. *The persuasive interviewer should assure the freedom to choose of the interviewee by allowing the time and space to make a decision without pressure.*

10. *Persuasive interviewers should be willing to accept the decision of the interviewee even if it runs contrary to their own agenda.*

Summary

In a persuasive interview, an interviewer seeks to influence the actions or choices of an interviewee through the use of questions, logical arguments, and emotional appeals. Sales interviews, in which the interviewer seeks to persuade an interviewee to purchase some commodity or service, are the most common form of persuasive interviews. Persuasion is the process of influencing the choices of another through communication, particularly logical arguments and emotional appeals. Persuasion is mutual, noncoercive, and nonmanipulative; it respects the autonomy and right of the interviewee to choose .

The phases of the persuasive interview include winning trust, assessing needs through questions, proposing solutions, assuring free choice, and accepting the decision made. The ethical guidelines governing persuasive interviews grow out of and seek to preserve the fundamental recognition of the individual's right to choose.

Discussion Questions

1. Was the opening interview of this chapter truly an interview? Why or why not?
2. Considering the controversy over legalized abortion in the United States, what are some of the rational and emotional appeals that might be employed by interviewers on both sides seeking to persuade a woman about what choice to make concerning an unwanted pregnancy?
3. In your own experience, are most sales encounters also sales interviews? Discuss some examples and evaluate what makes them interviews or not.
4. Some scholars believe that all communication is persuasive. In other words, they believe that we always seek to influence the other when we communicate. Discuss whether you accept this idea.
5. Are emotional appeals by their nature coercive or manipulative? Use examples from your own experience to decide.

Suggested Activities

1. Rewrite the opening interview to transform it into a persuasive interview as defined in this chapter.
2. Develop a list of examples of what you consider to be manipulative emotional appeals that you have encountered or experienced in persuasive interviews. Share your list with a group of peers to seek consensus about which appeals are manipulative. Identify what distinguishes manipulative from non-manipulative emotional appeals.
3. Develop suggestions for how the following interviewers could win the trust of their interviewees:

A public health nurse seeking to persuade a reluctant parent of the value of using the whooping cough vaccine on her infant.

A guidance counselor seeking to persuade a student planning to drop out to remain in school.

A veterinarian seeking to persuade an elderly gentleman to have his terminally ill pet euthanized.

A student seeking to persuade her teacher to hand out a study guide for the final exam.

Related Readings

Bettinghaus, Erwin P. and Cody, Michael J. *Persuasive Communication,* 4th ed. New York: Holt, Rinehart and Winston, 1987.

Jamieson, G. H. *Communication and Persuasion.* London: Croom Helm, 1985.

Johannesen, Richard L. *Ethics in Human Communication.* Prospect Heights, IL: Waveland Press, Inc., 1978.

Larson, Charles U. *Persuasion: Reception and Responsibility,* 5th ed. Belmont, CA: Wadsworth Publishing Company, 1989.

Woodward, Gary C. and Denton, Robert E., Jr. *Persuasion and Influence in American Life,* 2nd ed. Prospect Heights, IL: Waveland Press, Inc., 1992.

Endnotes

1. This interview was adapted, with permission, from a description of an actual experience provided by Kathy Magaña, a student at Indiana University-Purdue University, Fort Wayne.

2. Gary C. Woodward and Robert E. Denton Jr., *Persuasion and Influence in American Life,* 2nd ed. (Prospect Heights, IL: Waveland Press, Inc., 1992), 20.

3. Herbert W. Simons, *Persuasion: Understanding, Practice, and Analysis,* 2nd ed. (New York: Random House, 1986), 121.

4. Ronald Emery Lee and Karen King Lee, *Arguing Persuasively* (New York: Longman, 1989), 15.

5. Adapted from a definition of "coerce" in *Webster's New World Dictionary,* Third College Edition (Cleveland: Webster's New World, 1988), 270.

6. Lee and Lee (1989), 23.

7. Martha Cooper, *Analyzing Public Discourse* (Prospect Heights, IL: Waveland Press, Inc., 1989), 138–39.

8. Lee and Lee (1989), 21.

9. Cooper (1989), 141–42.

10. For discussion about basic issues related to credibility, see Carl I. Hovland, Irving L. Janis, and Harold H. Kelley, *Communication and Persuasion* (New Haven: Yale University Press, 1953); Jesse Delia,"A constructivist analysis of the concept of credibility," *Quarterly Journal of Speech* 62 (1976), 36–-75; and Dominic A. Infante, Andrew S. Rancer, and Deanna F. Womack, *Building Communication Theory* (Prospect Heights, IL: Waveland Press, 1990), 16–-94.

11. Aristotle, *Rhetoric,* translated by W. Rhys Roberts and *Poetics,* translated by Ingram Bywater (New York: The Modern Library, 1954), 24–25.

12. David K. Berlo, James B. Lemert, and Robert J. Mertz, "Dimensions of evaluating the acceptability of message sources," *Public Opinion Quarterly* 15 (1951), 635–50.

13. G.H. Jamieson, *Communication and Persuasion* (London: Croom Helm, 1985), 31.

14. Dorothy Leeds, *Marketing Yourself: The Ultimate Job Seeker's Guide* (New York: Harper Collins Publishers, 1991), 43–44.

15. Richard L. Johannesen, *Ethics in Human Communication* (Prospect Heights, IL: Waveland Press, Inc., 1978), 11–12.

Assistance Interviews

Chapter 12

Employee Intervention and Disciplinary Interviews

*"Life becomes about learning
how to use what you have left."*
—Robert Dole, in Character:
America's Search for Leadership
by Gail Sheehy, New York:
William Morrow, 1988, 130.

Stewart "Stu" Lambrusci's receptionist, Frankie Tucker, has not been answering the telephone in the morning until 8:30 or 8:45, even though she is supposed to be at her desk at 8 o'clock sharp. Stu has tried to call her from his office several times and has gotten no answer. Now Stu's boss, Ms. Redman, has also noticed that no one answers until after 8:30, and she has told Stu to "look into it and get it taken care of right away." Stu has called Frankie into his office on Friday afternoon. She enters cheerfully.

Frankie: You wanted to see me?

Stu: Uh, yeah, Frankie, sit down. Wait, before you sit, would you mind closing the door?

Frankie: (Looks up questioningly.) Sure. (Closes door.) What's up?

Stu: Have a seat. (She sits down.) Well, we've got a problem.

Frankie: What's that?

Stu: Well, I've called into the office in the morning a couple of times this week, and nobody answers.

Frankie: (Squirms in seat.) Oh.

Stu: Now I've not been happy about it, but I figured you were caught in traffic or something, so I was waiting to talk to you about it. Now Redman has found out. She's been trying to get a hold of me each morning this week, and guess what? Nobody answers the damned phone.

Frankie: Oh.

Stu: Well, what's going on? I didn't know it was happening a lot, but Redman says she has tried every single day, and there's no answer. That makes me look great.

Frankie: (Suddenly begins sobbing.) I (sob) . . . oh (sob) . . . I feel awful (sob).

Stu: (Surprised, offers her a tissue box.) What's wrong?

Frankie: (Can't talk because of sobbing.)

Stu: Well, uh, well, uh, do you want to talk later? What's wrong? Is there something I can do?

Frankie: (Trying to stop crying.) I'm really sorry. (Sobs.) I've been trying to keep it a secret, but I guess I can't.

Stu: What?

Frankie: Well, it's my Dad. He, uh, he's been really really sick . . . he's had emphysema for years, and now he can't hardly take care of himself. (Sobbing subsides.) Each day after work I go to his house to take care of him. Then I go home and feed my own family. He's just so stubborn that he won't come to live with us and he won't go into a nursing home. So now we have to have a visiting nurse come every day to his house to help him with the oxygen unit. I have to help with that because he's so bullheaded that he won't let the nurse do it. Well, the nurse can't get there till quarter to eight. By the time she gets the tank set up and I can go, I'm late to work. I keep hoping the nurse can get there by 7:00, and she says she will, but she never does. So I get here late. I've been hoping you wouldn't notice. But now I've made you look bad with Ms. Redman. I feel terrible. I'm just so overwhelmed with this thing with Dad—and he's getting weaker and weaker—and I hardly know my own kids because I have to be over there so much. I just don't know how to make it. I'm just so sorry. Should I just quit? I don't want to ruin your reputation. Mine's already ruined.

Stu: Wait, here. Let's not rush into things.

Frankie: But there's no way I can do it all. I'm stretched so much now I don't know what I can do.

Stu: Well, let's think about it for a minute. I wonder if . . .

Frankie: I should just quit. I'm being a terrible worker. I don't want to get you into any more trouble.

Stu: Now just a minute . . . I'm wondering if we could flex here a little while you get things at home under control. Let me think. (Silence) How about this idea? Since I'm always in the office at eight, how about we forward the calls from your desk to mine until you get here in the morning? I could take care of the early morning stuff and then as soon as you get to the phone you can cancel the forwarding command. You can keep track of the time you're late and make it up at lunch or in the afternoon. We couldn't do this permanently, but I think it might work until things at home settle down.

Frankie: Oh, I couldn't let you do that. This is my problem and I ought to take care of it. You shouldn't have to answer the phone!

Stu: Listen, Frankie, you've worked here almost six years. You're a good receptionist. I don't want to lose you, but at the same time I need to make sure the office runs professionally. I think we can do this for the short run. You do all you can to get the visiting nurse schedule straightened out. Let's plan to do it this way starting tomorrow. Then you let me know next Friday what you've been able to set up with the nurses.

Frankie: Thanks.

Stu: If your Dad's needs continue, we'll have to do something different, but I think this will work for now. What do you think?

Frankie: I really appreciate your understanding. This has been the worst time of my life, but I didn't want to quit my job because we need the money. I promise I'll get here as soon as I can. And I'll keep talking to the visiting nurse office to see if we can rearrange the schedule. I really appreciate your help.

Stu: Okay, then, let's get back to work. Hang in there, Frankie.

Frankie: Right. I know things will work out, but it's really a mess now.

Stu: Well, it'll be okay.

Frankie: Thanks. (Leaves office.)

Chapter Goals

- To define employee intervention interview.
- To propose interviewer adaptations to problems that employees bring to intervention interviews.
- To suggest appropriate topics and interviewer responses for employee intervention interviews.
- To define disciplinary interview.
- To propose ways for interviewers to prepare for, set the climate, and participate in disciplinary interviews.
- To suggest appropriate topics and responses for disciplinary interviewers.

Introduction

Workplace supervisors often find themselves in interviews that do not fit neatly into any of the categories that this book has already discussed. For example, they interview workers who need to change their work schedules because of family crises, such as the interview at the opening of this chapter. Other times supervisors interview employees who have used obscene language around customers. Although family problems and obscenities may seem unrelated, they both represent employee problems that have a harmful effect on work performance. Employee problems may lead to low morale, unrest, increased grievances, and turnover. They can also affect the organization by reducing productivity and lowering the quality of goods and services. They are contagious.

Industrial psychologists assume that many organizational problems are the result of personal and interpersonal problems in their employees' lives.[1] Some organizations deal with these interviews reactively; that is, the supervisors simply respond to individual employee problems as they arise without any formal interview system to ensure consistency. Other organizations develop elaborate programs to deal with employee problems. Such programs, however large or small, suggest that workplace interviews can help solve employees' problems directly (e.g., through on-site professional counseling services) or indirectly (e.g., through appropriate referrals to other agencies). These interviews, whether they are designed to intervene to help employees solve personal problems or to discipline workers who have violated organizational rules, can improve the quality of work life for employees and boost organizational productivity.

What do these two types of interviews—intervention and discipline—have in common? They are both prompted by trouble. Consequently, unlike appraisal interviews they occur irregularly. They focus on a specific problem, and as a result, the participants are often unusually defensive, angry, or anxious. These two characteristics—their irregularity and their emotional intensity—make them more intimidating than other kinds of on the job interviews. Moreover, their problem-centered nature is another reason they are often stressful for both parties.

Despite their unpleasantness, employee intervention and disciplinary interviews are a necessary part of work life. They are highly individualized, since specific personal problems make them necessary. Because certain kinds of problems are common topics for intervention and disciplinary interviews, this chapter will focus on specific problems that come up frequently in these interviews as well as on more general techniques for conducting the interviews. This chapter will provide guidelines for constructive responses to problems that arise in intervention and disciplinary interview situations.

Employee Intervention Interviews

Employee intervention interviews occur between employers and workers when the employee's problems have a noticeable negative impact on job performance. Worker problems such as family financial difficulties, audits by the Internal

Revenue Service, terminally ill children, and transportation problems are a few of the personal problems that can impair work performance. A worker who has a sick child may interrupt work many times during a day to telephone home to check in on the child. Both the employee's worry about the child and the frequent phoning diminish work effectiveness. Another worker whose unreliable car has broken down on the freeway may arrive late to work and have to leave at lunch to check that the towing company has gotten the car to the repair shop. Personal problems affect productivity. When they do, organizations often choose to intervene to help solve the problem so that work performance returns as soon as possible to an acceptable level.

In large organizations, this intervention often occurs within the structure of a formal **Employee Assistance Program (EAP)** or an **Employee Counseling Program (ECP).** These are organization-based systems to help workers solve personal problems.[2] These programs, administered differently by different organizations, are often promoted as part of employee benefits.[3] Recruiters and selection interviewers sometimes tell potential employees about the employee assistance opportunities during their selection interviews to increase the attractiveness of their organizations. The assumption behind this recruiting strategy is the belief that organizations that have such programs have a real concern for their employees' welfare.

Large EAPs follow extensive procedures to develop effective programs. For example, organizations develop clear rationales for the existence of their programs; negotiate professional contracts for the services provided (e.g., mental health counseling, credit counseling, etc.); develop guidelines for confidential and accurate record keeping; and create and maintain professional relationships with providers of services.[4] These highly organized programs have dual and interrelated goals; namely, to improve organizational productivity and to assist employees with difficult problems. Interestingly, a survey of numerous companies with EAPs found that the purposes of the EAPs were described by more than one-half of the EAP personnel as being primarily of benefit to the employer and by about one-fourth as of benefit to employees.[5] This suggests that EAPs serve multiple purposes for organizations. They are good recruiting tools, they provide needed services to workers, and they save money and other resources for the organizations.

Whatever the motives for the assistance process, many organizations provide helpful assistance to employees through intervention interviews. Before supervisors conduct intervention interviews, they need to examine their own motivations. We will examine preparations for intervention interviews, methods for conducting the interviews, and specific issues that are typically discussed in intervention interviews. Let us look first at the interviewer's motives prior to the actual interview.

Before the Intervention Interview

Many supervisors and employee-assistance program staff members find it difficult to initiate intervention interviews, even when personal problems are clearly affecting job performance. A survey of organizations, for example, found that supervisors referred their workers to EAPs on the average of one time every six years.[6] The infrequency of supervisor initiated intervention stems from a variety of reasons. For example, Pawlick and Kleiner found that supervisors were often hesitant to initiate or participate in intervention interviews because of time pressures, intimidation, pity for the worker, friendship with the worker, fears of legal complications, lack of interviewing or referral skills, and concessions to seniority.[7] Therefore, although many supervisors want to help their workers who are experiencing problems, many different reasons keep them from doing so.

In the face of this supervisory hesitance to initiate the assistance process, how do workers who need help get access to intervention interviews? In large part, they refer themselves. In fact, one survey of organizations found that 85 percent of the referrals for assistance were by the employees themselves.[8] Employees whose work is affected by personal problems actively seek assistance to solve those problems. Rather than waiting for their supervisors to begin the process, they seek it out themselves.

Supervisors who respond to employees' self-referrals or who initiate intervention interviews need to consider several questions before conducting the actual interview. These questions allow interviewers to decide whether the interview has the potential for positive change and, if so, how best to approach the employee and the problem.

Although intervention interviews are often stressful for both parties, constructive responses and solutions can result.

As Figure 12.1 suggests, interviewers need to ask themselves several important questions before scheduling intervention interviews. They need to consider whether the problem is a temporary one that would likely solve itself without outside intervention or whether it is a more persistent one that needs outside help. If it is a temporary problem, then the supervisor may decide to keep quiet about the short-term difficulties and allow the worker time to take care of the situation personally. Second, interviewers need to realize that people have different work styles and different approaches to problems. Sometimes supervisors' work styles are very different from the work styles of their employees, although both styles may be productive. Difference in work style is not necessarily a problem: it may just be a difference. Supervisors need to consider whether what seems like a problem might just be that the employee approaches work differently from the supervisor. In many of these cases, no intervention is needed.

Third, how does the supervisor know a problem exists? There are many different ways to become aware of problems, some of them credible and reliable and others not. Before a supervisor intervenes to help an employee with a problem, the supervisor needs to have credible evidence—from observation, credible complaints, records—that a problem exists and that intervention has the potential to solve it. Fourth, supervisors need to consider their motives for intervening in employee problems. Are their motives clear? Do they center on assisting the worker? Are complicating motives present, such as supervisory nosiness, a desire to control others' lives, or a desire to try out and practice a new counseling strategy? Intervention interviewers should only schedule interviews when their motives are to improve worker job performance by helping the worker solve an immediate problem.

1. Is it a persistent problem that needs assistance from outside or a temporary one best left alone?

2. Does the fact that the employee deals with things differently than I do necessarily make this issue a problem?

3. How do I really know there is a problem? Hearsay? Observation? Complaints? Intuition?

4. What is my real motive for speaking with this worker?

5. What specifically do I want to ask and say?

6. What are my expectations for how the employee will respond? Pessimistic? Optimistic? How might my expectations affect the interview?

7. What have I learned from similar past experiences that may be informative to me in this situation?

FIGURE 12.1   Questions to Consider Before the Intervention Interview

Adapted from Cavanaugh, Michael M. "Employee Problems: Prevention and Intervention," *Personal Journal* 66 (1987), 36.

Fifth, supervisors need to consider exactly what they want to inquire about and why. Intervention interviews should focus on the problem that has precipitated the interview. Only information pertinent to that problem should be elicited by the supervisor. Prior to the interviews, supervisors can also consider how they want to talk about certain issues. They may, for example, consider how to discuss sensitive topics without heightening defensiveness in the employee. Finally, supervisors need to realize that their expectations for worker response may affect the eventual outcome. If they are pessimistic about the worker being able to respond and think, for example, "George is really too old to be able to make these changes," they will convey those pessimistic expectations which will, in turn, affect George. Supervisors need to be aware of their expectations for employee change and realize that these expectations affect the eventual outcome of the intervention interview.

Preparation for the intervention interview involves careful thought about motives and expectations because both affect choices the interviewer will make. Once these issues have been considered, it is time to conduct the interview.

During the Intervention Interview

Climate. A supportive climate is very important for an intervention interview, particularly since the interview focuses directly on a worker problem. As discussed in chapter 10, workers find interviews focusing on their deficiencies and problems unpleasant. One characteristic of a supportive communication climate is what Gibb called "problem orientation."[9] Problem orientation is an approach in which the interviewer demonstrates a desire to collaborate with the worker to define a problem and solve it.[10] Such an approach contrasts to those of more controlling supervisors who might insist that workers understand the problem in the supervisors' terms and do exactly what the supervisors suggest as a solution. For example, a worker might enter an intervention interview, as did Frankie at the beginning of the chapter, with a specific family problem, an ill, aging parent whose needs interrupt the work schedule. A supervisor who wants to create a supportive climate, like Stu, examines the problem along with Frankie and together they arrive at a mutually satisfying solution. A less supportive supervisor might say, "Well, you need to get a different nurse to come in to change the oxygen tanks." Such a response demonstrates no empathy nor consideration for the complexities of Frankie's problem. As a result, the response may increase the worker's frustration, defensiveness, and discouragement. Other characteristics of supportive communication behaviors discussed in relation to appraisal interviews also improve effectiveness of intervention interviews; namely, provisionalism, description, and spontaneity (see chapter 10).

Skill at Assessment and Referral. In addition to creating a supportive climate, intervention interviewers need to sharpen their skills in assessing problems and referring workers to appropriate agencies or solutions. Assessment and referral skills have been identified as the most important abilities required of people who staff EAPs.[11] **Assessment** is the identification of the nature of the problem, its extent, and seriousness. Many people believe that referral means only the ability to tell people where to go to get help. In actuality, **referral** includes knowledge of appropriate sources of help as well as assistance in preparing troubled employees for entry into treatment and helping them to obtain the assistance in a way that minimizes bureaucratic complications.[12] Workers who have problems with elderly parent care, for example, may be referred to federal health care agencies for deserved treatment. If, however, scheduling appointments with these agencies, receiving accurate billing, and obtaining direct answers to questions is too bureaucratic and complicated, then the referral may create more problems than it solves. The interviewer, therefore, needs the skills to determine the employees' problems and to assure appropriate referrals. Having assessment and referral skills allows the interviewer to provide the most helpful interview. Interviewers who pay attention to their previous experiences learn from them.

Confidentiality.   Confidentiality is a complicated issue in the workplace. At times, workers may risk negative appraisal or even loss of jobs if the company learns about their problems. For example, an employee who has diabetes may want to discuss that issue with a supervisor in order to get permission to keep food at her desk. She may be concerned about making this information public, however, because she knows that she is eligible for a promotion soon and is afraid the department head who will decide on the promotion may decide she lacks the physical stamina necessary for the new position. Her disclosure about her illness to her supervisor could risk the loss of a promotion if her department head has inaccurate information about diabetes.

Organizations need to ensure the confidentiality of all problems discussed in intervention interviews. This assurance is complicated by requirements in many insurance programs for detailed information about employees' insurance claims. The need to give personal information in insurance claims and the need for the company to maintain these records suggests that confidentiality is not limited to the information shared between the supervisor and the worker. Other professionals in the organization may have access to the information. Their positions, however, mandate confidentiality also. Confidentiality needs to extend to record keeping such as computer operators who record health information, receptionists who take and make telephone calls, and all other individuals involved in the intervention process.[13]

Listening.   Good listening is essential in an intervention interview. Intervention interviewers need to listen empathetically, that is, they need to listen both for content (i.e., the problem) and for affect (i.e., the worker's feelings about the problem). Chapter 2 discusses listening in ways that are particularly useful for intervention interviews. Effective listening allows the interviewer to appreciate the employee's concerns. It is a ". . . matter of feeling *with* the other person."[14] Listening closely to the employee has three advantages. First, it demonstrates to the employee that the interviewer genuinely cares about the employee and wants to work cooperatively to find an acceptable solution to the problem. Second, it increases the interviewee's sense of security.[15] Security is the sense that the interview is confidential and that the supervisor can be trusted to use information constructively. Workers who feel more secure in the interview setting are more likely to relax, give honest and full information, and work collaboratively to solve the problem. Third, good listening increases the likelihood that the interviewer will understand the situation accurately. Careful listening leads to a more complete and accurate understanding of the problem because the interviewer is able to receive and remember more information. These three results of careful listening—demonstration of concern, increased worker security, and accurate understanding—all work together to solve what can be very complicated problems.

Interview Structure.   In order to work collaboratively with the employee to understand and address a problem, the intervention interviewer needs to proceed through a series of steps. Rapport building is the first step in an effective intervention interview. A harmonious opening or connection is important in intervention interviews because it assures both parties that they are there to work together on the problem. Sometimes rapport is valued for its own sake,[16] but in the intervention interview it serves an instrumental function. Rapport becomes an instrument that enables other things to happen. In intervention interviews, rapport allows interviewers and interviewees to do their work. Rapport allows them to interact in ways that allow accurate and full understanding of a problem and its solution.

A second step is the interviewer's statement of the purpose of the interview, which may include a description of the specific problem. Both parties need to understand the boundaries of their discussion. Intervention interviews do not include general appraisal of the worker's job performance. Instead, their purpose is to solve a specific personal situation that has had a negative effect on work performance. In this second step, it is helpful for the interviewer to get feedback and information from the worker about how she or he understands the problem. This feedback allows the two of them to agree that there is a problem and what it is. Unless this agreement occurs, a collaborative solution is unlikely.

Third, it is important that the supervisor and employee work together to arrive at a possible solution. The fact that the intervention interview is occurring suggests that the employee has been unable to solve the problem alone, so the two parties should cooperate to reach a workable, desirable solution. After discussing the problem and the solution, the interviewer needs to be sure that the employee understands that she or he is finally accountable for a solution to the problem. Although the organization will help find assistance and support the worker, ultimately the worker is responsible for solving the problem.

Fourth, if the interviewer makes a referral, it should be specific and precise so that the employee understands very clearly what needs to be done. Referrals often require that an employee go to an unfamiliar agency. Most people find this to be a difficult activity. Because an appointment may require scheduling complications and because it is with an unfamiliar person, an employee may find reasons not to follow through on the referral. Specific, assisted referrals increase the likelihood of employee compliance and follow through because they contain fewer ambiguities that provide the worker with excuses for noncompliance.

Finally, the intervention interview should end with a summary of the problem and solution and a statement about how the interviewer will follow up on the decisions that have been reached. Moreover, if the interviewee is expected to follow up in a specific way, the interviewer will refer to that. The parties may, for example, agree that the interviewer will arrange an appointment with a counselor and that the interviewee will go. They may also agree to meet with one another again in three weeks to discuss progress (see Figure 12.2).

The U.S. Department of Health and Human Services suggests some general guidelines for effective interviewer behaviors in the intervention interview.[17] They suggest:

Do focus entirely on problems in work performance and your offer of help.

Do let specific job problems (and written documentation about them) speak for themselves.

Do maintain a professional and considerate attitude.

Do explain all the help that the organization has available.

Do emphasize that this interview and all follow up is confidential.

Do remind the employee that how s/he deals with the job-related aspects of the problem may be considered in later appraisals.

Don't get personally involved in the worker's life.

Don't draw inferences about motivation from work performance.

Don't moralize; keep the focus on work performance.

Don't be guiled by sympathy ploys; focus on specific work performance.

Don't threaten discipline unless you are able and willing to follow through on the threats.

Conducting intervention interviews involves a supportive climate, respect for confidentiality, ability to assess and make referrals, good listening, and systematic steps for problem solving. Interviews may involve varying dimensions of each of these, but together these qualities make good problem solving possible. Now let us focus on some of the typical specific employee problems that often instigate intervention interviews. Although each interview is unique, certain problems recur in ways that affect job performance. We will look at some of these specific problems and offer some information that interviewers might find helpful as they deal with their own employees.

1. **Rapport**

    "Come on in Raquel. It's nice to see you again! I wasn't sure you'd survived the volleyball game last Friday."

2. **Purpose of Interview**

    State purpose

    "I'd like to tell you why I asked you in today."

    Discuss the presenting problem

    "I've noticed that you've been taking more than ten personal phone calls during the day."

    Invite employee ideas about the problem

    "Tell me what you can about all these calls."

    Seek agreement that problem exists and what its dimensions are

    "I appreciate your honesty. Can you see how your personal calls are making it harder for others in the department to get their work done?"

3. **Solution**

    Remind employee of accountability

    "We'll be happy to adapt while Toby is sick, but you need to realize that you must do what's necessary for you to get your work done without relying unfairly on others in the department."

    Make specific referral (if appropriate)

    "I'll call the director of the day care center for sick kids and make an appointment for you. My call will help you get an appointment sooner than if you call her directly."

4. **Summary**

    Summarize problem, next steps

    "So, we've decided that you need to cut down on these personal calls and that you need help with Toby while he's sick. What we want to do is work with you to get you the help you need so you can do your work."

5. **Follow up**

    Supervisory follow up

    "I'll call the child care center this afternoon."

    Employee follow up

    "You call them tomorrow and get help with Toby's needs. Let me know what you get set up with them as soon as you've talked to them."

    Cooperative follow up

    "Let's meet next week to see what progress we've made on this. I'm really glad you're working here, and I'm optimistic that we can adapt to Toby's illness so you can do your work while you're here."

FIGURE 12.2   Steps in the Intervention Interview

Typical Problems for Intervention Interviews

Family Problems.   Employees do not work in a vacuum. They have lives outside their occupations, and often their personal lives interfere with work. Typical family problems for workers include (but are certainly not limited to) problems like: sick children, troubled children, aging parents, and family members in legal difficulties. The federal government has implemented a nationwide family policy, the Family Leave Bill of 1993, and many organizations provide varied services for families with problems. Intervention interviewers need to know the extent of family support services offered in their organizations and make the full extent of these resources available to employees who need them. Some organizations, for example, provide excellent on-site child care. When organizations do not provide assistance directly, referrals to community agencies, such as child care centers, care facilities for sick children, and adult child care centers, can be made. Families with ill members may benefit from services of hospices and visiting nurse agencies. Organizations can offer **flextime,** a work schedule that can be adapted both to the organization's and the worker's needs. Organizations can also offer **job sharing,** a situation in which two or three workers share one full-time position, dividing the duties and schedule of the position among themselves. All of these and other organizational adaptations allow organizations to fulfill their purposes at the same time that employees' personal constraints are honored.

Stress and Burnout.   Many popular magazines feature articles about stress and burnout. Because of a rash of publicity about these problems, some supervisors have misconceptions about them. For example, some supervisors erroneously believe that burnout (a reaction to chronic job stress) is an excuse for not working, that people who like their jobs do not burn out, that physically and psychologically strong people are not susceptible to burnout, and that burnout is always job related.[18] A supervisor who believes these misconceptions may miss valuable opportunities to improve work performance and employee satisfaction by responding inaccurately to stress and burnout. Contrary to common misconceptions, burnout is a real condition. It affects strong people, including those who like and those who dislike their jobs. It tends to affect employees who are idealistic, self-motivated, and who have high goals.[19] Burnout is a phenomenon that deserves serious attention.

Stress manifests itself in physical symptoms such as decreased physical energy and even weakened immune systems. Employees who experience excessive stress may have difficulties with concentration, fatigue, impaired memory, diminished patience, poor motivation, and fluctuations in mood.[20] Employees whose stress levels are excessive and who exhibit symptoms of burnout may need to be referred to personal counselors who specialize in stress-related disorders. Others whose stressors may be temporary often find that stress is lowered when they get into better physical condition, use stress reduction exercises, leave the workplace during the day to refresh themselves (such as lunch break), talk about their stress with a trusted person, and deal with job-related stressors directly.[21] Every individual experiences stress differently, and supervisors who understand stress can offer helpful suggestions for managing it better.

Alcohol and Drug Problems.   At times, problems related to alcohol and drug use require disciplinary attention, which will be discussed later in this chapter. At other times, alcohol and other substance use may require a less dramatic response. Although some writers contend that substance abuse affects 12 percent of the workforce,[22] Weiss suggests that the problem is grossly overestimated.[23] For example, Weiss surveyed records from over 300 corporate assistance programs and found that not one of these identified an alcoholism level of even 5 percent.[24] Alcoholism and other forms of substance abuse, however, can impede job performance. An employee who voluntarily seeks assistance with such problems can be referred to formal alcohol and substance abuse rehabilitation programs. In intervention interviews, employees are generally willing to cooperate with suggested solutions. However, if workers do not cooperate with necessary referral for substance abuse, their jobs can be threatened. Such a threat, called "constructive confrontation,"[25] has been more effective in dealing with substance abusers than with individuals who have different types of problems. Supervisors whose employees seek assistance for substance abuse problems should work assertively on their behalf, reminding them ultimately that they are responsible for the outcome, so that the problems do not become discipline problems which may result eventually in dismissal.

Physical Health Problems.   Physical problems can become job problems if they cause excessive absences, create danger to the worker or coworkers, or impede effective job performance. Workers, for example, who do not get medical help for common bacterial infections such as bronchitis may miss many days of work unnecessarily. Other employees who do not take prescription medications such as insulin regularly may find their energy lower than necessary to complete the amount of work they have been assigned. Supervisors, when observing relevant job-related consequences, need to consider whether the medical condition is work related, whether improvement is likely, and whether alternative work in the organization might help relieve the problem. Supervisors should educate the worker about any relevant support programs such as health insurance benefits, disability coverage, flexible spending programs, and health maintenance organizations (HMO's). If the available benefits are insufficient for dealing with the employee's medical needs and expenses, the supervisor can recommend that the worker use other agencies such as governmental health services, community-based charitable health services, and social security. The supervisor can serve as an educator for workers who may not have had a need to learn about health services prior to the problem.

If a person has been on disability leave, an intervention interviewer can also create a rehabilitative assignment to help the person make a constructive transition back into full-time work. For example, some organizations provide alternative assignments to people who have been on disability because of physical problems. These assignments include office jobs, telephone sales, light manufacturing, recycling, cleaning, clerical work, and inspection.[26] By providing flexible, meaningful work for the person who has been ill, the supervisor helps both the worker and the organization.

Psychological Health Problems.   Some health problems relate more to mental than physical ailments. Common problems that affect worker performance include problems ranging from neurosis to psychosis; external problems such as battering, incest, rape, or crime victimage; sexual problems; depression and suicide attempts; divorce and marital problems; retirement adjustments; and legal and financial problems.[27] These problems obviously vary in their severity and in their potential effect on work. Some may have almost no effect at all while others make work nearly impossible.

The interviewer should make the best possible assessment of the situation and make appropriate referrals. Unless the interviewer is a trained and experienced mental health professional, the worker should be referred elsewhere for professional assistance. The interviewer should be careful not to stigmatize the worker so that the worker feels abnormal because she or he is experiencing mental health problems. Many mental health difficulties are normal responses to life crises. Others have organic causes. Regardless of their origins, mental health difficulties can make life and work difficult for employees. Efforts to get appropriate assistance will maximize the likelihood that employees can make timely returns to their roles as productive workers. Chapter 14 addresses issues pertinent to selection of skilled counselors.

Fatigue.   Sometimes a worker's job performance drops because she or he is tired. Obviously, fatigue can have many different origins. The intervention interviewer needs to work with the employee to discern the cause of the fatigue. If the cause is physical (e.g., caused by chronic depression or insomnia), then appropriate medical attention can provide relief. If the problem stems from the fact that the employee is working at a second or third job, then the supervisor needs to handle the difficulty differently. Some organizations, for instance, have policies against moonlighting, which is the practice of working at several jobs. If this is the case, the employee needs to be reminded of the policy. If the organization does not prohibit moonlighting, then the supervisor and worker need to collaborate to find a way to ensure that work standards at the current job are sustained. The focus in either instance should be on solving the immediate, specific job problem caused by the fatigue.

Career Development.   Some employees seek assistance concerning their own career development from their supervisors. A problem such as frustration at the lack of advancement may prompt the interviewee to seek assistance. These kinds of interviews serve a **mentoring** function for the worker; that is, they give information and guidance that contribute positively to the worker's professional development.[28] Unlike other intervention interviews, these can be affirming interactions that focus more on strengths than on a specific problem. Historically, mentoring interviews have not been as readily available for women and minorities as for male employees.[29] As a result, some large organizations have established formal mentor programs so that all workers have access to the guidance that can come from such interviews.

Personal Financial Problems.   Many people develop difficulties in their personal finances during their lifetimes. These problems can affect work performance if they increase personal stress, divert attention and labor away from work, result in telephone calls from collection agencies, or generate extra paperwork in the organization because of garnishment of wages. **Garnishment** of wages is the mandatory direct withdrawal of money from worker paychecks to pay other obligations before the paychecks are given to the workers. Workers whose financial problems impair their job performance can benefit from intervention interviews that guide them to resources that might be helpful. In particular, workers with financial problems can often benefit from the professional services of a consumer credit counselor. Many communities provide such services on a sliding fee scale or for no charge at all. Supervisors should be aware of the resources in their communities so that they can refer troubled employees to those agencies.

Retirement Transition Planning.   As employees near retirement, some exhibit a decrease in job effectiveness because of concerns about retirement. People nearing retirement may be anxious about health benefits after retirement, retirement income, personal adjustments such as spending full time at home, and many other substantial concerns. If the interviewer can refer the employees to appropriate information sources, often the unanswered questions or unfounded worries that have been hurting their work will become less powerful.

In summary, many specific and intensely personal problems confront intervention interviewers. Employees may find that their work is impaired by family problems, stress, substance abuse, physical health problems, mental health problems, fatigue, career development concerns, personal financial problems, and concerns about the transition into retirement. Alert interviewers can assess the seriousness of these matters and their impact on work performance and then refer the employees to appropriate agencies for assistance.

Disciplinary Interviews

Workers get in trouble. When they do, their supervisors must conduct **disciplinary interviews,** which are those interviews where an employer deals with an employee who has violated a condition of work. Numerous violations that vary in seriousness precipitate disciplinary interviews, including disrupting the work of others, insubordination, carelessness with resources, chronic absenteeism, and noncompliance with safety regulations. Because disciplinary interviews occur only when a work violation has occurred, they happen irregularly, and the supervisor almost always initiates them. They are also inherently evaluative, like appraisal interviews.

Disciplinary interviews often take place within a climate of anger and frustration; nonetheless, it is necessary that the supervisor schedule them as soon as possible after the infraction has been discovered. The supervisor must schedule the interview and prepare to focus the entire content of the interview on the immediate problem that has prompted the interview. Ideally, disciplinary interviews occur in a private setting. At times, in certain work settings, a union representative or attorney will also be present at the disciplinary interview.

Before the Disciplinary Interview

Facts.   Supervisors should base disciplinary decisions and actions on factual information. Therefore, complete records—including attendance records, results from drug tests, direct observation, testimony from witnesses, or credible complaints from customers and coworkers—provide the basis for a swift and effective disciplinary interview. Supervisors need to check the credibility of the sources of all facts so that the information is accurate and complete. All accusations, ultimatums, and recommendations should be based on factual information. As one writer said, "Deal in facts, not opinions."[30] Before the disciplinary interview, supervisors should also consider specifically how they will handle the particular infraction.

Progressive Discipline.   Most organizations attempt to incorporate a form of progressive discipline into their policies. **Progressive discipline** is a discipline system that gives employees a series of warnings about their unacceptable conduct and provides opportunities for them to improve their actions before they are dismissed. Progressive discipline has two important characteristics. First, the system of discipline moves through a series of warnings; and second, each warning contains an added element designed to draw the employee's attention to the urgency of the need for change.[31] Typically, a supervisor orally warns an employee who has violated a particular rule. In this initial warning, the supervisor also tells the worker that if the violation occurs again within a specified period of time that certain disciplinary actions will occur. If the employee commits the same infraction again within that specified time, a written warning goes into the worker's personnel file and an additional warning about repeating the offense is given. If another violation occurs within the time specified, the employee will be suspended for a particular time period without pay and a final warning will be given. If yet another violation occurs, the employee will be discharged from employment. The term *progressive* suggests that the disciplinary warnings move through a series of increasingly serious steps.

Due Process.   Legal considerations affect the procedures that organizations use to deal with disciplinary problems with their employees. Discipline must deal with individual violations. Discipline must not be used to discriminate against a particular ethnic, religious, or racial group. When disciplinary actions occur, the organization must abide by a system of **due process,** which is a procedure that ensures an employee's right to be treated fairly during the investigation of an alleged offense and the administration of disciplinary action.[32] A system of discipline designed to protect employees' rights always recognizes certain principles of due process. A standard list of such rights follows in Figure 12.3.

One aspect of this listing of rights is especially important; namely, employees need to know the rules and the consequences for breaking them. When employees have this information before they get into trouble, the disciplinary interviewer is much more able to deal effectively with the violation. A key element in the disciplinary interview is the supervisor's reference to the rule that has been violated. Employees need to know these rules in order to understand their violations. Without such understanding, the change that the supervisor wants will not make sense to the worker. Thus, organizations should have policies and rules that are reasonable, necessary, consistent, applicable to all employees, clear, and distributed to everyone. It is essential that all pertinent policies and rules be available to all employees and that the system of disciplinary procedures be available also. Not just supervisors should know the rules. All employees should know them. To make them available, the organization can disseminate them through company handbooks, labor union representatives, newsletters, and bulletin boards. An organization's expectations about employee behaviors should be clear to all who work there.

---

1. Employees have the right to know what their organization expects of them and what the specific consequences for violation of those expectations are.

2. Employees have the right to receive reactions to violations of the rules that are consistent with what other employees have received.

3. Employees have the right to receive discipline based on facts.

4. Employees have the right to defend themselves when they are charged with disciplinary violations.

5. Employees have the right to appeal disciplinary decisions.

6. Employees have the right to progressive disciplinary actions.

7. Employees have the right to be considered as individuals.

FIGURE 12.3   Employee Rights of Due Process

From Redeken, James R. *Employee Discipline: Policies and Practices* (Washington, D.C.: Bureau of National Affairs,Inc., 1989), 25–35.

During the Disciplinary Interview

Disciplinary interviews are usually brief and straightforward. The supervisor who has requested the meeting with the employee who has committed the infraction begins the interview with minimal small talk. Because both parties know that this is an interview prompted by a serious problem, the interviewer moves directly into the substance of the interview. First, the interviewer *states the problem* and provides supporting facts so that the employee understands the infraction that has occurred and the reasons that the supervisor has for believing that it has occurred. The focus of the supervisor's comments should be the problem, not the person.

The interviewer then *describes the policy* regarding such infractions and states clearly what the outcome of the interview needs to be. If the employee wants to speak, the supervisor needs to listen. As long as the employee is sharing pertinent information, there is no need to rush the meeting. When the worker has contributed sufficiently, the interviewer clearly *states the outcome;* that is, what behavior needs to change, under what conditions this change needs to occur, and what is the acceptable level of change.[33] As long as the employee understands the violation and is willing to respond positively to the consequences imposed by the organization, the disciplinary interview has accomplished its purpose. The interviewer then describes the *follow up* that will occur after the interview. An example of the appropriate sequence of interviewer behaviors is provided in Figure 12.4.

A factor that can undermine the clarity of the disciplinary purpose is the level of anger that is often present in disciplinary interviews. Anger in disciplinary interviews stems from varied sources. Sometimes the employee is angry at getting caught. Sometimes the supervisor is angry because the employee has been warned repeatedly and still continues the violation. At any rate, it is not uncommon for disciplinary interview participants to be angry during the interview. For women supervisors, this emotional dimension can be especially problematic. For example, a recent study about gender differences in expressions of anger have found that women have a harder time expressing negative assertions (e.g., angry statements) than men.[34] Because people make different attributions to behaviors exhibited by men and women, women also perceive angry episodes to be more costly professionally (e.g., they hurt supervisor-subordinate relationships) and personally (e.g., they hurt self-esteem).[35] These studies suggest that women supervisors and employees may experience more hesitance to participate fully in disciplinary interviews when one or both of the parties is overtly angry. Nonetheless, disciplinary interviews need to occur promptly when the violation is discovered. Hence, even individuals who feel uncomfortable with the emotional intensity need to move directly to handle the problem.

As with intervention interviews, certain problems are more typical than others for disciplinary interviews. In the section that follows, we will discuss the most common types of problems that lead to disciplinary interviews and will suggest issues for the interviewer to consider in dealing with them.

State the problem:
"Michelle, I have received two serious complaints from customers that you used threats to get them to increase their insurance coverage. One told me that you said his future claims would not be processed if he didn't buy more coverage; and the other told me this morning that you said unless she added coverage, we would drop her as a customer."

Review the policy:
"You know that we have a firm policy about being honest with customers, and your threats were not honest reflections of our sales policy that you got your first day here."

State the outcome:
"Call both of these customers as soon as you leave my office. I want you to apologize for giving them wrong information."

Use follow up:
"I want to see you back here at 3 o'clock to tell me the substance of those conversations. I will also be calling those people later."

Clarify consequences of repeating the violation:
"If this ever happens again, you will be dismissed on the spot. I am putting a letter about this in your file, and this is your last chance to correct this problem. Are you clear about what must happen now and about the consequences of future violations?"

FIGURE 12.4   Sequence of Interview Behaviors for a Disciplinary Interview

Types of Presenting Problems for Disciplinary Interviews

Although many different rule violations necessitate disciplinary interviews, most violations fall into certain categories. Many of these disciplinary problems have been studied carefully by legal scholars so that both the organization's right to discipline employees and the employee's right to fair treatment are respected.

Absenteeism and Tardiness.   One of the most common worker infractions is in the area of attendance and promptness. Organizations have the right to expect their workers to be at work on time consistently. Attendance policies must be reasonable, widely publicized, and consistently enforced across all workers with clear consequences for infractions. Employees whose attendance violates those policies because it is sporadic, chronic, or unreported (i.e, the employee does not notify the organization of the absence) can be disciplined for those problems. The discipline provided should follow the principles of progressive discipline with warnings, chances to improve, and clear consequences for failure to do so. In the disciplinary interview, the supervisor needs to describe the specific attendance or tardiness violation, state the consequences for the infraction, tell the employee what improvement is needed, and provide a clear description of what will happen if another violation occurs.

Abusive or Profane Language. Whether or not a worker's use of profane language violates policy depends upon the nature of the workplace. If the workplace is an elementary school, then worker profanity is likely to elicit a disciplinary response. If the workplace is a production line in a factory, on the other hand, obscene language is more likely to be tolerated because the culture of the workplace may both permit and encourage use of obscenities. The question about whether profanity or abusive language violates policy also depends on the target of the language outburst. For example, if abusive language is aimed in a threatening way at a supervisor, it is more likely to result in disciplinary action than if it is used in a casual manner toward a peer.

How widely the offensive language was heard is also a consideration. If the language was heard only by employees and supervisors, it is less likely to result in discipline than if it was heard by customers. Finally, abusive or profane language that is prompted by another person's abuse may be less likely to be the cause of a disciplinary action than similar language that is unprovoked. If, for example, a male worker speaks to a female worker using insulting sexist language and if she responds with profanity, then her profanity is less likely to be considered a reason for discipline since it was provoked by insulting language.

The supervisor who is speaking to an employee about the use of abusive or profane language should limit the interview to the specific infraction, refer to the actual language that led to the problem, review the consequences of the infraction, and set into place consequences for any recurrent use of such language.

Alcohol or Drug Problems. To discipline an employee because of alcohol or drug abuse, the employee must have done something that has directly impeded work performance. Employers who know of work-related problems that result from alcohol or drug abuse are obligated to intervene to instigate change. Although employers do not have the right to interfere with their workers' personal lives, they do have the right to impose standards for work performance. Alcoholism, alcohol-related conduct, and drug-related conduct can impair work performance.

Alcoholism itself is not a cause for disciplinary intervention by an organization unless the problem impedes work performance. Much has been written about alcoholism and alcohol- and drug-related conduct in the workplace.[36] Basically, the disciplinary consequences depend on the conditions of the first major offense, the pattern of effect on work performance, the violation of policy by an employee, and the willingness of the employee to admit and work on the problem. Because alcohol and substance abuse are often harmful in the workplace, supervisors need to deal with observable problems directly. If the supervisor observes work that is impaired by alcohol or other substance abuse, and particularly if it is observed repeatedly, the supervisor must intervene to tell the worker of the work-related aspects of the problem and to suggest programs for rehabilitation. Many organizations work assertively with their employees who have shown a desire to change by participating in credible rehabilitation programs.

Disloyalty or Disrespectful Attitude. Organizations may discipline employees whose behaviors reflect blatant disloyalty or disrespect toward their employers. To discipline for disloyalty, however, requires that (a) the disloyal behaviors be combined with other problems that impair work performance and (b) the behavior must have affected customers or other workers. Disciplinary interviews dealing with disloyalty and/or disrespect must be based on specific, factual instances of worker behaviors. Supervisors do not have adequate evidence of these problems if they want to discipline a worker for having a "bad attitude." The violation of policy must be specific, verified, and harmful to the work of the organization.

In the disciplinary interview, the supervisor needs to describe the specific behaviors that have generated the complaint, make recommendations about behavioral changes to rectify the problem, and warn about consequences of repeat infractions. The more factual the description of the problem, the more likely that the worker will understand what changes are expected.

Dishonesty or Falsification of Records. Organizations have the right to expect honesty and accurate treatment of records by their workers. If an employee violates policies about honesty and record keeping, the organization may invoke disciplinary action. Most organizations and labor unions consider dishonesty and falsification of records to be very serious issues. The organization that disciplines a worker must demonstrate that the worker acted with (a) knowledge that the action was wrong and (b) an intent to defraud the organization. If the first steps of progressive discipline suggest that the employee did not meet the first condition, (i.e., knowledge that the action was a violation of policy), then the organization's response will be different than in situations where both conditions are met. Because the infraction of dishonesty and falsification of records is considered so serious, the employee's work history is less of a mitigating factor than in some other areas of discipline.

The degree of disciplinary response must take into account several factors; namely, whether the action harmed the organization, whether the company acted quickly when the infraction was discovered, and whether similar problems have been treated similarly in the past. Considering these factors, the supervisor confronts the worker with facts about the violation, informs the worker about the consequences of the violation, and warns the worker about consequences of subsequent violations.

Dress or Grooming. Although organizations do not have the right to dictate how their employees live their private lives, they do have the right to discipline employees for work infractions related to dress and grooming. Discipline is only in order if the dress and grooming code is reasonable, well-publicized, consistent with labor agreement, consistently enforced, and related to BFOQs (*bona fide* occupational qualifications). For example, it is considered reasonable to have grooming policies that relate to health and safety issues. Some employers have a "no facial hair" regulation for employees who use respirators since facial hair affects respiratory seal.[37] A "no facial hair" policy would not be considered reasonable in circumstances where facial hair is irrelevant to the satisfactory completion of job requirements. Dress and grooming policies cannot be implemented or enforced in a way that constraints religious expression. For example, an Amish woman working as a checker in a grocery should be allowed to wear the religiously prescribed hair covering of her choice despite a general policy against check out clerks wearing hats.

Disciplinary interviews about dress and grooming are easily focused on the issue. The supervisor can directly point to policy regulations, the infraction, its consequences, and consequences of recurring violations of the regulation.

Gambling.   Many organizations have clear policies about on-site gambling by their employees. Obviously, organizations are not required to have disciplinary policies that are redundant with state and federal regulations about gambling because employees who violate the law are vulnerable to prosecution by the state, not just to disciplinary violations in their workplace. When gambling occurs on the work grounds and when it has a detrimental effect on other workers and on productivity, supervisors can begin disciplinary actions toward the employees who participate in it. Like other disciplinary interviews, the supervisor needs to describe the specific offense and the consequences of the violation. A warning about subsequent violations should be a part of the interview.

Insubordination.   Insubordination is a situation in which an employee understands the supervisor's directions but intentionally disobeys or disregards those directions. For example, if an employee who has been accused of sexual harassment is directed by the supervisor to stop calling female coworkers "darling" but persists in doing so, the supervisor can discipline the employee for insubordination. The worker's willful choice to disregard the direct order of the supervisor fits the definition of insubordination.

Insubordination must be based on factual accounts of the intentional disobedience or ignoring of an order. Supervisors must take into account any mitigating factors that might explain or justify what appears to be insubordination. First, a charge of insubordination must take into account the possibility of supervisor misconduct. For example, if a supervisor uses profane language to give an order, such as "Get off your fat a__ and get that truck unloaded, you lazy SOB," and if the worker says, "Do it yourself, b_____," a charge of insubordination may be inappropriate. The supervisor should not have used insulting profanity to give instructions to the worker, and as a result, disciplining the worker for insubordination is not likely the most constructive response to this workplace problem.

Second, a worker who refuses to cooperate with an order because of threat of physical danger should not be charged with insubordination. For example, a supervisor who smells natural gas coming from a storeroom cannot expect a worker to obey an order to "go in there and see what's wrong." In cases where compliance with the order poses danger to the worker, a worker who does not comply should not be charged with insubordination.

In disciplinary interviews concerning insubordination, the supervisor should document the charge with reference to specific behaviors that led to it. The supervisor should then discharge the punishment associated with the violation and warn the employee about what will happen if the insubordination continues.

Fighting.   Organizations can expect "reasonable" social behavior from their workers.[38] Before disciplining an employee for fighting at work, the supervisor must consider how intentional the worker's participation in the fight was, the degree of potential for physical injury or damage to property, the general atmosphere of the workplace, whether improvement in social behavior seems likely, the employee's work history, whether weapons were used, and whether the fighting was provoked. This complex mixture of factors must be considered before an individual worker is disciplined for participating in a fight. Most companies have straightforward policies about fighting in the workplace. Supervisors can consider mitigating circumstances (e.g., whether the fighting was provoked or the worker's previous history) when implementing the punishments associated with the regulations.

In a heated atmosphere immediately following a fight, the disciplinary interviewer must report specifically what the worker has done that violates policy and what punishments will be imposed. If the workers remain openly hostile and belligerent during the disciplinary interview, additional punishments may result as a consequence of those interview behaviors. Supervisors have the responsibility to halt workplace fighting, and a firm, prompt disciplinary response is the best way to halt it.

Work Slow Downs.   Sometimes employees intentionally slow down production or customer service in order to register their dissatisfaction with contract negotiations or frustration with management. Such worker slow downs often violate organizational policy. When they do, supervisors have to demonstrate that the slow down was done purposefully, that it was not justified, and that it had a harmful effect on the organization. Because slow downs are considered a very serious infraction, the employee's work history may not mitigate the seriousness of the offense in the organization's eyes.

Since slow downs are difficult to prove, the supervisor must enter the interview with firm, specific factual information about the violation. An example of such verification might be a videotape of a television news story in which an employee has openly stated to a reporter, "We plan to do the absolute minimum in terms of customer service and to do it as slowly as we can until this contract is agreed on." The supervisor can then deliver the appropriate penalty and give a warning about subsequent behaviors. Work slow downs are very difficult to prove and are often complicated by strained labor union and management relations.

Carelessness and Negligence. Supervisors should discuss chronic carelessness and negligence with employees during regular appraisal interviews. At times, however, because of particular safety policies individual acts of carelessness mandate special discipline. For example, an airline may have a policy requiring that any employee who damages equipment because of negligence will receive a one-day suspension without pay. In an instance like this, the supervisor describes the specific incident and imposes the standard penalty. If the carelessness is frequent and if repeated warnings have not improved the situation, then the penalties will be increasingly stringent. Factors that also need to be considered include the worker's ability, how costly the problems, how much time was lost, the extent of damage, and the danger that the carelessness created. As with other disciplinary infractions, supervisors need to impose a consistent set of penalties across employees.

Disciplinary Interviews and Termination

In some circumstances any of the preceding infractions can, if not improved, lead to termination. Termination must occur only because of problems in job performance and only after progressive discipline has been used. Employees should not be terminated because of irrelevant issues. Supervisors need to consider the following legal and ethical issues in Figure 12.5 before suggesting termination.

Before terminating an employee for a disciplinary problem, consider:

1. Could this termination be viewed as resulting from the employee's *legal* right to file a harassment complaint or blow the whistle on illegal activities?

2. Is this termination really because of the worker's disciplinary problem or because the company needs to lay off workers? Are others more deserving of termination?

3. Has the disciplinary problem been mentioned earlier? Has it been documented? Has the worker had the opportunity to solve the problem?

4. During the disciplinary process, has the employee been treated fairly, consistently, and respectfully?

5. If this employee files a law suit or a grievance, are the company's records and practices defensible?

FIGURE 12.5   Why Terminate an Employee?

Adapted from: "Employment at Will: New Restrictions on the Right," *Business Report* 13 (1988), 61.

At the Conclusion of the Disciplinary Interview

Because disciplinary interviews are sharply focused and often brief, the conclusion arrives quickly. In the conclusion, the supervisor needs to clarify the specific changes that are expected, what measures will be used to check whether those changes have occurred, and a timetable for improvement. The supervisor can reiterate any pertinent warnings about subsequent problems.[39] If a written record of the interview is going into the worker's personnel file, the interviewer should inform the worker of this fact. The supervisor should end the interview professionally.

Summary

Problems provoke two kinds of interviews in organizations; namely, intervention interviews and disciplinary interviews. Supervisors or organizational staff members in employee assistance programs participate in intervention interviews to provide assessment and referral services to employees with problems. Creating a communication climate conducive to good problem solving can be done by building rapport, demonstrating respect for worker confidentiality, and listening carefully. Typical presenting problems for disciplinary interviews include family problems, stress and burnout, alcohol and drug problems, physical health difficulties, mental health difficulties, fatigue, career development, financial difficulties, and retirement concerns.

Disciplinary interviews occur when an employee has violated an organizational regulation or policy. Disciplinary interviews must be based on factual evidence and are most effective if the organization has used a system of progressive discipline. Typical disciplinary interview topics include: absenteeism, abusive language, alcohol or drug conduct, disloyalty, dishonesty, dress or grooming violations, gambling, insubordination, fighting, work slow downs, or negligence. Terminations should only occur after progressive discipline has been unsuccessful in correcting work-related problems. Employee disciplinary interviews should always focus on job-related problems.

Discussion Questions

1. Discuss factors that supervisors should take into account when they are trying to decide whether to discuss a problem (e.g., fatigue on the job) with an employee. What problems are not the business of the organization? What situations deserve immediate attention from a supervisor?

2. In what ways did the interview at the beginning of this chapter demonstrate a supportive communication climate? What were the possible effects of the interviewer's supportive behaviors on the interviewee's responses? (See chapter 10 for full discussion of supportive and defensive behaviors.)

3. What possible ethical dilemmas are raised when employees participate in employee assistance programs (EAPs)? What are ethical concerns for the organizations? For the employees?

4. Why don't some employees respond to progressive discipline and change their behaviors? How can organizations adapt to these employees to help them improve and change?

5. This text suggests that disciplinary interviews should not have much rapport building at the beginning. Do you agree with that position? What might be some advantages to spending time building rapport? Would rapport building in disciplinary interviews increase the likelihood that employees would comply with the suggested changes?

Suggested Activities

1. Write a three to four page paper about the following hypothetical situation: You are a supervisor whose two best workers have just had a fist fight. One is yelling that the other sabotaged his work station and the second is denying the charge. Although they have been separated by other workers, they are both furious. They are sitting outside your office, one in the workroom and one near the secretary's desk. You need to talk to them.

   Will you talk to them individually? Separately?

   How serious is this offense in your mind?

   How comfortable will you be with the intensity of their anger?

   Will you offer to hear their versions of what happened?

   Will you seek information from witnesses?

   What will you do if either gets loud, angry, and disrespectful toward you?

   How will you feel?

   To what organizational policies will you refer?

   To what extent will you consider their work histories as you deal with the problem?

   What kind of progressive discipline will you administer?

2. In groups of three or four, discuss how you would find out information about the following resources in your community:

   Day care for adults

   Credit counseling for individuals with financial problems

   Child care for sick children

   Workshops or counselors who teach ways to reduce job stress

   Alcohol treatment

3. In groups of three or four, list as many possible resources related to child care in your community as you can. If possible, use a telephone book to develop a list of resources with telephone numbers.

4. Divide into dyads. Discuss the common stereotype that people have about mentally ill persons. If you were supervising a worker who had a treatable mental illness like chronic depression, what could you do in an intervention interview to minimize the negative stigma associated with mental illness? After the dyads have talked for ten minutes, return to the larger group and share your ideas. Persons who are interested in reading more about the stigma of mental illness may want to read J. Dan Rothwell's book *Telling It Like It Isn't*, published by Prentice Hall, 1982.

Related Readings

Byars, Lloyd L., and Rue, Leslie W. *Human Resource Management,* 4th ed. Homewood, IL: Irwin, 1993.

Ivancevich, John M. *Human Resource Management: Foundations of Personnel,* 5th ed. Homewood, IL: Irwin, 1992.

Masi, Dale A. *Designing Employee Assistance Programs.* New York: American Management Association, 1984.

Redeker, James R. *Employee Discipline: Policies and Practices.* Washington, D.C.: Bureau of National Affairs, Inc., 1989.

Weiss, Stephen M., Fielding, Jonathan E., and Baum, Andrew. *Health at Work.* Hillsdale, NJ: Lawrence Erlbaum Associates, Publishers, 1991.

Endnotes

1. Harold V. Schmitz, *The Handbook of Employee Counseling Programs* (New York: The New York Business Group on Health, 1982), 16.

2. William J. Sonnenstuhl and Harrison M. Trice, *Strategies for Employee Assistance Programs: The Crucial Balance,* 2nd ed. (Ithaca, NY: ILR Press, Cornell University, 1990), 13.

3. J. Spicer, *The EAP Solution: Current Trends and Future Issues* (Center City, MN: Hazelden Educational Materials, 1987).

4. Sandra S. Lee and Elizabeth A. Rose, "Employee Counseling Services: Ethical Dilemmas," *Personnel and Guidance Journal 62* (Jan. 1984), 279.

5. Keith McClellan and Richard E. Miller, "EAPs in Transition: Purpose and Scope of Services, *Employee Assistance Quarterly 3* (1988), 29.

6. D.A. Harley, "Impaired Job Performance and Worksite Trigger Incidents: Factors Influencing Supervisory EAP Referrals," *Employee Assistance Quarterly 6* (1991), 59–60.

7. Vicki Pawlick and Brian H. Kleiner, "On-the-job Employee Counseling: Focus on Performance," *Personnel Journal 65* (1986), 31–32.

8. David W. Martin, Virginia M. Heckel, G. Kenneth Goodrick, Janet M. Schreiber, and Virginia L. Young, "The Relationship between Referral Types, Work Performance, and Employee Problems," *Employee Assistance Quarterly 1* (1985–1986), 28.

9. Jack Gibb, "Defensive Communication," *Journal of Communication 11* (1961), 143.

10. Jack Gibb, (1961), 145.

11. Keith McClellan, and Richard E. Miller, (1988), 35.

12. Harold V. Schmitz, (1982), 29.

13. Dale A. Masi, *Designing Employee Assistance Programs* (New York: American Management Association, 1984), 201–03.

14. James J. Floyd, *Listening: A Practical Approach* (Glenview, IL: Scott, Foresman, and Company, 1985), 119.

15. Harold Hackney and Sherilyn N. Cormier, *Counseling Strategies and Interventions,* 3rd ed. (Englewood Cliffs, NJ: Prentice Hall, 1988), 31.

16. Jane Jorgenson, "Communication, Rapport, and the Interview: A Social Perspective," *Communication Theory 2* (1992), 148.

17. Department of Health and Human Services, Employee Counseling Services (ECS) Program: Supervisory Training, *Trainer's Manual* (Prepared by Management Concepts, Washington, D.C., 1981), Handout #6, 3–6.

18. Michael Cavanagh, "What You Don't Know About Stress," *Personnel Journal 67* (1988), 56–57.

19. Sarah Sanderson King, "The Relationship between Stress and Communication in the Organizational Context," Kevin L. Hutchinson (ed.), *Readings in Organizational*

Communication (Dubuque, IA: William C. Brown Publishers, 1992), 383–392.

20. Michael Cavanagh, (1988), 55.

21. Michael Cavanagh, (1988), 57–58.

22. John M. Ivancevich, *Human Resource Management: Foundations of Personnel*, 5th ed. (Homewood, IL: Irwin, 1992), 591.

23. Richard M. Weiss, "Writing Under the Influence: Science Versus Fiction in the Analysis of Corporate Alcoholism Programs," *Personnel Psychology* 40 (1987), 342.

24. Richard M. Weiss, *Dealing with Alcoholism in the Workplace* (New York: The Conference Board, 1980), 182.

25. "Constructive confrontation" was first termed "constructive coercion" in H.M. Trice, *Alcoholism and Industry*, 3rd ed. (New York: Christopher B. Smithers Foundation, 1969). It was later renamed "constructive confrontation" in H.M. Trice, *Alcoholism and Industry*, 5th ed. (New York: Christopher B. Smithers Foundation, 1972).

26. Sheila H. Akabas, "Transitional Employment Encourages Earlier Return to Work," *HR Focus* 69 (1992), 21.

27. Dale A. Masi, (1984), 118.

28. K.E. Kram, *Mentoring at Work* (Glenview, IL: Scott, Foresman, and Company, 1984).

29. Sebywyn Fernstein, "Women and Minority Workers in Business Find a Mentor Can Be a Rare Commodity," *The Wall Street Journal* (November 10, 1987), 31.

30. Joseph T. Straub, "Disciplinary Interviews: The Buck Stops with You," *Supervisory Management* 36 (1991), 1.

31. James R. Redeker, *Employee Discipline: Policies and Practices* (Washington, D.C.: Bureau of National Affairs, Inc., 1989), 53.

32. Lloyd L. Byars, and Leslie W. Rue, *Human Resource Management*, 4th ed. (Homewood, IL: Irwin Publishers, 1993), 455.

33. Harold Hackney and N. Sherilyn Cormier, (1988), 112.

34. M. J. Blier, and L.A. Blier-Wilson, "Gender Differences in Self-rated Emotional Expressiveness," *Sex Roles* 21 (1989), 287–95.

35. Mark A. Davis, Patricia A. LaRosa, and Donald P. Foshee, "Emotion Work in Supervisor-subordinate Relations: Gender Differences in the Perception of Angry Displays," *Sex Roles* 26 (1992), 513–31.

36. See, for example, William J. Sonnenstuhl, and Harrison M. Trice, (1990); J. Spicer, (1987); Dale A. Masi, (1984); and Richard M. Weiss, (1987).

37. See legal precedent, E.I. duPont de Nemours and Company (Light), 78 LA 327.

38. James R. Redeker, (1989), 306.

39. Joseph T. Straub, (1991), 2.

$$C\ h\ a\ p\ t\ e\ r \quad 13$$

Diagnostic Problem-Solving Interviews

*"To write prescriptions is easy, but to come
to an understanding with people is hard."*
—Franz Kafka, "A Country Doctor," Willa and Edwin
Muir (Trans.) Selected Short Stories of Franz Kafka
(New York: The Modern Library, 1952), 152.

Wilson White has been sitting in the examining room of the busy neighborhood family practice clinic for twenty minutes, waiting to see a doctor about his sore throat. The nurse has taken his temperature and blood pressure, inquired about his symptoms, and asked him to sit on the examining table until the doctor comes. He hears the rustle of papers outside the door, it opens, and Dr. Kaplan enters, reading the chart. Without looking up, Dr. Kaplan speaks.

Dr. Kaplan: I'm Dr. Kaplan.

Wilson: Hi.

Dr. Kaplan: So you've got a sore throat.

Wilson: Yeah.

Dr. Kaplan: How long has it been bothering you? (Still looking at chart.)

Wilson: About a week. I thought it would go away, but it just kept getting worse. (Dr. Kaplan writes on chart.)

Dr. Kaplan: Any other problems?

Wilson: No, just my throat.

Dr. Kaplan: Have you had a runny nose?

Wilson: No.

Dr. Kaplan: Headaches?

Wilson: No.

Dr. Kaplan: Earaches?

Wilson: No.

Dr. Kaplan: Well, let's have a look. (Examines throat, looks into ears, and checks breathing with a stethoscope.) Breathe in deep. Let it out. Breathe in again. Let it out. Breathe in. Let it out. Breathe in. Let it out. Well, your lungs sound clear. (Puts away equipment, sits down in chair, and begins to write on prescription pad.) You've got a throat infection. I'll give you this prescription. You need to take it until you're completely finished with it. Don't stop taking the pills just because you start feeling better. Take them all. (Talks while writing on chart.) Try to drink lots of fluids and get some rest. You'll feel better in a day or so. But be sure you take all the medicine. Any questions?

Wilson: No.

Dr. Kaplan: (Hands prescription to Wilson.) OK. See you. (Leaves room.)

Chapter Goals

- To define the diagnostic problem-solving interview.
- To identify particular challenges for diagnostic interviewers.
- To introduce issues of preparation and implementation for diagnostic interviewers.
- To suggest ways that interviewees can prepare and participate in diagnostic problem-solving interviews actively.

Introduction

At different times in their lives, people need help. They may need assistance in paying overdue bills, finding temporary housing for foster children, getting rid of a sore throat, or finding why their dog's fur is falling out. Interviews often play a key role in solving these problems. Such problem-solving interviews are called diagnostic problem solving interviews. In **diagnostic problem-solving interviews,** one party (i.e., the interviewer) has knowledge or abilities needed by another party (i.e., the interviewee) to diagnose and solve a problem. Usually, although not always, the interviewee seeks help from the interviewer.

Diagnostic problem-solving interviews are common. Typical kinds of diagnostic interviews are those between social workers and their clients, consumer credit counselors and individuals with credit problems, and customer service representatives and customers. The most ubiquitous or widespread type of diagnostic interview is between health care providers and their patients. These health care interviews occur between patients and a variety of physicians, nurses, nutritionists, chiropractors, dentists, physical therapists, hospital social workers, and laboratory technicians. They also occur between veterinarians and animal owners. All diagnostic interviews share certain characteristics; namely, the interviewee has a problem and has sought out or been referred to the interviewer as an expert who can assist in solving it.

The interviewee's goal is simple: to get effective help to solve a problem. The nature of the problems vary, but each problem indicates a difference between how the interviewees think things are and how they believe they ought to be. The problem could be related to economic conditions, such as working with a consumer credit counselor to rectify a bad credit rating by consolidating bills and improving spending habits. It could be a problem related to the return of defective merchandise, or it could be a health problem. All of these problems bring interviewees to experts (e.g., a credit counselor, a customer service representative, or a physician) to help solve them.

The goal of the interviewer is complex because it has several components. The interviewer must (a) obtain relevant and necessary information from the interviewee and other sources, (b) make an accurate diagnosis, and (c) recommend an effective solution. To be effective, proposed solutions must be workable and advantageous to the interviewee. While the interviewee is the primary information source, information can also come from other places such as credit records (for the interview with the credit counselor), receipts (for the interview about the defective merchandise), or physical examinations or laboratory tests (for the health care interview).

Many persons who conduct diagnostic interviews regularly use standard interview guides based on previous experiences with similar problems. A social worker, for example, may have a standard set of questions to ask all clients seeking particular services. This checklist of questions allows the social worker to meet the client's needs in the most efficient way possible. Using these standard questions can actually make a more individualized interaction with the interviewee possible if the interviewer realizes that ". . . a *scientific* approach to history taking permits and reinforces an *artful* approach to the patient."[1] Getting basic information from the standard questions in a systematic way allows time for the interviewer to give individualized attention to the unique needs of each client. Answers to the standard questions provide the interviewer with basic information to use in diagnosing the problem. Additional questions tailored individually to each interviewee allow the interviewer to adapt the diagnosis and subsequent solution to the specific interviewee. For example, in the opening interview of this chapter, Dr. Kaplan did not take advantage of his opportunity to give individualized attention to Wilson White. Instead, he took the expedient approach and wrote a prescription without trying to understand the individual circumstances of his patient. He could have used the standard questions for a patient with a sore throat and also gone beyond those questions to adapt to the special needs of this particular patient. A diagnostic interviewer who listens closely to individual interviewees acts as a kind of "multilingual interpreter"[2] who attends to the interviewee's concerns, seeks information to reach an accurate diagnosis, and works with the interviewee for a workable solution. To be an effective interpreter, the interviewer needs to establish a constructive working relationship with the client, obtain relevant information, discard irrelevant information, and implement good solutions. These are challenging tasks.

In fact, diagnostic interviews are often difficult. Many diagnostic interviewers complain that their interviewees are "poor historians." This is a common label for an interviewee who does not provide information in a way that makes it easy for the interviewer to diagnose the problem. Interviewers often hold interviewees responsible for not volunteering helpful information in an organized way. The label "poor historian" actually reflects a joint problem; that is, both the interviewer and interviewee may not have participated fully and effectively in the diagnostic interview. The success of the interview depends on both parties' abilities to communicate effectively with one another.[3] Mutual respect and credibility are necessary for good communication. A good relationship between the interviewers and interviewees affects whether the interviewees will find acceptable resolutions to the problem that brought them to the diagnostic interviews in the first place.

Poor histories result from various barriers that hinder effective communication in diagnostic interviews. Some of these barriers have their roots in the interviewees' fear and embarrassment about the situations that brought them to the interviews, and others stem from poor interviewer questioning. Each of these barriers can hurt the effectiveness of a diagnostic interview. Let us consider them separately.

Interviewees often bring a sense of shame or embarrassment to diagnostic interviews. They may be embarrassed by a variety of behaviors or conditions. For example, they have bounced checks, are unemployed, have not had their teeth cleaned for a decade, or have ignored a noticeable lump in the abdomen. Embarrassment often occurs when people fear that they do not measure up to their own or others' expectations. Because of fear, shame, and preference for privacy, some people avoid diagnostic interviews. Many do not keep return appointments with their physicians.[4] Some fear that the interview may require them to volunteer information that makes them vulnerable to criticism or ridicule. Others may fear they will be ridiculed for their ignorance about their situations.[5] Interviewee reticence and shame make effective communication difficult because people who are ashamed may not share important information freely.

Interviewers also contribute barriers to diagnostic interviews. Simply put, many diagnostic interviewers do not ask questions in ways that elicit the information needed to make accurate and helpful diagnoses. Too often they interrupt, ask too many questions, or neglect to elicit important information. Research in the field of medicine, for example, is telling. Beckman and Frankel found that over two-thirds of the time physicians interrupted their patients' opening statements before the patients were done speaking.[6] Another study of senior medical students found that in one-fourth of all diagnostic interviews, medical students failed to ask questions and conduct examinations in such a way that they could identify the patient's main problem within 15 minutes.[7] Related research with experienced primary care physicians (i.e., family practice and internal medicine physicians) found that, on the average, they elicited only half of the facts relevant to a complete diagnosis from their patients during initial diagnostic interviews.[8] Clearly, some interviewers in these health-related diagnostic interviews do not ask questions that get the information they need to make accurate diagnoses.

Both interviewers and interviewees need to bring understanding and skill to diagnostic interviews to meet their goals. The remainder of this chapter will discuss how interviewers can work effectively in diagnostic interviews. It will also discuss how interviewees can choose effective helpers and participate in the diagnostic interviews to maximize their effectiveness in reaching good resolutions to the interviewees' problems.

The Interviewer in the Diagnostic Interview

A diagnostic interviewer faces many challenges. Increased appreciation for the (1) interviewee's perspective, (2) the role of empathy in diagnosis, and (3) changing attitudes toward diagnostic interviewers allows interviewers to communicate more effectively in diagnostic interviews. We will look at these three issues as well as the role of training in diagnostic techniques, the need for interview preparation, and the ways to conduct the interview. First, let us consider the issues of interviewee perspective, empathy, and the role of the diagnostic interviewer.

Issues Affecting Diagnostic Interviews

The Unique Perspective of the Interviewee. An interviewer works most effectively in diagnostic interviews when she or he understands and appreciates the perspective of the interviewee within the diagnostic interview structure. Effective interviewers realize that interviewees bring two kinds of important knowledge to the interview; namely, the ability to describe their problem and their own assessments of the problematic condition. Some clients even bring their own solutions to interviews and seek diagnostic approval. In health care interviews, the interviewee's perspective on the problem is called *"health understanding,"*[9] that is, the patient's own attitudes and beliefs about health, illness, and medical treatment in general. Before patients seek medical care, for example, they try to understand what is wrong with them, how serious it is, whether it is treatable, and how it fits into the whole nature of being sick. Medical patients come into diagnostic interviews having already "organized" their illnesses so that they make sense to themselves.[10] Health care providers need to realize that they are interviewing patients who have already tried to understand what has happened to their bodies. Cassell has said that you don't just speak to patients; you speak to their sets of beliefs about the world.[11] The effective interviewer pays attention to the individual patient, the symptoms that are presented, *and* the information that allows the interviewer to see, at least in part, how the patient understands the situation. Interviewers, in other words, must listen for patients' points of view.[12]

Paying attention to how patients understand the medical situation helps the interviewer decide what questions are necessary, how to word them, and what kinds of courses of treatment would make sense to the patients. If the interviewer detects that a patient is understanding the medical problem differently, the interviewer can ask outright: "I wonder what your ideas are about why this might be happening to you."[13] The answer to this question allows the interviewer to determine whether different perspectives are affecting the communication in the interview.

Let us look at an example of the impact of interviewee perspective in a medical interview. A woman with breast cancer believes her cancer is punishment for an abortion that she had when she was a teenager. If she tells this to her physician, the physician is able to explain other possible causes—heredity, risk factors, diet, and previous injury. While appreciating the patient's point of view, the physician can offer less guilt-producing explanations and, in doing this, possibly create in the patient more hope for cure. Finding out what the patient thinks sometimes provides the health care provider with helpful clues about the patient's problem and its possible solutions.

Appreciating the Role of Empathy in Diagnosis.   **Empathy**, the capacity to understand another's ideas and emotions, is powerful in diagnostic interviews. The reason for this is simple. For some problems, interviewers can diagnose better when they understand the situation from the interviewee's point of view. In trying to help another solve a problem, an interviewer benefits from knowing both what the person thinks about the situation *and* how the person feels about the problem. To be empathic, the interviewer needs to pay attention both to thoughts and feelings.

Consider, for example, a recent college graduate who has financial difficulties because of using several credit cards that had been sent to him in the mail upon graduation. After six months, he finds himself more than $8,000 in debt, and unable to make even the minimum payments on the accounts despite the fact that he is earning decent wages in his new position. He meets with a consumer credit counselor and tells the counselor about his problem. The counselor, striving for empathy, listens "between the lines" and learns not only about the graduate's specific financial problem, but also about his feelings of intense fear about losing his car and even his job if his employer learns of his debt.

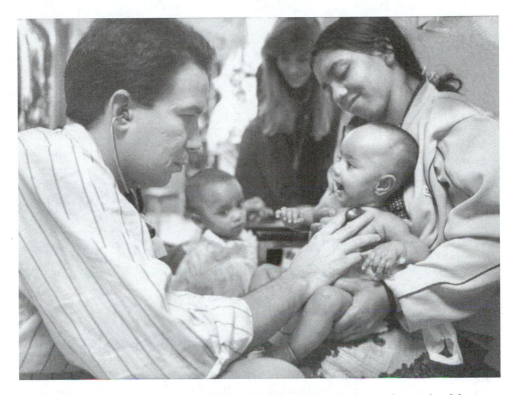

By paying attention to both thoughts and feelings, the interviewer is able to make a better diagnosis.

The counselor, sensing the man's fear, is able to provide both the information *and* the assurance that other people had been in comparable predicaments and have gotten out of them successfully. Moreover, the counselor explains quite carefully how a consolidation account can bring all the bills together into one payment, gradually reduce his debt, allow him to keep his car, and keep his employer from learning of the problem. Because the counselor understands the graduate's thoughts (his description of the situation) *and* feelings (fear and panic), she is able to respond both to the problem and to the man's fear about what would happen next. Interviewing empathetically allows the interviewer to be more helpful to the interviewee by making better diagnoses and recommending solutions that respond to the needs of the whole person.

Appreciating Changing Attitudes Toward Diagnostic Interviewers. Ongoing research suggests that people of different ages bring different attitudes toward the diagnostic interviewers. In health care interviews, for example, research about patient satisfaction with health care providers suggests that younger consumers are less satisfied with diagnostic interactions than are their older counterparts. A study of internal medicine physicians and their patients found the younger patients to be significantly less satisfied with diagnostic interviews with their physicians than were the older patients.[14] Likewise, a survey of patients in an anesthesiology clinic found that younger patients were significantly more dissatisfied with their interactions with physicians than were the older patients.[15] This trend in health care represents a movement toward less consumer willingness to assume that "the doctor knows best."[16]

This trend in patient perceptions suggests that interviewers in diagnostic situations can no longer assume that interviewees will automatically accept the diagnosis and recommended treatments. This change in attitude on the part of interviewees points to the need for the interview to include a shared search for information and for a solution to the problem which incorporates *both* the expertise of the interviewer and the insights and needs of the interviewee. This change in attitudes also suggests that interviewers may want to provide information about their own training and experience so that interviewees are better informed about the interviewer's expertise. Interviewers may, for example, discuss their professional training and experiences with problems like the interviewee's own. All these activities can enhance interviewer credibility at a time when younger consumers are more critical.

The Power of Interviewer Training.   Training for diagnostic interviewers is important for them to be effective. Many persons who conduct diagnostic interviews receive such training regularly. Most social workers, for example, learn to conduct interviews during supervised internships, while working with clients under the supervision of experienced social workers and receiving critical feedback from them about their diagnostic-interviewing skills. In retail settings, customer service representatives who field complaints from customers also receive training about how to interview those customers. In some companies, interview training includes the use of videotapes and role playing. In many medical settings, nurses receive training in communication. In most medical schools, however, training in diagnostic interviewing is often limited to what the residents can pick up through observing more experienced physicians. Nonetheless, diagnostic-interviewing skills can be improved with training. A study of medical students, for example, found that students who had received an extra lesson about the specific disease their patient had did not necessarily conduct better diagnostic interviews. More advanced students who had completed a course that included specific training on interviewing, however, were significantly more effective at making accurate diagnoses.[17]

Various methods of interview training are available and effective. These include role playing, modelling, video playback, homework assigned to practice in the field, group training, and on-the-job training.[18] Role playing techniques place persons into specific roles in hypothetical problem-solving interview situations. Participants communicate as effectively as possible to solve the problem, even though they may be in a role that is not familiar. Participants then discuss and analyze the simulated interview to learn from their strengths and weaknesses.

The technique of modelling uses effective interviewers as examples for interviewers in training. The principle is that observing and learning from good interviewers allows novice interviewers to incorporate certain questioning, listening, and responding skills in their own work. Other methods for interview training include the videotaping of actual or simulated interviews so that in consultation with colleagues interviewers can evaluate and improve their skills. Some training programs give interviewers homework assignments to practice during actual interviews. For example, an interviewer may be assigned the task of expressing more empathy toward her clients. In the interviews conducted during the next week, she would then work on that assignment, trying to demonstrate more empathy in actual interviews. In-service training also helps interviewers improve. For example, training programs that incorporate all the previously mentioned techniques can be done during on-the-job training. Moreover, all of these techniques can be adapted to groups of interviewees so that they improve their individual skills with encouragement and feedback from their professional colleagues. Not only does such training teach questioning skills, but even elusive interpersonal skills such as empathy can also be broken down into components and improved effectively.[19]

Research and experience are clear: interviewing training helps interviewers. An appreciation for the importance of training and a commitment to participate in it is crucial for an effective diagnostic interviewer.

Interviewer Preparation

Preparation for diagnostic interviews involves activities that range from long-term education to furniture arrangement. The primary preparation for diagnostic interviewing is becoming an expert in the areas of concern to the client. For diagnostic interviewers who are social workers, this means getting the best social work education possible. For problem solvers in retail or nonprofit community services, preparation may include formal education and specialized in-service training. For health care interviewers, formal training and supervised practice provide the skills to become an expert in health-related fields. Obviously, the necessary expertise to diagnose and solve client problems must come from individual fields of knowledge and training. Once an interviewer has the necessary background to diagnose and solve problems in a particular field, then it is time to focus on preparation for effective interviewing. The preparation for diagnostic interviewing includes: (a) developing a respectful attitude toward interviewees, and (b) planning a setting conducive to effective problem solving.

Developing a Respectful Attitude. Diagnostic interviewers reach more accurate diagnoses and suggest more effective resolutions to problems when they interview with respect, genuineness, and empathy toward the interviewees.[20] Diagnostic interviewers can demonstrate respect for interviewees in many ways. For example, as mentioned earlier, an interviewer needs to gain a sense about how the interviewee understands the problem. At times, the interviewee's understanding may reflect ignorance. For example, a patient with hypertension (i.e., high blood pressure) may report that she has followed the doctor's orders and restricted her intake of salt. She may also say that she doesn't eat salty foods like pretzels. Instead, she eats healthier foods like dill pickles and Spanish olives. Being ignorant about nutrition, the patient might not realize that pickles and olives are high salt items. The health care provider needs to educate the patient, taking care not to ridicule or become impatient with areas of ignorance.

At other times, interviewee understanding of situations may be based on superstition, such as a welfare client who is convinced that the fire in his oven was caused by his breaking a mirror (and bringing bad luck on himself) rather than by a malfunctioning pilot light. Interviewers need to realize that such superstitions are a serious concern to those who hold them. As such, they deserve respect, but not agreement. The social worker might respond: "I know you think that when you broke the mirror last week, you brought bad luck to your family for seven years. But I don't think this fire was because of it. The person from the gas company left the pilot for us to look at. (Hands part of the pilot light unit to the client.) You can see here that the whole side of it along here (points to side) was cracked because it was so old and worn. That's probably what caused the fire. The gas seeped out and got into the flame and the fire started."

Another attribute of respect is interviewer planning for interviewees who do not speak English. If the interviewer knows ahead of time of that possibility, then it is possible to make arrangements for a capable interpreter to be present.[21] Interviewers need to adapt to clients' language capabilities in all circumstances. In order for communication to be clear, interviewers need to speak to clients in the language and at the level of that language that's understandable to them. Many interviewers forget that clients do not understand technical language or jargon because they do not use it as frequently as interviewers do. Imagine how a first-year college student, who is the first in her family to attend college, feels at her initial problem-solving interview with her adviser during orientation. The adviser begins: "All we have to do today is consult the bulletin, figure out what classes you need for your fifteen credit hours, check prerequisites, and go to the bursar's office. You'll get your syllabus later. Don't forget how important it is to keep up your GPA. It'll just kill you if it gets down to 1.5 because it's so hard to raise it." The new student may be wondering: "What is a bulletin? Credit hours? Prerequisites? Bursar? Syllabus? GPA? 1.5?" For this problem-solving interview to work, the adviser needs to adapt to a new student for whom the technical jargon of university life is foreign. All key terms need to be explained clearly, not because the interviewee is stupid, but because this is a new vocabulary for her. In order for the student to understand and participate fully in the interview, the interviewer needs to adapt the language to her.

A diagnostic interviewer also needs to be genuine in the diagnostic interview. Although the constraints of the role mean that diagnostic interviewers are not always forthcoming about what they are thinking each moment, they do need to express themselves during the interview. They should plan to represent themselves, their knowledge, their thoughts about the problem, and their diagnosis and prognosis honestly with the interviewee. For example, a consumer credit counselor might say directly to a financially troubled client: "I appreciate all the information you've shared with me about your debts and assets. Taking it all into account, I think we can work on a repayment plan that will get you out of this mess within two or three years. It's because you seem so committed to changing your spending habits that I'm going to suggest this plan. It's a harder plan than many people are willing to work on, but you strike me as a very motivated person. Let's look at it."

Finally, as mentioned earlier, diagnostic interviewers should enter each interview with the goal of being empathic with the interviewee. Diagnostic interviewers who try to answer the question "How would I feel if this were happening to me?" are more likely to understand the content and emotion that the interviewee is expressing. A family practice physician reported that she cried when she told a family about the death of their three-year-old son. Her awareness of how she might feel if this were happening to her had created her tears. Although she reported discomfort about her losing her composure in her professional role, the family with whom she talked, years after their child's death, still speaks highly of her empathy and compassion for them during a difficult time.

Creating a Conducive Setting for the Interview.   A second preparatory step is creating a setting that facilitates effective problem solving. When possible, the diagnostic interview should occur in a safe, comfortable, and private place.[22] If privacy is not possible in situations such as a hospital emergency room, then the interviewer should make workable adaptations to bring as much comfort and privacy as possible to the interaction. This might include behaviors such as closing a curtain, standing close to the patient, and touching in appropriate ways.

If possible, the seating arrangement should allow the interviewee and interviewer to face each other at the same horizontal level.[23] This allows for a more balanced, less threatening physical interaction. Persons with problems, as mentioned earlier, often feel intimidated about having to seek help. If seating accentuates the difference between the client and the expert, such as an unclothed patient lying prone while the physician stands, embarrassment can increase. Even physicians who are busy on their rounds report that sitting face-to-face with patients facilitates more open information sharing. Likewise, if chairs are arranged so that two people can see each other easily, without large pieces of furniture or great distance between them, interaction is better. Pietroni, for example, found that persons using the seating arrangement A–C interacted six times more than those in the A–B arrangement and three times more than those seated in the A–D arrangement.[24]

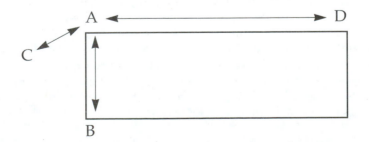

Becoming a qualified expert, maintaining a respectful attitude toward the interviewee, and developing a setting conducive to problem solving are all important aspects of interviewer preparation.

Conducting the Interview

Creating a Supportive Climate.   The responsibility for creating a nondefensive climate in which good problem solving can occur belongs to the interviewer. A diagnostic interviewer should give the interviewee a sense of being welcome, care, interviewer competence, and respect.[25] This can be done in many ways. While they wait, the seating for interviewees should be comfortable and safe. Lighting should be bright enough so they can read and relax. Delays should be minimal. Information that the interviewees might need (e.g., forms to complete, hours of operation, check-in procedures) should be readily available and easy to understand. If possible, a helpful and informed person should be accessible to assist interviewees with questions.

At the start of the interviews, diagnostic interviewers should introduce themselves and identify their roles in the organization.[26] "Hi, I'm Helen Melton. I'm the customer service manager for this store." If the interview involves young children, such as a child's visit with a pediatrician, the interviewer should give the children time to grow comfortable with the health care provider. Children are often nervous with strangers, and a wise diagnostic interviewer does not move too abruptly into the interview. In addition, interviewers who show they are glad that the interviewees have sought them out build a supportive foundation for problem solving. For example, instead of saying, "I've been assigned to work on your problem with the catalogue return," the interviewer can indicate interest by saying, "I'm here to learn more about your catalogue return to see how we can solve the problem you're experiencing." The difference here is not dramatic, but it conveys to the interviewee the interviewer's interest in diagnosing and solving the problem.

Interviewers should call new clients, customers, and patients by their surnames. Although some people prefer an informal interaction with diagnostic interviewers, others do not. It is important for many interviewees, particularly for those from cultures where the use of first names by strangers is considered disrespectful,[27] that they be called by their surnames. It is simple for interviewers to begin with surnames and ask clients what they want to be called. This lets the interviewees initiate changes if they want.

If multiple interviewees are present, the interviewer should introduce her/himself to each one and learn their relationships to one another. This might occur, for example, if a child is hospitalized and the physician is talking with several family members. It is important not to make assumptions about the relationships of various interviewees. A supportive approach is to ask politely about the relationships during the introductions so that accurate perceptions are established from the outset. Interviewees are more satisfied when they perceive that interviewers have treated them courteously.[28]

In addition to these specific techniques, diagnostic interviewers should try to create supportive climates for all interviews when it is possible. Chapter 10 discussed the characteristics of defensive and supportive climates in detail.

Asking Appropriate Questions.   Diagnostic interviewers generally structure their questions in response to what is commonly called the interviewee's "chief complaint" or "presenting problem." The **chief complaint** is the specific issue that has brought the interviewee to seek assistance. The interviewer needs to discover the answer to the question "Why did this person come to me now?" in order to move toward a diagnosis and constructive solution. Harry Stack Sullivan summarized succinctly: "Who is this person and how did [s]he come to be here?"[29]

Usually, when asked, the interviewee simply states the presenting problem. For example, "I finally came in because I just can't get my checking account balance to match the one your bank sends me each month," or "I've had a fever for four days, and I ache all over." These are clearly stated chief complaints or presenting problems. At times, however, the stated chief complaint is really not the major problem that the interviewee wants to discuss. Sometimes an initial description of a chief complaint is really a kind of admission ticket to gain access to the expert for help with other concerns. A family practice physician, for example, described a time that his nurse told him the patient's chief complaint was that he had been coughing a lot. When the physician entered the examining room and discussed the symptoms with the patient, however, the physician soon learned that what the patient really wanted to discuss was a problem with impotence. The patient was too embarrassed to tell the scheduling nurse and the examining nurse his real concern; the complaint about coughing was his admission ticket for private access to the physician.

People are often embarrassed to talk about such problems as those having to do with sexual practices, hygiene, finances, and personal relationships. Diagnostic interviewers can relieve some of that embarrassment by asking clients if there are other concerns in addition to the chief complaint. Interviewers can help further by avoiding judgment and assuring their interviewees that many people have such problems or concerns. For example, a diagnostic interviewer might say, "Lots of people are having financial problems right now. Tell me what has happened in your family budget that brings you here today" or "It's very common for teenagers to have questions about birth control because there are so many different stories out there. What questions do you have for me?"

Once the chief complaint is clear to the interviewer, then questions can be structured in a basic pattern.[30]

> Begin with general, open questions: "What brings you here today?" Include nudging probes to elicit more information: " . . . and then?" ". . . yes?"

> Utilize open questions on more specific topics: "Tell me more about the problem with the creditor at the Rent-All Bargain Center." "Describe the pain for me."

Continue with "WH" questions (Where? What? When? How?): "Where in your head is the headache worse?" "What does it feel like?" "When do you get these headaches?" "How have you been treating them?"or "Where is the television set now?" "What did the creditor say would happen next?" "When will you talk with them again?" "How do you plan to pay the late fee?"

Use moderately closed questions with limited answers to get more details: "Did the creditors say they would pick it up or you would have to bring it in?" "What is the deadline for the payment?"

Use yes/no questions in emergency situations where information must be gathered quickly and where the interviewee may not be functioning at 100 percent capacity: "Can you feel this?" "What's the grandparents' phone number?"

As in other interview contexts, certain kinds of questions should be avoided in diagnostic interviews.[31] Leading questions are inappropriate because it is the interviewee's description of the situation that will allow the interviewer to make a good diagnosis. Questions that are overly complex or contain multiple inquiries may confuse interviewees and should not be used. Finally, any questions or explanations that use technical jargon—the specialized vocabulary of a field—should be omitted. If jargon is essential in the question, the interviewer should define and explain it to the interviewee.

Asking questions well in any interview is important. In diagnostic interviews, good questions are often the deciding factor in whether an appropriate diagnosis and solution are provided.

Listening to the Interviewee's Story

The more the interviewee is like the interviewer, the easier the interviewer's job.[32] Like other forms of human interaction, personal similarities (e.g., age, ethnicity, education, work) make communication easier because the parties have more in common. Often in diagnostic interviews, however, the two parties are very different in socioeconomic background or education. Consider, for example, the vivid socioeconomic and educational differences between many welfare clients and their college-educated social workers or between hospital emergency room patients and their physicians. The interviewer has the responsibility to bridge those differences and minimize the negative impact they might have on the interview. It is not the responsibility of the interviewee to learn social work theory in order to be able to speak easily to the social worker. Instead, it is the social worker's responsibility to try to understand the client's life situation and level of understanding to bridge the socioeconomic and educational barriers that exist between them.

Trenholm and Jensen suggest ways to bridge these gaps by increasing subcultural understanding.[33] They encourage these steps to bridge subcultural differences effectively: (1) expand your circle of contacts to include people from different subcultures, (2) learn more about different subcultures, (3) reflect on your stereotypes and the reasons for them, and (4) develop more empathy for people with different life experiences. If interviewers sense that personal differences may interfere with communication, they can always say, "I have not known many people from your background and so we may have some difficulty understanding each other at first."[34] Another statement might be: "I want to understand you and have you understand me—please help me do this." These statements convey interest in and respect for the interviewee. They also suggest that the interviewer is genuinely interested in the interviewee's story.

Whether interviewees are similar or dissimilar from their interviewers, they have relevant stories to tell. A common interviewer error in diagnostic interviews is reluctance to listen to the interviewees' stories. In their study of primary care physicians in an outpatient clinic, Beckman and Frankel found that the physicians only let patients speak on the average of 18 seconds before interrupting them.[35] Likewise, Weiner and Nathanson found that health care interviewers tend to ask patients too many questions, to "over question them,"[36] rather than allow them to

The interviewer has the responsibility to bridge differences of age, ethnicity, education, etc. between the two parties.

tell their own stories. Interviewees' stories are the primary sources of information needed for diagnosis. While interviewers can guide interviewees to provide pertinent information, they should not impede or interrupt stories as long as the interviewees are generating salient information.

Also, interviewers should broaden their assumptions about what kinds of information are salient. At times, information that appears peripheral to the chief complaint may be very important for a good diagnosis and solution. For example, parents who have come to a teacher to discuss their daughter's fights on the playground during afternoon recess need to tell their story to the teacher. As they discuss what their daughter is like at home, how she interacts with her brothers and sisters and the ways she helps her grandparents, they may share information about her craving for sugary snacks like candy bars. Some teachers might assume that eating habits do not have any bearing on playground behavior, but others might realize that this seemingly unrelated issue could explain her fights during the afternoon recesses. The teacher and parents might decide together that the girl see a pediatrician to see whether her strong need for sugar might affect her playground interactions. What might seem like irrelevant information might actually be the secret to a good diagnosis and solution.

Diagnostic interviewers need to listen carefully. In health care settings, patient satisfaction is correlated with nonverbal measures of listening. Research by Larsen and Smith found that the more health care providers listened to their patients, the more satisfied the patients were with their care.[37] Health care providers and other diagnostic interviewers can increase interviewee satisfaction by careful listening. Interviewer listening skills enhance credibility and increase the information that the interviewee shares. Not only does listening well elicit information, but "simply listening to patients in an empathic manner can be therapeutic."[38]

Two kinds of probes are particularly effective for diagnostic interviewers to demonstrate their listening: the *mirror probe* and the *paraphrase for content.* Mirror probes, as explained earlier, are reflective responses that restate what the interviewee has said.

Interviewee: I'm so scared they're going to take the house if I can't pay the bills!

Interviewer: You're really scared about losing your house if you can't pay the bills.

Interviewee: Exactly! It terrifies me. I can't even sleep.

Paraphrases for content are responses that restate the interviewee's message but in different words.

Interviewee: I'm so scared that I'm going to lose the house if I can't pay the bills.

Interviewer: You're really afraid at the possibility of not having a roof over your head if those debts aren't caught up.

Interviewee: Exactly! I'm terrified. That's exactly how I feel.

Both mirror probes and content paraphrases reflect good listening. Moreover, they indicate empathy with the interviewee. The interviewer does not inject personal views into a mirror probe or a paraphrase. Instead, these kinds of probes nonjudgmentally restate or reflect what the interviewee has said. Good listening and careful responses contribute to the success of the diagnosis.

Sharing Information with the Interviewee

"Good explanations take time," suggest Billings and Stoeckle.[39] Diagnostic interviews meet the goals of both the interviewee and interviewer more effectively when the interviewer allows adequate time to provide a thorough explanation of the diagnosis and the suggested solution. Interviewees are generally more satisfied with interviews when plenty of information is provided. Research on patient satisfaction has found that patient satisfaction with health care providers is positively correlated with the amount of time that the health care providers spend with them discussing preventive care.[40] Health care providers who discuss issues fully have more satisfied patients.

Equally important is the finding that after health care interviews, patients are more likely to comply with a course of treatment when they have been satisfied with their interviews with health care personnel.[41] Why is compliance so important? Amazingly, few patients do what their physicians have told them to do. Eraker, Kirscht, and Becker found that patients comply with physicians' orders only about 50 percent of the time.[42] Lack of patient compliance often puts patients at risk and clearly undermines standard courses of treatment for disease. Roter and Hall found that patients were much more likely to comply with a physicians' orders when their physicians provided more information.[43]

Moreover, physicians who provide more information found that their patients, in turn, give them more information. Additional information from patients clearly assists health care professionals to make accurate diagnoses. If a satisfactory resolution of the health problem relies on accurate diagnosis and treatment, it is obvious why patients need to comply with the course of treatment recommended by the health care experts. The same need exists in other diagnostic contexts. For example, the recommendations of a credit counselor must be followed in order for a client to reduce the level of debt. Clients who do not agree with the recommended treatment plan can tell the interviewer. The interviewer can then explain the plan further, change it, or suggest that the patient seek a second opinion. A full and appropriate amount of information from both the interviewer and interviewee generally increases compliance with the recommended course of action.

Another factor also increases compliance. When interviewers describe their expectations about what will happen as a result of a suggested course of treatment, interviewees are more likely to cooperate fully in that treatment. Buller and Street studied physicians and patients in a pain clinic where some physicians who recommended their patients use biofeedback in their pain treatments told the patients that they had very positive expectations about the ability of biofeedback to help them.[44] Patients' self-reports about their participation in the biofeedback treatment regimen indicated that when physicians expressed these positive expectations about the potential value of the treatment, patients were more likely to do what the physicians had recommended.

Overall, interviewers need to give complete information to the people who seek their assistance. Giving appropriate and abundant information increases both interviewee satisfaction with the interview and compliance with the recommended course of action.

Concluding the Interview

Most constructive diagnostic interviews allow the interviewee enough time to provide all pertinent information and to ask all questions that the discussion has raised. In addition, the interviewer can take time to offer complete explanations of recommendations. As the interviewer negotiates and discusses a solution to the interviewee's problem with the interviewee, the interviewer's approach to the problem can increase the likelihood that the plan will work and that the interviewee will cooperate with it. The interviewer should discuss the suggested plan in language that is clear and explicit, explaining any prescriptions or suggestions that the interviewee needs to follow. An actual interview might sound like this:

Physician: Your throat condition seems to be pharyngitis. That is a bacterial infection in your throat. My visual examination of your throat and the way you described the soreness match the symptoms of pharyngitis. Your lab tests confirmed that it is not strep throat. Now what is needed is for you to take these antibiotics for ten days. They may upset your stomach a little bit, but if you take them with meals, it shouldn't be a problem. Your throat will start feeling better in a day or two, but make sure you finish all the antibiotics because taking them the whole ten days ensures that we have killed off the strongest bacteria. If you stop too soon, the strongest bacteria may still remain. If you take all these antibiotics, the whole infection will be gone in ten days and you shouldn't have to worry about a recurrence.

Notice that the physician has summarized the diagnosis and its basis, explained the treatment and its side effects, and conveyed a positive expectation for what will happen when the patient cooperates with the course of treatment. This information is in contrast to the physician in the interview at the beginning of the chapter. That physician gave almost no rationale for the recommended course of treatment. A summary and explanation of future actions is an important step in providing closure to the diagnostic interview.

After explaining a course of action, interviewers should go even further. If there is any doubt about whether the patient understands the diagnosis and treatment plan, the interviewee should ask the patient to repeat the explanation. This request allows the interviewer to learn whether the interviewee really has understood what was said. Although it takes additional time, this step provides an effective safeguard against misunderstandings. Moreover, the interviewee should be provided with written information, such as the names of medications, schedules of office hours, and telephone numbers of health care providers, to reinforce information that has been given orally. Clients are often nervous during diagnostic interviews; consequently, they may forget many details. Writing important facts or sharing informative brochures increases the likelihood for interviewee understanding and compliance.

Finally, ending the interview with a positive, encouraging statement increases compliance and satisfaction. In diagnostic interviews, like in parent-teacher conferences, for example, a teacher can use the end of the interview to confirm the parents as "capable and collaborative partner[s]" in their child's education.[45] Unlike the physician in our opening interview who only said, "OK. See you," as he left the examining room, an effective diagnostic interviewer will use concluding statements to thank interviewees for seeking assistance and to encourage them to believe that the proposed resolutions will work to solve their problem.

The Interviewee in the Diagnostic Interview

The interviewee's role in the diagnostic interview is often overlooked. Some believe that the interviewee is a passive participant in the interview and is there only to respond to questions. For diagnostic interviews to work, however, interviewees must recognize the importance of their roles as active partners. Diagnostic interviewees can improve diagnosis in several ways: by finding a good expert, working as active participants in the interview, volunteering information, asking questions, and knowing their rights and responsibilities. Let us consider each of these areas individually.

Find an Appropriate Expert

Individuals needing assistance will only obtain useful assistance if they select a competent person to help them. It is appropriate that diagnostic interviewees follow the recommendations of credible friends and colleagues as well as professional associations in choosing persons from whom to seek help. Professional associations include such agencies as the Better Business Bureau, local or regional medical and legal associations, local mental health associations, and regional educational accrediting agencies. Appropriate questions to consider about a potential interviewer include:

What is the person's training?
Is the person licensed by an accredited agency? (if relevant)
How does the person stay up to date in the field?

> Does this person work as a part of a group agency or individually?
> How available is the person? Hours? Emergency availability?
> What payment options are possible?
> Does this person adapt to the individual problems of clients?
> Can this person be understood by "regular" people?
> Will this person refer clients to other professionals, if necessary?

To be effective, the interviewers must be trustworthy to the interviewee. To do so, the interviewers should be demonstrably expert in their areas of expertise. In addition, the interviewer should have a reputation as an effective, empathic interviewer.

Being an Active Participant in the Diagnostic Process

Many interviewees see themselves as pawns in the diagnostic interview. What has caused this perception of the interviewee's role as a passive one? Leeds and Strauss suggest that medical patients have often been passive in diagnostic interviews because of three mistaken beliefs. First, patients do not want to offend their physicians. Second, patients assume that all physicians are competent just because they are physicians. Third, patients believe they need medication, not information, or explanations.[46] In medical interviews, apparently many interviewees do not feel entitled to ask questions or request explanations.

Nonetheless, most patients want more than a prescription to take to the pharmacy: they want information about what is wrong with them and how they can get better. Wilson White, the patient in the interview at the start of the chapter, left his medical interview with a prescription, but it was unlikely that he was satisfied with the interaction there. Why? The physician scarcely listened to him, provided little information, and gave no explanation about the illness or its treatment. Likewise, interviewees in other kinds of diagnostic interviews are entitled to information and explanations, not just quick solutions. Considering the diagnostic interview as a partnership encourages interviewees to believe they can achieve their goals by working actively in the interviews.

Becoming Informed

Several specific behaviors can accomplish this increased partnership. First, interviewees should *communicate their desire for information and explanations.* Many interviewers assume that clients only want solutions, not information. Clients must correct this false assumption. Moreover, interviewees can be more constructive participants in interviews if they understand what the interviewer is doing and thinking. A client talking with a child-support official might say, "I don't just want to get last month's check figured out. What I want to understand is how the whole thing works. When does he pay? Where does that money go before I get it? Why does it come to me more than a month after he pays it? How can I get it more on schedule with my budget? I need to know how the whole setup works."

Statements like these let interviewers know that their clients want to act as partners in the problem-solving process.

Second, interviewees can become more active in the process by assertively *seeking information in advance of the interview.* There are many different places to get information about social, educational, consumer, and health problems. Interviewees who learn as much as they can in advance of the interview function better in the interview. Medical patients, for example, can learn about illnesses or treatments by reading books such as those listed in the Related Readings section at the end of this chapter, drug company brochures, educational pamphlets from physicians' offices and clinics, and publications about health care from the National Institute of Health. Persons seeking care for mental illness can find comparable resources. For nonreaders, major medical centers often have audio tapes and videotapes available to explain services. Customers registering complaints with customer service offices can read the store's policies for exchanges and returns, which are often posted in the vicinity of the customer service offices.

Learning as much as possible about the problem before the interview helps to become a better consumer of diagnostic information. Learning about the problem and stating to the interviewer your desire to be involved in the diagnostic process moves the diagnostic interview toward a partnership of shared responsibility.

Volunteering Information

Effective interviewees share with their interviewers information that might help in accurate diagnoses. Volunteering information is one of the interviewee's responsibilities in a diagnostic interview. An example of a woman who did not believe that interviewees had such responsibilities demonstrates the problems that can result. When she was asked by her adult son if she had told her doctor about her fainting spells, an elderly woman reported proudly, "No I did not! He did not ask about them, so I didn't tell him." People who believe that it is solely the interviewer's ability to request all relevant information undermine the interviewer's ability to reach an accurate diagnosis. This woman's fainting spells may have been a symptom of a serious problem. Because the doctor did not inquire about fainting and because the patient believed the doctor should ask for all information rather than her volunteering it, valuable information was lost to the doctor. Accurate diagnosis was impaired. A productive interviewee volunteers all information that may be related to the problem. In the case of a medical interview, certainly all current physical symptoms may be relevant.

In order to provide pertinent information, two practical suggestions often help interviewees. First, many interviewees find it helpful to *prepare a list* of issues to discuss before the diagnostic visit.[47] This list could include factual information about the specific problem to discuss, examples of times the problem occurred, previous attempts to solve the problem, specific questions and concerns, and other such details. This list enables interviewees to make sure that all of their pertinent questions are answered.

Second, for accurate diagnosis, it is important that interviewees *not* withhold information. Embarrassment about weaknesses, previous mistakes, or personal habits can tempt interviewees to omit some information. Interviewees must remember that the interview goal is to get a good solution to a serious problem. The interviewer can only provide a good solution if an accurate diagnosis is made. To make such a diagnosis, all pertinent information needs to be considered. For example, a person seeking public assistance to find housing needs to provide an accurate history to the social worker, even if it means telling about a prison record. A social worker who is eventually required to provide references to apartment managers will be much more able to find appropriate and available housing if the interviewee gives this information at the outset.

Also, interviewees may be tempted to omit certain information in other interview contexts. For example, patients who drink large quantities of alcohol regularly should report that to their physicians even if they are embarrassed by that practice. Reporting the use of illegal, over-the-counter, or prescription drugs is equally important. The physician needs this information in order to understand and make sense of certain symptoms. Clients who share information, even about illegal drug use, are protected by a physician's obligation to keep this information confidential. Moreover, in prescribing a course of treatment, this information is essential for patient safety because of possible drug and alcohol interactions.

Embarrassment and shame often lead interviewees to withhold important information, but doing so inevitably prevents interviewers from helping their clients. Interviewees who have chosen trustworthy experts to assist them will get the best help when they volunteer all pertinent information.

Asking the Right Questions

Different kinds of diagnostic interviews raise different questions and concerns for interviewees. A customer seeking the replacement of defective merchandise might ask a customer service representative questions like these:

What is your policy about returns?
What if I do not have my receipt with me?
Can I return the merchandise if I just don't like it?
What is the deadline for returns?
Can I get a refund of my money?

Customers deserve answers to these kinds of questions, and most customer service representatives will cooperate in providing the answers. Different questions can make health-care diagnostic interviews more productive. Leeds has provided extensive lists of sample questions to ask about medical tests and examinations:[48]

What is the name of the test? (How is it spelled?)
What are you looking for with this examination?

Where do I go for the tests?
Does it make a difference that I might be pregnant?
How will I feel during the procedure? Afterwards?
What risks are involved?
Can it be done on an outpatient basis so I don't have to check into the hospital overnight?
How will I find out the test results?
How much will these tests cost?

Comparable questions can be asked about surgeries, treatment plans, drugs, and other health care issues. In fact, the U.S. Department of Health and Human Services suggests that patients get answers to these questions before they undergo any non-emergency surgeries:[49]

What is the doctor's diagnosis of the problem?
What operation does the doctor plan to do?
What are the benefits of the surgery?
What are the risks of the surgery? How likely are they to occur?
What is the length of the recovery period?
What does the recovery entail?
What are the costs for this surgery? Does my insurance cover them?

Usually, some questions like these will be answered before they need to be asked. But some health care providers, like Dr. Kaplan at the opening of the chapter, give very little information. Moreover, some insurance companies insist on answers to these and other questions before authorizing payment. Patients deserve the answers to these questions, and one way to get the answers is to ask the questions. Interviewees in other contexts can also ask questions when the information they want is not otherwise provided.

Knowing One's Rights and Responsibilities as a Patient

Diagnostic interviewees have rights and responsibilities. These rights and responsibilities have been clearly articulated for medical patients by various authors and medical groups.[50] Likewise, various social service agencies and consumer organizations have such lists of clients' rights and responsibilities. Guidelines for diagnostic interviews in varied contexts suggest that interviewees can and should take an active role in the process. The rights and responsibilities of interviewees adapted from a health care setting by Maurer[51] include the interviewee's *right* to:

1. Have as much information as desired about the problem.
2. Receive adequate time to ask questions and share concerns.
3. Have reasonable access to the interviewer.
4. Be able to participate appropriately in decisions about a course of action.
5. Determine who other than the interviewer has access to information shared in the interview.

6. Know in advance the approximate charges and payment options.
7. Be seen within a reasonable time of the scheduled appointment.
8. Be allowed to transfer records to another interviewer if the first relationship is not productive at solving the problem.

Interviewees also have the *responsibility* to:

1. Disclose all pertinent information to the interviewer.
2. Keep appointment or cancel in advance.
3. Plan for visits in advance (e.g., prepare a list of questions to discuss).
4. Ask the interviewer for explanations when necessary.
5. Ask questions.
6. Follow the advice in the negotiated solution and report any pertinent problems that occur.
7. Pay in a timely manner for diagnostic services.

Interviewees have both rights and responsibilities in diagnostic interviews. If interviewees provide information and cooperate to fulfill their responsibilities, interviewers will be better able to provide accurate diagnoses and solutions. If interviewers do not provide the information, assistance, or course of action clients deserve, clients should terminate the relationship and seek assistance elsewhere. All kinds of diagnostic interviews—medical, social work, customer service, educational, and others—have particular rights and responsibilities that interviewees can assume.

Summary

Diagnostic interviews, those in which the interviewer has knowledge or abilities to diagnose and help solve the interviewee's problem, take place in many contexts (e.g., social work, customer service, education, and health care). Although interviewee embarrassment and poor questioning skills can create "poor histories," both parties can work productively to bridge communication barriers.

Interviewers need to appreciate the interviewee's perspective, the role of empathy, and the trend toward more critical interviewees. Moreover, interviewers need to realize that training improves interviewing skills for diagnostic interviewers. To prepare for the diagnostic interview, interviewers need to become expert in their area, develop respectful attitudes toward the interviewees, and create settings conducive to problem solving. During the actual interviews, interviewers are most productive when they create a supportive climate, ask appropriate questions, listen to the interviewee's stories, and share information and expectations with the interviewees. Closing diagnostic interviews with positive predictions about the likelihood that the solution will work increases interviewee satisfaction and compliance.

Interviewees also need to work as active participants in diagnostic interviews. They need to find appropriate experts from whom to seek help, work actively in the interview process by educating themselves, volunteer all pertinent information, ask questions, and understand their rights and responsibilities as interviewees.

Discussion Questions

1. There are several comments Dr. Kaplan could have made at the start of the interview with Wilson White that would have created more of a sense of partnership in that interview. Suggest some possibilities.

2. Why might Kafka's country doctor quoted at the chapter opening believe it is harder to try to reach understanding with an interviewee than to offer a quick solution to the problem? What are some examples of trying to reach such understanding as opposed to giving quick solutions in diagnostic interviews?

3. Besides making the interviewee reluctant to talk, what other effects might interviewee shame have on communication in a diagnostic interview?

4. Do you agree with the suggestion that diagnostic interviews initially greet and call interviewees by their surnames? Discuss the advantages and disadvantages of doing that. Consider individual differences such as cultural background, sex (in relation to the diagnostic interviewer), and age.

5. Discuss ways that you in your community could find an expert (a) social worker, (b) educator, and (c) physician to ask about a personal problem.

Suggested Activities

1. In groups of three or four, go around the group and have each individual describe a physician they consulted and really liked. Have each person identify what specific behaviors the physician exhibited that helped the diagnostic relationship. Then, without naming names, do the same for physicians who were not good communicators. Have the class reconvene and write the behaviors of the effective physicians and ineffective physicians at separate places on the board. Compare these observations to those in the chapter.

2. Write a brief paper (two to four pages) in which you propose a design for a building where welfare clients apply for food stamps, relief checks, housing, and other services. Try to design waiting areas and conference spaces that (a) create a sense of partnership between social worker and client, (b) counteract inter-

viewee shame, and (c) build a supportive problem-solving setting. Give reasons for each suggestion.

3. In groups of three or four, imagine that your retail store has asked your work team to develop a question guide to use with customers who are returning merchandise. Develop a set of five to ten standard questions for customer service representatives to use to determine the nature of the customers' problems, the legitimacy of the complaints, and fair solutions. If necessary, you can also create procedures and rules for your organization to use in handling merchandise returns.

4. In groups of three or four, imagine that you are school administrators planning a half day in-service training session for teachers on parent-teacher conferencing. Plan what you will teach them and how you will do it. Prepare a

goal for the workshop, a schedule, specific sessions, and the methods by which you will instruct teachers in interviewing skills. Submit your proposal in written form.

5. In groups of three or four, discuss the strengths and weaknesses of both parties in the interview between Dr. Kaplan and Wilson White at the beginning of the chapter. Consider ways that each person could have participated more constructively in the interview. Role play the interaction, assigning one group member to play Dr. Kaplan and the other to portray Wilson White. Try to demonstrate ways that both persons could have been more effective in the interview.

Related Readings

Billings, J. Andrew, and Stoeckle, John D. *The Clinical Encounter.* Chicago: Year Book Medical Publishers, Inc., 1989.

Coulehan, John L., and Block, Marian R. *The Medical Interview: A Primer for Students of the Art*, 2nd ed. Philadelphia: F.A. Davis Company, 1992.

Friedman, Paul G. *Communicating in Conferences: Parent-Teacher-Student Interaction.* Annandale, VA: Speech Communication Association, 1980.

Leeds, Dorothy, and Strauss, Jon M. *Smart Questions to Ask Your Doctor.* New York: Harper Paperbacks, 1992.

Maurer, Janet M. *How to Talk to Your Doctor: The Questions to Ask.* New York: Simon and Schuster, 1986.

Pell, Arthur R. *Diagnosing Your Doctor.* Minneapolis, MN: DCI/CHRONIMED Publishing, 1991.

Endnotes

1. John L. Coulehan and Marian R. Block, *The Medical Interview: A Primer for Students of the Art*, 2nd ed. (Philadelphia: F.A. Davis Company, 1992), 21.

2. Chase Patterson Kimball, "Techniques of Interviewing: 1. Interviewing and the Meaning of the Symptom," *Annals of Internal Medicine* 1 (1969), 148.

3. Mark Siegler, "The Physician-patient Accommodation," *Archives of Internal Medicine* 142 (1982), 1901.

4. Aaron Lazare, "Shame and Humiliation in the Medical Encounter," *Archives of Internal Medicine* 147 (1987), 1653.

5. T.E. Quill, "Recognizing and Adjusting to Barriers in Doctor-Patient Communication," *Annals of Internal Medicine* 111 (1989), 51.

6. H.B. Beckman and R.M. Frankel, "The Effect of Physician Behavior on the Collection of Data," *Annals of Internal Medicine* 101 (1984), 692–96.

7. G.P. Maguire and D.R. Rutter, "History-taking for Medical Students: Deficiencies in Performance," *Lancet ii* (1976), 556–58.

8. Debra L. Roter and Judith A. Hall, "Physicians' Interviewing Styles and Medical Information Obtained from Patients," *Journal of General Internal Medicine* 2 (1987), 327.

9. David Pendleton, "Doctor-Patient Communication: A Review. David Pendleton and John Hasler, (eds.), *Doctor-Patient Communication* (London: Academic Press, Inc., 1983), 5–53.

10. M. Balint, *The Doctor, His Patient, and the Illness* (New York, NY: International Universities Press, 1972).

11. E.J. Cassell, *Talking with Patients, Vol. 1: The Theory of Doctor-Patient Communication.* (Cambridge, Mass: MIT Press, 1985), 174.

12. Pater Pritchard, "Patient Participation." David Pendleton and John Hasler, (eds.),

Doctor-Patient Communication (London: Academic Press, Inc., 1983), 205.

13. T.E. Quill, (1989), 53.

14. Loretto M. Comstock, Elizabeth M. Hooper, Jean M. Goodwin, and James S. Goodwin, "Physician Behaviors that Correlate with Patient Satisfaction," *Journal of Medical Education* 57 (1982), 105–112.

15. David B. Buller and Richard L. Street, Jr., "The Role of Perceived Affect and Information in Patients' Evaluations of Health Care and Compliance Decisions," *The Southern Communication Journal* 56 (1991), 233–35.

16. Dorothy Leeds and Jon M. Strauss, *Smart Questions to Ask Your Doctor* (New York: Harper Paperbacks, 1992), 4.

17. Mark L. Wolraich, Mark Albanese, Stefanie Reiter-Thayer, and William Barratt, "Factors Affecting Physician Communication and Patient-physician Dialogues," *Journal of Medical Education* 57 (1982), 621–25.

18. Michael Argyle, "Doctor-Patient Skills." David Pendleton and John Hasler, (eds.), *Doctor-Patient Communication* (London: Academic Press, Inc., 1983), 70–73.

19. A.C. Ivey and J. Authier, *Microcounseling* (Springfield, IL: Charles C. Thomas, 1978).

20. John L. Coulehan and Marian R. Block, (1992), 30.

21. Cervando Martinez, Jr., "Interviewing Across Cultural and Language Differences." Robert L. Leon, *Psychiatric Interviewing: A Primer* (New York: Elsevier, 1982), 69.

22. T.E. Quill, (1989), 56.

23. John L. Coulehan, and Marian A. Block, (1992), 32 & 54.

24. P. Pietroni, "Non-verbal Communication in the General Practice Surgery." B. Tanner (ed.), *Language and Communication in General Practice* (London: Hodder, 1976), 167.

25. Aaron Lazare, (1987), 167.

26. John L. Coulehan, and Marian A. Block, (1992), 32.

27. Martinez Cervando, Jr. (1982), 69; Robert L. Leon, *Psychiatric Interviewing: A Primer* (New York: Elsevier, 1982), 16.

28. Loretto M. Comstock, *et al.* (1982), 107–109.

29. Robert L. Leon, (1982), 40.

30. John L. Coulehan and Marian A. Block, (1992), 64.

31. J. Andrew Billings and John D. Stoeckle, *The Clinical Encounter* (Chicago: Year Book Medical Publishers, Inc., 1989), 25–26.

32. Martinez Cervando, Jr., (1982), 67.

33. Sarah Trenholm and Arthur Jensen, *Interpersonal Communication*, 2nd ed. (Belmont, CA: Wadsworth Publishing Company, 1992), 404–405.

34. Martinez Cervando, Jr., (1982), 68.

35. H. B. Beckman and R. M. Frankel, (1984), 692–96.

36. Stanley Weiner and Morton Nathanson, "Physical Examination: Frequently Observed Errors," *Journal of the American Medical Association* 236 (1976), 853.

37. Kathryn M. Larsen and Charles Kent Smith, "Assessment of Nonverbal Communication in the Patient-Physician Interview," *The Journal of Family Practice* 12 (1981), 487.

38. John L. Coulehan and Marian A. Block, (1992), 25.

39. J. Andrew Billings and John D. Stoeckle, (1989), 65.

40. Kent Smith, Emily Polis, and Ralph Hadac, "Characteristics of the Initial Medical Interview Associated with Patient Satisfaction and Understanding," *The Journal of Family Practice* 12 (1981), 283–88.

41. W.B. Stiles, S.M. Putnam, M.H. Wolf, and S.A. James, "Interaction Exchange Structure and Patient Satisfaction with Medical Interviews," *Medical Care* 17 (1979), 667–81.

42. S.A. Eraker, J.P. Kirscht, and M.H. Becker, "Understanding and Improving Patient Compliance," *Annals of Internal Medicine* 100 (1984), 258–68.

43. Debra L. Roter and Judith A. Hall, (1987), 327.

44. David B. Buller and Richard L. Street, Jr., (1991), 234–35.

45. Paul G. Friedman, *Communication in Conferences: Parent-Teacher-Student Interaction,* (Annandale, VA: Speech Communication Association and Urbana, IL: ERIC Clearing-house on Reading and Communication Skills, 1980), 29.

46. Dorothy Leeds and John M. Strauss, (1992), 4.

47. Arthur R. Pell, *Diagnosing Your Doctor,* (Minneapolis, MN: DCI/CHRONIMED Publishing, 1991), 39.

48. Dorothy Leeds and Jon M. Strauss, (1992), 39–50.

49. U.S. Department of Health and Human Services, H.C.F.A. Pamphlet #02114 (Washington, D.C. 20201).

50. Janet M. Maurer, *How to Talk to Your Doctor: The Questions to Ask* (New York: Simon and Schuster, 1986), 15–20; Joint Commission on Accreditation of Hospitals, One Renaissance Blvd., Oakbrook Terrace, IL 60181. In Pell, Arthur R. (1991), 205–208.

51. Janet M. Maurer, (1986), 15–17.

C h a p t e r 14

================

Counseling Interviews

*"If I can provide a certain type of relationship,
the other person will discover within . . .
the capacity to use that relationship for growth,
and change and personal development will occur."*
—Carl Rogers, On Becoming A Person,
(Boston: Houghton Mifflin, 1970), 33.

Claire and Blaine Wellington have been married for five years. They have one child, a son named James, who is two. Claire and Blaine have arrived for their first appointment with a marriage counselor, David Steele. Claire made the initial telephone call to arrange the appointment.

Steele: Mr. and Mrs. Wellington—Claire, isn't it?

(Claire nods.)

Steele: And Blaine?

Blaine: Yes.

(The two men shake hands.)

Steele: I'm David Steele.

(He points to two chairs in his office.)

Steele: Please sit down.

(Steele takes a seat in a third chair not far away. The couple is silent.)

Steele: Now, Claire, it was you who called to make the appointment, is that right?

Claire: Yes, I did.

Steele: And, Blaine, did you know about that call before it was made?

Blaine: Yes, I knew. She asked if I would do this and I said I would.

Steele: Okay. I'd like to begin then by asking each of you why you're here today and what you hope to accomplish by talking with me. Claire, let's start with you.

Claire: I'm here because I want to save our marriage.

Steele: You believe, then, that your marriage is in trouble and that you need help?

(Claire nods.) Tears well up in her eyes.

Steele: May I ask why?

Claire: Ask him.

(She points at Blaine.)

Steele: I'd rather hear what you have to say before asking Blaine for his perspective.

Claire: Please, I can't talk right now. I need a minute to collect myself.

(She dabs at her eyes with a tissue.)

Steele: Okay. Blaine, why are you here today and what do you hope to accomplish?

Blaine: Honestly? I'm here because she begged me to come. As for what I hope to accomplish, well, I hope talking to you will help her accept that our marriage is over and there's nothing she can do about it.

Steele: May I ask why?

Blaine: Sure. Look: it's like I explained it to her. Ever since James was born, I don't exist for her anymore. She doesn't want to be with me; she doesn't want to go out; she doesn't want to talk about anything but James, James, James. I'm sick of it. All she's wanted for two years is to be with the kid. So, the truth is, I've found some-one else.

(Claire sits weeping.)

Steele: So you're involved in another relationship.

Blaine: Yes. And I want to marry her, and she wants to marry me. But Claire wanted us to talk to someone before I moved out and filed divorce papers, so I said I would, and here we are.

Steele: I see. Claire, you knew all this before you called?

(Claire nods.)

Steele: And did you—do you—believe you could change things by coming to talk to me?

Claire: I hoped he would come to his senses. I hoped you would make him see what he is throwing away.

Steele: I'm sorry I can't do that, Claire. I can assist couples when both of them are committed to finding a way through the trouble they're in, but when only one person wants to save the marriage and the other is determined to get out, there's really nothing I can do to resolve their differences.

Blaine: Thanks, Steele. I was hoping you'd set her straight.

Steele: I'm not really trying to assist you here, Blaine, or to give you permission to do what you have chosen to do. I'm trying to help Claire see that neither she nor I can fix what you insist is irretrievably broken.

Blaine: That's for sure. I don't want it fixed. Like I said, I'm sick of it. I want a new life.

(They sit in silence for a minute.)

Blaine: (To Claire) Can we go now?

(Claire nods and stands.)

Steele: Claire, I'm sorry I couldn't help you accomplish what you wanted to accomplish here today, but if you'd like some help dealing with what has happened and adjusting to the changes yet to come, I'd be glad to refer you to a colleague of mine who counsels women affected by divorce.

(Claire shakes her head and turns to go.)

Steele: That's fine, but if you change your mind later, just give me a call.

Blaine: Thanks, Steele.

(Steele and Blaine shake hands and the couple leaves.)

Chapter Goals

- To discover the nature of counseling interviews, their goals and parties, and the settings and situations in which they occur.
- To examine and move past some popular misconceptions about counseling, including misconceptions about who needs it and who offers it.
- To explore the nature of directive, nondirective, and mixed approaches to counseling interviews.
- To understand the interviewer's needs and the guidelines for conducting a counseling interview.
- To consider the interviewee's needs and concerns in counseling interviews.

Introduction

Whatever our career plans and whatever our own mental states, sooner or later counseling interviews will affect our lives directly. Many churches, for example, currently require premarital counseling for all couples seeking to be wed. School and career counselors help individuals to decide important issues concerning academic and job choices. Schools and other agencies sometimes employ peer-counseling systems as a means of offering ongoing support to their members.

Additionally, all human beings experience periods of profound crisis in the course of their lives, whether the cause of crisis is death, divorce, job loss, or a loss of faith or hope in their own goals and plans. The couple in our opening interview was in a state of crisis when they sought the assistance of a marriage counselor. When crisis occurs—when individuals, couples, or families reach a turning point of some kind in their lives—counseling interviews are a viable, sometimes vital, avenue of assistance to help them through times of upheaval and change.

In this chapter, we will begin by exploring the nature of counseling interviews in general, as well as various settings and situations in which counseling interviews take place. Next, we will turn our attention to psychotherapeutic counseling, which is the most common form of counseling interviews. We will consider some popular cultural misconceptions about therapeutic-counseling interviews that discourage some individuals from making use of them. Then we will examine the general structure of directive and nondirective counseling interviews, consider methods to evaluate treatment, and offer ethical guidelines to govern the role of the counseling interviewer. Finally, we will turn our attention to interviewee considerations in counseling, including the choice of a therapist, the expectations of counseling, and the evaluation of the counseling experience.

The Nature of Counseling Interviews

Counseling interviews are helping interviews occurring within the context of a relationship in which the interviewer offers the interviewee(s) the opportunity for self-discovery and change through the use of empathic listening, questions, confidentiality and safety, feedback, and, in some cases, active direction toward change. We will examine the various elements of this definition one at a time.

Ivey distinguishes between *interviewing* as a "basic process" of gathering and dispensing information, problem solving, and advising; *counseling* as a "more intensive" process in which interviewing occurs; and *psychotherapy* as a more deeply intensive process focused on basic personality and behavioral problems.[1] For our purposes, however, we will use these terms somewhat interchangeably, understanding that counseling interviews are a process within a process, imbedded in the context of a helping relationship. The goal of the counseling interviewer is to allow the formation of a helping relationship that enables client growth.

Holmes and Lindley define *psychotherapy*, a common context for counseling interviews, as "the systematic use of a *relationship* between therapist and patient

. . . to produce changes in cognition, feelings and behaviour."[2] Frank and Frank define psychotherapy as those types of influential relationships characterized by (1) a "healing agent," the therapist, who need not be a professional, (2) a sufferer who seeks help from the healing agent, and (3) "a healing relationship—that is, a circumscribed, *more or less structured series of contacts* between the healer and sufferer in which the healer, often with the aid of a group, tries to bring about relief of symptoms."[3]

It is these "more or less structured contacts" occurring within the context of a healing relationship that constitute counseling interviews. A psychotherapist working with a depressed client may be involved over time in dozens of interviews with that individual. Likewise, a school counselor may have many interviews with a high school student planning a college career. Even an employment counselor may meet several times with an out-of-work client, while exploring employment options and offering advice on job search strategies. Because they are part of an ongoing relationship of some duration, most counseling interviews differ from other forms of interviewing that often occur just once between strangers.

Initial counseling interviews, such as the one at the chapter opening, have the goal of determining whether a helping relationship is feasible and desirable. These early interviews allow both interviewer and interviewee to explore the possibility of relationship formation. In certain settings, such as academic and vocational placement services, helping interviews may be sporadic and not necessarily imbedded within the context of an ongoing relationship. As a general rule, however, counseling interviews occur within the context of ongoing relationships.

Essential interviewer qualities for counseling interviews are empathic listening and acceptance and the ability to make judgments and offer perceptions about actions without condemnation of the person. The counseling interviewer must be able to win and sustain the trust of the interviewee through the assurance of confidentiality, the creation of a private setting in which to meet, and consistent supportive responses to interviewee needs.

Essential qualities for the interviewee include motivation to participate, an expectation that good can be derived from counseling, and a felt need to change. A laid-off employee utilizing outplacement counseling needs to be willing to explore new employment options in order to benefit from the counseling. A high school sophomore obtaining academic counseling must have a genuine desire to plan his academic future in order to make use of a helping relationship with a counselor. Without interviewee motivation, successful counseling is unlikely.

The desired result of counseling interviews is positive change in the interviewee. This growth, depending on the nature and setting of the counseling, may consist of deciding on a college major, developing a strategy for changing careers, or obtaining freedom from an eating disorder or relief from years of depression. The degree of change sought and/or obtained depends on the particular circumstances and needs of the individual interviewee.

Many different philosophies and types of therapy exist. The interviewee may arrive at growth or change in a helping relationship irrespective of the type of therapy. Holmes and Lindley cite evidence that there "is no one major type of psychotherapy that is consistently more effective than others."[4] The authors also state that: "Some therapists produce better results than other therapists. This applies whatever school the therapist belongs to. . . . The view of Carl Rogers that accurate empathy, nonpossessive warmth, and honesty are the essential attributes of an effective therapist has stood the test of time."[5] Regardless of therapeutic orientation, effective counseling interviewers are empathic, warm, and honest in their interactions with clients.

Who counsels? Frank and Frank include in their list of counselors clinical psychologists, psychiatrists, social workers, psychiatric nurses, and various other professionals and nonprofessionals.[6] Whatever their training or therapeutic model, effective counselors seek to provide the context, setting, and response skills that allow a helping relationship to grow and thrive.

Counseling Interview Settings and Situations

Woody, Hansen, and Rossberg include the following range of counseling interview settings and situations in their text on counseling psychology: vocational and educational counseling, individual counseling and therapy, group counseling and therapy, and family therapy.[7] To this list we will add rehabilitative counseling in hospital settings, and, because of its increasing popularity, peer counseling. Let's begin by briefly examining typical settings for vocational and educational counseling, rehabilitative counseling, and peer counseling. Then we will turn our attention to settings in which psychotherapeutic counseling occurs.

Vocational and Educational Counseling

Vocational counseling occurs in many settings and sometimes overlaps with the career development work of academic guidance counselors. The vocational counselor usually conducts interviews within an **institutional framework;** that is, within specific guidelines and constraints imposed by the school or organization in which the counseling occurs. This institutional framework inevitably imposes limits and standards on a counselor's interactions with interviewees. An outplacement counselor who works with laid-off employees in a large private business may be limited to a set number of interviews per client and her/his activities may be restricted to providing referrals to other agencies or organizations. Likewise, a vocational counselor for a federally funded job project will have to abide by the regulations imposed by the funding source.

Academic counseling occurs in schools. This institutional framework frequently imposes limits and requirements on the amount, duration, and nature of the counseling provided. An urban high school with a student population of 2,000, for example, might have only one or two counselors on its staff. In such a setting, a counselor's contacts with individual students will be sporadic and brief.

A school counselor at a small private high school or college, on the other hand, may have both the time and the institutional encouragement to develop ongoing relationships with students. These relationships might consist of interviews con-

Academic and vocational counselors listen to the needs, hopes, and concerns of interviewees in order to provide assistance.

ducted at regular intervals to assess student satisfaction with courses of study, plans for the future, and even personal concerns that affect academic performance and careers. For the most part, school and vocational counseling interviews are conducted in the counselor's office at the employing institution and focus primarily on individual academic or employment careers.

Another institutional constraint on academic and vocational counselors is that counselors usually maintain detailed records of interviewee contacts to meet requirements of the employing agency. These records may be made available to other staff at the institution. In these settings counseling interviews may be confidential only in the sense that information will not be shared outside the institution.

Academic and vocational counseling interviews involve effective listening to the needs, concerns, hopes, and plans of the interviewee in order to provide assistance. Unlike other forms of counseling interviews, vocational and academic counseling interviews are often specific and **directive,** providing concrete information about requirements and recommendations. An academic counseling interviewer might provide a student interviewee with the admission requirements at a certain university and then assist the student in planning coursework to meet those requirements prior to graduation.

Woody, Hansen, and Rossberg describe academic counseling in school settings as the early stages of life-long career development carried out by school and career counselors.[8] These authors suggest that school counseling should include: (1) at the elementary level, focus on work values and habits, self-exploration and self-assessment, and identification of occupational and role models; (2) at the middle school level, matching occupational goals to interests and abilities, and planning educational options; and (3), at the high school level, specific assessment, career planning, treatment or referral for those who need additional knowledge or skills, and assistance with academic or occupational placement as is appropriate to the individual student.[9]

The primary assistance offered by academic counselors is guidance concerning long-range academic goals. The primary assistance offered by vocational counselors involves matching individuals with career options and offering assistance with placement and job-seeking strategies.

Both academic and vocational counseling interviews are helping interviews occurring within institutional frameworks that may or may not allow for ongoing relationships. They offer interviewees the opportunity to plan their futures through effective listening and specific, directive assistance. Academic and vocational counseling interviewers must be knowledgeable about options open to their interviewees while conforming to the constraints of employing institutions.

Rehabilitative Counseling

Rehabilitative counseling is a helping relationship that seeks to assist those recovering from disabilities with social and psychological issues arising from their life changes. Rehabilitative counseling, too, normally occurs within institutional settings that make their own demands on the counseling process. Rehabilitative counseling usually occurs in health care settings, particularly in hospitals devoted to treatment of persons who have been permanently disabled. Persons in need of rehabilitative counseling include those who have become paralyzed as a result of accident or injury, those recovering from strokes or other brain injuries, and those who have lost their eyesight or limbs. Sometimes rehabilitative counselors work with persons whose disabilities are congenital or stem from birth traumas and who need help adapting to their conditions.

According to Jaques and Kauppi, the rehabilitation process includes the following tasks: facing societal attitudes toward the disability; assessing and making use of the client's assets; encouraging the client to cope effectively with personal barriers such as despair, anger and bitterness; helping the client to develop necessary life skills; and assisting the client in making responsible choices about the future.[10] Frank and Frank state, "Because emotional factors frequently contribute more than bodily damage to the distress and disability of patients with chronic disease, rehabilitative methods increasingly incorporate psychotherapeutic principles."[11]

Rehabilitative counseling allows affected individuals to develop to the highest possible level of functioning with and acceptance of their disability or disease.

Sometimes rehabilitation counselors also help family and friends of disabled individuals to accept the reality and limitations of the disability. Because social responses to persons with disabilities influence the self-concept of disabled individuals, educating those in the disabled person's network of family and friends is vital to the individual's healing and self-acceptance.

Peer Counseling

Peer counseling involves the use of nonprofessionals who share some quality or qualities in common—who are peers, in other words—to provide helping relationships for one another. Peer counseling programs can be found in many high schools and universities, as well as at women's centers and various other support networks for specific groups of individuals. The worldwide Alcoholics Anonymous organization (AA) utilizes an individual peer counseling system, as well as group programs to aid individuals in recovery. Volunteer suicide or trauma hotlines are another example of nonprofessional counseling programs.

In most cases, peer counseling involves pairings of like persons who meet to listen and provide support. Within AA, for example, newly recovering alcoholics are paired with a same-sex peer who has a longer history of sobriety. A research survey compiled by Luborsky and others found eighteen studies supporting the notion that patients and therapists who have similar interests, values, social class, and other qualities are more likely to achieve positive outcomes from therapy.[12] Taken alone, this research is a positive argument in favor of peer counseling where matching of similar persons has occurred. As we shall see, however, the degree of patient-therapist match is not the whole story when it comes to successful outcomes of counseling.

Usually, one member of the peer counseling pair fulfills the role of counselor. Often, peer counseling programs have some level of supervision and direction for the designated counselors. Frequently, as in AA, they occur within a larger framework of group support and even hospitalization treatment programs. In some cases, peer counseling is a means of providing a helping relationship at little or no cost to persons in need of assistance.

We include peer counseling in this chapter because of its existence and popularity. In certain settings and frameworks, with appropriate training and supervision, it can be helpful. However, we also want to offer some cautions concerning it. Emotional and psychological counseling interviews are delicate and difficult work. By its nature the therapeutic relationship is one that gives great power and control to the counselor. The counselor is the designated healer; the interviewee comes into the relationship in a vulnerable state as a result of a crisis. Luborsky and his coauthors cite numerous research studies that link the skills, experience, and mental health of the therapist to the likelihood of positive outcomes from therapy.[13]

Peer counselors are often minimally trained for their important work. The quality of the supervision provided to peer counselors in different settings varies. While all of us are called upon at times by family and friends to listen and provide support in times of crisis, it is important to be aware of our own limitations and to do no more than we have the skills and experience to do. A chapter in a text, or even a training program of several days' duration, does not make a skilled counselor.

In some settings, however, such as on a college campus where upperclass students are assigned to advise and support incoming first-year students on adjustment to college life, or in the well-established and multi-faceted self-help programs such as AA, peer counseling can be of real use. On the other hand, anyone engaged in peer counseling should be alert to problems beyond the skill level of the designated counselor. Serious crises deserve the most skilled assistance available. In most communities mental health clinics provide services at reduced rates to those whose finances are limited.

Psychotherapeutic Counseling

Currently, much psychotherapeutic counseling takes place in public mental health centers or in hospitals where the existing institutional framework imposes various demands and limitations upon the counseling interviewer's work. Within hospital settings, for example, insurance companies often impose standard recommended limits on length of stay for the client's treatment. Also, different hospitals have different preferred methods of treatment, from the types of counseling employed to the types of medications most often dispensed.

In outpatient mental health clinics, institutional limitations and biases are also often in place. A local or county-funded clinic, for example, may provide treatment in six-week intervals with a required reassessment of whether treatment should continue at each interval. In these settings, emphasis on short-term treatment is the goal of patient-therapist contacts. Some agencies focus primarily on group as opposed to individual treatment. While other settings may be more flexible, there are often standard treatment plans in place. One of the authors, for example, worked at a county mental health agency at which treatment teams assessed client needs, recommended individual or group counseling, and assigned clients to therapists. Ongoing therapy groups were available for adult women, adolescents, and couples.

Many counseling relationships take place within settings known loosely as "private practice," in which an individual therapist or small group of therapists practice together out of a suite of offices. Within private practice settings, institutional constraints may be minimal, with the individual counselor given virtually free rein in treatment choices. Often, however, even within group private practice settings, individual therapists seek supervision and feedback from one another concerning treatment plans. Often, too, groups of therapists form a private practice because they share common counseling philosophies. Individual practitioners or private practice teams of therapists may have areas of specialization. A husband and wife therapist team in private practice in the authors' hometown specialize in the treatment of children and families affected by divorce. Another therapist may work only with adult survivors of childhood sexual abuse, violent men, or families in crisis. Therapists in private practice obtain their clients by referral from public mental health agencies and/or by client referrals.

Individual, group, and family therapy are the three common forms of counseling. Group counseling was founded on the premise that individuals can benefit from the feedback and support of peers within a structured setting in which a therapist or counselor sets limits and provides direction. Because group therapy differs significantly from individual counseling and involves an understanding of group dynamics beyond the scope of this book, we will not examine this therapeutic context here. Likewise, while we will refer to family or marital counseling at times, our primary focus in the remainder of this chapter will be on one-on-one counseling interviews within the context of ongoing helping relationships.

Whether in individual, group, marital, or family therapy, the client enters into a helping relationship because it offers the opportunity for growth through the use of listening, safety, feedback and, possibly, active direction toward change. "Because they are clearly distinguished from daily life, all therapeutic settings provide a relatively protected environment where patients can feel free to express forbidden thoughts, release pent-up emotions, or experiment with new ways of behaving without fear of consequences."[14]

We will turn our focus now to individual counseling, looking first at popular misconceptions about counseling. Next, we will consider some basic approaches to individual therapy, followed by a look at the interviewing skills involved in conducting counseling interviews. Finally, we will offer suggestions concerning interviewee considerations in counseling interviews.

Individual Counseling Relationships

Popular Misconceptions about Counseling Interviews

Our culture places great value on individualism and personal strength. We speak with awe or admiration of the "self-made" person; namely, the individual who "pulls herself up" from poverty or other devastation. We admire those who "go it alone." There is, within our cultural belief system, the implicit value or demand that we must be able to make our way through our lives without relying on the assistance of others. (Meanwhile, of course, ours is a highly addictive culture, in which dependencies on drugs, including alcohol, are widespread.)

At any rate, partially as a result of our beliefs in individualism and personal independence, counseling and those who make use of it within our culture are often viewed negatively. Those who seek therapeutic assistance are often seen as flawed and unable to make it on their own, weak, and not "normal." Counseling or therapy is seen as an admission of failure rather than as a sign of strength on the part of those who seek it.

These misconceived notions about counseling have made it difficult for some persons who would benefit from counseling to seek it. These myths are false. Pennebaker expresses the truth that counseling is not for the few, but for the many:

We are all humans simmering in the same stew. Our lives oscillate from exhilarating highs to devastating lows. We can usually cope with the highs. It's the lows that are a problem. Most of us will face one or more horrible experiences in our lives—death of a loved one, divorce, loss of a job, crime—the list is endless. How we cope with those events will dictate our happiness for months or even years afterward.[15]

As for the notion that counseling is for the weak, exhaustive research conducted by the Penn Psychotherapy Project found these pretreatment client qualities were the best predictors of successful psychotherapy or counseling: high motivation for change; positive attitudes about self, therapist and treatment; interest in and capacity for human relations; intellectual functioning; healthy personality traits and coping styles; and ability, as opposed to helplessness and passivity.[16] People possessing these qualities benefited most from counseling. These are qualities not of weakness but of strength. Counseling is for the strong.

It is important to recognize the existence of misconceptions about counseling and the falsehood of these misconceptions. While it is certainly true that there are some profoundly disturbed persons involved in counseling interviews, these people are neither the majority nor necessarily the persons who will benefit most from counseling interviews. Most of those people who benefit from the helping relationship are everyday people like ourselves.

One additional question is sometimes voiced about counseling or psychotherapy: "What good does it do to talk to someone anyway?" Pennebaker engaged in various research projects where individuals were instructed to share their experiences and feelings, either in oral or written form. His findings provide strong evidence not only of improvement in the mental health of those who confided in others, but also of remarkable improvement in their physical well-being, including heightened immune function.[17] Likewise, the Penn Psychotherapy Project found physical as well as emotional improvement in those treated by psychotherapy. In addition, these researchers found that most of the gains made by those who obtained counseling were maintained long after counseling was done.[18]

"Not disclosing our thoughts and feelings can be unhealthy," Pennebaker writes. "Divulging them can be healthy."[19] What good is it to talk to another? "Specifically, the act of talking can change the ways we think and feel about traumatic events and about ourselves."[20]

Approaches to Counseling

Different writers on the subject of counseling classify approaches or philosophies of counseling in various ways. Frank and Frank state: "The variety of psychotherapeutic procedures precludes any neat classification, especially since their aims and methods overlap."[21] Specific approaches to therapy include: *behavior therapy*, which focuses on problematic client behaviors and is highly directive (i.e., offers specific prescriptions for change); *cognitive behavior therapy*, which focuses on faulty beliefs and thoughts and directs the client to new ways of thinking; *Gestalt therapy*, which utilizes exercises in directed imagination to allow clients to experience their feelings; *psychoanalysis*, a nondirective therapy in which the client chooses the subject matter and the therapist offers interpretations but not prescriptions; *Rogerian, person-centered therapy* in which the nondirective therapist offers empathy, genuineness, and warmth and seeks to reflect back or paraphrase client insights without imposing interpretation; and *systemic therapy*, used often in family therapy, which views individual problems as a result of dysfunctional relationship systems and offers behavioral direction for change.[22] Figure 14.1 shows a therapeutic continuum of therapies, using the previous approaches. Ivey has created a chart depicting the use of various interviewing skills by those of differing theoretical orientations. It is presented in part in Figure 14.2

The previous discussion provides some indication of the ways that various practices of therapy differ. While there is no easy way to classify these approaches, we can say that they range from directive to nondirective and that they make variable use of a variety of interviewing skills. But how are they similar?

Pennebaker says: "Psychotherapy offers a powerful setting for the disclosure of secrets, thoughts, and emotions. Therapists usually provide the essential ingredients of honest self-disclosure, trust, nonjudgmental feedback, and safety from recrimination. Distressed individuals also receive specific information on ways to cope with the source and symptoms of their stress."[23] In other words, all therapies seek to provide a helping relationship to the client. The provision of a helping relationship is an important similarity among the various therapeutic approaches.

Pennebaker also reports that, "In studying individuals who have faced major traumas such as rape, psychoanalyst Mardi Horowitz reports that people typically progress through three general stages: denial, working through, and completion. The goal of therapy, in Horowitz's view, is to aid in the working-through phase so that completion or assimilation is attained."[24] Therapists try to help interviewees to work on problems until they are resolved. Assistance with the resolution of problems is a second important similarity among therapies.

Frank and Frank state: "All psychotherapies share at least four effective features: An emotionally charged, confiding relationship with a helping person . . . A healing setting . . . A plausible explanation for the patient's symptoms . . . [and] A ritual or procedure that requires the active participation of both patient and therapist and that is believed to be the means of restoring the patient's health."[25] These authors add to the similarities of (1) a helping relationship which (2) seeks

Highly Directive					Nondirective
Behavior therapy	Cognitive behavior therapy	Systemic therapy	Gestalt therapy	Psychoanalysis	Rogerian therapy

FIGURE 14.1   Directive/Nondirective Continuum of Common Therapies

		1.	2.	3.	4.	5.
1. Nondirective	F = frequent use					
2. Rogerian	C = common use					
3. Behavioral	I = infrequent use					
4. Psychodynamic						
5. Gestalt						
ATTENDING SKILLS:						
Open question		I	I	C	C	F
Closed question		I	I	F	I	C
Encourage		C	C	C	I	C
Paraphrase		F	F	C	C	I
Reflect feeling		F	F	I	C	I
Reflect meaning		C	F	I	C	I
Summarization		C	C	C	I	I
INFLUENCING SKILLS:						
Feedback		I	F	I	I	C
Advice/info/ instruct/other		I	I	C	I	I
Self-disclosure		I	F	I	I	I
Interpretation		I	I	I	F	F
Directive		I	I	F	I	F
AMOUNT OF INTERVIEWER TALK TIME		Low	Med	High	Low	High

FIGURE 14.2   Interviewing Skills Employed by Counselors of Various Common Theoretical Orientations

Adapted from "Table 1.1 Examples of microskill leads used by interviewers of differing theoretical orientations," in Ivey, Allen E., *Intentional Interviewing and Counseling: Facilitating Client Development*, 2nd ed. (Pacific Grove, CA: Brook/Cole Publishing Company, 1988), 15. Used with permission.

the resolution of problems: (3) a specific therapeutic setting, (4) a plan of treatment, and (5) a method for accomplishing that plan. Frank and Frank also contend that a "universal feature of successful psychotherapies" is "their ability to arouse the patient's expectation of help."[26] The importance of (6) the patient's positive expectation of healing is the sixth similarity of the various therapies. This similarity is also supported by studies reported by Luborsky, who found that the positive prophecy of the therapist is important to a successful outcome.[27]

Guidano offers these conclusions about commonalities of experience in therapy: "No change seems possible without emotions" and "The structure and quality of change depend to a large extent on the level and quality of self-awareness with which the subject carries out the reorganization process."[28] While some cognitive or behavioral therapists might disagree with the need for emotions, all would agree that (7) client self-awareness is essential in order to facilitate change. Client self-awareness is yet another similarity between therapies.

Last, Pipes and Davenport define the common elements of all psychotherapies in these terms: "1. An emotionally charged relationship—which by providing an optimum balance of challenge, support, and involvement offers an opportunity for development or restoration of the self in a more or less healthy interpersonal environment. 2. A new way of looking at the problem (including a rationale for it) and potential solutions in relationship to the self. 3. Encouragement to try new and more adaptive behavior. 4. An influential person (the therapist) who models and encourages self-acceptance and courage."[29] In addition to recognition of the importance of a healing relationship, these authors add three additional similarities to our growing list: (8) a new way of viewing the problem, (9) support for trying new and more effective behaviors, and (10) a therapist who serves as a model for self-acceptance and the courage to change.

We can summarize the similarities between the various approaches to therapy in this way:

1. A helping relationship
2. Support for working through problems until resolved
3. A specific therapeutic setting
4. A plan of treatment
5. A method for accomplishing that plan
6. A positive expectation of help
7. Client self-awareness as the basis for change
8. A new way of viewing the problem
9. Support for trying out new behaviors and
10. A therapist who is a model of self-acceptance and the courage to change.

These commonalities are the fundamental building blocks of all therapeutic relationships regardless of philosophy or orientation.

Conducting the Counseling Interview

Preparing the Setting

We have already discussed the importance of feeling safe and being assured of confidentiality to the success of counseling. The counseling interviewer must create an interview space which is comfortable, quiet, and secure, where the interviewee needn't fear being overheard by others, and where the consistency and safety of the setting encourage the interviewee to view the experience as trustworthy and set apart from the confines of everyday life.

Ideally, there should be seating options for clients when they enter the room, so that they feel they have some choice or control in their proxemic relation to the interviewer. Most often, the counseling setting also contains visible evidence in the form of diplomas and certificates of the training and expertise of the interviewer. This evidence helps create a positive expectation of competent assistance in the interviewee.

The Early Interviews

Clients arriving for a first counseling interview usually come with some idea in mind of what is wrong. They also come with concerns and fears about the interviewer and the counseling process.

Frank and Frank suggest demoralization as the common characteristic of individuals seeking psychotherapy. They define demoralization as the consciousness "of having failed to meet their own expectations or those of others, or of being unable to cope with some pressing problem" and a sense of powerlessness "to change the situation or themselves" and to "extricate themselves from their predicament."[30] It is this vulnerable person in crisis whom the counseling interviewer must meet.

The standard interview opening phase of rapport building in the counseling context is usually brief and professional. It includes a warm welcome, an invitation to choose a comfortable seat, and then the question of concern, variously worded as "Why are you here today?" or "What made you decide to seek counseling at this time?" "The outset," Guidano writes, "is generally marked by the classic question: `What problem has brought you here?'"[31] The interviewer's first responsibility in the earliest session is to ask this central question, listen for the answer, and seek a clear sense of the client's problem.

Even as the interviewer seeks a clear understanding of the client's problem, she or he also strives to be aware of and to allay the interviewee's most immediate fears and concerns. Pipes and Davenport categorize client fears into three general content areas: (1) How will I be treated? (2) How will I be viewed as a client? (3) Will I like the effects of counseling? Under treatment concerns, the authors list the following: a desire to be treated with honesty, like a person, taken seriously, with understanding, without pressure, with confidentiality, without fear of abandonment, by a competent therapist. Under concerns about how the interviewee will be perceived, the authors include such fears as being viewed as a bad person by the therapist or by friends, being perceived as crazy, having secrets forced from them, and being perceived as foolish or weak. And in the category of concerns about the effects of therapy, the authors list fears about learning what one doesn't want to know, losing control of one's emotions, finding there's no hope for change, and experiencing disruption of one's existing relationships.[32]

Each of these fears may be present at some level of consciousness when an interviewee arrives for that first session. What can the interviewer do to allay them? First, through the use of what Ivey calls "attending behavior," the interviewer communicates interest and establishes rapport. **Attending behavior**

Interviewers who adapt to the needs and concerns of clients will forge a stronger alliance between themselves and the clients.

demonstrates that the interviewer is listening. It includes eye contact, attentive body language, vocal qualities that affirm interest, and verbal tracking. *Verbal tracking* is sticking to the topic of concern indicated by the client without changing the subject.[33] Effective use of attending behavior helps allay client concerns about being taken seriously as a person, with understanding, and without judgment.

In addition to attending behavior, the interviewer can help alleviate interviewee fears by providing information about the therapeutic process, suggestions on what to expect from the process, and assurance of positive outcomes. Frank and Frank state: "Psychotherapeutic success depends in part on a congruence between the expectations a patient brings to treatment and what actually occurs; hence, shaping those expectations by means of instructions or a preliminary role-induction interview enhances the effectiveness of short-term psychotherapy."[34]

In order to allay client fears and shape positive expectations, the interviewer can also assure the client of the confidentiality of what is shared and the security of the setting. The interviewer can provide information about her/his experience and therapeutic orientation, commitment to assist without coercion or manipulation, philosophy and methods, and hope.

Pipes and Davenport offer these suggestions to interviewers for early sessions: "When in doubt, *listen* . . . . Interact unapologetically . . . . Offer appropriate hope."[35] According to Pipes and Davenport, interviewers should offer: assurances that change is possible; "accurate and empathic labeling of client concerns" to assure interviewees that their concerns are real, identifiable, and *heard*; and therapeutic direction which includes "references to [a] client's perceived strengths."[36] These authors also recommend that interviewers strive to forge an alliance between themselves and their clients through the use of provisional wordings and a general willingness to adapt to the needs and concerns of the clients. "Indicate willingness to learn. . . . you are the expert on therapy but . . . clients need to be the experts on themselves."[37] All of these efforts do much to allay interviewee fears.

The interviewer's responsibilities, in early as well as later sessions, are to be clear about the primary goal of helping the client, to be open to the client, to seek objective assessment of the client's status and needs, to possess the necessary knowledge and skills to counsel, and to have sufficient self-understanding to view the client and the process with accuracy.[38] In order to be able to arrive at an accurate assessment of client status and needs, most counseling interviewers employ interview guides for initial or early interviews (sometimes called intake interviews), which ask questions to clarify certain basic counseling concerns. A sample intake interview guide is provided in Figure 14.3.

During the Interview

Ivey recommends that interviewers use the "basic listening sequence" in the conduct of interviews. He defines this sequence as the use of questioning and observation, encouraging, paraphrasing, reflection of feeling, and summarizing.[39]

A skillful use of open and closed questions is essential to effective counseling at every stage. Open questions such as "What concerns do you bring with you today?" at the start of the interview encourage the interviewee to select a focus for the session. As in any interview, questions also invite elaboration and detail, allowing the interviewer to probe more deeply into behaviors, problems, and concerns. Likewise, questions aid in diagnosis. Ivey describes a set of diagnostic questions suggested by George Kelly: *Who* is the client? *What* is the problem? *When* does it happen? *Where*? *How* does the client respond? *Why* does the problem occur?[40]

Questions can also encourage and assure. For example, a counselor might ask, "Can you identify the personal strengths in the actions you took?" or "Do you have any questions or concerns about this relationship that you want to share with me?"

Problems occur when questions, either because of their nature or frequency, cause defensiveness in the interviewee or wrest control of the focus of the interview from the client. For the interviewer, the use of questions requires a delicate balancing act of encouraging, seeking, and probing to elicit continuing self-discovery and self-disclosure without at the same time asking for more or different information than the client is able to confront or experience at a given moment.

In addition to the use of questions, the counseling interviewer utilizes observation of the client's verbal and nonverbal responses, noticing incongruities and/or indicators of anxiety and other emotions. Through sharing observations,

I. Presenting Problem:
    A. What brings you here?
    B. Onset of difficulties?
    C. Feelings about situation?
    D. Any other issues or concerns?

II. Relevant Information:

    A. Current living situation
    B. Personal history
    C. Previous counseling
    D. Family history

III. Counseling Issues:

    A. Expectations of counseling
    B. Fears or concerns about counseling
    C. Commitment to or motivation for counseling

IV. Assessment:

    A. Appropriateness of counseling
    B. Seriousness of crisis
    C. Risk to self or others
    D. Range of symptoms

FIGURE 14.3   Sample Intake Interview Guide

Adapted from: "Appendix A: Outline of an Intake Interview" in Pipes, Randolph B. and Davenport, Donna S., Introduction to Psychotheraphy: Common Clinical Wisdom (Englewood Cliffs: Prentice Hall, 1990), 123.

paraphrasing client descriptions, and reflecting on client feelings, the interviewer confirms understanding and affirms acceptance of the feelings and concerns of the other. Through verbal and nonverbal encouragement, the interviewer reassures the interviewee and offers acceptance and positive regard.

These skills, as outlined in Ivey's basic listening sequence, represent the traditional Anglo-European approach to counseling. Interviewers need to be aware of the differing cultural origins and cultural communication styles of their clients, however, and to seek an approach and a communication style adapted to those styles.[41] Sue and Sue suggest that the emphasis on attending skills rather than influencing skills in many of the traditional western forms of counseling may be inappropriate for counseling efforts with individuals from many other cultural groups. "Mental health training programs tend to emphasize the more passive attending skills. Counselors so trained may be ill equipped to work with culturally different clients who might find the active approach more relevant to their own needs and values."[42] These authors suggest, for example, that Asian Americans who are reluctant to express feelings but seek concrete instruction would have a difficult time with traditional therapeutic responses and would prefer short-term treatment with a therapist who actively offers solutions to problems.[43]

Counseling Interview Structure.   The rapport-building and orientation stage of counseling interviews involves the use of questions, assurances, and information to win the client's trust and develop an understanding of the client's situation. The information-gathering stage further utilizes questions to probe more deeply into the problem and aid both interviewer and interviewee understanding. A third stage involves utilizing questions designed to learn the client's own goals and desires. What does the client want? How would she or he like to behave? What are her/his goals in therapy?

Another stage of counseling interviews involves the summary and application of lessons learned. Depending on the theoretical orientation of the interviewer, this stage may involve offering directives or agendas for action and carryover between sessions. "You have identified a desire to stop blaming yourself for what happened in childhood," an interviewer might suggest. "Between now and our next session, I'd like you to pay attention to the self-blaming messages you give yourself when you think about the past. Try to identify and make note of what those messages are and what beliefs they express." In this stage, Ivey suggests, the interviewer learns how committed the interviewee is to change.[44]

Closing and Evaluation.   Closing the counseling interview may consist of providing assignments or follow-through as previously suggested, or it may consist primarily of affirming when the next session is and offering a warm farewell. Like the opening, the closing of the counseling interview is generally quite brief. Its most important element consists in an unspoken assurance of continuity from session to session.

After the session, the counselor employs the method of record keeping and evaluation deemed appropriate by the agency or individual counselor. The evaluation process may consist of noting behavioral changes, responses of the interviewee, issues discussed, follow-through from previous sessions, and future assignments. On an ongoing basis, the interviewer will observe and note evidence of change in the client and the effectiveness of the therapeutic approach. Often, as was mentioned earlier, this evaluation process is carried out in consultation with another therapist who offers a different perspective and feedback on the therapeutic relationship.

Mistakes Interviewers Make

Pipes and Davenport provide an insightful compilation of common mistakes made by counseling interviewers.[45] We summarize them briefly here. Counselors can get into verbal response habits of overusing certain patterns of response, for example, saying "Tell me more about that" after many client statements.

Interviewers may engage in inappropriate behaviors such as chatting or nervous laughter. Sometimes interviewers push too quickly for change or self-disclosure. Others attempt to solve the client's problem before they have fully understood it.

Other common mistakes include focusing on someone other than the client ("Tell me more about your husband's behavior"), striving for friendship rather than a professional helping relationship, asking too many questions, filling the silences before the client has a chance to speak, not probing deeply enough, and not sharing enough of oneself. "All therapists, whether experienced or inexperienced, make mistakes . . . . [T]he issue is not whether one makes a mistake but rather how one recovers from it."[46]

Counseling Interviewer Ethics

The primary ethical governance of the counselor must lie in the fundamental goal of helping the client to heal. Various professional organizations such as the American Psychological Association and the American Association of Counseling and Development have ethical guidelines for their members.[47] According to Lindley and Holmes, a code of ethics has three functions: to specify the goals of the profession, to indicate ideal standards of conduct, and "to protect clients or patients from bad practice."[48] These authors recommend the development of a "code of practice" which would include both mandatory requirements and recommended behaviors for all persons practicing psychotherapy.[49]

Ethical Principles of Psychologists, published by the American Psychological Association in 1981, lists various principles governing psychotherapist behavior. Some of these include the necessity: to represent one's training accurately; to recognize the limits of one's own competence; to make use of supervision; to be responsive to individual client differences in culture, gender, etc.; to be aware of one's own personal issues and problems and their impact on one's counseling work; to respect, within the limits of insurance disclosure regulations and legal demands, the need to protect client confidentiality; to avoid sexual intimacies with clients; and to terminate therapy with persons who are not benefiting from it.[50]

Actions undertaken as healing efforts should be tested through discussion with peers and supervisors, and in accordance with recommendations for treatment contained within the body of research in the field, in order to be sure that personal motivations are not distorting the therapist's vision. Not all counselors follow this guideline. An estimated 10 percent of U.S. psychiatrists in a nationwide survey admitted to having sexual contact with their clients, many with more than one client; most of these contacts were between male therapists and female clients.[51] Similar results were found in a survey of psychologists.[52] It is safe to assume that, had any of these individuals asked their peers about the healing value of these actions, they would have been discouraged from pursuing sexual relationships. According to Pipes and Davenport, a growing body of evidence suggests that sexual relationships between therapists and clients are damaging, not healing, in their impact.[53] Lindley and Holmes state: "Therapists who allow sexual relationships to develop with patients . . . lack the heightened sense of moral responsibility which we have argued is an essential characteristic of a good therapist."[54]

Interviewee Considerations in Counseling

Counseling Interviewee Rights

Many times persons seeking counseling enter into these relationships with no prior knowledge of the therapist or of the therapeutic process. Because the territory is unfamiliar, they find themselves vulnerable and uncertain. These new clients often do not think of themselves as consumers with the right to obtain information and make judgments about the service they are buying, but they are.

Counseling interviewees have the right to obtain a therapeutic relationship in which they can place their trust, which does not damage them, which promotes their self-discovery, healing and change; and which conforms to certain ethical standards and mutual expectations. If, for example, an interviewee seeks a therapist who will listen empathically and provide insight and direction, she or he is entitled to ask for those qualities and seek referral elsewhere if the first therapist consulted does not provide them.

Interviewees entering into therapeutic relationships should ask questions in order to allay their fears and concerns and to be assured that the form of counseling they are entering into is compatible with their values and likely to promote healing. If the interviewer seems cold or judgmental and the interviewee does not feel welcomed or accepted, the interviewee should feel free to express these perceptions or leave the relationship in search of another. If the interviewer seems not to hear or accept what the client believes to be her or his primary current concerns, the client is entitled to ask that the concerns be taken seriously.

A sample client information form developed by Handelsman and Galvin follows in Figure 14.4; it suggests a variety of questions in a range of topic areas which clients can explore, but these questions are not exhaustive. Any interviewee in a counseling relationship should feel free to express questions, voice doubts, ask for information, and negotiate the nature and terms of the relationship. If the relationship cannot be negotiated to the mutual satisfaction of client and therapist, then a new therapeutic relationship should be sought.

Choosing a Counseling Relationship

A person seeking counseling should begin by asking trusted friends, ministers, or colleagues for recommendations. Before arranging an appointment, they should know something about the person or agency's approach and arrangements for counseling, including a clear understanding of fee arrangements and insurance coverage. They should enter into early sessions with the belief that they are assessing the potential benefits of this relationship. Interviewees should not feel that they are bound to that relationship unless they feel respected and welcomed there.

How does therapy work?
What risks are involved?
Will I improve?
How long will it take?
What if therapy doesn't seem to work for me?
Will I have to take tests of any kind?

What other kinds of help are available?
What risks are involved in them?
Would I improve with these kinds of help?

How do I schedule appointments?
How long are sessions?
What do they cost?
How do I pay—monthly, weekly?
What if I can't pay?
What if I have an emergency?
What if I cancel an appointment?

Who has access to your records?
Who will you talk to about what we talk about here?

What training and experience do you have?
If I have a problem with our therapy that we can't work out, who can I talk to about it?

FIGURE 14.4   Sample Client Information Form: Questions You Have A Right To Ask

Adapted from: Handelsman, M. and Galvin, M., "Facilitating Informed Consent for Outpatient Psychotherapy: A Suggested Written Format,"*Professional Psychology: Research and Practice* 19 (1988), 223-25.

Client Responsibilities

Once a productive helping relationship has been found, the client must be willing to make an emotional commitment to the relationship and to the process. This commitment must include openness to change, receptivity to the insights and guidance of the therapist, willingness to explore feelings; and willingness to make new behavioral choices, to try out alternative habits, patterns, or responses, to risk change.[55]

Likewise, the client should understand that coming to terms with crises or traumas takes time; that facing problems is painful in the short run but provides long-term gains; and that even the impact of old traumas can be eased by self-expression and self-understanding.[56] Interviewees must be willing to risk honesty, to experience the full range of emotions, and to trust in the healing relationship in order to gain from the therapeutic process.

Evaluating the Counseling Process

Periodically, through the course of therapy, clients should take time to examine and assess what they have gained. Have their symptoms subsided? Do they feel more or less in control of their lives? Has the crisis which brought them into therapy subsided? If they have doubts about progress or change, they should feel free to ask the counselor for perceptions and assessments of what has transpired. After each session, they should consider what was experienced, what was learned, and what was gained. They should not feel afraid to test their judgments against those of the therapist nor to trust their own judgments about what is taking place, keeping in mind, however, that the process needs to be painful at times in order to be liberating. Interviewees are co-creators of the therapeutic relationship. In order to be effective co-creators, they must be informed, honest, and willing to negotiate the therapeutic process.

Summary

Counseling interviews are helping interviews that occur within the context of a relationship where the interviewer offers the interviewee(s) the opportunity for self-discovery and change through the effective use of empathic listening, questions, confidentiality, safety, feedback, and, sometimes, active direction toward change. The goal of counseling interviews is positive benefit for the interviewees. Counseling interviews include vocational and educational counseling, rehabilitative counseling, peer counseling, and individual, family, and group therapies. Counseling interviews are affected by the institutional framework in which they occur.

Academic, vocational, and rehabilitative counseling offer specific assistance regarding school or work careers and adjustment to disabilities. Peer counseling is used within various organizations and institutions as a means of providing informal support to individuals. Psychotherapeutic counseling offers more generalized treatment in a variety of settings for individuals experiencing emotional crisis.

U.S. culture contains pervasive misconceptions that counseling is for the weak and the abnormal, as well as doubts about what benefit can be obtained from talking to another person about personal difficulties. Contrary to popular understanding, those who use counseling effectively are both "normal" and strong. Documented evidence exists of the physical and emotional benefits of confiding in others.

There are many approaches to therapy. Each approach utilizes a variety of interviewing skills. They share the goal of healing, the role of the healing relationship, a new perspective on the problem, and hope for change.

In conducting the counseling interview, the setting must be safe. Clients enter into counseling with many concerns about the process and the relationship. Interviewers can allay these fears by attending behavior, assurances of confidentiality and safety, careful listening, and the offer of real hope for change.

The conduct of the interview involves the use of a basic listening sequence, encouragement, paraphrasing, reflection of feeling, and summarizing. The structure of the interview includes rapport building, information gathering, assessment, summary and application.

Interviewers should be guided by ethical standards, taking care not to engage in actions that coerce or manipulate or are not in accord with the goal of healing.

Interviewees should be informed and aware of their rights and responsibilities as co-creators of the helping relationship. They should feel free to ask questions, express concerns, and make frequent personal assessments of the benefits being obtained. They should make informed choices about with whom to counsel and should be willing, once a suitable relationship is found, to be committed to the process and willing to risk honesty and pain.

Discussion Questions

1. What kinds of traumas or crises have led people you know to seek counseling?

2. How many forms of helping interviews have you experienced in your life this far? How were they different? How were they the same? Were they helpful?

3. If your were to seek personal counseling for yourself or someone you care about after a death in the family, what kinds of qualities would you look for in a counselor?

4. Which of the common approaches to therapy mentioned in this chapter seems most appealing or sensible to you? Why?

5. If you were a counseling interviewer, what aspects of the counseling process would you find most difficult? Why?

Suggested Activities

1. Re-read the opening interview for this chapter. Consider whether an alternative set of responses on the part of the interviewer might have changed the outcome of the interview. Discuss the interview with a group of your peers and decide what alternative responses, if any, might have changed the course of the interview.

2. Write a three to five page paper about a time in your own life when someone turned to you for help. What skills did you attempt to use in your responses to this person? What do you wish you had done differently? If you had been in a peer counseling relationship with the person, what training would you have wanted before engaging in your helping encounter?

3. Develop a tentative interview guide for an initial interview with a client who is coming to you for help in adjusting to the death of a family member. What would you want or need to know? What information, guidance, or encouragement would you want to offer?

4. Design an office setting suitable for counseling interviews. Write a two to three page rationale for your design.

Related Readings

Carpenter, John, and Treacher, Andy. *Problems and Solutions in Marital and Family Therapy.* Oxford: Basil Blackwell, 1989.

Holmes, Jeremy, and Lindley, Richard. *The Values of Psychotherapy.* Oxford: Oxford University Press, 1989.

Ivey, Allen E. *Intentional Interviewing and Counseling: Facilitating Client Development,* 2nd ed. Pacific Grove, CA: Brooks/Cole Publishing Company, 1988.

Modell, Arnold H. *Other Times, Other Realities: Toward A Theory of Psychoanalytic Treatment.* Cambridge, MA: Harvard University Press, 1990.

Pennebaker, James W. *Opening Up: The Healing Power of Confiding in Others.* New York: William Morrow and Company, Inc., 1990.

Pipes, Randolph B., and Davenport, Donna S. *Introduction to Psychotherapy: Common Clinical Wisdom.* Englewood Cliffs: Prentice Hall, 1990.

Sue, Derald Wing, and Sue, David. *Counseling the Culturally Different: Theory and Practice,* 2nd ed. New York: John Wiley and Sons , 1990.

Endnotes

1. Allen E. Ivey, *Intentional Interviewing and Counseling: Facilitating Client Development,* 2nd ed. (Pacific Grove, CA: Brooks/Cole Publishing Company, 1988), 9–10.

2. Jeremy Holmes and Richard Lindley, *The Values of Psychotherapy* (Oxford: Oxford University Press, 1989), 3.

3. Jerome D. Frank and Julia B. Frank, *Persuasion and Healing: A Comparative Study of Psychotherapy,* 3rd ed. (Baltimore: The Johns Hopkins University Press, 1991), 2.

4. Holmes and Lindley (1989), 37.

5. Holmes and Lindley (1989), 37.

6. Frank and Frank (1991), 15.

7. Robert Woody, James Hansen and Robert Rossberg, *Counseling Psychology: Strategies and Services* (Pacific Grove, CA: Brooks/Cole Publishing Company, 1989), 4–7.

8. Woody, *et al.* (1989), 97.

9. Woody, *et al.* (1989), 97–99.

10. M.E. Jaques and D.R. Kauppi, "Vocational Rehabilitation and Its Relationship to Vocational Psychology," (1983). As reported in Woody, *et al.* (1989), 102.

11. Frank and Frank (1991), 11–12.

12. Lester Luborsky, Paul Crits-Christoph, Jim Mintz, and Arthur Auerbach, *Who will Benefit from Psychotherapy? Predicting Therapeutic Outcomes* (New York: Basic Books, Inc., Publishers, 1988), 362–366.

13. Luborsky *et al.* (1988), 340–343.

14. Frank and Frank (1991), 188.

15. James W. Pennebaker, *Opening Up: The Healing Power of Confiding in Others* (New York: William Morrow and Company, Inc., 1990), 7.

16. Luborsky, *et al.* (1988), 283–285.

17. Pennebaker (1990). See especially pp. 38–49.

18. Lubrosky, *et al.* (1988), Chapters 5 and 19.

19. Pennebaker (1990), 14.

20. Pennebaker (1990), 38.

21. Frank and Frank (1991), 188.

22. Holmes and Lindley (1989), 249–251.

23. Pennebaker (1990), 122–123.

24. Pennebaker (1990), 86.

25. Frank and Frank (1991), 40–43.

26. Frank and Frank (1991), 132.

27. Luborsky, *et al.* (1988), 284, 295.

28. Vittorio F. Grudano, *The Self in Process: Toward a Post-Rationalist Cognitive Therapy* (New York: The Guilford Press, 1991), 96–97.

29. Randolph B. Pipes and Donna S. Davenport, *Introduction to Psychotherapy: Common Clinical Wisdom* (Englewood Cliffs: Prentice Hall, 1990), 5.

30. Frank and Frank (1991), 34–35.

31. Guidano (1991), 113.

32. Pipes and Davenport (1990), 63–88.

33. Ivey (1988), 22.

34. Frank and Frank (1991), 153.

35. Pipes and Davenport (1990), 132–135.
36. Pipes and Davenport (1990), 133–134.
37. Pipes and Davenport (1990), 136.
38. Pipes and Davenport (1990), 128–130.
39. Ivey (1988), 124–147.
40. Ivey (1988), 51. ,
41. Derald Wing Sue and David Sue, *Counseling the Culturally Different: Theory and Practice*, 2nd ed. (New York: John Wiley and Sons, 1990), 159–174.
42. Sue and Sue (1990), 70.
43. Sue and Sue (1990), 198.
44. Ivey (1990), 132–140.
45. Pipes and Davenport (1990), 188–207.
46. Pipes and Davenport (1990), 207.
47. Ivey (1988), 239.
48. Holmes and Lindley (1989), 193–195.
49. Holmes and Lindley (1989), 201–203.
50. Pipes and Davenport (1990), 210–217.
51. Holmes and Lindley (1989), 157.
52. Holmes and Lindley (1989), 157.
53. Pipes and Davenport (1990), 214.
54. Holmes and Lindley (1989), 161.
55. Pipes and Davenport (1990), 131–132.
56. Pennebaker (1990), 97–99.

Conclusion:
Guiding Principles

Fourteen chapters ago we began with general concepts and basic components of interviews. We have now completed a rather lengthy journey through the needs and practices of many specific interviewing contexts. One task remains; namely, to pull together the various paths we have explored with the goal of arriving at a useful synthesis of guiding principles for the artful interviewer to apply with confidence in any interviewing context. To do so, we will go back to the beginning and attempt to pull from each chapter the overarching principles useful to both parties in the interview.

Guiding Principles for Interviewers and Interviewees

1. *Understanding increases options.* The more the parties to the interview appreciate the complex communicative realities involved in the process, the better able they are to negotiate that process with ease and to obtain their desired goals.

2. *Know your goals.* Each party to the interview should be clear on what she or he hopes to accomplish from the interaction. Recognition of goals allows for clear choices and actions in the interview, so that each party may employ questions and answers effectively (verbal and nonverbal communication) to influence the other and obtain the desired ends.

3. *Interviewing is a transactional process,* in which both parties work together in a reciprocal, mutual exchange to attain individual and/or collective goals.

4. *Interviewing involves a variety of messages* that serve both informational and relationship-building needs and that may or may not be intended.

5. *Interviews are governed by rules and norms* that create expectations in all parties against which the actual interview is judged.

6.   *Communication in interviews, as elsewhere, is imperfect.* Information gets lost or misunderstood, and obstacles of many kinds interfere with the goals of the interview parties.

7.   *Interviews involve the application of skills and techniques and artful adaptation to the other within the given context.*

8.   *Accurate perception and effective listening are essential to the success of interviews.*

9.   *Both listening and perception involve aural, visual and mental processes, as well as feedback, in order to obtain understanding despite obstacles in the communication process.*

10.   *Listening is enhanced by goal setting, focused attention, adaptation to obstacles, and accurate record keeping.*

11.   *All parties in interviews actively implement varying degrees of control.*

12.   *Interviews have structure.* Each phase of the interview serves important purposes for all parties.

13.   *Questions and answers are the fundamental tools* used by the parties in interviews to pursue their goals.

14.   *The nature of the questions exerts powerful influence on the nature, validity and depth of the answers.*

15.   *The parties in interviews are influenced by their cultures.* One's cultural framework is inherently ethnocentric and fosters stereotyping and discriminatory responses to others.

16.   *Knowledge of one's own and the other's culture increases options for accurate perception.*

17.   *Where interviews are governed by laws, both parties to the interview should be informed and act with regard to those laws.*

18.   *Interviewers adapt the information sought and the information obtained to the needs of the particular interview context.*

19.   *Probes are an essential tool of the interviewer.*

20.   *Parties to the interview should make informed choices about their own behaviors in light of the ethical issues affecting their particular context.*

21.   *Preparation is essential to all parties seeking to effectively negotiate an interview.* Research is necessary in order to enter knowledgeably into the interview.

22.   *Interviews obtain different kinds of information and in differing form, depending on the goals and/or hypotheses with which they are undertaken.*

23.   *Interviews are more effective when they are conducted in a supportive climate.*

24.   *All interviews are persuasive; all persuasion involves ethical choices.* Persuasion that does not allow free choice on the part of the other is coercive or manipulative and unethical.

25.   *Empathy is an important interviewing skill.*

26.   *Both parties to the interview have rights and responsibilities.*

27.   *Each specific interviewing context informs our understanding of the others* because each throws a different light on the qualities and requirements of the interview.

Examination of journalistic interviewing enhances our understanding of the need to adapt interviews to the intended audience. Research interviews enrich our appreciation of the impact of goals and questions on the information obtained. Selection interviews highlight the need for preparation and the reality of mutual persuasion in interviews. Sales interviews allow us to see ethical issues clearly. Disciplinary and appraisal interviews enhance our understanding of the impact of defensive versus supportive climates. Diagnostic interviews develop our appreciation of the vital importance of obtaining accurate information. Counseling interviews enhance our awareness of the role of empathy and prophecy in determining the outcomes of interviews. For the student of interviews, no interviewing context is irrelevant to her or his own needed skills and understanding. The study of each context strengthens our understanding of them all.

Glossary

Accuracy-checking Probe: A secondary question designed to check whether the answer to an earlier question has been understood correctly.

Amplification Probe: A secondary question that seeks elaboration of an earlier answer.

Appraisal: The assessment or evaluation of an employee's work.

Appraisal Interview: An interview based on carefully collected data that allows organizations and workers to assess worker performance, set goals, and improve productivity.

Assessment: The process of identifying the nature and seriousness of a worker's problem to prepare for an employee intervention interview.

Attending Behavior: Actions that demonstrate that the interviewer is listening, including eye contact, attentive body language, vocal qualities which affirm interest, and "verbal tracking."

Behaviorally Anchored Rating Scales (BARS): Rating scales used for appraisal interviews that include short statements that describe particular work behaviors related to a specific position in the organization.

Bipolar Question: A closed question that allows interviewees to choose between two responses.

Body: The lengthiest part of the interview where the content "work" of the interview occurs through use of sequenced questions and answers.

Bona Fide Occupational Qualifications (BFOQs): The specific qualifications a person needs in order to do a job successfully.

Business Necessity: Concrete evidence that certain hiring patterns are necessary for the success of the business.

Category Rating Systems: Employee evaluation procedures in which the supervisor rates an employee's level of performance on a series of predetermined categories.

Checklist: A rating method in which the supervisor checks those statements that best describe the employee's work performance from a given list of statements.

Chief Complaint: The specific issue that brings an interviewee to seek another party (the interviewer) to diagnose and solve a problem.

Clearinghouse Probe: Question near the end of an interview that invites the parties to raise any issues that have not been discussed earlier in the interview.

Closed Question: A question that restricts possible answers.

Coercion: The act of compelling another to act or change through the use of power, threats, or intimidation.

Communication Climate: The atmosphere of a communication event; the degree to which people feel valued in a communication interaction.

Communication Obstacles: The many factors that can interfere with the accurate reception of a message, sometimes called "noise."

Conclusion: Final, brief portion of the interview that serves three functions: to summarize, finalize business, and create closure.

Content Messages: Messages that focus on the actual topic of discussion in the interview.

Counseling Interviews: Helping interviews occurring within the context of a relationship in which the interviewer offers the interviewee(s) an opportunity for self-discovery and change through the use of empathic listening, questions, confidentiality and safety, feedback, and, in some cases, active direction toward change.

Convenience Sample: A survey interview method that involves interviewing people who are easily available and willing to participate.

Cover Letter: A letter of introduction to a prospective employer, usually accompanied by a resume, in which a job applicant expresses an interest in working for a company.

Critical Incident Method: A method of employee appraisal in which the evaluator keeps a written record of the employee's most and least effective work performances.

Cultural Differences: Differences in verbal and nonverbal communication, values, expectations and beliefs which might impede effective communication of meanings.

Cultural Obstacles: Misunderstandings of intended meanings as a result of different cultural backgrounds and experiences.

Culture: A group's world view or frame of reference, formed by collective history, which defines and limits its perceptions of reality.

Depth Interviews: Interviews that probe deeply into individual experiences, interviewing a few persons at great depth, to learn about their experiences in their own words, and to arrive at descriptive rather than numerical results.

Diagnostic Problem-solving Interview: An interview in which one party (interviewer) has knowledge or abilities needed by another party (interviewee) to diagnose and solve a problem.

Directional Control: The power of an interview participant to influence what topics are covered in an interview.

Directive Interview: An interview in which the interviewer provides concrete information about requirements and recommendations.

Disciplinary Interview: Interview in which an employer deals with an employee who has violated a condition of work.

Double-barreled Question: Problem question that contains two questions in the guise of one.

Due Process: A procedure that ensures an employee's right to be treated fairly during the investigation of an alleged offense and the administration of disciplinary action.

Emotional Appeals: Arguments that seek to persuade or influence another by involving their feelings and emotional attachments in the decision-making process.

Empathy: The capacity to understand another person's thoughts and feelings from that person's perspective.

Employee Assistance Programs (EAPs): Organization-based programs designed to help workers solve personal problems that interfere with their work performance.

Employee Counseling Programs (ECPs): Organization-based programs designed to help workers solve personal problems that interfere with their work performance.

Employee Intervention Interviews: Interviews that occur between employers and workers when the employees' personal problems have a noticeable negative impact on job performance.

Environmental Obstacles: Physical noises and distractions in the interview setting that interfere with effective communication.

Essay Method: A method of employee appraisal in which supervisors write brief essays describing each worker's performance.

Ethical Guidelines: Standards or values that reflect what an individual or group believes is right and fair behavior.

Ethnocentrism: Literally, means "nation-centered," the belief in the inherent superiority of one's own racial or ethnic group, gender, neighborhood, school, or nation of origin.

Ethnography: The process of collecting information about cultural groupings through interviews and/or observational research.

Ethnology: The descriptive study of contemporary cultural groupings.

Exit Interviews: Interviews conducted with employees who are leaving or have left a company, for the purpose of getting reliable information about the organization.

Feedback: The ongoing verbal and nonverbal responses of a listener to another's messages.

Flextime: A work schedule which the organization adapts so that it meets both the needs of the organization and the needs of individual workers.

Focus Group: A group of six to twelve persons, similar to an actual sample group demographically, who share their reactions to topics of research investigations or to interview guides.

Frame of Reference: The particular frame or focus that people bring to events.

Frequency Interval Scale: A scale that measures the number of occurrences per unit of time.

Funnel Sequence: Question sequence that moves from broad questions to more focused questions.

Garnishment: Mandatory direct withdrawal of money from worker paychecks to pay other obligations before paychecks are distributed to workers.

Glass Ceiling: The invisible barrier that many women and minorities encounter when they get to the top of mid-level management and are unable to break through to the highest levels of management.

Goal: The purpose that a party wants to accomplish during the interview.

Graphic Rating Scales: An appraisal technique that incorporates Likert scales to evaluate work performance.

Greeting Rituals: Culturally-specific patterns of recognizing others and beginning interaction with them.

Hearing: The auditory reception of sound waves.

Highly Closed Question: A question that can be answered with one or two words.

Highly Open Question: A question that gives few, if any, restrictions about how the interviewee can respond.

Highly Scheduled Guide: An interview guide with preworded questions that affords more flexibility in answers than does the standardized guide but still is highly controlled by the interviewer.

Highly Scheduled Standardized Guide: An interview guide that has a preset list of questions to be asked exactly as worded on the interview guide.

Hypothesis: A proposition or idea to be tested.

Hypothetical Questions: Questions that pose realistic descriptions of job-related incidents, actions, or problems and ask the applicant to describe how she or he would respond.

Implicit Personality Theory: An individual's unwritten ideas or beliefs about how groups of personality characteristics often appear together in other people.

Impression Management: The ways that persons present themselves to others to create a particular perception.

Informational Control: The power of an interview participant to control the amount and type of data shared with the other participant in an interview.

Institutional Framework: The guidelines and constraints imposed by the specific school or organization in which counseling interviews occur.

Interpersonal Coordination: The ways people "mesh their flow of behaviors with each other"(e.g., smiling to match the other person's smile).

Interview: A communication interaction in which at least two parties, at least one of whom has a goal, use questions and answers to exchange information and influence one another.

Interviewer Bias: An interviewer's impact on the interview which is so strong that it alters the outcome of the interview by affecting the responses offered by the interviewee, sometimes called "interviewer error."

Interview Guide: An interview outline that contains the interview purpose, a list of major questions, and possible probes to be asked.

Inverted Funnel Sequence: A question sequence that moves from specific, focused questions to more general ones.

Investigative Interviews: News interviews that seek to explore an issue in-depth for the purpose of coming to some conclusion or decision about it.

Jargon: Technical vocabulary for a specific subgroup of people.

Job Description: A formal written document that describes the title, duties, place in the organization, and requirements for a particular position.

Job Posting: A method of making persons aware of job vacancies and application deadlines by listing the jobs available in selected locations or through an in-house network.

Job Relatedness: A company's obligation to demonstrate that the procedures it uses to select and place employees are related and good predictors of an applicant's ability to be successful at that job.

Job Sharing: A situation in which two or three workers share one full-time job, including its salary and responsibilities.

Journalistic Interview: An information-seeking interview in which the interviewer seeks information of interest to a particular audience.

Leading Questions: Questions that suggest a desired response to the interviewee.

Libel: The malicious printing or broadcasting of false and injurious information about a person.

Likert Scale: Statement with which a rater can demonstrate degrees of agreement or disagreement.

Listening: The creative, intentional, and dynamic process of selectively receiving and attending to both aural and visual stimuli for the purpose of interpreting and responding appropriately to the messages of the other.

Management by Objectives (MBO): A method of employee assessment that combines goal setting with performance review and invites employees and supervisors to work together to establish goals for the employees.

Manipulation: An attempt on the part of the persuader to bring the audience to agreement or action through less than honest or forthright means.

Measurement Validity: Answers that actually reflect what the interviewer is attempting to learn.

Medium: Method of access to the audience (e.g., print, television, radio) through which the information gathered in a journalistic interview is disseminated.

Mentoring: The process in which an experienced worker gives information and guidance that helps a less experienced worker's professional development.

Mirror Probe: A follow-up response that reflects what the interviewee has said by virtually restating it, sometimes called an "accuracy-checking probe."

Moderately Closed Question: Question that seeks particular information and can be answered in several words.

Moderately Open Question: Question that asks about a specified topic and can be answered more briefly than a highly open question.

Moderately Scheduled Guide: An interview guide with a goal and outline of possible questions and probes.

Narrative: A story told in the language and from the unique point of view of the teller of the tale.

Networking: The deliberate effort on the part of job-seekers and others to expand their "whom you know" list in order to have contacts and potential links to information, job recommendations, and other career advantages.

News Feature Interview: A journalistic interview that goes beyond fact-finding to determine the how and why of a story.

News Interview: A journalistic interview that gathers information to generate fact-based stories for print or broadcast.

Nonpurposive Message: A message that communicates meanings to receivers, even though the sender does not intend to send them.

Nonscheduled Interview Guide: An interview guide with no questions prepared in advance that relies on information shared by the interviewee to guide the interaction.

Nonverbal Message: A message that is expressed in ways other than words.

Norm of Reciprocity: A norm that suggests that when one party provides a particular kind of information, the other party should give back similar information.

Norms: Powerful guidelines, often unstated, about what behaviors are typical and appropriate for particular situations.

Nudging Probe: A probe that uses one or two words to encourage a longer answer.

Numerical Scale: A unit of measure that can be used in an interval scale to express quantity of something.

Open Question: A question that allows a very broad response.

Opening: The brief, beginning segment of an interview with four functions: introductions, establishment of working relationship, rapport building, and interview preview.

Parallel Path Sequence: Question sequence in which all questions are of comparable breadth and structure.

Paraphrase: A response that restates the interviewee's message in different wording from that used by the interviewee.

Patterned Behavior Description Interviewing: An interviewing method that seeks to predict future performance on the basis of specific descriptions of past behaviors.

Perception: The process of noticing, organizing, and interpreting stimuli.

Perception Check: The process by which persons check whether their understandings of messages are accurate by asking those who sent the messages.

Person Perception: The process of noticing, organizing, and interpreting people; includes three basic stages: selection, organization, and interpretation.

Persuasion: Process of seeking to influence the thoughts or choices of an independent person through communication.

Persuasive Interviews: Interviews in which an interviewer seeks to influence the actions or attitudes of the interviewee(s) through the use of questions, rational arguments, and emotional appeals.

Poor Historian: An interviewee who does not provide information in a way that makes it easy for a diagnostic interviewer to reach an accurate diagnosis.

Presenting Problem: The specific issue that brings an interviewee to a diagnostic problem-solving interview, sometimes called the "chief complaint."

Pretesting: Administration of a survey interview, exactly as it will be administered to a sample group, with a smaller group of similar respondents as a way of testing and refining the instrument.

Primacy Effect: The belief that information about another individual received early in a relationship has a more powerful impact on the impressions formed than information received later.

Primary Question: Question that introduces a topic and makes sense when it stands apart from the context of the interview.

Probe: Secondary question designed to follow up on answers that have already been given.

Process: The concept that suggests that communication involves the ongoing transmission of meaning over time.

Profile Interview: A journalistic interview designed to gather information that will provide an in-depth look at one person.

Progressive Discipline: A disciplinary system that gives employees a series of warnings about their unacceptable conduct and provides opportunities for them to improve their actions before they are dismissed.

Psychological Obstacles: Those factors inside communicators that interfere with their clear understandings of messages, sometimes called "internal noise."

Purposive Message: A message that reflects a person's intended goal to communicate a particular message.

Qualitative Research Interviews: Interviews that probe deeply into individual experiences, interviewing a few persons at great depth, to learn about their experiences in their own words, and to arrive at descriptive rather than numerical results.

Quantitative Interviewing: Interviews with representative samples of particular human populations which gather information that is quantifiable and able to be subjected to statistical analysis.

Question Validity: The extent to which a specific question actually elicits the information sought.

Quintamensional Design Sequence: Five-question interview sequence designed to measure intensity of attitudes of large numbers of people.

Racism: Systematic justifications for the assumed inferiority of particular groups of individuals.

Ranking System: A method of employee appraisal that asks the evaluator to rank employees from best to worst in terms of job performance.

Rapport: Friendly compatibility in interaction.

Rational Arguments: Appeals that use facts, reason, and supporting evidence to win acceptance of an idea.

Realistic Job Previews: Information that provides job applicants with balanced information about both the strengths and weaknesses of the job and organization.

Reference Checking: The systematic process of contacting former employers and/or other references whose names are provided by the applicant for the purposes of verifying employment records and obtaining job-related information about the applicant's work or academic history.

Referral: Knowing and recommending appropriate sources of help for troubled interviewees.

Relational Messages: Messages by which interviewing parties let each other know how they define their relationship.

Reliability: Consistency in research procedures and techniques.

Representative Sample: A research sample that is a demographic microcosm of the population, possessing the same relative proportions of men, women, age groups, income levels, etc., as the population about which it claims to generalize.

Research Interviewing: Interviewing for the purpose of gathering information to test hypotheses or discover meanings.

Response Bias: Inaccurate answers from respondents attributed to misunderstanding of the questions or a felt need to provide socially desirable responses.

Response Rate: The percentage of people who have been asked to participate in a research project who actually agree to be interviewed.

Resume: A formal, one-to-two page summary of the academic, work, and professional experiences of an individual.

Roundtable Interviewing: Journalistic interviews with a group of experts and others designed to present a diverse range of views on an issue, sometimes called "round-up interviewing."

Sales Interview: An interview in which interviewers seek to persuade interviewees to purchase some commodity or service.

Salient Issues: Issues of great relevance to the respondent or of high current social interest to a larger group.

Sample: The representative group of persons who will be interviewed in quantitative research interviews.

Sample Point Random Sampling: A sampling method in which a geographic location is selected and the interviewers interview a certain number of persons by moving outward in a set pattern from a specified geographic starting point.

Sampling: A method of assessing the views of a large group of people (a population) by surveying a portion, or representative group, of the larger population.

Sapir-Whorf Hypothesis: The theory that, to a significant extent, language determines a culture's definition of reality.

Script: Any fixed set or sequence of events which come to be expected in certain interpersonal encounters.

Selective Perception: What the perceiver chooses to notice and interpret.

Self-Assessment: A method of employee appraisal in which the employees evaluate themselves and share that evaluation with their supervisors.

Simple Random Sampling: A sampling technique in which each member of the population has an equal chance of being selected.

Situational Interviewing: A process that predicts an employee's future performance by presenting a series of job-related hypothetical situations that ask applicants how they would respond under circumstances.

Skip Interval Random Sampling: A sampling technique that selects sample members who are found at certain intervals of the total population.

Snowball Sampling Technique: A nonrandom sampling method that involves identification of interviewees by persons known to the researcher that can yield representative samples.

Social Desirability Effect: Pressure to answer questions in a way that is perceived to be favorable to societal values and norms.

Social Organization: The specific ways that a society is bound together by laws, relationships, and status differences.

Stereotyping: The act of forming ideas about a group of people and then applying these impressions to individual members of the group without checking whether they really fit.

Stratified Random Sampling: A sampling technique that allows the demographic characteristics of the population to be represented in the same proportions in the sample as they exist in the population.

Subculture: A group of persons within a culture who share common (1) ethnic, social, gender or other experiences, (2) patterns of behavior, and/or (3) beliefs which exist apart from or in addition to other patterns of the larger culture.

Summary Probes: Secondary questions that provide a current account of what the interviewer thinks has happened during the interview.

Survey Instrument: The standardized schedule of questions to be used with every respondent in a survey interview project.

Survey Interviews: Interviews that gather information from large numbers of respondents for purposes of statistical comparison.

Transactional: A process that notes how both parties in the interview act as senders and receivers simultaneously, involved in a mutual exchange of meaning.

Topic List Guide: An interview guide made up of a list of possible issues to discuss in the interview.

Uncertainty Reduction Theory: Theory of communication based on the belief that people communicate in order to reduce ambiguity.

Validity: The accuracy of a research procedure, technique, or question at gathering the desired information they purport to gather; the extent to which we measure what we think we are measuring.

Verbal Communication: Using language to convey meaning.

World View: That set of perceptions and beliefs about life and others which define how people see the world.

Index